This is the most important book I've read in years. Whether you are subject or ally, My Baby Rides the Short Bus will open you—with its truth, humanity, and poetry. Lucky you to have found it. Now stick it in your heart.

Ariel Gore, author, *The Mother Trip: Hip Mama's Guide
to Staying Sane in the Chaos of Motherhood*

....

Smart, diverse, inspiring. My Baby Rides the Short Bus reminds us of what we all have in common and how much more work there still is to be done.

Vicki Forman, author, *This Lovely Life:
A Memoir of Premature Motherhood*

....

For the collection's diverse and candid discussion of such topics as diagnosis, education, family, community support, respite and relearning to stand up in order to be seen, heard, respected and believed, I hereby declare this book required reading for outsider parents of all stripes, their allies, school psychologists, therapists, social workers and child advocates!

Jessica Mills, author, *My Mother Wears Combat Boots:
A Parenting Guide for the Rest of Us*

....

If only that lady in the grocery store and all of those other so-called parenting experts would read this book! These true-life tales by mothers and fathers raising kids with "special needs" on the outer fringes of mainstream America are by turns empowering, heartbreaking, inspiring, maddening, and even humorous. Readers will be moved by the bold honesty of these voices, and by the fierce love and determination that rings throughout. This book is a vital addition to the public discourse on disability.

Suzanne Kamata, editor, *Love You to Pieces:
Creative Writers on Raising a Child with Special Needs*

The contributors of this important and necessary anthology span a range of decades from a time when "defective babies" were institutionalized, to the nascent civil rights movement, straight on to a new era of independent living. The families sharing these stories live and often struggle with the consequences of illness, injury, genetic inheritance, or sometimes a perplexing and mysterious combination of factors, insisting that the world recognize a basic fact: We are not science experiments.

Disability is a uniquely humbling and equal experience, sometimes expected, often striking without warning. These parents are honest about both the distressing and illuminating facts of their lives; the stories are caustic, exhilarating, fierce, funny, harrowing. Yet despite the intricate and often overwhelming challenges they face, these parents and children never succumb to maudlin stereotypes, because, as one contributor learns, "it isn't saintly to take care of someone you love."

Bee Lavender, author, *Lessons in Taxidermy: A Compendium of Safety and Danger*

....

There are smaller groups within every subculture, just the way there are mini revolutions within every larger revolution; and often, as well, the realization that everyone has not been included, after all. When any such group of people comes together to seek answers and share questions—uniting personal voice and experiences into a larger chorus—it creates a breakthrough that enriches all movements for social justice, as well as individual lives.

My Baby Rides the Short Bus is such a groundbreaking work—wonderful, thought-provoking, and diverse in different abilities of the different children. Little gems of life all buried in here, great tales. This book advances alternative parenting consciousness raising; and we need many more (on different separate themes within the multitude of those disenfranchised) in order to strive towards a community where no one will be left behind.

This is a collection of beautifully written stories, incredibly open and well articulated, complicated, and diverse: about human rights and human emotions. About love and difficulties; informative and supportive. Wise, non-conformist, and absolutely punk rock!

China Martens, author, *The Future Generation: The Zine-Book for Subculture Parents, Kids, Friends and Others*

My Baby Rides the Short Bus:
The Unabashedly Human Experience
of Raising Kids with Disabilities

My Baby Rides the Short Bus:
The Unabashedly Human Experience
of Raising Kids with Disabilities

Edited by
Yantra Bertelli, Jennifer Silverman,
and Sarah Talbot

My Baby Rides the Short Bus:

The Unabashedly Human Experience of Raising Kids with Disabilities

Edited by Yantra Bertelli, Jennifer Silverman, and Sarah Talbot

ISBN: 978-1-60486-109-9
LCCN: 2009901395

PM Press
PO Box 23912
Oakland, CA 94623
www.pmpress.org

Cover art by Liz Baillie
Index by Chris Dodge
Layout by Kersplebedeb

Printed in the USA, on recycled paper

Foreword

Almost ten years ago, three moms met on an online community bulletin board for "alternative" parents. We were activists, but it wasn't for a few more years that we discovered the most defining thing we would have in common: we are the parents of disabled kids. Our lives came together over the Internet and things changed. We all became parts of blended families as Yantra and Sarah became a couple, Jennifer remarried and eventually became a parent of two. Throughout, the diagnoses, the symptoms, and the services kept rolling in. We talked each other through advocating and strategizing, and we began to know a few things.

When friends from the online community Hipmama.com put together a conference in 2004, we offered a workshop on disabilities and parenting. In a windowless room, we chatted about what it felt like living with our kids while one of them obsessively watched the same movie for the 600th time and the other flipped pell-mell through a phonebook. Not a lot of other parents showed up, and most of them came only out of curiosity, not need. It didn't matter who showed up to the three of us, because for once we were subject, not object. We had pulled ourselves out of cautionary tales about things that can go wrong with babies, out of isolation, and pulled ourselves into the center of our own stories together.

We decided to put together a zine, and this book was born of our work.

Raising a child with a disability brings a whole new level of isolation to "alternative" parents, who do not fit into the mainstream through circumstance, identity, or choice, and who carefully consider the implications of our parenting. Disability forces us to reach back toward the mainstream while moving us irrevocably outside of it. We might have been planning to put our children in small, alternative schools before we knew they were disabled, and now, after the diagnosis, find ourselves fierce advocates of their inclusion in traditional classrooms. While we might have had home births planned, we may spend years in hospitals praying for the success of invasive medical procedures. While we might have fantasized about anarchist communes before our disabled babies entered our lives, we find ourselves lobbying the legislature for increases in funding to state bureaucracies. We, who had previously rejected the institutional structures of mainstream culture or found ourselves on the margins to begin with, discovered that we are clinging to the slim hope that they will save us after all.

We are remarkably absent from the public eye. When we are in the media, it's usually about a miracle cure that made some starlet's child more normal. Or there is the occasional story that spotlights a stereotypical American (white, middle-class, two-parent, heterosexual) family showing off the gifts of a savant or highlighting a feel-good donation made to a poor, struggling family with special needs kids. At worst, our families are objects of ridicule in alternative and mainstream press sources.

Take, for instance Denis Leary's 2008 book *Why We Suck*, in which he stated that kids diagnosed with autism are just stupid or lazy and their diagnoses are just for their parents who "want an explanation for why their dumb-ass kids can't compete academically."

Comments like this poke fun at the people in our society who are too visible for comfort, and they function to enforce invisibility. When your everyday experience only ruins a joke, you have to decide to stand out as both, "one of them" and humorless, or blend into the wallpaper of a mythical normalcy. These stories erase completely the reality that all children learn at varying rates, making our complex reality a bummer of a laugh-kill.

As parents of differently-abled children, we are often put on pedestals. People wonder in awe about how we cope, or hand us platitudes about how we have landed in a different but wonderful country where we need simply to dream new dreams for our special angel children. But when we're out in public, our "special angel children" are most often stared at and treated like enigmas. Our children are inconvenient, awkward, and difficult. Their parents—even those of us with a lot of tattoos—are usually struggling mightily to be less obtrusive. Those who wonder aloud how we do it are really just highlighting for themselves (and us) that they will never have to.

The truth is that our kids aren't angels; they're people with big challenges, and their challenges make our lives as parents incredibly complicated, messy, and sometimes heartbreaking, no matter how much we love them. As parents who are already marginalized by politics, sexual orientation, gender, race or ethnicity, parenting philosophy, our own disabilities, economic status, blue hair, piercings, or something else that makes us unlike the camera-friendly special needs family America knows and adores, it can be harder to find support among other parents or be taken seriously by the teachers, therapists, and other professionals on whom we often have to rely to get the services our kids need.

When we three parents made the leap of taking a small zine and turning it into an anthology, we strove to make the voices represented as inclusive as possible in terms of diversity—class, gender, race, and struggle—to distinguish this project from others. Part of valuing that diversity included working to preserve the authenticity of the work of the authors, including valuing voice over grammatical convention from time to time. As is the nature of anthologies, there was a submission process for accepting pieces, and we extended our deadline twice to encourage a wide range of writers to contribute. On many levels, we have succeeded: the contributors here range from a Burmese mother overcoming her own physical disability as she works through her son's challenges, to a lesbian minister who becomes a foster parent and advocate of a developmentally delayed teenager not much younger than she is, and a "quirky" single mama who quit school at the age of sixteen, yet successfully took on her son's school system to find an accessible placement that accommodated his cerebral palsy. Still, the racial and cultural diversity of the writers may not be immediately apparent to the reader, as some writers considered race and culture central to their story and some did not mention their backgrounds.

Statistically, the overwhelmingly female voice in this book makes sense. Numerous studies from the United States, United Kingdom, Canada, and Turkey have shown that women take on an especially high responsibility of caring for children with disabilities compared to men[*]. And while we definitely have an economic range within these contributors (mostly working-class to middle-class) we received almost no submissions from parents who are economically struggling the most. Having the time and space to

---

[*] R.Hassall, J. Rose, and J. McDonald, "Parenting Stress in Mothers of Children with an Intellectual Disability," *Journal of Intellectual Disability Research* 49 no.6 (June 2005); M. D'Ottavi, C. Spearin, and C. Andrzejewski, "The Division of Household Labor in Families with a Disabled Child: Insights from Quantitative and Qualitative Research" (Brown University; R. Ceylan and N. Aral, "Hopelessness Levels of Mothers with and without Disabled Children," *Pakistan Journal of Social Sciences* 4 no. 6 (2007).

write, especially while raising kids with special needs, is a privilege. We work, fight for, and look forward to the day when that is not the case.

My Baby Rides the Short Bus is meant as a *partial* antidote to the stories that misrepresent, ridicule, and objectify disabled kids and their parents. Here, you'll find parents of disabled kids telling their own subjective stories with humor and grace. In lives where there's a new diagnosis or drama every day, we know that the stories these authors have written will provide a giggle, a rock to stand on, a moment of reality held far enough from the heart to see clearly. From professional writers to academics to novice storytellers, *My Baby Rides the Short Bus* collects experiences from parents at the fringe of the fringes. We hope you will enjoy it.

Introduction

by Lisa Carver

I came home to find a police car in my driveway.

Again.

I knew they'd be there, from the message on my cell. My son Wolf's home aide called them when Wolf: A. started growling, B. tore his homework to bits, C. trampled the flowers he'd planted, and D. hurled himself repeatedly against the door, saying he didn't belong in this family, in this home; he was going to live in a tree.

Because my son hating himself or lacking adroitness in managing frustration, whichever you call it, was such a part of my life, that wasn't what I was focusing on when I got the call. Experience had taught me that what I needed to concentrate on right then was how I looked. Because the consequences that would result—for Wolf and for me—would depend on how well I could translate for him, explain the destructive things he does and reassure the stranger holding authority over our fate that we were doing all we could to get it under control. And how believable he would find me would depend on how serious, how *normal*, he found me.

When you have a special needs child, it's your attitude on trial, your lifestyle, and the judge and jury is every "helpful" stranger/family member/professional in the world.

I did the mental checklist. Did I happen to pick out conservative clothes today? Check. Tattoos covered? Check. Okay, now exit the vehicle with grocery bag in hand, so obviously I wasn't out doing jolly or countercultural things when I *should* be doing games and therapy with my child to practice the social/physical skills/reactions that don't come naturally to him.

I tried to maintain eye contact while explaining that Wolf has the mental capacity of an eight year old. The officer explained to me that he is not eight, he's thirteen, and at his age he could be charged with assault or malicious destruction of property.

I said, "It's his property he destroyed. It's himself he assaulted. Life is hard for him."

"You're making excuses for him," the officer replied. "Keep that up and your kid is going to end up in jail."

We don't make excuses. We make explanations. To all the people who don't know. To the people who have power over our child's life, and ours. Which is everyone. Our special child's peers, surgeons, therapists, teachers, guidance counselors, insurance companies, home aides, camp officials, independent living center directors, our own families. Sometimes we plead. Sometimes we threaten. Sometimes we hold it together and someone is actually listening. But there's only so much they can do.

We are tired. Something works, ten other things fail. You try everything, and eventually you burn out. Which can be a good thing. You start trusting yourself, trusting your child. My son got the short end of an awful lot of sticks, and no matter how hard I keep tugging on the other ends, those sticks ain't lengthening.

Not to take away from the value of when he was younger, when I was still a hopeful zealot. That is absolutely necessary. At some point, you will give up trying so hard, and come to trust yourself, trust your child, trust what *is*. But if you haven't beaten your head first against every wall, if you haven't tried until you cry for what *could be* you haven't done your job.

Still—it sure does help to have some acceptance and encouragement and commiseration along the way.

And along comes the Short Bus.

The various authors in this anthology may not have any cures to offer, but they have something infinitely more valuable: no cures. Understanding. They, too, have experienced society's impossible-to-fulfill expectations (demands) for parents of special needs children.

1. For actions: We must do everything we can to help our children to change what is different about them, make it *undifferent*, so they can integrate, so they can be as normal as possible. (To do that, *we* need to be normal first.) We must reprogram our children, go against their nature, go against nature itself. Constantly. It would be considered emotional abuse to do that to a "normal" child, to tell them every day in many ways they cannot be who they are.

2. For attitude: What can't be changed, we have to look at as a gift, *God's way of teaching us patience*; God gave us this child because *He* knew we had enough love to handle it. (To keep that positive attitude up in the midst of all this crap, one would have to be a total hypocrite, or on massive amounts of Xanax.) We are not allowed to be angry.

For our child, there are therapy, surgery, medication, and aides (home and school) aimed at achieving that first goal.

For *our* attitude, there are guidebooks and memoirs to help get that one right.

This book is not one of those.

You're not wayward here. Here you don't have to fight the outside world, and you don't have to fight the inside world of other parents of special needs kids with whom you have only that in common. The authors here are different in different ways—some by politics, some by orientation, others by poverty…all by attitude. Here, we don't say what we think one is supposed to say—we say what we know. Even if it's, as Christina Witkowski, whose child has spina bifida, admits: "Sometimes I hate being the parent of a special needs child." Or as Amy Saxon Bosworth jokes, she's sick of being told her three (!) special needs children are gifts, "like [I] won some disabled kid lotto." Of course, these moms love their children just as much as the ones who call them little angels…maybe more so, because they are honest and brave enough to get *all* the truths off their chest, not just the ones we're *supposed* to feel, and so they can see their children for who they are.

This is for you, the outsider parent who already didn't look at the world the way others did, and happening to have a child with, say, autism, is not going to make you suddenly able to relate to the attitude held by other parents and specialists of other autistic children. Of course you want to help your child to be a success. It's simply that you may have different ideas about the definition of success.

"If everything was beautiful and the same," explains Sabrina Chapadjiev's mother Magdalena, "it wouldn't be life."

So please, come ride this awkward Short Bus, where no passenger is alike, where there is no Right, there is no Truth. There are only some unusual, sometimes unpleasant, sometimes incredibly pure and beautiful, little truths. And, to paraphrase Tiny Tim in *A Christmas Carol*, God bless us, every fucked-up one.

Contents

Foreword..........v

Introduction by Lisa Carver..........ix

♦ ♦ ♦ CHAPTER 1
The Other Combat Boot Drops..........1

    Rebirth by Emily Zolten..........3

    A Bus(wo)man's Holiday by Kathy Bricetti..........7

    The Story So Far by Andrea McDowell..........20

    Paging Dr. House by Christina Witkowski..........28

    Evaluating Ezra by Kerry Cohen..........32

    The Head Game (diagnosis) by Kim Mahler..........41

    Popeye by Thida Cornes..........42

    The Letter for Services by Aileen Murphy..........53

♦ ♦ ♦ CHAPTER 2
**Enough Acronyms To Make Your Head Spin:
Navigating the System & Advocating For Our Kids**..........57

    *Exile To Bridlemile
or Where the @#$%&! is My Village?!* by Chloe Eudaly..........59

    After the IEP by Kim Mahler 72

    Play Therapy by Karen Wang..........73

    Accidental Unschoolers by Heather Newman..........79

    *An Inadvertently Compelling Argument for
National Health Care in Five Mutually Incriminating Scenes*
by Ayun Halliday..........86

    *Watching My Son Grow: An Illustrated Timeline
from Birth to Three Years Old* by Joe Dimino..........101

    Authentic Activism by Maria June..........117

    Interpreting the Signs by Andrea Winninghoff..........129

◆ ◆ ◆ CHAPTER 3

Seen, Heard, Respected, and Believed............**135**

What I Said, and What I Didn't Say by Sharis Ingram............137

Jackpot! by Amy Saxon Bosworth............144

What Should Have Been… by Megan Raines Wingert............152

Building Bridges into Ordinariness by Ziva Mann............159

Diagnosis Invisible by Stephanie Sleeper............167

A View through the Woods by Christy Everett............176

My Friend Christine by Marcy Sheiner............186

Scout by Robert Rummel-Hudson............192

◆ ◆ ◆ CHAPTER 4

How Do We Do It?
Respite, Community Support, and Transitions............**199**

My Mama Drove the Short Bus by Sabrina Chapadjiev............201

How I Met Jennyalice by Shannon Des Roches Rosa............212

No Use in Crying by Jennifer Byde Myers............219

Life Among the Doozies by Anonymous............227

Glass Houses by Sarah Talbot............234

Small Victories by Elizabeth Aquino............240

Dragonflies and Inky Blackness:
Raising a Child with Asperger's Syndrome
by Caryn Mirriam-Goldberg............242

♦ ♦ ♦ CHAPTER 5
Families: When the Balancing Act Induces Vertigo............253

Our Closet by Diana Robinson............255

"Because He's Retarded, Ass!" by Amber E. Taylor............260

And We Survive by Nina Packebush............267

Thanksgiving by Kim Mahler............276

Dual Parentship Status by Jennifer Silverman............277

Taking the First Step by Yantra Bertelli............285

This is What Love Looks Like by Andrea S. Givens............293

♦ ♦ ♦ CHAPTER 6
Righteous Resources
What Do You Know: A Little Practical Advice After All..........299

A User's Guide to Self-Help Literature
(Or, Who's the Real Expert Here, Anyway?)
by Dr. Mitzi Waltz............301

Special Needs Trusts: The Lowdown............307

Glossary of Terms............312

Resources............317

Contributors' Biographies............325

Acknowledgments............333

Index............335

CHAPTER 1
The Other Combat Boot Drops

"There's something wrong..." Three words that no parent wants to hear regarding their child.

Some of us knew it during pregnancy. Others found out at birth, during an adoption process, or months or even years later. For some of us, the process is ongoing. All of us find ourselves parents to kids with "special needs." Regardless of when we learned about these "special needs," most of us went through the same emotions trying to process the information: fear, confusion, anger, sadness, and hope. We met clueless (and some helpful) doctors, trudged through mountains of books, and turned to the Internet. We found some—but definitely not all—of the answers we were searching for. In the process we found our voices, symbolically put on our combat boots, and channeled our inner mama and papa bears to become advocates. But the learning curve has been steep, demanding, and often isolating.

With the exception of our one Canadian author, these writers joined the parents of the reported 17 percent of children in the United States with special needs. Marginalized by their own disabilities, liberal parenting philosophies, anti-consumerist lifestyles, and interests that set them outside conventional culture, many of these parents found it harder to be taken seriously by the professionals leading them through the diagnosis process.

The children of the parents in this chapter span eventual diagnoses from cri du chat syndrome to autism. Along the way, their parents learned as much about their kids' conditions as the "experts"—and became the best

1

experts possible on their own kids. Their stories here and throughout the book are alternately funny, challenging, triggering, and sobering. The humor and honesty in these tales of parents living on the margins and learning about their child's special needs sets them apart from the status quo.

Rebirth

by Emily Zolten

I have heard new mothers say time after time that they felt like they were reborn on the day that their babies were born. This has been true for me after the births of all three of my daughters. What was unexpected was the version of myself that would emerge after the birth of Lucy.

I had experienced labor twice before and so I thought that I knew exactly how I gave birth. That's why I was so surprised when my water broke late in the evening three weeks before my due date. My water did not break with my other children until right before they were born. There were many things about this pregnancy that were different and it was hard not feeling like something was wrong. As a midwife, I saw this all the time—women having their third baby and feeling like they had been so lucky before that their number was surely up. Things were bound to go wrong this time.

When my water broke, I jumped up from the couch in shock. I realized what this all meant, how things would change for me, and the pain that was about to begin. I told my husband and my daughters what was happening and what to expect. They were all so excited. We cuddled up with a book about having a new baby sibling and read our bedtime story. We all knew, but no one said, that this was the last time we would be this family of four sitting here together.

I woke up in the morning surprised that labor hadn't started yet. The kids got dressed and we headed out for a walk. It was the perfect Vermont spring day. The dirt road was a combination of hardened mud and hollowed out gravel filled with puddles. The air was heavy with mist. I walked while doing nipple stimulation to bring on labor, waving at my neighbors, and laughing as they looked at me with raised eyebrows. I knew that this walk we were taking together would bring us our new baby. As we reached the top of our unbelievably steep driveway, I knew that there was no turning back. I walked into the house, threw off my clothes, and got in the shower. I did a dance between inviting in the pain and trying to back away from it. It was time to call Gabe, my husband, home from his trip to the supermarket.

Shortly after labor had gotten serious, I knew that it would soon be over. I lay in the 250-gallon horse-watering trough that sat in my living room filled with warm water. It was a gray day outside the windows and my daughters hung on the sides of the tub encouraging me. I reached down and felt her head pushing into my palm. The baby and I began the work together as a team.

When Lucy was born I immediately noted her small size (5 lbs 14 oz) and her even smaller voice. She sounded just like a baby kitten. She had a herniated umbilical cord. Her ears were slightly low set, but barely. I had seen so many newborn babies in my experience as a midwife and I knew that there were things about Lucy that were different, but I explained away these things by her early arrival. It wasn't until the day the geneticist handed me the lab results that I knew how truly unique this little girl was. We had hit the genetic lottery. Lucy had a syndrome that occurs once in every 50,000 times a baby is born. The funny thing was, when the proof was there that something about her was unusual, it struck me that she was the same baby that I had been holding five minutes earlier when there was no diagnosis.

In that moment, I knew and continue to learn every day, that I am a different mother than I ever thought that I would be. Some days I am a better mother than I was before: I participate so fully in Lucy's therapy, I make excellent lunches for my other children, and we talk about all of our feelings and about Lucy's disability in such a mature way. Other days, I snap at my girls for the simplest of things because I am over-tired from not sleeping for nearly three years and my shoulder is bruised from Lucy banging her head all night. I snap at Lucy for banging her head, despite the fact that I know she would stop if she could. Sometimes I am not completely compliant with the things that the specialists and doctors have told me to do with Lucy. She refuses to wear her glasses, and I don't force her to. Lucy does not wear her orthotics for the entirety of her day. I love babies with bare feet. Worst of all, after years of making parenting choices that seemed so in line with nature and how I thought natural parenting was supposed to happen, I have made the decision to medicate my toddler so that she might sleep for even a few consecutive hours at night.

I am a mother who knows that each one of my children will have her own story. I know that all of the things I have hoped for them are only in my imagination, they will be exactly who they are meant to be. I often remember that moment when I was pushing Lucy out into the warm water of the birth tub, when we were working together, just like we do now. We teach her how to walk, albeit more slowly than I have ever done it before and with much more outside help than I ever thought was needed. At the same time, I am learning how to walk in the shoes of a parent who has a child with special needs; this also takes patience and the skill of fighting for your child without stepping on anyone's toes.

I am still learning who Lucy's mother is, which version of myself was born that day when she entered the water and pushed herself into my hands. I know now that the phrase "expecting a baby" is absolutely right in its sentiment. Expecting something is all you really are doing as a parent. You imagine the baby that you will have and all of the things that this child will do in his or her life, but those things are not real. When parents receive a diagnosis for their child there is often a lot of grief that follows, but what are you really grieving? The sense of loss is for something that never was, it existed as an illusion. When babies are born they come with their own story, and everyone faces some sort of trouble during their lifetime. Some of us come with our troubles right on the surface at birth. The important moments arrive when parents decide what to do next.

I have learned a lot about what I don't know. I don't know where Lucy will end up for preschool and how her classmates will receive her. I have learned that I will probably find defeat in the Individualized Education Program process numerous times before I learn the ropes and how to fight. I have learned to not to scream "Fuck you!" every time I open a condolence card or hear "I'm so sorry." I have learned not to say "Good thing for you that you were lucky enough to have all of your children born healthy and 'normal'" every time someone tries to say "Special kids get special parents." There is nothing special about me. I challenge people who say this to think about what they would do. Would they really just quit? Of course not, they would get up the next morning and feed their kid breakfast, if they were lucky enough to have a kid who could eat by mouth without a feeding tube, and they would go to therapy appointments, and they would do their best to parent even when they were at the end of their rope.

I have learned to be a fierce and strong advocate for my child, to have all of the uncomfortable conversations that I never want to have. I have learned to be charming and sweet while demanding not only what I want, but also what Lucy is due. I have learned to work hard with her and seize every moment of these immensely important formative years. I have learned that some of the things that seemed important to me before are so easily moved to the back burner now. Why not change careers at the age of thirty? Most importantly, though, I have learned to enjoy her, to let her just be a kid, and to help her achieve her maximum potential.

A Bus(wo)man's Holiday
by Kathy Bricetti

*Busman's holiday—noun: a vacation or day off from work spent in
an activity closely resembling one's work, as a bus driver taking a
long drive.*

On my first car, a bile-colored Datsun Honeybee, I stuck a bumper
sticker that read: I'D RATHER BE STIMMING. I loved it for its
obtuseness, for the private joke. Stimming is what autistic kids do: hand
flapping, head banging, humming or laughing, finger twiddling, spinning
toys, and waving a piece of yarn in front of one's face. One day, I stopped
at a red light, and a guy on a motorcycle pulled up next to me. Over the
drone of his engine he shouted, "What's stimming?" I wasn't sure how to
answer in the time before the light changed. "Self-stimulation!" I shouted
across the lane as the light turned green. "Well, all right!" he said, nodding
a couple of times and speeding away.

Around that time, I volunteered at a Saturday recreation program for
autistic kids in San Francisco. We took them to the zoo, to the beach, to the
snow one winter. I knew nothing about special education, goals, performance measures, testing, IEP meetings, or school psychologists. I wanted
to be a teacher. My favorite book in college was Virginia Axline's *Dibs in
Search of Self*, and I, too, wanted to cure children lost inside themselves.

Before I became a mother, I was a school psychologist. I tested deaf kids.
I tested hearing kids. I tested kids with learning disabilities. I tested kids
with emotional disabilities. I tested poor kids. I tested rich kids. I tested
retarded kids. I tested kids with IQs in the 120s and a couple in the 130s. I
tested kids in overheated, windowless rooms. I tested kids in the janitor's
closet. I drove from school to school to school to school, my test kits in the
trunk of my Datsun Honeybee.

My son is born. At two minutes, his Apgar score is 8. At five minutes, it is 10. He is perfect.

As a newborn, Benjamin rarely looked directly into our faces. Babies are supposed to prefer human faces to other shapes, but for months he explored the outline of our heads. "He's staring at our auras," Pam said.

"Maybe he's still connected to a higher consciousness," I said, trying for a joke. But something niggled at the edge of consciousness. Something was off.

In one hand, I carry my test kit, and in the other, I lug my rental breast pump into my office—a dusty book storage room in the elementary school, where I put up my TESTING: DO NOT DISTURB sign and lock the door three times a day so I can empty my aching, dripping breasts.

Holding
Being held is different from holding
someone—a baby, a child, a lover.
Being held is an arm's weight,
warmth, and the deep security
of being attached to the earth,
being reminded of gravity.

At the picture window, Ben waves good-bye to Pam and Morgan in the mornings, and then with the same hand makes the sign for "I love you" and then waves, alternating the two over and over. When Pam drives away without giving him one more "I love you," he whines.

He makes a best friend in his first week of preschool, and they play every morning together, mostly running, chasing, swinging, and climbing. One afternoon, when I come to pick him up, I find Ben and his buddy dancing with scarves to classical music the teacher has put on for them. Their faces are flowers fluttering in a soft breeze.

At home, though, my sweet boy is a stuttering, running, slamming, screaming, stomping, throwing, smashing, trashing, crying, out of control mess.

"No," he shouts. "This way. Stupid door. Stupid curtain. Stupid Cupid." I know he wants to say stupid Mommy, but it's prohibited because names hurt people's feelings. So he whispers it. "Stupid Mommy. Time out. Time out. Time out." Then, when I tell him to pick up the books and toys he threw across his room during a time out, he says in a tiger voice, "I'm angry at you."

"It's okay to be angry at me." At this moment, I'm calm. Two days ago I screamed at him in the loudest voice I've ever used with him; my throat hurt for hours afterwards. Now my stomach is tight, my head throbs. "Why are you angry at me?"

"I'm ANGRY at you." He growls, but doesn't answer.

This afternoon he finally took a nap after a week of none. When he woke up, and all the way until dinner time, we had our sweet boy back. Who will come out of that room tomorrow? A growling three-and-a half-year-old or my cuddly boy?

At our first parent-teacher conference at the preschool, Pam and I share our concerns over the tantrums and tell his teacher that time-outs seem to calm Ben. "He watches his clock, and knows when three minutes are up," Pam says. We are kind of proud of this.

"Young children can feel abandoned on time-outs," the teacher says. "It might be better to hold him during his upsets."

I leave the meeting feeling like a horrible mother. Like the old refrigerator mothers I learned about in graduate school in the early eighties. Or the schizophrenogenic mothers, who caused mental illness in their children. Now we know that serious disorders like schizophrenia are caused by genetic anomalies, not a mother's behavior, but still I wonder what I'm doing to my son to make him like this.

He calls us butthead, stupid, idiot, poo-poo head. He is five and he is furious, throwing his body on the floor, stomach down, head up like a tortoise leaning its long neck skyward. He plugs his ears against our voices, doesn't want us to repeat anything; it's poison to him. He splays his right hand out, palm up and curls his fingers inward, his gesture of extreme frustration.

His cries are sometimes angry wails, but sometimes when he is truly hurt, he sobs and I can hear the intake of breath between sobs coming from his gut.

"Why don't you just talk about feeling mad?" I say one evening. "You don't need to have a tantrum; you can scribble in your mad book or rip up some scrap paper. Why don't you just tell us you're mad?"

But he is silent, and I know he hates me when I send him on a time-out, five minutes now, solitary confinement in his room. He doesn't say "I hate you" yet, but I know I am frustrating him, turning away from him, pushing him away. And it's breaking my heart.

I don't hold him, like his teacher suggested and like Virginia Axline did with Dibs in therapy. I'm afraid of *rewarding the bad behavior*—my training in college and grad school was thorough. I understood behaviorism. Reward. Punish. Natural consequences. Logical consequences. Ignore the negative. Praise the positive. When I'm stressed, I fall back on this way of thinking, and it feels both right and wrong.

During calm times, when I want to embrace him, he pushes me away. He can't tolerate the feel of my skin on his; it is repulsive to him. When he's raging, I can't tolerate him. I don't want to hold him. I want to leave until it's finished. I want to go away. I am repulsed.

> IEP, or Individualized Education Plan, [noun]: a document, usually about fifteen pages long, outlining a special education student's present functioning, a list of goals for improvement, and what kind of special education program will meet his or her needs.
>
> IEP [noun]: a meeting of parent(s), teacher, support staff, and/or advocate(s) in which an IEP document is developed and approved by parents.
>
> IEP [verb]: the action of holding an IEP for a student; e.g., "We're going to IEP him next week."

School psychologists attend an IEP meeting for every student they assess. In a typical school year, a full-time school psychologist will attend seventy to eighty IEP meetings.

At work, the speech and language therapist and I begin noticing the couple of quirky kids we see every year who don't have friends, who only engage in conflicts with their classmates, who get along better with younger or older children. We wonder what we should be doing for them. Over the ten years at that school, I test 200 kids with learning disabilities. I get good at recognizing ADHD. I'm no longer one of the new psychologists. Younger ones are coming in. Sometimes they ask me for advice.

When he gets home, he kicks off his shoes by the door. And I notice for the first time that he walks on his toes in the house. His arches are so high they resemble the monument in St. Louis. Later, when he is jumping on a trampoline, I will tell him to put his heels down. "Your feet look like a Barbie doll's."

The speech and language therapist and I talk more about the kids who have poor social skills, the loners on the playground, the ones who have no one to eat lunch with. She shows me social stories she uses with the kids on her caseload, cartoons of kids facing daily social situations. She suggests we form a "Lunch Bunch" and pair these kids with socially adept students to model appropriate behavior. We are too busy with our assessments and therapy. We never get around to it.

A boy arrived at the elementary school where I tested and counseled kids and consulted with teachers about difficult students. He had been kicked out of a private school kindergarten because he toppled chairs and hid under tables, and his mother home-schooled him until it was time for first grade. I met with her immediately and set up accommodations for him. He needed to visit his new classroom before the school year began. He needed to arrive at school early every day to adjust to the classroom before his noisy classmates arrived. He needed a quiet escape when the cafeteria got too loud. He reminded me of Ben. He had a diagnosis of sensory integration disorder. But unlike Ben, he didn't hold it together during school and let it out at home; he let it out at school, too. His mother and I talked about our sons' sensitivities, their needing things to be a certain way, about how frustrating it could be, how draining.

At a visit to the pediatrician, Dr. C. poked the little plastic cone into Ben's ear and narrowed his eyes, not speaking until he'd checked both ears. Ben sat statue-like on the paper-covered table, facing the pediatrician but keeping his eyes trained right on me. I noticed he never rubbed his face after the doctor touched it. At home, if I grazed his chin while brushing his teeth, he immediately huffed and brushed off my touch. But here, like in the barber's chair, he always sat perfectly still. Perfectly behaved. Holding it all together outside, falling apart inside.

Teacher's report:
"I'm concerned that he doesn't seem to feel empathy for other people."
"He's not taking responsibility for his actions."
"He doesn't show any remorse."
"He treats other people," she hesitates, "in a mean way."
"He seems to have trouble judging people's body language and the nuances behind what they're saying."

At home, we disband at the end of the video, the four of us falling out of our spots on the couch, stretching, Pam and me saying together, "Time for bed."

I forget, but these times of transition from one way of being—enveloped by the soft, puffy couch and warmed by proximity—to the next state: standing, moving toward bedtime rituals, that this often is too much for him. I forget that this change, this requirement that he make an adjustment, must feel to him like jumping into an icy lake—a shock that would make anyone gasp.

A boy at the elementary school where I work walks the perimeter of the playground every recess. He has no friends but he does well in school. He gets special education services from the speech and language therapist for his difficulty with pragmatics. I keep forgetting what *pragmatics* means. That and *pedantic speech*. It's not my area.

It started like all the rest. After breakfast he didn't understand something Pam told him; he'd taken it literally and moved into his professor role, setting us straight, telling us what it *really* meant. When I tried to teach him the finer, more abstract meaning, he pressed his palms to his ears. But I pushed, told him that was rude, that he needed to listen to me. I pushed too much, or it was time, he was ready to blow anyway. The first explosion came almost immediately.

"Shut up Mommy! Just shut the fuck up!"

"Go to your room, Ben," I said. "Go calm down."

"I *am* calm!" he shouted.

It ended with Ben pounding on Pam's arms, me intervening again, and Pam calling the psychiatrist but not being able to speak after the woman at the answering service said, "What's the matter, hon?" this touch of humanity completely breaking any remaining defenses Pam might have had. With tears running down her cheeks and dripping onto the kitchen floor, she handed me the phone and when the doctor came on the line, I told him we were stopping the medicine, Ben was in his room smashing a baseball bat into the floor. This one ended with Pam and me canceling our dinner reservations, giving my mother, who had been planning on babysitting, our theater tickets. It ended with me sobbing at the kitchen counter and Morgan standing beside me rubbing my back. It ended with me telling Ben he had wrecked our evening, wrecked our whole day, and him retorting, "Well, you're wrecking my *life*!" It ended with me believing and not wanting to believe that I was wrecking his life. It ended with me sobbing because the believing it was winning.

I plod up the six wooden stairs to my bedroom, slippers flapping against my soles and then snapping against the floor. I close the door gently, although what I really want is to slam it so hard the glass in its upper half crashes to the floor. I want to make the house shake; I want my rage to slam through the door, its frame and the foundation of our house, shaking us from our center like Ben shakes my core.

I have to get out of the house or I will truly go crazy—pull-my-hair-out-in-fistfuls crazy, scream-until-my-throat-turns-raw crazy, cry-until-there-are-no-more-tears crazy.

I drive away. For forty-five minutes, up into the hills and back down again. Nothing to do. Nowhere to go.

When we get the diagnosis, I don't know how to spell Asperger's. Is it "burger"? No, it's "asp," like a snake.

We are at the top of the stairs, but he will not descend. I watch him as he screams, as he beats his hands on his thighs, as he takes shallow breaths and sobs. Tears are streaming down his face, landing on the hardwood floor beneath him. I know now that he cannot help this, that he is stuck because of a screwed-up circuit in his brain that prevents him from understanding me.

For a long time, I thought he was manipulating us, and sometimes he is, but now he is doing this because he believes Pam or I will back down, that we will make it right, or at least what he sees as right in his mind. Now I know he is not doing this to anger me, he is not enjoying it; he is miserable. He is physically stuck, and this knowledge wraps a protective layer around him. Around me. I am able to stay disengaged. I am not raging; even though I'm yelling, demanding to be heard, to be the authority, I'm not out of control, shouting from rage. I'm annoyed; I'm frustrated that what we're doing isn't working; I'm angry that he's not obeying because children should obey their parents, but there is a new feeling during this tantrum. Sympathy.

I feel so sorry for my boy when he's like this, crying, wiping his eyes with his palms; his voice is raw; his throat must be burning.

I have another image: that of an old LP record stuck in one groove, a record skipping, unable to proceed to the next one. I have an impulse to flick the needle, do something to jolt Ben out of this groove. But I know I cannot. I have tossed water at him, both Pam and I have slapped his face, I have clapped my hands loudly next to his ears. But, of course, these things only enrage him. For a person with normal sensory input, maybe some kind of surprise would jolt them out of the stuck place. But for a person with an extra-sensitive sensory system, the same thing must make them feel as if they are under attack, that they must protect themselves at all cost.

Now I know it's the Asperger's, not willful behavior, causing this. We have to help him learn how to get unstuck not by shocking or beating him. He's so smart, maybe if we present it logically, with no room for ambiguity—if such a thing is possible—maybe he'll learn. But I don't know how to do it yet. I wonder if it's even possible. Will we ever be able to teach him? Will someone?

He is lying on his back on the floor, sleeping bag pulled to his chin, hands nested on his chest like an old man's. I am on my side next to him on the scant inches of foam pad he has allotted me. There have been two tantrums today, and I've been wearing my hooded sweatshirt all day, wrapping myself in its softness, in its promise of protection, in its feeling of home and nurture. We are both breathing slowly, deeply. He is finally sleeping, finally in the magical place that turns all children into angelic beings, softens their features, softens their souls. Sleeping, they are no longer monsters who inspired us to devil rage during the day, but they are safe in their respite from reality. They are safe from us. And we from them.

I'm sleepy, but I force my eyes open to watch him. As he floats into sleep, I find my heart opening again and pulling him toward me. I remember seeing him for the first time, amniotic wet, then watching him holler in the brightly lit bassinette, his chest inflated into a barrel shape, like it is today when he stands straight and pounds on it like an excited gorilla. It's his chest that I like to pat with a flat palm, too. I like the sound of my patting, the hollowness of thudding, and how his burly chest feels under my palm, solid, substantial, significant.

April is Autism Awareness Month I read on the Internet today, during the intermission between explosions, eyes stinging from weeping and too much computer screen reading. "It's ironic," I told Pam earlier. "We sure got aware this month, didn't we?" I asked. "Do you think we're aware enough now?"

She laughed. "Maybe we should skip April next year."

I don't want to call the police because I don't want to offer ourselves up to the system and have everything taken out of our control. Two huge officers will storm into our house and throw him to the floor, press a knee into his back, and handcuff him. I would watch this scene wanting to shout, "be careful with him, he's just a kid!" I'll want to tell them to never mind. Let him go. We'll work it out. Doctors deciding to hospitalize him, how long he will stay, what medicines will go into his body. I don't want to call.

Three tantrums in one weekend, each more violent than ever before. He is taller than me, almost six feet tall now. He pummels the arms of both Pam and me, pounds on the window of her car when she leaves, tears a branch off a tree in front of our house, kicks a hole in the dining room wall, pulls the huge curtain at the front window off its track. I call.

The officer, a short but burly man in his early thirties, steps into our house, and I introduce us. "We're his mothers."

He asks us a few questions, and when I answer, I cry. I tell him about the medicine, about the psychiatrist, the family therapist. He looks at Ben.

Ben is silent, completely intimidated. And embarrassed, I think. He doesn't want people to know about the Asperger's, about his tantrums.

The officer speaks with Ben for several minutes about the consequences of his behavior. I'm relieved that he's calm and kind to Ben who answers his questions with a voice that is ragged from screaming. He is calm now, and I'm struck with how handsome he is, this tanned, tall blond boy. The officer explains the process for an involuntary hospitalization, a process I know from work. If we have to call again, the officer says, they'll have to take Ben to the hospital. And it won't be pleasant, he promises Ben.

Straightening Up: A Haiku
Put the box on top
Just like I had it before
Turned ninety degrees.

When he is twelve and a half, we still have to turn the shower on for Ben, still have to dry his hair with a towel. It is a ritual, and it drives me crazy.

"He needs to learn to do it himself," I say to Pam.

"It's no trouble to do it for him."

"But he relies on it too much; he needs to be more flexible, to be able to tolerate a change once in a while."

Pam and I argue. Do we keep towel drying his hair after his shower past puberty, or make him do it, risking his rebellion against the change.

"We need to modify the world for him," she says.

"But he needs to get along in the real world. Things aren't like this out there."

"If he was in a wheelchair, we wouldn't expect him to get around without ramps and other modifications."

This is right out of special education arguments. Modify the environment or teach the child to cope with it as it is. Pam and I are in opposite camps.

I'm assigned to a school for special education students who have autism, Asperger's, and other communication disabilities. Since about half our students have autism, I never know which kids will sing "hi" to me as they pass me in the hall and which will stare right past me, like I'm not there.

Sometimes, I feel like I'm in the movie *Invasion of the Body Snatchers* and I'm surrounded by people with Asperger's but I don't know who has it and who doesn't, and it's like a dream but I'm wide awake.

Just before Ben's fourteenth birthday, Morgan and I were whispering in the kitchen when Ben walked in. We stopped and looked up, caught. "What are you talking about?" Ben asked. "What to have for dinner," I said quickly, hoping to move on, get him to leave the room again so Morgan and I could continue talking about birthday plans. Ben stared at my face, and I knew the lie was right there, visible. "Did you just lie to me?" he asked. I struggled with my choices. Do I keep up the ruse to get him to go away, or do I come clean? I decided that since we want him to be able to read faces, it's important that I give him correct feedback. "Yes," I said. His eyes filled with tears. "Don't lie to me," he said.

It bothers me that so much of the press now, at the end of 2007, about Asperger's never fails to mention poor eye contact. I've worked with many kids on the autism spectrum whose eye contact is not noticeably different from their peers. And some kids with autism who stare so hard at me, I feel like they're taking measure of my soul. A better description than lack of eye contact might be unusual eye contact. A neuropsychological evaluation for Ben noted his eye contact as "fairly typical, though it appeared forced at times and seemed as if he was looking through the examiner, rather than at her." I'm so used to Ben's eye contact or lack of eye contact or unusual eye contact that I don't notice it anymore. I wear the rose-colored shades of motherhood.

I also know about the research done at Yale that mapped eye tracking and compared autistics with controls. While watching film clips of emotional moments (an argument in the movie *Who's Afraid of Virginia Wolf,* for example), non-autistic controls tended to watch the eyes of the speakers, so their computer-generated visual scanning maps have lines back and forth between the faces of two people. The maps of autistics show that they look at the speaker's mouths, the picture on the wall, the peoples' mouths, their belts, their mouths.

Once Ben and I were having an argument and I was yelling at him about something when he started to laugh. This made me yell more. "What are you laughing at?" I shouted. He smiled. "Your lips look funny right now."

He and I are walking home from somewhere when he lopes an arm over my shoulder. My god, he's touching me, he's showing affection. I haven't had an arm over my shoulder since high school or college or maybe when I was dating and some tall man playfully flopped an arm across my back and over my shoulder, maybe tugged me closer to him. Connecting.

But this is different. Ben isn't taller than me, and this is not a romantic gesture. But it is affection, physical, tactile affection and I am shocked it is coming from him. We take only three steps like this, and just as I wonder when he'll drop his arm and break the spell, I see why he has embraced me. With his arm around my shoulder, he has been nudging me to the left side of the sidewalk and I almost smash my face into a street sign pole. I dodge it and then give him a wounded look. He is laughing; it wasn't an embrace, it was an assault. To him, it was all a joke. And the sensation of his heavy, loving arm around me has faded to nothing.

In the car between home and work and work and home, I do not turn on the radio. I need the quiet. My car is my transition bubble: I'm leaving one place behind so I can reenter the other.

A pediatric neuropsychologist diagnosed one of our students with a non-verbal learning disability, a diagnosis with a huge overlap with Asperger's Syndrome. In her office, she found him eager to engage with her and using good eye contact, so she ruled out AS. When I observed him in his classroom, on the playground, and in the cafeteria, I saw a boy who did not engage with his kindergarten peers without a teacher's facilitation. I saw a boy who monopolized conversations, talking only about the most recent superhero movie he'd seen. And when I saw him walking the perimeter of both the fenced-in playground and the classroom while running his hand over the barriers—including his teacher's body—I knew. When I spoke with his mother before the IEP, she said she'd suspected it was indeed Asperger's. "I wish we'd had you evaluate him before the neuropsychologist," she said. My shining moment.

When I explain to parents what autism is, I hold up my hands as if I'm about to show them how long something is. "No one looks the same on this line," I say. I use the span of my hands to show where their kid is in relation to others. Once, in an IEP meeting, I set up my hands and placed the severely autistic group on my right hand and the mildly affected on my left. The child in question had high functioning autism, but I gestured toward my right hand when I said this. My colleague, a speech and language pathologist, looked at me and raised her eyebrows. "Did I—?" I asked. She nodded, and I corrected myself. The child's mother let out a huge breath.

I arrive fifteen minutes late to an IEP meeting that started at eight in the morning. We usually don't schedule meetings before 8:30 but have accommodated the developmental pediatrician's schedule. He's a busy and important man. He is the same developmental pediatrician who saw Ben when he was six, and gave us no diagnosis, instead referring us to an occupational therapist who confirmed our suspicion of sensory integration disorder. We paid this man $500 for nothing, and now I'm sitting across a table from him in our school's library.

Who the hell is this doctor to come as an expert when he still doesn't know enough about Asperger's to call it what it is? His report says the six-year-old in question has a developmental dysregulatory disorder. Fancy words for *the kid's got some delays for some unknown reason*. I say it's Asperger's Syndrome.

Before he leaves the meeting early, because he is a busy and important man, he crosses one leg over the other, takes a sip of his coffee and says, "This is one of the best IEPs I've had the pleasure of attending."

I want to slap him.

"I feel like such a failure," I tell the therapist, a woman who has been treating children with Asperger's Syndrome since before it was called Asperger's Syndrome. "About everything," I say. "About having no more patience, about losing my temper—I spanked him a few months ago." I can't hold the tears back any longer, and have to wait a moment before I can speak again. "It's just so hard to deal with him when he gets rigid, 'getting stuck' we call it. I know I shouldn't yell at him. It only intensifies the tantrum. And spanking him was the worst thing to do. It only makes him furious, makes him hate me. I'm a psychologist, for God's sake. I work with children. I'm supposed to know what to do."

She places her notebook on the table and leans forward. "It's harder for us, isn't it?" she says, and I let go a silent exhalation. "First there are the challenges of raising a child with special needs, and add to that the expectations that we will always know what to do, that we should be able to get everything right." I sink a little deeper into the leather couch. "And then, of course, there are the expectations we put on ourselves. Those can be pretty high, can't they?"

My tears now are those of drunken, delirious relief. She has borne witness to our secrets, and for the first time in months, if not years, I feel as if we might survive Ben's childhood.

The Story So Far
by Andrea McDowell

I am a Type 1 diabetic, so my pregnancy with Frances was rigorously planned. Before we started trying, I got my sugars under control, purchased an insulin pump and learned how to use it, visited all of the specialists to make sure I had no complications or other contraindications to pregnancy, and then it was hats to the wind.

By May of 2003, I was pregnant. The estimated due date was January 22, 2004, which was a relief; it wouldn't be a Christmas baby. Goodness knows how much of an inconvenience that would be—birthday parties and the holidays right together, buying two sets of presents at once. I cracked down even more on my blood sugar control and managed to maintain healthy average blood sugars. I took my folic acid and my prenatal vitamins. I cut caffeine down to less than 100 mg a day. I didn't dye my hair. I abstained from alcohol, except for half a glass of champagne at my brother's wedding and a shot of Limoncello on my trip to Italy. I sewed bright yellow tab curtains for the baby's window to go along with the bright, granny-smith-apple-green walls. I sewed a floor pillow in the shape of a bear. I bought a big diaper bag that looked like a stuffed dog, a little soft yellow stuffed elephant, some nice outfits size 0–3 months, lots of books and magazines on pregnancy and motherhood; in short, I did everything I was supposed to do.

It didn't work. It didn't keep the bogeyman away.

On November 13, 2003, I was thirty weeks pregnant. I sat down in the nurse's room of the ob/gyn high-risk practice that was following me (due to the diabetes). The nurse bit her lip, looked at her feet and said, "The doctor is going to want to talk to you about the results of your last ultrasound," then left the room.

I learned from the doctor that the "problem" was that the baby had "short femurs." The baby's size was normal, its head was normal, all the organs were there and working properly, but the thigh bones were short. I was told they were three weeks behind expected measurement and that this meant the baby might have a "mild form of dwarfism," but it was probably because I'm short (I'm 5'8") or my legs are short (they aren't). The doctor said I shouldn't worry because the baby wouldn't die and you can't even tell that people have this form of dwarfism, they are just short. I had no idea what any of this meant. All I had heard was that there might be something wrong with my baby, my little baby who squirmed and kicked and mooned the world all day and all night long. My little baby who had a bright cheery room, many little clothes already washed and folded in her dresser. My little baby who I'd waited so long for and worked so hard for and done everything I was supposed to for.

My dream of a perfect baby died that day, and nothing would ever bring it back.

I had loved being pregnant up until then, even though I'd been terribly sick for the first eighteen weeks, but now it was tainted. I closed the door to the baby's room. Sometimes I would forget I was pregnant at all—then look down at my stomach and be shocked to see it, swollen and round.

I did a lot of research. I read hundreds and hundreds of pages from medical journals on ultrasound screening, achondroplasia and hypochondroplasia (the "mild" form of dwarfism), diagnosis, accuracy, false positives, as well as what the lives of people with these disorders were like. Would my baby be happy? What would life be like? What did I need to know?

I learned that the definition of "short femur" used to screen for true dwarfism (achondroplasia) was much shorter than three weeks behind, and that "weeks behind" didn't mean anything anyway because it was diagnosed by percentiles (third percentile or less) and my baby's legs were at about the fifth percentile. I read that the majority of people with legs this short were just people with short legs, that the risk of a person with legs below the third percentile having achondroplasia was approximately 1/200. I did not learn any of this from the doctors. I had to find out by myself in the library.

We met with a geneticist at about thirty-two weeks along who told us that the risk of achondroplasia, she felt, was minimal to non-existent. There was a possibility it was hypochondroplasia (the mildest form of dwarfism), and it could also be Down's or another chromosomal disorder like Turner syndrome. I asked her what the risks of those were, based on our ultrasound results. "Oh," she said, looking shocked, "I couldn't possibly say." *Isn't that your job?* I wanted to ask her. *Isn't this what you get paid to tell people?*

I got copies of all the ultrasound test results. Then I found a site on-line that calculates the numeric risk of Down syndrome based on ultra-sounds and found out that my risk was approximately 1/300, or almost great enough to justify an amniocentesis. I'd been told that if I wanted an amnio, it should be after thirty-six weeks because it might trigger prema-ture labor and we didn't want a premature baby.

In the meantime we went for more ultrasounds to track the growth of baby's legs. They stayed three weeks behind, which was a good sign—they weren't getting any shorter relative to the rest of her. I scanned the images on the computer screen desperately, trying to prove to myself that she had no secondary signs. No frontal bossing on her forehead, no trident hands. Sometimes I thought I saw it, other times I thought I didn't.

I vacillated terribly on the question of the amnio. Some days I felt rela-tively good, that the risks were low and in any case we could handle what-ever happened. Some days I felt desperate, struggled to adjust to a new real-ity and a new life I had never prepared for. On those days I went shopping and spent a lot of money— "My baby deserves the best of everything," I told myself, "whether she's 'perfect' or not. She's perfect to ME. She's beautiful to ME." After spending so many months reading pregnancy and parent-ing magazines in which perfect little babies slept perfectly in perfect little rooms while wearing perfect little outfits, these purchases made me feel as if at least one part of that equation was still within my control, even though it was in complete contradiction to how I'd lived the rest of my life: as an anti-consumerist environmentalist, not to mention anti-pink-for-girls. Up until then, I'd made her whatever I could just on principle. My largest concern had been how to ensure that my little person grew up properly feminist and politically progressive, and how exactly I could communicate my Wiccan beliefs to her without telling her she ought to follow them herself.

Some days I was torn by a terrible needing to know, a choking awful feeling of grief, and on those days I needed the amnio. If only so that the birth of this desperately wanted baby could again be joyful, instead of ter-rifying—if only so I wouldn't be ambushed in the delivery room—if only so I could prepare and work on acceptance.

I never did make up my mind.

On Sunday, December 21, 2003 (35w4d), I had a surprise baby shower. I returned home and went to bed. Shortly after midnight I awoke to a wet mattress and what I thought were gas pains. Soon I realized that my water had broken and I was in labor—the contractions were three minutes apart. I hadn't even packed my bag yet. I quickly did, pausing when contractions hit, and then at 3:00 am when they were still strong and getting stronger, I awoke my husband (he was sleeping in a separate bed that week because he had a cold) and we went to the hospital, still half convinced that it was a false alarm and they'd send me home.

But no: on Monday, December 22, 2003 at almost 10:00 am, Frances was born—exactly one month early and weighing 5 lbs 1 oz and just over 15 inches long. In case you're wondering—that's very short. It's under the third percentile line on the preemie growth charts.

Frances spent eight days in the NICU while the nurses pretty well did whatever they pleased with her. They fed her from bottles even though I asked them not to—they gave her pacifiers even though I asked them not to. She ended up with nipple confusion (which the nurses said didn't happen to preemies). After she'd been home several weeks, she still wasn't taking the breast, and I was losing my mind using the nipple shield (which I hated) and pumping all the time to supplement her. We broke her of the silicone habit by feeding her expressed milk from a dropper and teaspoon for thirty-six hours, after which she refused to eat from anything—including bottles and nipple shields—for six hours.

I thought about sending the nurses a thank-you note, but never did.

The high-risk pediatrician determined that she did not have Down syndrome and showed no signs of dwarfism. They took a blood test for chromosomal abnormalities and that, too, came back negative. Our baby was (briefly) normal.

Meanwhile, she wasn't growing very fast. Her length shot up relatively quickly over the first month or two and she briefly hit the tenth percentile, but her weight was increasing very slowly. First hypothesis: reflux. She was spitting up huge amounts after almost every feeding, and screaming afterwards for hours (in retrospect, this is almost certainly because the nurses told us to supplement her with a bottle of expressed milk after every feeding to "make her grow," and it was too much for her stomach to hold). We couldn't put her down at an angle of less than forty-five degrees for even a few minutes or she would spit up everything in her little tummy and scream. I learned to get by on one meal a day, without peeing, without showering, and without getting dressed. Leaving the house was a joke. Her car seat bunched up her tummy and made her spit up, and from the driver's seat I would hear her choking on it and crying. Already scared and worried over her low weight gain, I did not dare put her down during the day unless it was absolutely necessary. She slept held upright on my chest all night, and I dozed leaning upright against the headboard. She went on Zantac, and it helped, but not so much that I didn't have to do all of these things.

The reflux slowly got better, but her weight gain did not improve. Our family doctor had been seeing her and was nervous about this; she had been pushing formula not very subtly for months. I resisted because it would make the reflux worse, and have a family history of allergies, asthma and diabetes, the risks of all of which are increased in someone fed formula during the first year. I did not believe it had anything to do with the breast-feeding, as she had lots of wet diapers and poops, was active and alert for many hours each day, and meeting her milestones on target.

At one appointment her doctor recommended that we take her to the geneticist's again because her eyes were "too big."

"She has her father's eyes," I replied.

I went home and cried. Her eyes, her beautiful big blue eyes, were one of the things I loved most about her. How could they mean that anything was wrong?

We got in to see the high-risk pediatrician who'd seen her at the hospital and he agreed to take her on. This was a huge relief; he didn't push formula or panic over her unusually slow growth (by then she was below the charts in length again as well). But he did want us to see the geneticist. Our respite, our period of having a "normal" baby, was over.

We saw the geneticist. She agreed that Frances' eyes were unusually prominent, and that she was very small. Furthermore her ears were low-set and her anterior fontanel (the one on top) was very large and closing slowly. I discovered that as painful as it is to hear about a problem with the baby-to-be, it is nothing like being a mother and hearing a doctor discuss your child's "abnormalities." She suspected a craniosynostosis disorder, possibly Crouzon's or Pfeiffer's syndrome. The wide-open fontanel gave her pause—craniosynostosis is when the sutures in the skull fuse too early, not leaving the brain room enough to grow. She said we could have a blood test taken and the genes analyzed to be sure. That's what we decided to do.

I was paranoid about her "unusual" appearance for a while. People looking at her made me feel sensitive and strange. I didn't want to leave the house with her and expose her to other people who might think she was "unusual." Like the lady who led one of the baby programs at the community center, who said she had a niece who looked "like a turtle" when she was a baby, and now she was a really pretty girl! So I shouldn't worry because one day Frances would be perfect, too. I took great comfort in the many, many lovely people who stopped us when we were out to compliment her on her big mop of blond hair, her sweet demeanor, and her huge blue eyes.

I took my five-month, not-yet-ten-pound baby to the lab, and a nurse and I pinned her to a gurney while she screamed so another nurse could take several vials of blood out of her little broomstick arm. I put my face against hers and kissed her cheek while we both cried. I was told I should have the results in "a few weeks."

It took four months.

The results were negative. She did not have a craniosynostosis disorder.

So back to the geneticist's we went because if she's short, her fontanel is closing slowly, her ears are low-set and her eyes are too big, there has got to be something "wrong" with her, right?

Right?

We spent the next year traveling from expert to expert, specialist to specialist, trying to get an answer to that question. She remained very small, very happy, and very bright. She continued to get compliments on her smile and her big blue eyes. The doctors never did get us any answers. They guessed at pyknodysostosis and 3M syndrome, both of which turned out to be negative after much fussing and testing and anxiety, and after which they had no new ideas. For the 3M syndrome misdiagnosis, her photograph and genetic test results had to be sent to a special laboratory in Paris, France. We haven't been back to the experts since then; it's been almost three years.

Frances is still tiny at four and a half—the height of an average two year old. To accommodate her size, we bought her a lot of footstools and small toilet seats and my father built her a special table and chairs set, since all of the kiddie furniture in the stores is much too big. She still wears 2T clothing and is mistaken for a baby in the mall ("I'm not a baby!" she yells back). She is adored by her classmates and teachers and family. Her fontanel is still open. Her head is still a bit larger proportionately than you would expect for her size—it's the only part of her that fits on the standard growth charts. It all adds up to a genetic quirk of some kind, though whatever it is, is so rare (and overall so benign) that we don't have a diagnosis and don't expect ever to get one. The last syndrome to be ruled out, 3M, has only been diagnosed in forty people ever worldwide. The last expert estimate of her adult height was four feet; I think she is growing a little faster than they expected, so she might hit 4'3". Dwarfism, medically speaking, applies to anyone with an adult height of less than 4'10", so whichever gene it is that's quirking, she is certainly a dwarf, however hesitant I am to apply the label.

That is our long story.

If you are a parent with a "different" child then you already know all of this, don't you? Only maybe you think I'm whining and spoiled because, after all, my baby isn't sick and doesn't need surgery (though we thought for a while that she would, on her skull) and is meeting her developmental milestones. I do feel blessed for this. It could have been so much worse.

If you, too, are living in a permanent limbo-land of some presumed di-agnosis that never materializes, then you will know already about the con-stant anxiety that never quite fades. How sometimes when you are staring at your child's beautiful face you will also be evaluating their "unusual" features, to see what it is the doctor sees, and if maybe they're right.

This is not the whole story.

Of course it isn't.

This story that I've written here is the story of all the terrible things that I did not expect, but which I somehow survived and got used to. You didn't read here about how much I love her. You didn't read about how perfect and flawless she is to me, how I would not trade a hair on her head, how if those two years between the first ultrasound and the official non-diagnosis were the price I had to pay for Frances to be the loveable little person she is, then I would pay it over again. How I would never trade her for a "normal" baby or even her made somehow normal.

You didn't read here about the charming, sweet, giggly, smart, amazing little individual person she is. About all the days in between the weigh-ins and the appointments and the tests and results, when I hardly even thought about this. You didn't read here about our picnics in the park, about how much she laughs, or how much she loved to play kissytickles or belly biting baby (it is what it sounds like). How she loves chocolate and cheesies. How well she does with strangers, how social she is. You didn't read here about how happy she is, about how much she loves to correct me, how scandalized she is when I say "jammies" instead of "pajamas," and how she is convinced that if I am putting her to bed when the sun is still up that it must be some conspiracy to have all the fun after she is asleep. You didn't read about what good care she takes of her stuffed toys, how she loves to put them to bed and kiss their owies, how much she adores the older girl who lives next door. You didn't read about how I secretly sometimes love her small size, because I can still pick her up and carry her around, burying my nose in the crook of her neck, kissing the top of her head, her arms and legs wrapped around me; how I can still toss her in the air to make her laugh.

Life with her is amazingly, overwhelmingly good.

I couldn't have pictured this back at that doctor's appointment, when I first got *the news* (which turned out to be wrong anyway).

But it's true.

There was a time I could not have imagined things being this okay. I could not picture my life with a child who was "different." When I was pregnant, the only thing that reassured me was that they might be wrong. I could not have pictured myself coping with any of this and remaining relatively sane and even happy.

But that was before I knew Frances. Now I love her so much, I can't picture her any other way, and whatever "condition" she has is such a small part of our life together. I only see her big blue eyes, adorably pointed chin, soft round cheeks, impossible grin, her long dark-blond hair, and her little hands twitching in the air as she asks for a hug.

Our life has not become her diagnosis, or lack thereof.

Paging Dr. House
by Christina Witkowski

I am thirty-one weeks pregnant; this has been a pregnancy riddled with issues following two miscarriages. I have asked the doctor for an ultrasound to confirm that my soon-to-be born son wasn't going to weigh fifteen pounds and tear me a new one when I delivered him. The ultrasound tech grew quiet while taking pictures of our son. I asked her what was wrong, and she looked at me with a sympathetic face and told me she'd have to have the doctor take a look at the scans. A gruff doctor walked in and roughly rubbed the ultrasound across my belly, alternating between shooting daggers at my husband and me and furrowing his brow at the ultrasound screen. I asked the doctor what was wrong. He pointed to the screen and said "Do you see that? You have a child with spina bifida, are you happy? Who's your OB? Go see him now and see how he deals with it." With that shocking statement, he stood up and left the room.

Spina bifida. Spina bifida. What the hell was spina bifida? Why couldn't we find any relevant or current information on spina bifida? Why were all the books telling us our child would be born deformed; why did all of the books tell us he'd be brain damaged and unable to do anything at all? Why did our doctor's office only have one pamphlet on spina bifida that didn't tell us ANYTHING at all? Why did the high-risk specialists advise me at thirty-two weeks of pregnancy to have an abortion? Why did the smug, arrogant bastard at the ultrasound tell me that it was MY fault my child had spina bifida?

After six agonizing weeks and countless doctors appointments, Gabriel Alexander came into this world screaming his head off. He was only hours old and was being thrust into the medical world that would soon become the norm for him. Sixteen days and two surgeries later, we were finally able to take Gabriel home and start trying to live our lives as a young family, a young family with a special needs child. We contacted Early Intervention; we met with our pediatrician, orthopedic surgeon, neurologist, nephrologists, and a genetic counselor.

Our first interaction with these medical professionals was rushed and done quickly; they were all very busy people and had many other children to attend to. We dealt with Early Intervention sparingly, at their request, not ours. At Gabriel's one-year evaluation, we were told that we needed to start thinking about a preschool for him. I assured our caseworker that preschool would not be an issue, as Gabriel had been coming to my classroom since he was three months old. Miss Caseworker sighed deeply and informed me that a Montessori classroom was no place for a child "like Gabriel." Like Gabriel? I asked her what she meant; did she mean Montessori discriminated against cute blond boys? I had it on good authority that they did NOT do anything of the sort. Did she mean that Montessori did not accept children who had a scruffy puppy dog that went everywhere with them? What did she mean, that's what I wanted to know? She gently said "Well, you know what I mean, a child like HIM, disabled, not functioning, besides, it's very expensive and your money would be best spent somewhere else. After all I can't afford a Montessori education for MY children, why should your child have that sort of education; he's DISABLED." I smiled sweetly and told her that she could find her way to the door and get into her shiny new Lexus and leave. I cried harder than I had ever cried at that point. Gabriel was a year old and already being told what he could and could not do by people who didn't truly know him.

Soon after the Early Intervention debacle, Gabriel started physical therapy with a wonderfully tough physical therapist. She pushed him to become more independent and to stand on his two feet and walk for himself. Two months before he turned two, he did just that. He took steps with no assistance from anyone; just from a pair of tiny foot orthotics in his cute little sneakers. In the last four years, we have seen many physical therapists, each one more wonderful than the last. All of them truly have Gabe's best interest at heart. He is not just a name, he is not just a patient, he is Gabriel; and he is their only focus when we are at therapy.

I have learned more about spina bifida from our physical therapists than from any of the other doctors we have met along our journey of raising Gabriel. I have learned that mother's intuition is a good thing, that trusting your instinct when it comes to your own child really does benefit your child.

Gabriel's spina bifida lesion is on the L5/S1 vertebrae of the spine, which gives him a fairly high functioning level. He had a closed lesion, so none of the nerves were "eaten away" by amniotic fluid, which, incidentally, I am told causes most of the damage in individuals with spina bifida. Gabriel didn't walk until he was twenty-two months old and wears braces to help strengthen his right ankle, which seems to be the only thing below the waist affected by the spina bifida. He had a shunt placed at ten days old to relieve the excess pressure on his brain. Gabe still receives occupational therapy to work on some fine motor-skill issues and also works on sensory integration issues such as eating and not gagging when he tries something new.

There is no manual for parents facing life with a disabled child. There are books full of suggestions and "this worked for me" but at the end of the day, none of these things means squat when it comes to your own family. Gabriel is a typical four-year-old child in most ways; he is obsessed with Hot Wheels cars, dogs, and potty humor. He likes to watch *Animal Planet* and read books about penguins. He pushes his sister, throws tantrums when we won't allow him to have ice cream for dinner, and has been known to spit on the carpet in front of house guests. Lord knows no one is perfect, let alone a four-year-old little boy with more energy than he knows what to do with who doesn't always have the ability to release that energy.

Have you seen the essay comparing having a special needs child to taking a trip to Holland as opposed to going to Italy? If one more well-meaning person forwards it to my inbox, I may scream. Do I love Gabriel more than anything else? Do I absolutely hate seeing him struggle to do things that other four-year-olds have no problem doing? Of course I do, I am his mother. Does that mean that I should feel sad that I am not in "Italy" with him? Does that mean that his life means anything less than his "normal" fourteen-month-old sister? Should I be sitting around gnashing my teeth and wailing?

Sometimes I hate being the parent of a special needs child. I absolutely hate it. There, I said it, now, anyone else who is the parent of a special needs child and hates it, please raise your hand. Look around, you're not alone. I don't enjoy the stares, the ignorant questions, or the assumptions people make. It's not easy, it's not fun, and it's certainly not cheap.

We've taken endless trips to doctors and specialists who can't tell us anything we don't already know, we've read countless books on our child's disability, and we've Google searched for hours at time in the wee hours of the night looking for answers. We look at other families with envy that they don't have to deal with the issues with which we are dealing. We silently seethe when yet another person, well meaning or not, suggests that perhaps your non-walking child shouldn't be carried so damn much and then they'll walk. We think about punching the next person who tells us that our child with autism would be fine if we'd just give them a good spanking and not allow them to throw temper tantrums in the middle of a packed grocery store. We smile and nod, pretending to agree when someone tells us that if we'd just stop giving our child with ADHD sugar, we'd have it so much easier.

Doctors, therapists, counselors, and advocates come into the lives of special needs children willingly. They CHOOSE to deal all day with our children, I sometimes wonder why. The best reason I can figure is that they understand how hard it is to raise a child with a special need; they understand that these families need good, caring professionals in their lives. They understand the need for a support network and willingly join that support network.

Gabriel is about to get a new support network soon; he is going to start school in a few months. In September, the short bus is going to come and pick him up so he can go to school with twenty-eight other children. The short bus. My child is going to ride the short bus. I don't know whether to laugh or cry, and truth be told, I've done both in the last few months. I'm scared and nervous about the next step, but if experience has taught me anything it's that there are people in the world with my child's best interests at heart, it's not just me, it's not just my family; he will have another support network, more people who care about him and the progress he makes.

Evaluating Ezra

by Kerry Cohen

The first time I hear the word autism associated with my son, he is only a year old, and it comes from his young babysitter, right before she leaves after her final day with us.

"One thing I want to be sure to say, though," she starts, "because I wouldn't be able to forgive myself if I didn't."

I wait. I have no sense of the huge thing she's about to say, no sense that life will forever be altered.

"I think Ezra's on the autistic spectrum."

Here's what happens to me in this moment: an electric bolt shoots through my body. I think—*Rain Man*. Institutions. Mental retardation. Rocking. Wordless. Empty. Alone. I think, *Please God, no*. She lists a couple reasons she thinks this. She says he has a tendency to get very involved with something, and that he doesn't look at her unless she's singing. He's picky about eating. He stays very focused on whatever toy he's playing with. He doesn't seem to understand much of what she says.

I know these things. He's my child. I have been with him since the beginning, have held him close to me, inside me, since he was a drop of possibility. I know every inch of him, the beauty mark on his belly, the way his skin turns red when he's upset. I know these things she's said about him, and yet they've never caused me concern. Not even an ounce. He's a happy baby. A loving, affectionate baby. He *is* engaged, you just have to know how to engage him. So he loves music. So what? As for understanding, well, he's only a year old. Surely, he'll catch up.

I go back to that moment again and again, holding it in my hand like an iridescent shell, turning it this way and that, trying to understand. Because that one small exchange effectively ended my innocence as a mother. From that day on, until he was around four, I couldn't see my little boy clearly.

He grew blurry, far away. Everything became cause for evaluation. I examined other children his age and wondered how they were different, how my child was maybe not right. I lost sight of him, my small, precious, beautiful blond love, and to this day I feel furious about it. I want to get that time back. I want to go back to that moment when she said, "One thing I want to be sure to say, though," and say, "No, say nothing," and push her more quickly out the door. I want to never have hired her at all.

Eventually, I would have noticed that Ezra's development was different, sure. Eventually I would have worried enough about his eating to seek help. But my right to that process, my right to my son, was stolen from me. When I hear people now tell their righteous, heroic stories of letting parents know they see something concerning in a child, that old rage comes back. When they claim other parents are in denial, I want to scream, *How dare you! How dare you think you know what other people need, what they know and don't know about their children! How dare you take their process of discovery from them!* Some may argue that the earlier a child is given services the better. The sooner you get them into therapies and programs, the sooner they will change. I don't believe in the small-window-of-time theory any more than I believe that all parents need to be anxious to change how their children interact with the world. Nobody seems to think about the harm that can come to a family, to a child, from pushing them into the world all special needs families must enter, one full of evaluations and interventions and schedules and do something fast now quick or else or else or else. No one considers that a family might do better, might have enough wherewithal even, to make its own choices about what's right for only them.

But I'm getting ahead of myself, because the day that babysitter says the words "autistic spectrum" to me, I'm not there yet. I'm suddenly not anywhere. I'm knocked off the world I thought I knew. It will be a long time before I feel this anger, a long time before I understand what was done to my family, what is mandatory experience for all families with a special need. For now, I am singly, unbearably terrified. For now, I am too scared to move.

That same night the babysitter leaves, after I get Ezra to sleep, I go online, my stomach hollow and aching, my body alive and pinging with fear. Fear of...fear of the only notion I have about autism: that it will destroy my son. It is the beginning of everything I will come to know about autism, just the tip of a beginning. It is the first day of what will quickly become the rest of my life. It is the day autism throws open the door of my house, the doorknob banging against the back wall. The day autism begins weaving its way through my every moment, standing at my shoulder while I'm on the phone with a friend, while I'm buttering toast, while I'm brushing my teeth, having sex with my husband. Tonight, autism comes into my house and settles into the cushions of my couch. As of tonight, autism is here to stay. It will not be leaving, not ever again, and tonight that idea terrifies me.

In my training to become a psychotherapist, I learned the abstract facts about autism in a child psychology course—it's defined by communication delays, social delays, and repetitive behaviors. I learned about autism only as a severe affliction, one that would never alter in the course of a person's life. I learned about autism as catastrophe. I try to see myself as a student, taking neat notes during the lecture. Ezra was already growing in my belly, a little fish, twisting and waving, becoming.

Tonight, I learn from a parents' perspective—the red flags that include not pointing or waving by twelve months, neither of which Ezra does. He hasn't adopted any of the sign language I've been diligently trying to teach him since he was nine months old—a vestige of my good parenting plan I created before he was born. I had so many plans: cloth diapers, no television, organic food. One by one, I had been watching my plans fall. One by one, I've been realizing how little I know about how to parent my son. He cries when a music CD ends, wanting it to play again and again. I had broken down months earlier and bought tons of videos to teach him to sign, and now he had to watch them over and over, or else he would cry. He will eat almost nothing, and so I offer him anything and everything, organic and healthy be damned, just trying to get him nourished.

But there's also so much about the spectrum that he doesn't fit. He has normal eye-contact, at least once he is comfortable with someone. He initiates peek-a-boo and chasing games. He plays normally with toys, albeit sometimes in rigid ways. He engages us as long as we do things that interest him. He's affectionate, doesn't mind loud noises or sudden changes or if we want to join him in his play or mess with what he's already doing. He's one, still a baby. It's so hard to know. Children can be weird. Children can develop at different rates.

At eighteen months, Ezra learns sign language for "more." I have been trying to teach him the better part of a year, pushing my fingertips against each other again and again, saying, "*More*, Ezra. Look at my hands. *More, more.*" We're in a grocery store, and I'm handing him one cheese puff at a time, trying to get him to ask. He looks at the bag, leans toward it, says,

"Mm mm mm." Finally, he does it. He presses his chubby dimpled hands together. "More!" I yell. "You signed more!" I hand him the puff and he sticks it in his mouth, unfazed.

I tell Michael that evening, and he lights up. He hasn't been burdened by my fears. Not yet. He heard the word "autism" and waved his hand dismissively. "No way," he said. He and Ezra play intensely. Michael chases him while Ezra squeals. He throws Ezra into the air and catches him. They have set games: Michael says, "Get out of here. Go on." And Ezra starts to walk away. Then Michael grabs Ezra's shirt and says, "Get back here," and they erupt into giggles.

Ezra isn't consistent with the signing, though, and he still has no words, so I call Early Intervention.

"What sorts of things are you concerned about?" the coordinator asks me on the phone.

"I'm not *concerned*," I say. I'm aware I'm pacing as we talk. "But I know he's supposed to have a few words by now, and I figure speech therapy could help."

"So, he isn't talking yet. How old is he again?"

I tell her, not wanting to. He's twenty-one months.

"Any other concerns?"

His poor eating. No pointing. Crying when songs end. He cries in terrible despair if someone sings one his favorite songs. "No," I say. "No. Just the words."

We set a date and time, and I immediately set about dreading the coming appointment. In moments, I am stricken with instinctual fear. What have I done? Allowing others to get their sticky something-is-wrong-with-your-son hands on my boy? Somehow I know that the moment they walk into our house, things will get out of hand. Somehow I understand they will take my son, grip him in their claws, in their estimation of who he is, based on his imperfections. That I will have to scramble to keep him safe.

The day of the evaluation, Ezra is in a good mood. He has gotten a good night's sleep and has been playing all morning. The team—a lead evaluator (with whom I spoke on the phone), a pregnant speech therapist, and occupational therapist—march into the house with a bag full of toys and eye Ezra. My heart batters against my chest. I know they're here to *evaluate* him. I'm not an idiot. But every bit of me doesn't want it. I know they will examine my child as though he were bacteria in a Petri dish, and short of making them leave, I won't be able to stop it. I want to get him speech therapy, I remind myself. I want him to get a chance to catch up. Unfortunately, this is what we have to endure to get there.

Almost as though Ezra knows what they are here for, almost as though he intends to shake things up, get this party started, he flips over a toy car and spins its wheels—a classic autism move. And something he has never ever done before. *Boom!* They perk up.

"Is this something he does often?" the lead asks.

"He's never done that before in his life," I say. They watch him, excited.

"As far as you know," the pregnant one corrects.

I shoot a look her way. *What is that supposed to mean?* I already don't like her. I don't like the way she glanced around my house after they got settled, evaluating not just Ezra, apparently, but my decorating. I don't like that she asked to use the bathroom, pointing to her belly, and when she came out, said, "Those are the same colors we're painting our nursery." I don't like that she's caught up in thinking about her own life, and, more than that, something about the way she referred to her precious belly, something makes me certain she believes herself immune to the possibility of having a child with special needs herself.

Next, the lead evaluator begins with the questions I will hear often over the next couple years, questions I will answer again and again about Ezra's behavior and my pregnancy with him, questions that will never lead to anything useful.

Meanwhile, one of the evaluators, the occupational therapist, is busy with Ezra. I keep looking over nervously, seeing Ezra grow frustrated each time she shows him a toy, tells him how to play with it, watches him play with it for a few moments in his own way, and then takes it away. She wears that same quizzical look, the one all evaluators are apparently required to wear. By the time a half hour has passed, Ezra is fully upset. He runs toward me, sobbing.

"Mama!" he calls, although I'm pretty sure it's just word sounds he made when upset.

"I see he says 'mama'," the lead evaluator says without emotion, while Ezra clings to me. She jots this into her notebook.

I hold him, his small, soft body, and nod, wanting Ezra to get this one positive mark today. When they finally leave, I get Ezra down for his nap, and then I sit on the couch and cry. I call Michael.

"You don't know how they look at him," I tell him. "Like he's not even a person. He's just a baby."

"Then why are we doing this?" he asks.

"I feel like I'm supposed to," I explain. "To be a good mom, I have to get him help."

I have to pull myself together. I have to be stronger, more resilient. I have to be a better mom. We have another evaluation coming up in just a couple months, this one with a private hospital's rehabilitation center, which is covered by our insurance. I want him to get as much speech therapy as possible, and, although I'm certain he'll qualify for services with Early Intervention, they warned me early on that their budget rarely allows for therapy more often than every other week. I wish we could just ask for speech therapy. I wish I could interview them, not the other way around. That I could be trusted, as my son's mother, to know what he needs. But this isn't the way it works. They have to determine for themselves that he needs it, and for that to happen, we have to endure more horrible evaluations.

In the waiting room of the children's rehabilitation center, I feel stupidly optimistic. I have learned nothing yet. I haven't yet suffered through enough specialists eyeing my child with that particular mix of scrutiny and judgment, as though he were a strange creature in a cage. I haven't yet listened to enough experts tell me that my son is disordered, that he will never do this and might always do that. I haven't yet come to know that the world will not welcome my child.

Ezra watches the fish in the aquarium they have set up here. I crouch down with him and point out the different fish, modeling the words. "Blue fish. And there! A yellow fish. So pretty." He stares into the tank, smiling at the fish. I just found out a few weeks ago that I'm pregnant again. I'm constantly fighting nausea and fatigue. With all the concerns that have begun to bore down on us—on me—about Ezra since Early Intervention's visit, I feel uncertain about having another baby. It's not that I worry this baby will be disabled. I worry that I don't have it in me to care as much about another human being. I fear my heart might explode once there are two.

We received a copy of EI's report a few days earlier. How can I describe the pain in reading such a document about my son? Substandard scores, observed doing this and not doing that. Your child—the same one who giggles, who pushes his truck along the floor, who claps and dances—he is not doing x, y, and z. He is doing w, but only about as well as 10 percent of the other kids his age. He is in the bottom percentile for this, and doesn't even get on the charts for that. He doesn't do v when we ask him to, which must mean he can't do v at all. He is no good. He is no good at all.

The speech pathologist leads us into a room no bigger than a closet. A ball, dirty and played with to death, lies against the wall. She shuts the door behind us.

"Hi, Ezra!" the woman says, insincere and too loud. Ezra ignores her.

"I think he's coming down with something," I say, already starting what will become a long habit of making excuses to protect him from others' judgment. She nods and writes this down, but I can tell by the way she examines Ezra that nothing is going to keep her from making whatever assumptions she's going to make.

Ezra looks around the room.

"Don't you have any toys for him to play with?" I ask.

"We take out one at a time to see what he does with them." She points to the ball and says in that same fake voice, "There's a ball, Ezra. See the ball?"

Ezra glances at the ball and goes to the door. He reaches for the knob. He's about to start crying.

"He's not into balls," I say. "Can we please get something else for him?"

The woman looks at me evenly. "He doesn't like balls?"

My palms feel sweaty. "He used to," I say defensively, but it's too late. She writes down this fact that Ezra doesn't play with balls. Ezra begins to cry, and she writes this as well.

"Come here, Ez," I say. "Come have nursies."

He climbs on my lap, sobbing. The woman eyes us.

"Does he nurse often for comfort?"

"He still nurses, yes," I say. I add defensively, "The World Health Organization recommends at least two years of breastfeeding." If nothing else, at least I accomplished this for Ezra. Will she take this from me too? Will I have nothing left in my small, useless armory to give my son?

She cocks her head but doesn't say anything. Nervous in the silence, I go on.

"He nurses less now that I'm pregnant," I tell her. "I think my milk is starting to dry up."

Suddenly she smiles, the first genuine smile I've seen from her, and she puts her hand on her belly. "I'm pregnant, too!" she exclaims. "Four months."

Another pregnant evaluator. What luck.

She unlocks a cabinet and takes out blocks. I'm beginning to get a headache.

"You know, Ezra's not really into blocks either," I tell her.

She gives him another analyzing stare. "He has limited play."

"No," I say. "He plays with lots of things. Just not balls and blocks." I can hear how pathetic I sound, how desperate. Ezra still tugs away on my nipple. I don't look at him, ashamed of my need to have this woman think he's good enough. "He's been putting the shapes in his shape sorter in the correct holes since he was sixteen months. And he's stacked his cups in the right order since fifteen months."

The woman nods. She wears nothing in her expression, no empathy, no emotion of any kind. I have never hated anyone more.

Ezra pops off, relaxed now, and she calls him over to look at the blocks. They are small, all the primary colors. To my surprise, he starts stacking them, building a little tower, saving the blue and red ones for last, like he always does.

"Blue and red, always last," I say, delighted, proud, but seeing her face, I immediately wish I'd kept my mouth shut.

"What do you mean?"

"He usually saves the blue and red pieces for last," I say quietly.

"With every toy?"

"Not *every* toy." Most every toy.

"Hmm." She gets up and scribbles that on her pad.

As soon as she does, Ezra goes to the door again and starts to whimper. I'm pretty sure he's feeling my stress, my energy pulled tight like a stretched rubber band.

She watches him as his cries turn into full on sobs. "Have you considered PDD?" she asks me. "That stands for Pervasive Developmental Disorders," she adds.

I start gathering my stuff. "I know what PDD is," I say. "I thought we were here to do an evaluation for speech therapy. If I'm not mistaken, speech therapists can't diagnose."

She puts a hand over her belly, protective. I know what she's thinking. I know she, like that therapist who came to my house, believes her own body could never bring forth anything that wasn't perfect. I know she believes Ezra isn't.

"I want you to do everything you can for Ezra," she says in a calm, condescending voice, one they must teach child therapists to use with parents. "I want him to get all the help he needs."

I want to say, *How dare you, how dare you.* But I say, "He's fine. I've got it."

Ezra is still crying, jiggling the door handle to get out.

"Lots of children look fine, but they're really not," she argues.

I wish I could formulate what I want to say, what it will take me years to know how to say: there is nothing wrong with him. He has a severe speech and comprehension delay, yes. But there is nothing *wrong*. I don't have the right words yet, and even someday when I do, I will still be misunderstood. People will still assume they know better than I do what my son needs. People will still accuse me—even though I will always get him services, always make sure he gets the therapies he needs—I'm not doing enough for my son. Unless I hate the things that make him different from other children, I will always be considered a wayward mother.

I scoop him up and we head toward the exit.

"Thank you," I say, though I wish now I didn't.

The Head Game (diagnosis)
by Kim Mahler

Though I've seen one pickled or as a pink
plastic model—quartered and labeled,
the bloodless organ baffles. *Cerebellum*
sounds like a secret in the tongue.

Scans can now match activity—red, inaction—blue,
fear. They can refashion a skull out of plaster,
giving tissue room to engorge.

Why isn't there more than theories:
mirror neurons, mercury, no cause, cure.
I want to know my son's brain, the way

a woman knows herself on the inside.
Do I have to crack it open to see that wet bouquet?
Give me something beyond these papers
to send my brain to Harvard in an ice chest.

Popeye

by Thida Cornes

Shrinking Popeye arm and growing boy body

September 16, 2004

My natural childbirth came to a jarring halt with the crowning of my son's head. The rest of his body stuck firmly inside me, I pushed harder than I ever had in my life while three doctors pushed and tugged and turned. He emerged, cold and blue. I waited for the cry that never came as doctors struggled to revive him. He required ten transfusions just to be stabilized. I sat for three hours in a wheelchair trying to memorize every detail of his face. I didn't know if this was the last time I would see him alive. I could only live with the reality by focusing on his dark eyes staring up me, hazy with pain. Then he was whisked away in an ambulance to another hospital.

I lay alone in my hospital bed and stared up at the ceiling reliving every detail of childbirth. A nurse had felt what I now knew was his hugely swollen arm. "I think it's his head." I heard the edginess in her voice, the undertone of something's wrong. The obstetrician didn't listen. She was pissed off at me because I'd adamantly refused Pitocin. She responded to the nurse, "His head is where it should be." She whipped out the ultrasound wand and waved it quickly on the spot where his head nestled. "See!" she said. The nurse frowned, but said nothing. Why hadn't I insisted that she check exactly where the nurse felt?

The phone rang. "He's not going to make it," a resident told me, "He needs surgery right away to try to save his life." The surgery would essentially amputate his left arm. He had lost a great deal of blood and was hemorrhaging constantly. I knew that this surgery would kill him. I closed my eyes and saw skin taut with blood burst open as the scalpel cut into it. I heard the monitor alarm and could smell blood's metallic stench. I opened my eyes and crumpled under the weight of my previous failures. The resident insisted again and I quietly agreed to the surgery.

I climbed into the shower but nothing could warm my heart. I touched my rounded belly and watched the water dew at my belly button. IVs bore into my son's belly button. I heard the beep of the monitor. You killed him. I shied away from thinking about a life without this child I had known for nine months and seen for just three hours and never touched with my hands. Why hadn't I spoken up about how worried I felt during my entire pregnancy? Why had I accepted "your baby will be fine" (because your first child is healthy)? I listened to the water on my back and drowned out the voices in my head. I scrubbed myself, trying to remove what I had done and not done.

The phone rang again and I jumped out of the shower soaking wet. I stood there in a puddle of water and listened to another doctor "Your son's been stabilized. I'm so sorry"—I caught my breath—"about the first call. I hadn't been contacted yet. The surgery's too dangerous right now." That doctor saved my son's life, he never had surgery, and the first phone call changed my life. I never again agreed to something I knew in my heart was wrong.

At last, I was released from the hospital after two days and could visit my son. A nurse with a hook nose and a crooked smile stood by his crib and carefully explained the litany of equipment and tests. I felt stuck in a bad story and the nurse reminded me of the good witch disguised. As we were about to leave, she asked, "Can I be your son's primary nurse?" I stared at her, afraid to say yes. She understood we were still like deer in the headlights stunned by the cacophony of the Neonatal Intensive Care Unit. Every NICU book recommends getting a primary nurse and she turned out to be one of the best NICU nurses in the hospital. Very well respected, she made sure my son was well taken care of. When she wasn't there, I felt bereft in the sea of doctors who came by to visit my son, a unique and interesting case at this top national children's hospital. Every resident paraded by his crib in the NICU: "Kasabach Merritt syndrome, last seen twelve years ago. Usually appears at a year old, never at birth."

His clinical reality presented as a cartoon. Capillaries wrapped and swelled in a massive tumor forming a grotesque Popeye arm. Blood flowed to his left arm and stuck in the maze of his tumor. Meanwhile the rest of his body starved for blood. I had jokingly called him a vampire in-utero as I had developed an aversion to garlic. His need for blood seemed insatiable.

43

My husband and I tried to make sense of the unknown. We dropped off our older daughter at preschool and tried to respond to kind inquiries from other parents and teachers. Words failed to describe our situation, and we swam in medical jargon. "Hemangioma" describes technically what my son has, but it's as far removed from a strawberry birthmark usually associated with this medical term. One acquaintance misunderstanding the diagnosis said to me, "My brother had bad eczema and he got over it. I'm sure your son will do fine." Another exclaimed, "I didn't know your son was so sick." After flailing for a while, we discovered that the short and shocking word "tumor" helped quell the clueless comments and covered it best.

We pored over medical journal articles and gave them to our doctors. Other NICU parents expressed shock. "Weren't the doctors insulted?" We replied "No, why would they be? He was our only medical concern. While a unique case, he was one of many patients they had to treat. We never implied that they should follow the treatments prescribed in the other cases, but merely they might prove useful."

And in fact our "willingness to educate ourselves" and the backing of our primary nurse allowed our son to be released earlier than his long list of medical issues might suggest. My husband learned how to clean a Broviac, an arterial line directly to his heart and how to inject chemotherapy. Even so, our insurance initially wouldn't pay for the medical supplies we needed. He would have even gone home a day earlier except the hospital and insurance had a standoff with my son staying an extra day until the approvals came through. In other situations NICU patients simply stayed. One NICU baby stayed in the hospital because her family lacked the resources to wrap her clubfoot.

The first time my disability, dystonia, clashed with my son's special needs began when I started pumping breast milk. My basal ganglia, a small region at the base of the brain, doesn't coordinate the signals between muscles and brain properly. Especially during fine motor tasks, my arms twist at awkward angles, my muscles seize up and I jerk. I'd learned to breastfeed my older daughter in a few days, but she latched on the second time and clamped on tight. However, trying to hold two vibrating breast pump flanges attached to two bottles filled with "liquid gold" breast milk had never been part of my mothering. The pressure not to waste milk proved too much. Unlike most pumping moms, my rebellious hands would throw milk across the room and like many moms, I cried over the spilled milk. So my husband held the flanges on me and sadly this often did not work.

Half the time my husband fell asleep standing there; sleep-deprived from long nights at the NICU.

I want to say I loathe pumping, but that implies passion and pumping was so clinical. I squirted with a slow rhythm as the pump swished softly—genteel and bucolic as breastfeeding is described in most parenting books. I sat utterly bored tethered to a droning machine until the squirting slowed to a drip. Then I had to milk my own breasts. I jerked too much for the C-shape milking suggested in the La Leche pamphlet. Instead, I jerked off like a bad porn rendition of nipple play, complete with squirting juice, but it got the job done. After it was over, my nipples were sore, my wrists hurt, and I'd had no release because the pump never really gave me that oxytocin fix.

Only the hope that someday he might actually breastfeed kept me going. One day Good Witch NICU nurse said "You can breastfeed him." She meant I could breastfeed him once. My son broke the bucolic fantasy of the breastfeeding books. I offered him my nipple and he twisted away and screamed at me. NICU monitors blared and nurses bustled about next to him. "Don't take it personally," they said. I thought sardonically, at least he's moving more to get away from me.

Good Witch assured me with twenty-five years of experience behind her, "Everything will be better once he gets home. He'll breastfeed." My friends said "There's nothing wrong with formula," in soothing tones. My husband said "Honey, do what you think is best," in the sort of voice that means he's afraid to say anything. I found a halter that held the breast pump flanges in place, so his role became limited to pump parts washer. Pumping generates a lot of dirty parts, so it kept him busy.

Every day at the hospital, I sat alone in a little room and pumped. After days of screaming, as though Good Witch waved her magic wand, my son latched on hard and breastfed. When he finally came home after six weeks in the NICU, he was still breastfeeding once a day.

The hospital sent us home with the same equipment that they used—a gravity feeding system. I, the stay-at-home parent, couldn't use this system and no one had ever shown me how. My work had been relegated to that private little room in the hospital. And I never spoke about my disability. I tried to solve the problem by breastfeeding frequently, but he just wailed. I wondered if he'd ever get it.

One morning he woke up and screamed at me incessantly. I tried changing his diaper, rocking him, giving him Tylenol. Finally I figured out he wanted to breastfeed. He latched on eagerly. After two and a half long months, he had finally got the nursing habit and he breastfed exclusively for a few months.

Sadly, Good Witch's powers didn't last and our breastfeeding story had no fairy-tale ending. When he was four months old, his tumor started growing again and he received chemo again. I overflowed with milk, but the chemo killed his appetite and he refused to nurse. He was diagnosed with failure to thrive. I viewed it as failure to nurse, failure to mother. I went back to pumping anyway.

We agreed to put a nasogastric feeding tube down his nose, down the back of his throat and into his stomach. He vomited several times a day. His GI doctor prescribed a pump at night to slowly drip milk into him. His doctor told us to make sure he could "tolerate the pump"—anything from vomiting to choking. We slept very close to him, listening. With each new sound, I'd startle awake to see if he had choked, or turned blue. After several nights of little sleep, we decided that he would survive the pump and his vomiting decreased. I slept six hours straight for the first time in months. I awoke and declared this pump was the best invention ever. I was hooked.

In June 2005, his Broviac catheter, the central line to his heart got infected and he developed sepsis, a life-threatening infection. After seven long days, doctors declared he was "out of the woods." I kept on pumping even though he had become too sick to eat.

Shortly after he came home, I sat there tethered to the pump as usual and my older two-year-old daughter wanted to play. I said, "I can't play. I'm pumping." "You're always pumping!" she screamed at me. She threw herself on the ground. I continued to pump. Later that night, I thought about how long pumping took. Each session took an hour when you combined prep and washing. I pumped four to six times a day, so I was spending four to six hours a day on the pump. I decided I had to stop. I faced the sad truth that I'd also have to spend time teaching him how to breastfeed again.

I tried cutting down my pumping, but it made me sad. Pumping kept my hope alive he would nurse again, but in my heart I knew even if I got him to breastfeed, he would stop again due to some medical crisis. My daughter would pay the price as I couldn't help the hormonal depression that abrupt withdrawal from breastfeeding causes. For once, I put my daughter first. Through many medical crises, I had developed a form of denial that is healthy. I told myself he had weaned himself cold turkey. Never mind the breastfeeding booklets that said he was too young. In these booklets, breastfeeding benefited the entire family. Breastfeeding represented the ultimate in nurturing motherhood. I couldn't stand thinking about how my son was too sick to accept "the best." How the NICU books also claimed it was the best (implying the only thing) you could do and yet breastfeeding was frankly a constant struggle for both of us due to the clash of our special needs. And he showed all signs of being done with the struggle to breastfeed. My son still refused to eat, and in July he had surgery to install a G-tube that went directly to his stomach.

Unfortunately, dramatic change also costs. I went into heavy withdrawal and started to slide into depression. In fairy tales, people die from grief when they refuse to eat. And in my darkest moments, I wondered if his refusal to eat meant he wanted to die. I knew he was getting all the nutrition he needed via tube and he had begun to laugh. But I kept reading "Breast milk is best" on the formula can. I had struggled so hard to breastfeed, but this time I had failed. Just as I started to hit bottom, he started to eat again, but only from a bottle.

He couldn't hold the bottle and neither could I. I bought a bottle prop, anathema to all attachment parents, and that broke my breastfeeding guilt. I quashed the little voice that told me only neglectful mothers use them. I imagine my son's legs kicking that voice vigorously in the teeth. I started to appreciate what I had done. I'm still a huge advocate of breastfeeding, but I think that there's not enough information and support for moms who are dealing with disabilities.

Sadly, I had little time to contemplate the end of our breastfeeding relationship before his tumor starting growing again. My son's chemo killed his appetite and he refused the bottle. This gave me the secret guilty satisfaction that it wasn't just me he rejected, but food in general. His weight started to slide down.

We switched to Resource 1.5, a sweet syrup of vitamins and minerals. The smell made me gag and I felt secret embarrassment I was feeding such junk to my son. Each week we bought organic produce from the local farmers' market. No formula touched my daughter's lips until she was six months old. But this time my mother instinct told me that Resource 1.5 would help my son survive and he loved it. He slurped it down mostly via pump but also by mouth and his weight began to climb at last. His head grew and he showed every sign of the intelligence I'd seen in his eyes the day he was born. The rest of his body grew in centimeters measured carefully at each doctor's visit. I celebrated any sign of growth.

Our struggles to help him grow changed after his physical growth improved and we began to pay additional attention to his developmental growth. When he was six months old, between bouts of hospitalizations, we had a brief window without beeping medical monitors to consider his development. Naively, I thought that a child who couldn't lift his head or kick his legs at six months would qualify for occupational therapy. I was wrong and I had to fight a large bureaucracy to get him the help he needed.

When he was released from the NICU, the hospital sent his medical records to California Children's Services (CCS), a government agency that provides occupational therapy and physical therapy for every child who qualifies, as well as general medical care for the poor. We only have some of his many records and even those are enough to fill a three-ring binder. Evidently CCS was in a hurry because we received a form letter stating that we didn't qualify for services we had not even asked for yet, based on our income. I asked the hospital to send another letter and CCS didn't respond. So I brought my son to a CCS open house with his threadbare hair and emaciated features due to chemo. He lay there serene and smiling. The head therapist admitted, "Yes, he needs help." We expected to receive a letter approving therapy. Instead, we received another rejection stating his "diagnosis does not qualify." Among his reams of medical records, the doctors had not highlighted the right diagnosis.

I turned to a Yahoo! group of parents with special needs kids. Everyone was dealing with a variety of disabilities, but they understood my battles. Their support put me on the right path. Without them, my son would have languished another several months as I tried to figure out what to do.

I found the CCS website. I struggled to read the legal language and relate the list of diagnoses that CCS covered to the laundry list of my son's conditions. I found a match! I asked a doctor to write a letter stating my son had that particular diagnosis and how services would benefit him. We received another form stating my son "qualified for occupational therapy only." The CCS head therapist who had met him earlier gave him therapy once a week.

Even with occupational therapy, my son needed more help. I had finally started to feel okay about giving up breastfeeding. And I started on the path to a more sane way of mothering a child with needs that were only partially met by a team of doctors and therapists. I started accepting that failure to meet his needs was not about my failings as a mother, but about the complexity of what he needed. I'd always been an advocate for my son, but I felt speaking up about my special needs was a reflection of inadequacy. I simply agreed to what professionals said and rarely mentioned that it was going to be a huge struggle for me, or even that I couldn't physically do what they suggested. Giving up breastfeeding was a turning point for me—that the "best way" to proceed, the way others had planned for my son, didn't necessarily work for me. I needed to advocate more for myself. And in doing so, I freed myself to do more for him and the entire family.

With the assistance of people on the parent Yahoo! group, I learned that I should contact Early Start, an agency that provides a number of services for children under three in the hopes that early intervention will mean they will need fewer services later. I called several times and nobody returned my calls. The government rules state that Early Start must respond within sixty days. My son's hospital had sent Early Start a letter upon his discharge from the NICU. I got another doctor to write another letter. Within a week, a pretty social worker and another woman interviewed us at our home. I only clearly remember the social worker, because my son smiled and smiled at her. He's always loved pretty people. Never mind that just before the interview, his neck had bulged out like the Incredible Hulk as he screamed at me in a steroid rage.

I trotted out our hospital vignettes carefully edited to match the angel before them. I stressed his high cognitive and social abilities and his limited physical abilities. I told his stories and my own. I wanted them to remember him. I talked about how I never received help for my disability. I had never learned how to do things ergonomically and now my body was breaking down from the ways I learned to do things on my own. I felt humbled by admitting this to strangers, and I'd never spoken about what I couldn't do to close friends or family. Yet I laid open my vulnerabilities and pain to get my son the help he needed. The caseworker stared at him, "He's so engaging." My son looked every part the special angel, lying there smiling with his chemo hair. Finally, when my son was seven months old, a hand specialist occupational therapist came once a week as his "intervention specialist."

He kicked his legs, at first a slow soft jab one at a time, then both at once, kicking us away when we wanted to perform some painful medical procedure. I started explaining my needs to every medical professional from whom we needed help. I found it embarrassing but helpful. Therapists and doctors found alternative ways for me to do things, and got help for my exhausted husband as well as. We measured each milestone, hoping he would kick his legs like a bicycle.

Over the next few months, he rolled over and began to babble. Then his tumor swallowed much of his progress. The second round of chemo stilled his legs and paralyzed his vocal cords. The loudest he could cry was a raspy whisper. I joked he would have been the perfect baby to take to restaurants if only we could have brought him out of the house. Even after he cried again, he never babbled. Instead he spoke to me in a tonal language consisting of five tones of "ba." I could only hear three, but my Chinese-American husband understood all five. He would repeat "ba" several times and then scream at me in frustration when I didn't understand. At times, I got frustrated, too. Then he stopped ba'ing all together and I felt terrible. I felt he had given up on talking to someone too stupid to understand his language. Then one day, at twelve months, as we dropped off his sister at preschool, he clearly said "Bye." We were filled with joy. And he began to speak, but not to talk. He spoke one word a day and I mean literally one single solitary word a day offered to us like a precious gift. One day he might say "car" and the next day "mama." His five-word vocabulary sounded great for his age, but he did not talk. I tried to explain, but the Early Start interventionists could not comprehend his development. I couldn't quite believe it myself. Surely, someday he would start talking. But months went by and his vocabulary grew, but he never talked.

In our strange world, the turning point came when his tumor grew again and he had to go back on steroids. His word offerings stopped. A child who stopped speaking was something the system understood. And when he was sixteen months old, a pretty blond speech therapist arrived at our house. She spoke to him in a sweet voice and discovered his passion for bubbles. He could blow bubbles if he would say "bu." For a while, he spoke only to his speech therapist. I sat listening and felt jealous that she received all his bounty of words. Slowly, he began to speak.

Unfortunately, at almost two years old, he showed no signs of walking. An inventive boy, he had learned to shuffle along on his butt using his functional right arm for support. His left side remained weaker, but Early Start said it was just his left arm and he'd learn to walk in his own time. I felt he needed help. I even asked a fellow parent who was a physical therapist to look at him, but she didn't see what I saw.

He would suddenly lose his balance and fall. I wanted to believe it was just his huge head shifting the weight of his body, but denial can only last for so long. While sitting, he fell, conking his head hard on the side of a chair. He had been sitting for months.

A top neurologist examined his three-month-old brain scans and examined my son. The diagnosis came back: "spastic diplegic cerebral palsy." I felt it was just one more diagnosis in a long list, but my son's visits to neurologists forced me to discuss topics with my parents that I'd not broached since I was a teen. My parents took me to top neurologists when I was two. "Mentally retarded" was their diagnosis. My mom had a sister with Down's syndrome, so she knew a face of mental retardation and it was not me. "No, she's a bright child," my mother replied. "You're overachievers who can't see her as she is," the doctors insisted. To prove their point, they gave me test after test and the same test again and again. Eventually fed up, I would give up and fail. My mother saw me literally jamming a square peg into a round hole with a mutinous look on my face. My parents persisted for a while. The occupational therapy helped a little, but the medicine made me cry. One day my mom heard an occupational therapist say "Good girl!" "As you would say to a dog," my mom says to this day. And that was it. My mom took me away and we never went back.

It's hard to explain to my parents how things have changed and yet stayed the same. No one has called my child mentally retarded even when he couldn't speak or move. "Cerebral palsy" no longer is synonymous with mental retardation and was treated as a physical issue.

The diagnosis of cerebral palsy allowed him to get physical therapy to help with his balance and coordination. He finally began to walk at twenty-five months old. We had been doing the usual things parents do to assist walking rather than helping him learn to get up himself. His physical therapist said he needed to learn how to balance his left arm that still hung as an extra weight. She bounced him on a big ball and positioned his hips. I also learned exercises to help my own balance and coordination.

After he started walking, his spindly legs became more obvious, especially as people would make comments when he'd fall down. He could walk and talk, but he still wouldn't eat.

I decided to see a holistic medical doctor. She ran "alternative" blood, urine, and fecal tests and told us, "He's starving, because he can't convert fat to sugar." She suggested supplements, which we had to balance against the drugs he was still taking to shrink his tumor. He drank down chocolate whey power for body builders and cod liver oil with gusto.

He started eating solid food, though he ate as if each morsel might be poison. He took a small bite then took the morsel of food out, inspected it and then repeated the process for each bite. It could take him twenty minutes to eat. At a party, an out-of-town friend offered him a pinto bean from her chili. He ate it in one bite. She kept feeding him single beans and he ate twenty beans in all.

He started eating without inspecting and began to grow. We'll never know if the supplements really helped or if he just decided to eat. What I do know is his G-tube was removed way ahead of schedule. He's no longer mistaken for a toddler due to his small size and delayed development. We still have Resource 1.5 sealed in individual boxes, considered "contaminated," that we can't give back. My son drinks them occasionally with a straw.

Sometimes people watch my son trotting. I notice his sturdy legs pump up and down, his constant stream of words, his bright smile. Sometimes others critique, he can't run and his left arm is covered in the red mottling of his still shrinking tumor. He holds it stiff by his side, his hand clenched into a fist. It feels so good to hug him without a G-tube poking me and to feel his broad and sturdy back. After spending so long below the growth charts, he's in the eighth percentile in height and twenty-fifth percentile in weight. I say, "He's come a long way" to sum up all that has happened. I've come a long way too. I've always thought of myself as an assertive woman not afraid of what people think, but I had never learned to ask for help or to insist even when I had nothing but my heartfelt belief. In the fairy story I sometimes tell people, I say my son has taught me these things. The truth is far more complex.

The Letter for Services
by Aileen Murphy

(a found poem)

Dear Dr. O----
I had the opportunity to see Henry H.
on 9/17/97
regarding his complex neurobehavioral pattern.
He is accompanied by his mother, father, and younger sister
for this visit.
They serve as the sole historians.
Henry attends Kipps Elementary School.
There he has been in kindergarten
but has shown excessive amounts of aggression
leading to significant concerns
over his overall behavior
and academic performance.
He shows the unique pattern of behavior
which you had discussed in great detail.
During the appointment which lasted well over an hour
we reviewed the characteristics of these issues
and I discussed with the family the significance
and my perception and assessment of these features.
In summary Henry shows excellent verbal skills.
He has had some formal testing performed
and preliminary reports are that he shows some marked scatter.
In some areas he is markedly above average
while in other areas he is in the average range.
There is apparently a big scatter in his initial test performance.

His social skills are very limited.
He does not tend to interact with children his own age
though he does a significant amount of parallel play.
He may be very focused on certain tasks
and may spend a long time working on complex issues.
His aggression has been variable.
In the past it has been directed toward his mother.
It has fluctuated and apparently had significantly attenuated
but has resurfaced this year at kindergarten.
Neurological examination shows a head circumference of 53.8 cms
which is 80th percentile.
Blood pressure is 90/40 and pulse is 90.
Significant findings are that Henry's running
does not show reciprocal movements.
His motor tone is slightly decreased.
His heel-shin and rapid alternative movements
are mildly impaired
as are his fine and gross motor performances.
He shows a consistent right-handed pattern
but works left-handed at least on occasion.
There are no neurocutaneous signs present.
Summary:
Henry presents a very complex neurobehavioral syndrome.
I discussed in great detail my overall perception
of such neurodevelopmental difficulties.
Many of Henry's behaviors are characteristic
of autistic spectrum disorder.
Based on the previously described pattern
Henry has many characteristics of Asperger's syndrome.
I have provided two articles to Mr. and Mrs. H.
regarding this diagnostic entity.
At the same time I emphasized to them
that Henry's situation is unique
and many different terms may be applied.
These may include attention deficit disorder
as well oppositional defiant disorder
as well as pervasive developmental disorder.

The most important thing
is that his specific areas of difficulty be identified
and appropriate behavioral interventions be initiated.
I do not see a place for pharmacologic interventions
at this point.
I have reassured them that the high quality of his present school
will address these issues with great insight

and provide excellent support for them.
I emphasized that Henry's discrepancies
in terms of his areas of great skill
need to be capitalized upon and efforts made
to keep his areas of weaknesses from holding him back.
Social skills will obviously be a problem for him.
Insight behavioral efforts will be beneficial for him
once he is able to identify the issues
which need to be addressed.
I appreciate the opportunity to evaluate
this complex young man.
I would be happy to see him back at any point
in the future
but have not scheduled him for a set follow-up.
Sincerely
James W-----, M.D.

CHAPTER 2

Enough Acronyms
To Make Your Head Spin:
Navigating the System
& Advocating For Our Kids

Many of the writers in this chapter walked into parenting children with disabilities with no formed opinions of their own, and so found themselves tossed in a wind of contradictory advice. Others chose to raise children who have disabilities through foster and adoptive placements, but even those of us who walked voluntarily into the land of many letters find ourselves occasionally baffled by all these acronyms we have to keep in our mouths: NICU, IV, SLP, IEP, ECE, ADA, IDEA, FAPE, LRE ... The list can go on infinitely, even as a child's disability fades.

Parents of disabled children who are prepared and unprepared have to form new opinions about schooling, therapy, and medical care. Parents who thought they would homeschool find themselves fighting for mainstream inclusion; others, who never considered it, are unschooling our kids. It didn't take any of us long to figure out that opinions matter; they might be as harmful to our children as they are helpful. All of us feel the tension between our own struggle to parent children with intense needs and our attempts to manage the way other adults interact with our children. We are the experts, but we often don't know what we're doing.

This chapter contains the stories of parents who've had to fight for their children to have meaningful opportunities to learn. We have fought school systems to have our child included. We have fought medical professionals who insisted on traumatic therapy models that didn't work. We have fought our own instincts, our families' misconceptions, and a culture that would as soon throw away our kids as see them for the learning, growing beings they are.

The phrase comes up again and again, "No situation is perfect." Even when they finally let our kids into the high-achieving school with all the cool parents, we find that we're not walking into paradise when we come to pick them up. Some of the parents in this chapter won the fight; some realized they were battling windmills and just walked away; two talk about the experience most of us end up facing sooner or later—the compromise of what we thought we knew for what works best given the limits of our kids, ourselves, our cultures, and our world.

Exile To Bridlemile
or Where the @#$%&! is My Village?!
by Chloe Eudaly

We took the scenic route on the way to my son Henry's first day of kindergarten. As we ascended Vista Avenue in my fifteen-year-old hand-me-down Toyota, the houses got bigger, luxury cars and SUVs proliferated, the signs for the Republican candidate for governor suddenly materialized—surprising in a city typically thought of as a bastion of liberalism—and there were a preponderance of dead raccoons along the side of the road. Bad omens abounding, we forged ahead and over the hills to Bridlemile, an elementary school in an affluent suburb six slow and winding miles away from home, a nearly hour-long daily commute. I had the feeling we weren't in Portland anymore.

Why wasn't I waving a tearful goodbye as the school bus pulled away for the first time that morning? Why weren't we walking the twelve blocks from our house to our neighborhood school, or even the one block to the K-12 alternative school that I myself had attended as a last ditch effort to redeem my own high school career? I'll give you a hint: it weighs 50 lbs., cost more than my car is worth, and it's on wheels.

Henry is a bright, adorable, funny, and in many ways typical seven-year-old who happens to have a severe form of cerebral palsy which affects his motor control. He needs a wheelchair or walker to get around, uses augmentative communication tools as he has very limited speech, requires full assistance with all daily activities, and struggles with secondary health conditions caused by his cerebral palsy. The need for a wheelchair is really the least of his challenges, but it has been a major obstacle to school and community inclusion at the most basic level—physical access—and it has impacted the already complicated placement process that often comes along with special education services.

Through casual conversation and informal online polling, I've found that most people are under the impression that public schools are required to be wheelchair accessible. They're usually as surprised as I was when they find out otherwise. It's true that it's been a requirement in the last three decades or so for new facilities, and since the passage of the Americans with Disabilities Act of 1990, school districts have had to make "reasonable accommodations" in their older facilities as well. However, they are not required to retrofit them to a level of full accessibility. So while you can probably access the first floor of most public schools (if the wheelchair entrance happens to be unlocked), many vital areas—gyms, cafeterias, auditoriums, basement classrooms, entire second floors, and don't even get me started on the playgrounds—remain inaccessible. In our district, roughly half of the elementary schools are not accessible, especially the inner city schools which tend to be among the oldest, and happen to be near where we call home.

At this point you may be wondering what happens to a student (not to mention parent, faculty, or community member) who uses a wheelchair or cannot otherwise navigate stairs, if their neighborhood school is not accessible? While students with disabilities are guaranteed a free and appropriate public education, they are not guaranteed access to a specific facility. By law, the first placement that should be considered is their neighborhood school; but in many cases, if students can be bussed to another school, up to an hour away from their homes, it will be difficult to compel a school district to make accommodations it deems unreasonable in order to send them there. To complicate matters, some districts opt to set up self-contained classrooms and special programs, so even if accessibility is not an issue, students may still be prevented from attending their home school if their educational plans require supports that aren't being provided at their home schools.

In 1975, I boarded the school bus for my first day of kindergarten, and so did thousands of children across the country, who in years prior had been denied access to public education altogether as a result of their disabilities, thanks to the passage of what is now known as the Individuals with Disabilities Education Act (IDEA). Of course, I was unaware of this at the time, and as disability was a normal part of my life—I had both family and friends with disabilities—I was not at all surprised to encounter children who had disabilities at my school. However, I only saw these kids, who were all different ages and whose disabilities were varied, at recess and lunchtime. They were more restricted in where they could learn, eat, and play than the rest of us, and eventually we learned they were in a "special" class called the Resource Room. It was a mystery to us what it was, but somehow we knew it wasn't good, and none of us wanted to be sent there.

Even at that early age we could sense the stigma attached to special education and by extension, disability. While some of us initially interacted on the playground, the division between the kids from the Resource Room and the rest of us intensified as we progressed through the grades and they stayed put. Not only were these students not full participants in the classroom or on the playground; they didn't seem to be a part of our community outside of school either. I don't remember ever seeing them at after school activities, Girl Scouts, community events, or birthday parties. In this small, rural town where hippies, farmers, and migrant workers comingled at the corner store, these kids and their families were nowhere to be found.

Thirty years later, I got an inkling of why this was, when my child entered the public school system. The bumpy road to Bridlemile had begun during Henry's idyllic year at a neighborhood preschool where he was accepted, included, and accommodated without question. He received all his early childhood services in his preschool classroom, where his classmates would often join in his therapy sessions. He made fast friends with many of them—nearly his whole class came to his fifth birthday party—several of whom would graduate along with him to the same elementary school, or so I thought.

When the time came, I attended the Kindergarten Roundup at our neighborhood school, one of the better schools in our district. As I sat in the auditorium soaking up the charm of the well-kept 1920s building, listening to teachers rave about the level of parent involvement and community support—and the special art, music, and science programs they were able to afford because of it—I felt fortunate that I didn't have to brave the school choice lottery system, because we had already won by virtue of living in the neighborhood.

As the crowd of parents broke off into groups for a tour of the school, I casually inquired as to where the elevator was located and was met with a blank stare. I explained that my son was in a wheelchair. The parent volunteer in charge of our group wasn't sure that there was one and nervously redirected me to the principal, who quickly explained that not only was there not an elevator, there wouldn't be one any time soon. She then relayed a story that perfectly and painfully sums up the separate and unequal policies for students with disabilities in which I would soon be receiving a crash course.

Apparently the year prior, a family from the neighborhood with twin boys, one in a wheelchair and one not, attended the roundup and asked the same question and received the same answer as I had. Not satisfied, they pushed the issue along the chain of command at the district level until they received the final verdict—since the student in a wheelchair could be bussed to another school that was accessible, no accommodation would be made for him at his neighborhood school. I imagine the parents already feeling cheated, didn't feel that both their sons should be denied access to their far superior neighborhood school, and so on the first day of kindergarten one brother headed there and the other was bussed across town, out of his community, away from his friends and family.

It was early in the year—January or February—when I hit this first roadblock, so there was still time to research our options. As I mentioned, our district has a school choice system. Families choose their top three schools and enter a lottery; chances are good they will land in one of them. While we weren't prevented from participating, I knew there was no guarantee we would be allowed to enroll in our school of choice as our district reserves the right to dictate the school assignment of students receiving special education services. So I set out to research what the best options were among the most likely candidates.

First, I contacted the district to ask what school Henry would be placed in, seeing as our neighborhood school could not accommodate him, but they couldn't tell me as apparently there isn't a clear protocol in place and they hadn't decided yet. I requested a list of wheelchair accessible schools in order to narrow the search, which they also couldn't provide me. I attended a district-wide showcase where parents could "shop" for schools by visiting booths staffed by administrators, teachers, and parent volunteers touting the strengths and benefits of their respective neighborhoods, magnet and charter schools, which are almost all competing for new enrollments. While I was there, I visited the special education booth and asked what I thought was a reasonable question, "What schools have the best special education programs and do the best job with inclusion?" The answer I received from the somewhat disconcerted assistant director of special education was something to the effect that my child would receive the same quality of education at any school in the district. Of course I knew that was patently false, otherwise what were we all doing there? But it would take real-life experience for me to realize how different each school and even classroom within them could be, depending on the climate created by the principal, the effectiveness of the IEP team and special education staff, the motivation and skill of the aides, the attitudes and experience of the general ed teachers, the available resources, and the level of parent involvement and community support.

I came away from this process with very little information, certainly not enough to make an informed choice. I saw little point in trying to lottery into a school if I didn't know in advance whether they were willing and able to accommodate my child. However there was one school that I thought might be the answer to our problem. The alternative school across the street wasn't my first choice, but there was a lot to like about it—it was K-12, so there wouldn't be any traumatic transitions, it had a non-competitive atmosphere, and a cooperative and individualized approach to learning. Known as a safe haven for quirky kids, a number of my friends already had kids at the school, and last but not least, although it was two stories and was around a century old, they had an elevator.

This particular school didn't participate in the lottery process, as administrators preferred to handpick their families, due to the school's educational philosophy not being a good fit for everyone. We submitted an application, made the first cut, and were scheduled for an interview. That day, Henry's dad and I walked him past the playground (which we usually avoided if we weren't going to stop and swing) and instead of heading off to preschool, we entered the building.

Henry likes his routines, and thus didn't appreciate our little detour and he became agitated as soon as we entered the principal's office. I asked his dad to take him on to preschool and finished the interview on my own. I'm glad that he wasn't there to hear the ensuing conversation. After asking me to tell her why I felt the school was a good choice for Henry, she explained in no uncertain terms why she felt it wasn't, using her brief observation of his behavior, his wheelchair, and her assumptions about his disability as the main reasons. I took issue with many of her comments and concerns and she became hostile when challenged, denying that her position had anything to do with his disability, even though she had just rattled off a list of issues directly related to it.

I reported my experience to the Special Education Department and once again asked for information that would help guide us in our decision making process. No action was taken, and they did not respond to my request. Feeling defeated and demoralized, not wanting to put our family through further rejection, and with only days to go before the lottery deadline, I decided to give up on exercising our "choice" and left the placement up to the district.

Months later, we finally got our answer. Henry had been assigned to Bridlemile and would be bussed to the suburbs, despite the fact that there were three schools in our immediate neighborhood, and several more across the river that were closer both in distance and demographics. At the same time, the transition team recommended fulltime Life Skills class, much to our dismay. We had hoped that Henry's successful preschool experience would support an inclusive placement for kindergarten and we thought we had federal law on our side. If special education is supposed to be a service, not a place, why couldn't they bring it to him in the kindergarten classroom?

How did they plan on demonstrating that he couldn't learn in the general education environment—the only reason a child should be removed—if they were never going to place him there? I asked if they could provide me with studies or statistics that demonstrated the efficacy of segregating children with disabilities, as I could offer piles of information that showed that children, both with and without disabilities, benefit from an inclusive educational environment given the proper supports and modifications. They adroitly deflected my many arguments, and sensing impending defeat, I dropped the R-bomb, paraphrasing something I had recently heard a speaker say at a parent training. I pointed out that the best way to learn a new language or skill was immersion, and asked what the self-contained classroom was but retarded immersion? Henry needed maximum language exposure, intellectual stimulation, and social opportunities. He needed the benefit of being surrounded by peers who were able to ask the questions that he could not, and to hear the answers. He would get none of this if he was relegated to the Life Skills classroom. I'm sure there were some stifled gasps and ruffled feathers around the table, but my disquieting assertion seemed to turn the conversation in a new direction.

It took another lengthy meeting, but finally both sides made concessions and we agreed Henry would be enrolled in half-day kindergarten with an aide, and no pullouts, and he would spend the second half of the day in the Life Skills class where he would receive all his special services.

This seemed like a reasonable compromise, although some of my more seasoned advocate friends were against it. They feared allowing Henry to spend half his day in Life Skills would undermine our ability to advocate for inclusion down the line, but it was a risk we were willing to take in order to get his foot in the door of kindergarten, avoid a lengthy dispute, and move forward.

Later that summer, I drove out to the school to get the lay of the land and to enroll Henry in kindergarten. The principal, who upon first meeting me assumed that I was just another neighborhood parent, did little to disguise the considerable downshift in her enthusiasm when she realized who I was. Apparently my reputation had preceded me, and she almost immediately let me know that she didn't agree with Henry's placement. She made several discouraging comments, including remarking that it would be difficult to accommodate him in the kindergarten classroom because of the way it was set up, and suggested that we might change our minds about inclusion once we realized how hard it would be and that it wasn't really in his best interest. I politely explained that I didn't agree with her, that we were exercising the rights guaranteed to Henry by federal law, and that if there was a problem with accessibility in the classroom, they should plan on rearranging it.

When transportation contacted me, they wanted Henry at the curb at 6:45 am for an hour-long bus ride. I didn't think this was reasonable, as he would have a long day ahead of him and it would necessitate us getting up around 5:00 am, so I chose to drive him myself. Instead of wheeling Henry out the front door and up the street, I would be breaking down his chair, hoisting it into my car, driving him to school, and performing the task in reverse on the other end. Unlike our daily walks to preschool during which we might encounter friends, neighbors and other familiar faces, we would be navigating morning rush-hour traffic. Pick-ups in the afternoons had previously been a time to interact with other families, grab some groceries, and meet friends at the park. But because there was no affordable, inclusive, after school child care available at Bridlemile, I would be rushing home every day at 3:00 pm to meet him at the bus stop. Between the commute and the lack of childcare options, more than ten hours would be sheared off my workweek.

After living part-time in disability world for the past five years—multiple weekly therapy appointments, doctor's appointments, specialty clinics, early intervention sessions, support groups, and advocacy training—I was accustomed to being the "funky" mom, the "quirky" mom, the oddest mom among the odd moms out. When I had my first and only child at thirty, I was unmarried, and by the time Henry was three, single. I lived in shared housing, preferred my Schwinn Cruiser to my car, and among my favorite pastimes were reading obscure literature, shopping at thrift stores, and singing karaoke. I was a small business owner, but my specialty bookshop devoted to zines, alternative comics, and independent media was tough to sum up for the uninitiated. I hadn't gone to college, spent my youth at punk shows and political rallies, and had once been described in our local paper as a "self-identified anarchist" after attendees at a show I had helped organize ran wild in the streets in response to being confronted by a wall of cops in riot gear, who were under the impression that we were plotting the violent overthrow of the American government amidst relentless three-chord aural assaults.

Alternative lifestyle aside, being socially adaptable, not remotely shy, and interested in other people's opinions, ideas and experiences, I could successfully navigate most social settings. But I was truly out of my element at Bridlemile. It wasn't that I didn't have experience with this particular social strata—mostly white, middle and upper middle class, conservative-leaning suburbanites—I had spent my middle and truncated high school years among them, and I had quit school and left home at sixteen in order to escape them, among other things. I spent the next decade and a half finding and building community, surrounded by relatively likeminded people who shared my values and lived comfortably outside of the mainstream. But all of a sudden here I was, back in their midst, trying to swallow insecurities that hadn't reared up since my own school days with little hope that my very vulnerable kid would fare any better.

The next few days did little to ease my fears. Neither classroom seemed prepared or had been provided with the equipment Henry needed to successfully participate in class. His kindergarten teacher demonstrated through her actions and words that she did not welcome Henry as a full member of her classroom. His aide—a sweet and enthusiastic, albeit inexperienced, young man—was instructed to respond to Henry's outbursts of frustration and boredom by repeatedly removing him from the classroom, a punishment that functioned as a reward and reinforcement for the behavior, as it was exactly what Henry wanted. I feared that he was being set up for failure and that the IEP team would use this as an excuse to roll back on his level of inclusion.

I wasn't faring much better. I had been an involved parent at Henry's preschool but because of the commute and my work schedule, it was impractical for me to put much time in at Henry's new school, even if I had felt welcomed. On the first day of school, the principal had asked me to be the room parent for the Life Skills classroom, and although I had happily accepted the task, she replaced me a few days later with another parent whom she deemed more capable because I had a job and the other parent was a well-to-do stay-at-home mom. I struggled with conflicting impulses to cover my car in the most offensive bumper stickers I could find or buy a minivan. I didn't want to succumb to the stifling conformity of the suburbs but I didn't want my kid to suffer the consequences of having a freak for a mom. For the most part, I kept my head down and tried not to stand out, making few meaningful connections in the process.

There were many more disheartening experiences that year, regular reminders that Henry was not regarded as a full member of his class—from his kindergarten teacher making special nametags for every child except him on the first day, to the school neglecting to arrange transportation for field trips, to Henry's picture being left off his class photo—and while I addressed these issues as they arose and they were swiftly dealt with, I couldn't shake the feeling that we were unwelcome guests and the cruel joke was that we couldn't go home.

The cumulative effect that his assignment to Bridlemile had on our quality of life was significant. I was spending more time and money to get Henry to school while I had less time to work, which diminished my income. Our brisk walks to and from preschool afforded me nearly an hour a day of exercise; I was now spending that time in the car. Our social opportunities on both ends of the commute were diminished. I was already experiencing a high-level stress brought on by the demands of being a self-employed, single parent, and managing Henry's extraordinary needs and health issues, but this was the first year that anxiety and depression became the prevailing state of being for me.

In the middle of the school year we were displaced from our long-time rental home due to the property selling. Henry was also in the midst of a health crisis that would ultimately end in surgery and a lengthy recovery period. We moved to another neighborhood across the river and once again, although the school was so close I could hear the bells ring every morning, Henry could not attend due to accessibility issues. The alternative the district offered was not appealing, so rather than disrupt his school year and possibly transfer to a third school for first grade, I chose to keep him at Bridlemile and resigned myself to an even longer commute.

When it came time for Henry's next IEP meeting to discuss placement for first grade, I let them know what we expected—a wheelchair accessible school, in or near our neighborhood, that he could stay at for the duration of his elementary school education. A nearby school materialized; it was not on a par with our neighborhood school, but met many of my other requirements. It was also in a neighborhood we frequented, and we already knew a number of families there. It was not entirely wheelchair accessible, but we were assured that Henry wouldn't need to access the second floor until third grade and since they had just sited a new Life Skills class there, the school would be prioritized for upgrades.

Unfortunately, none of that proved to be true. Shortly after school began, I learned that the music room, computer room, and learning center were all located on the second floor, and no accommodations were made to bring these resources to the kids who couldn't reach them. They also failed to mention that while the school was K–8, the Life Skills class was only K–2, so even if the elevator did materialize, which it did not, Henry would probably have to change schools again for third grade, as at that time it was felt that he needed the support of a special education teacher and classroom despite the fact he was now only spending 20 percent of his day outside of general ed.

Despite these disappointments, we had a much better year and I had hopes that we could find a way to stay in the long run. His new school couldn't have been more different from Bridlemile; it was an inner city Title I school, predominantly families of color, in a neighborhood that, while gentrifying, remained one of the most economically and ethnically diverse areas in the city. Although he could take a short bus ride, I frequently dropped him off or picked him up myself, which afforded us opportunities to interact with other kids and families and enjoy our neighborhood. The first-grade teacher was more receptive to having Henry in her classroom. He made new friends. Although it wasn't perfect, things were going better and through our nightly homework sessions, I knew that he was learning and making progress towards his IEP goals, which is what we needed to demonstrate in order to keep him on the inclusion track. I became involved with the PTO, helped organize several family night events, and adopted the book exchange as my pet project. I had a good rapport with most staff, including the principal, and made new friends myself.

I had even been nominated to chair the PTO for the upcoming school year, but the day before that was to be made official, we received word that the district was moving the Life Skills class, after one year, to another school and Henry would not be able to return for second grade.

As you can imagine, I was angry and distraught. I felt we had been misled by the district, I feared they would repeat this pattern throughout Henry's school years, and it seemed that they were deliberately keeping information from us that we needed in order to make informed decisions. We were being exiled once again, from a community that had valued and embraced us.

I knew with each move Henry's ties to friends were being severed and they would become increasingly harder to make as he got older. His school assignment for second grade was unknown. He certainly wasn't going to follow the Life Skills class to one of the worst schools in the district. Because they had announced this decision so late in the year, we had missed the school choice lottery deadline by several weeks. We prepared ourselves for a contentious meeting with the IEP team and district representatives. We brought a friend, an IEP partner, and considered hiring an attorney.

I had braced myself for another round of meetings similar to our transition to kindergarten, but the district representatives were surprisingly sympathetic to our plight. I don't know if we lucked out with whom they sent or they just realized how royally they had screwed up, but one of them actually apologized for what we had gone through. The recommended placement was at a great school, and while not in our immediate neighborhood, a reasonable distance and a short bus ride away. All vital areas are accessible and there is a continuum of special education services through eighth grade, so we don't anticipate another transfer until high school.

The school year is now under way and I'm happy to report that it's going well. The teachers and staff have been welcoming and supportive. We are both slowly making new connections. I've adopted a couple of projects. Henry's inclusive placement feels more secure for now, and at the time of this writing, his "case" is being transferred to the learning center teacher, which means he will no longer be tied to the Life Skills class in which the district tried to stick him three years ago.

Every parent has their own way of coming to terms with the unexpected. Henry's disability was caused by a birth injury. One minute he was okay and the next everything changed forever. There was a clear cause, and it was probably preventable or could have been minimized, but no one was really to blame. A series of choices made by a number of people, none of them bad or wrong on their own, had contributed to the outcome.

I remember a moment I had when he was one or two and we were out for a walk in our neighborhood. I was thinking about how I had dealt with trauma in the past and that often I could find consolation in the fact that I had absorbed some abuse or burden so that someone else didn't have to, but in the case of Henry's injury that logic did not hold. If anything, I had an unwitting hand in creating more suffering in the world and the recipient was my own child. I let myself wallow in that particular pit of despair for only a few moments before I resolved that there would be a purpose to what had happened to our family—I would share my experience with others in the hopes that they could make better informed choices than we had, and I knew by virtue of fighting for what I thought was right for Henry, that we would help make life a little better for the families that followed in our footsteps, just as we were benefiting from the struggles of those who came before us.

When Henry was three, thanks to stumbling upon a used copy of *Disability is Natural* by Kathie Snow, I learned about and ended up attending a yearlong intensive advocacy-training program called Partners in Policymaking. During his preschool years, I frequently attended informational meetings and support groups, during which time I connected with a group of moms who also had kids with significant disabilities and were advocating for inclusion. When Henry entered kindergarten, I began working as a coordinator for a community partnership project aimed at families with young children (birth to five) with disabilities in our county.

The transition to kindergarten was difficult for nearly all the families with whom I was in contact, and if we were struggling despite our knowledge and experience, I could only imagine how hard it was for families who didn't have the resources that we had. The family-centered and inclusion-focused early childhood program and affiliated parent group through which we had connected had no parallel for school-age families. A group of us continued to get together on a monthly basis for cocktails and occasionally the topic of starting a school age parent group would come up, but we were unsure how to go about it. We'd all joined and benefited from existing groups and many of us had taken on leadership roles, but this was uncharted territory.

During Henry's first-grade year, I joined a district family involvement committee, primarily aimed at cultivating participation among under-represented and under-involved populations. I was there to represent but mostly to learn new strategies to engage families. I had been mulling over an idea that I couldn't quite wrap my brain around. I knew that there were special education PTAs (SEPTA), but the notion had always struck me as contrary to my values and goals. Wouldn't having a "special" PTA just reinforce segregation and discourage inclusion?

When the Life Skills class closure was announced at Henry's school, it finally hit me—if we were going to be denied access to our neighborhood schools and the same rights and choices that other families enjoyed, then we needed to make a home for ourselves not subject to the whims of the district budget shortfalls, or public opinion. As contrary as it might sound, creating a special interest group to network, educate, and empower families with kids with disabilities is a logical step toward our ultimate goal of school and community inclusion.

The idea was enthusiastically received by most of the moms in my group and many of them are now serving on the executive committee or as committee chairs. We're an official unit now and are planning our first district-wide public meeting. We have sketched out a few goals—to make sure parents know what their rights are, to connect them with any available resources and perhaps most importantly with each other—but we are anxious to discover what other needs may exist in the larger community. We hope to eventually have representatives at every elementary school in the district, and that our members will become more involved at their respective schools. We'll know we've accomplished our goals when our organization no longer needs to exist.

I never cared for the "it takes a village" adage; I liked it even less when my family became an outcast. It's been lonely out here at times in the disability hinterlands, what with the underdeveloped infrastructure, unfunded mandates, and sheer ignorance of some of the gatekeepers, but I've found kindred spirits along with way. What we're building is more akin to a refugee camp, as we have no intention of staying here. I hope the village is ready for us.

After the IEP
by Kim Mahler

She says it's natural to lick the lime pulp
off the glass rim of Tanqueray. To eat
off the kitchen floor ignoring hair,
crumbs. Natural the mind drops to the word *backsliding*;
group armed with leather bibles, cartoon
tracts stuffed in their pockets crossing
the mall, park, to save a backslider
in 1979 from hell. Pray for the waitress;
they leave tracts instead of tips.
Curling into the fetal position, that's
natural. Hearing voices, mama's little
gonna buy baby a mocking *Hush* bird.

Note: IEP is an acronym for Individualized Education Plan

Play Therapy
by Karen Wang

I'm a little embarrassed whenever I welcome visitors to my home. Outside, the landscaping has been neglected for years and is now full of weeds and badly overgrown. Inside, I never have a free moment to tidy up or to improve my own ragged appearance. Toys are everywhere because we're always playing. Louie's kindergarten papers, photo collages, and art projects cover the walls haphazardly, inevitably ending up on the floor. The scuff marks on the ceiling are from the time my husband Oliver held Louie upside down so that he could walk on the paper moon I had taped up there, right next to the handmade signs instructing, "Please walk naked," "Please flop," and "Please walk steady on the ceiling."

There is a sort of organization to it all, I tell my guests. The living room has soft toys as well as extra pillows and blankets for snuggling. We have an arsenal of tools for gross and fine motor, vestibular, and proprioceptive movement, and for collaborative play, which is Louie's latest developmental breakthrough; a slide, small climbing structure, balance board, and mini trampoline, craft supplies, and play-dough kits. The bathroom is the place for tactile sensory play—soap, lotions, shaving cream, and water—and it's where we painstakingly teach Louie about self-care. Around every corner in our house, young visitors are delighted to discover stacks of jam-packed toy boxes. This is my family's work in progress, our labor of love. I smile to myself as I recall the stories behind each little mess in our wreck of a house, the stories of five-year-old Louie's growth through play therapy.

I think most adults underestimate what playing with a child, giving a child full attention for short periods throughout the day, can do for the child's health and development. When I explained to my sister that we planned to pursue one-on-one play with our son as his primary therapy, she told other family members that we had chosen to do "nothing" for our autistic son. I'm not sure I would have believed in the benefits myself without seeing them firsthand in my son Louie.

He was an unusually active, alert baby, often fussy and anxious. I was looking for ways to balance his intense emotions and energy. I knew instinctively that the balance had to begin with our mother-child relationship. I sought out activities that brought peace and joy to us both: long walks, singing, reading, puzzles, and balls. But my son was still missing out on something big: at nineteen months, he was having panic attacks and could not tolerate any length or type of separation from me. Various therapies were recommended to us, but none of them were viable because they all required a trained therapist, and Louie was terrified of strangers. Enforcing separation from me and introducing new therapists caused new phobias and more frequent panic attacks. Louie's bond with me was his strength and his greatest comfort. To relieve his anxiety, Louie needed to learn the most basic social skills from the ground up, and the only people qualified to teach him were those to whom he was most attached, his parents.

Play therapy begins with wordless interaction. In his hyperlexic pattern of development, my little Louie skipped all the pre-verbal relationship skills, which most babies develop in their first year of life, and went straight to reading and spelling words before he was two years old. Hyperlexic autism is characterized by early literacy complicated by poor comprehension, and often accompanied by severe anxiety and unusual phobias. I had to take my son back to his emotional infancy to re-learn and remediate. My favorite part of each day was the moment Louie first woke up in the morning. Resting my head on the mattress beside him, we would gaze silently into each other's eyes for a few precious moments. Sometimes I'd break the spell, but usually Louie would rev up his engine and zoom off to start his adventure. I thought that no matter what happened during the day, he would have that warm beginning moment with me as solace. He wanted constant physical stimulation, so I gave it to him at varying speeds. Rolling and play-wrestling together gave him confidence and a sense of power, but slower movements such as massaging his hands or dancing to lullabies brought him back to a secure, loving place. As he learned to match his movements to mine, I was able to hop, skip, and jump with him, and even to play "airplane" and "skin-the-cat." Instead of running away from me, he wanted to hold my hand to walk with me. Louie still panicked in many situations, but I had found a way to get inside his head to calm him.

I remember my husband once saying, "Louie has work to do. Play is his work." Play is the most important thing that happens in our house. Everything, and I mean everything, comes after it. We don't cook or do housework unless we can find a way to involve Louie playfully; laundry, dishes and vacuuming are all standard "games" around here.

All children express their fears and questions through play, and it can be difficult to find the answers they seek. Spinning in circles, arranging fifty Hot Wheels cars in a perfectly straight line, and repeatedly pressing elevator buttons are reflections of an inner emotional question. When a child's environment is unbearably overwhelming, he will find one little thing that he can rigidly control, blocking all other sensory input. But hyper-focusing in this way, only compounds the initial anxiety as more and more control is required. Sometimes Louie gets stuck in a repetitive pattern (often representing his anxiety) that needs to be playfully disrupted. One day he was repeating a story over and over: "Once upon a time Louie was crying because the pool was closed." He turned to me and asked me to retell the same story. I held him gently so that our faces were almost touching. I kissed him softly and said, "Once upon a time Mommy ate Louie's ear (nibble). Once upon a time Mommy ate Louie's nose (nibble). Once upon a time Mommy gave Louie a raspberry (big raspberry on the tummy). Once upon a time Louie gave Mommy a razberry." Laughing, he collapsed in my arms, comforted at last. We had returned to our safe place in each other's arms, even as we relinquished control over the day's disappointments.

For tactile and sensory play, I started buying cheap cans of shaving cream. "I want to make a mess," Louie said to me one rainy afternoon. "Yes, we can make a big mess in the bathroom!" I gleefully responded. He helped me put away all the shampoo bottles and toothbrushes first, then I handed him the shaving cream. Because of his fine motor delay, I had to teach him how to press down on the button to release a fluffy cloud of shaving cream but he was a motivated learner. Within a few minutes, the counters, sink, and cabinet doors were covered in shaving cream and we were both sporting "Santa Claus beards." We "painted" each other's arms, traced words on the snowy surfaces, and clapped our hands to make the foam fly around in a surreal wintry scene. There was an academic method to our giddy madness. I had read about using shaving cream to reduce my son's sensory issues; I also wanted to create a new situation to stimulate conversational and emotional exchanges, eye contact, and shared attention. My scheme worked: Louie was giggly and chatty, and far from fearing the squishy texture of the shaving cream, he explored and fully enjoyed it. He kept looking up into my eyes to share his excitement and happiness, and I felt my heart ready to burst from his sweetness. When the can of shaving cream was finally empty, Louie announced that it was time to clean up. We wiped everything down with damp washcloths and watched the thinned-out froth dissolve down the sink. The bathroom sparkled for the cost of sixty seven cents and a dash of imagination, but all I saw was the spark between us.

If raspberries and shaving cream are the mortar, then bean bags are the cornerstones of play therapy. My little monkey-boy was bouncing off the walls and climbing the bookcases by the time he was ten months old, but he always became calm and attentive when his body sank down firmly in his big red bean bag. Every time I saw bean bags, chairs, and giant pillows on clearance, I bought more. We began making bean bag towers and forts, playing pillow catch and, at the end of the day, sitting back and listening to music together. Before we knew it, the family room was decorated entirely in bean bags, devoid of any other furniture.

Play has a way of breathing new life into the odds and ends around our house. A spatula and an empty oatmeal carton make a nice drum set, and I always clean out and save the big yogurt containers with lids for our "What Is It?" game. I sneak a little something into each container and start shaking to get Louie's attention. "What is it?" I ask. It could be nail clippers, a granola bar, a sock, or anything inside. Louie changed this game into "Christmas in July" by wrapping up old toys and stacking them in the living room. We guess at the contents and make our discoveries together. A treasure hunt is another game that uses everyday items for a new purpose. Sometimes I make a list of items on a piece of paper, or I may put Xs and arrows around the house to direct Louie's attention to forgotten household debris. At the end of the treasure hunt, I have a surprise that he doesn't usually get to play with, such as my digital camera. His prize is to play with it for a few uninterrupted minutes. Louie knows that masking tape on the wall means a treasure hunt, but masking tape on the floor makes an obstacle course. I just love to hear my son laugh while we hold hands and hop forwards and backwards, crawl, skip, and wheelbarrow walk across the house according to the directions on the floor. The games always end on the sofa with all those extra pillows and blankets, our attachment deepening and expanding.

Mealtimes also present an opportunity to play and experiment. I was leery when Oliver suggested a candlelight dinner: I imagined our house reduced to ashes and all of us covered in burns. But the candlelight had a calming effect, and Louie enjoyed the different scents on each candle. The spice rack is another place that is often overlooked. With a plate of scrambled eggs for breakfast, we allowed Louie to select the spices he wanted to try. We had no idea that Louie loved paprika and every type of pepper until we did this. We put those scrambled eggs under the category of "edible play dough," and I've been trying new variations on that theme ever since. Quick-cooking oats, sunflower seed butter, applesauce, flax meal, raisins, honey, sesame seeds, water, and whatever I've got in the back of the cupboard can all be combined somehow to work with Louie on his tolerance of taste and texture. The biggest mess is the most delicious fun. Sensory integration begins in the kitchen!

With all this roughhousing, I keep wearing out my pants—every last pair, in fact. It happened again last week. The knee ripped open, as it always does, while I was playing on the floor with Louie. We were driving the cars in his toy parking garage, and he was telling me where his little people were going: to a concert, to a bookstore, then back home. He was re-enacting things that we had recently done together, transferring his ideas, memories and feelings to his characters. I had never seen him do this before. I was witnessing a developmental leap: the long-awaited leap into imaginative play. My closet full of ruined pants was paid for in that moment.

One night, sitting cozily in our bean bags, my husband and I talked about Louie's play goals for the week. "Most therapies seek to change the behavior of an autistic child," Oliver mused. "But really, it makes more sense to change the behavior of the parents so that we can better support our child's natural development." My assignment was to work on building block towers with him and to act out certain scenarios with the towers. But when we woke up the next morning, the rain had finally stopped and the sun was shining. Louie and I snuggled under the covers to read some books, and after breakfast we walked through the wet grass and mud to the park. (I was wearing a pair of pants with a small hole in the right knee.) Before school, my son drew a picture of his best friend and his best friend's little brother and he asked me to invite them over to play. When I dropped off Louie at preschool, he made me promise that he could ride his bike "around the block the long way" if it wasn't raining after school. At 3:30, the weather was glorious, so Louie raced ahead of me on his bike, smiling and pointing out everything that interested him, occasionally pausing to allow me to catch up with him.

In my mind I saw the clinical textbooks stating, "The autistic child is unable to co-ordinate eye contact, verbalization, and gestures simultaneously; he may speak in a monotone and his face may bear a flat affect." I laughed aloud at the thought. When my husband came home from work, Louie greeted his dad with a hug, gazed lovingly into his eyes and said, "Louie is happy today." All of our other goals vanished.

Resources for play therapy

Cohen, Lawrence. *Playful Parenting*. New York: Ballentine Books, 2002. This book explains how one-on-one play enriches the development of all children: http://www.playfulparenting.com.

Greenspan, Stanley. *The Child with Special Needs*. New York: Perseus Books, 1998.

Greenspan, Stanley and Serena Wieder. *Engaging Autism*. New York: First Da Capo Books, 2006. Dr. Greenspan recommends following a child's interest and lead in play, then gradually introducing new patterns into play. This method is widely practiced for children with developmental disabilities: http://www.floortime.org.

Gutstein, Steven and Rachelle Seely. *Relationship Development Intervention with Young Children*. London: Jessica Kingsley Publishers, 2002. These authors follow a developmental model similar to Dr. Greenspan's Floortime, except that the parent leads the child through each playful exercise. Special emphasis is given to the development of "episodic memory," the integration of emotion, cognition and past experience that allows individuals to adapt to new experiences. All of my bean bag games come from this book: http://www.rdiconnect.com.

Kranowitz, Carol. *The Out-Of-Sync Child Has Fun*. New York: Peregee, 2003. This book is full of messy ideas to help children with extremely high or low sensitivity to texture, taste, smell, sound, and light. I found the shaving cream idea here.

Jenkins, Peggy Joy. *The Joyful Child: A Sourcebook of Activities and Ideas for Releasing Children's Natural Joy*. Santa Rosa, CA: Harvest House Publishers, 1996. The author writes in a New Agey, hippie style that may grate on some people's nerves, but her point is that joy is tangible and contagious. The first song my son ever sang was "I Am Happy" from this book.

Accidental Unschoolers

by Heather Newman

I would like to establish a few things about myself: I am not a saint, nor am I unusually patient. In fact, on most days, I would argue that I am decidedly impatient. I have not been "blessed" with my boys because I am in some way more worthy or special than you, and you probably could imagine how I do it every day, you just don't want to because it makes you uncomfortable. I am a mother of three loud, chaotic, creative, affectionate boys. The two youngest are labeled "special needs" (with no specific diagnosis or syndrome) although their needs do not seem any more special to me than our oldest who has been tagged with the word "gifted" (read: high energy and emotionally intense). We don't care for these labels in our home because they don't have any connection to real life. They exist in a bubble where the therapists, specialists, and school systems use them to justify services given or refused. My question is: what happens to these labels when our boys are grown? I don't identify myself by my shortcomings when meeting people or applying for a job. How can our sons be successful if we condition them to see themselves as deficient by focusing intensely on their difficulties from preschool through graduation?

We have chosen a different path in our home. It is one that can be lonely, and it is one that sometimes puts us at odds with the beliefs of the people who work with our sons. We are unschoolers. There is no curriculum in our house, no hours of therapy, no rigid schedule, no written goals to be marked off quarterly. Our boys grow by living life and being curious. My husband and I are learning to trust that our kids will learn what they need to know when they are ready and that they do not need a timetable for when information or skills should be mastered.

This was not our original journey, the one that my husband and I imagined when our boys were babes. I don't know that anyone experiences parenthood as they envision it before their first is born, but my life bears no resemblance to the daydreams of my pregnancies. Those were the ones where our kids hit the baby book milestones on (or before!) the average ages, suffer the usual childhood illnesses, and head off to school to join the other neighborhood kids in a journey to graduation. Four years ago, our oldest son was enrolled in a highly recommended private school and our middle son was attending a preschool with a mix of kids who had Individual Education Plans and kids who were considered neurotypical. By this time, our oldest was in second grade and miserable. Every day was a battle to get him out of bed, to school on time, and at the end of the long day, to finish his homework. We were tired of the constant stress and unhappiness in our lives, decided to make a leap of faith and brought him home (as he so succinctly phrased it) to the best day of his life. The path for our middle son, at that time, remained the same. We felt that he needed a schedule and an array of experts guiding his every step, telling us what was best for his development. I still believed that we could work with the system to meet his unique needs.

In my early twenties, I worked with adults with special needs and although I questioned some of the methods and decisions of the company I worked for, I did not realize that there could or should be another way. One of the policies of this particular company was that every person in the program had to go out into the community for two hours each day, regardless of whether or not they had an interest in doing so. One gentleman did not enjoy his daily community visits; going out once a week for coffee was sufficient to satisfy his needs. As he had spent his childhood in a horrific institution, it would seem that he had earned the right to spend his remaining time as he wished. Not so. We were informed that everyone went out because it was a company goal. Never mind that he would sit in the middle of the parking lot after leaving the vehicle, refusing to budge, creating a dangerous situation for himself and providing the general public something to gawk at. Personal dignity be damned, it looked good in the paperwork. When I left that job, I informed my husband that if we ever had a child with special needs, I would not allow that kind of situation to occur. Prophetic words.

Fewer than ten years later, there were two boys with special needs in my life. Watching our middle son withdraw in the face of the experts and preschool, my vow of years past resurfaced. After three years of intensive speech therapy, he still was not speaking any more than he had when he began. Well, at least not while he was at school; at home, he would talk about dinosaurs, Spider-Man, and African animals, with a combination of his limited vocabulary, signs, and gestures. It took some time to understand him and for him to formulate his ideas—time that the schools did not have. As the physical and occupational therapy reports listed dozens of activities in the hour and a half allotted every week, I began to question their methods; there was no discernible improvement in any of the areas listed. It turned out that they were rushing him through multiple activities without giving him any time to actually learn the skills presented. I explained that our son learns much better when he is given time to become accustomed to a task: that pushing him on a swing, rushing him through a tunnel, and then asking him to jump on a mini trampoline all in the space of five minutes was overwhelming him. Those words fell on deaf ears. They were the experts, not me. Besides, it looked good in the paperwork. I felt so frustrated and powerless to truly help him. He continued to withdraw.

In the spring before he was scheduled to begin kindergarten (whether or not he was ready), I met with his preschool teacher to review his pre-K assessment. He scored about as well as a rag doll, doing poorly on things that I KNEW that he knew. His teacher expressed concern that it was difficult to get him to answer questions or participate in most classroom tasks. It seemed that our son had already learned how to play the system. He realized that if he didn't feel like doing an activity, all he had to do was wait. If he waited long enough, the class had to move on to the next thing on the list. This conversation, his slow retreat into himself, and the fact that I had witnessed incidents on the playground during which he had been treated badly and had no way to communicate this to the teachers, left us disillusioned with the system and our ability to work within its confines. We decided that he deserved the freedom to be himself, work at his own pace, and feel good about his achievements and skills, just as his older brother had. He had the right to be exempt from testing, judgment, labels, and exclusion.

As we struggled to find our way, we initially repeated some of the mistakes that the schools had made. School at home was a spectacular failure: they hated it and so did I. Note to self: if it didn't work in the big brick building, it ain't gonna work anywhere else. Looking for another approach, we learned more about unschooling, which led us to question the accuracy of the tests our children had been given, the results of which were used to shape their educational experiences. Under serious scrutiny, the flaws in the process became unbelievably obvious. The results could be inaccurate for many reasons. Did our boys connect with, feel comfortable with, or even understand the language used by the tester? Were they in an environment that felt familiar and safe? Were they tired, hungry, not in the mood to answer questions that had no real purpose for them? Did they understand the images they were shown? One Early Intervention assessment required our son to find a picture of a cup, but the illustration depicted a teacup and saucer. He couldn't find the cup. His world at the age of one-and-a-half was all about the sippy cup; the images had no relationship to his reality. Did the testing method tap into their learning styles? Our youngest son has a difficult time with worksheet type images, but if the same information is presented with real objects, or even in a computer game, he can answer easily with little instruction. There is no room for flexibility in these tests and many of their IEP goals were based on this narrow method.

The next step in the process was to examine the necessity of some of the IEP goals. Were they relevant to the life our children lead and were they skills that they are ready, and most importantly, willing, to learn? The idea that children need to know the alphabet, numbers, and colors by the age of five is arbitrary. Will they never learn these things if they don't have a se-ries of goals to be checked off of a list? As adults, we are learning new skills all of the time as our interests change and grow. Why do we think that it is different for our children? Letting go of the notions that we had lived with all of our lives enabled us to see that everything in our sons' lives is learn-ing, and by the same reasoning, everything is therapy. Allowing our sons the freedom to follow their interests and respecting their desires has given them the chance to blossom and gain abilities faster than they ever did at school. Best of all, I get to be there to see this process, watching their eyes light up as they make a connection or learn a new skill.

My husband and I have now begun to discuss what tools we believe are necessary for our sons to be successful adults. The ability to find informa-tion, debate and discuss ideas logically, enjoy reading, and be proficient enough in math to be able to maintain their personal finances are all im-portant to us. Our youngest is not as severely delayed as our middle boy, our oldest is a fairly typical eleven-year-old, and we are reasonably certain that both will be able to live independently as adults. Unless circumstances change dramatically, our middle son will need a high level of care through-out adulthood. We have to define what will be important for him. He has a very difficult time understanding the concept of numbers and words, if we push him hard, he may be able to count to five or ten, name some letters, and recognize simple sight words—certainly not enough to learn to read and balance a checkbook or a budget. Do we make him miserable forcing him to learn scraps of information that will be of no use to him? We don't believe that his happiness should be sacrificed to learn what would amount to a parlor trick.

All of these changes occurred before our youngest son was preschool age, and as a result, his experience has been very different from that of his older brothers. He attends a local preschool two afternoons a week because he enjoys the program. On the days that he wants to stay home, or another opportunity comes up that he would rather do, he simply doesn't go. We are fortunate that his teacher feels that children at this age learn by playing, choosing interests and activities, and that everything to be learned does not require a therapy goal. This enables our youngest to simply enjoy the games, toys, and friends. Is it still a school environment? Yes, but our son is in control by viewing it as his choice to be there. We also nixed a lot of the goals presented for his IEP. Some, like chewing a certain number of times before swallowing at snack time, were ridiculous and demeaning. Others, like knowing a certain number of letters by a certain date, had no relevance to him as he already knows most of his letters. Perhaps he did not feel like discussing the alphabet the day that they decided to ask him. If the therapist had chosen to ask me when setting these goals, I could have clued her in.

Our middle son has also enjoyed the changes in our approach to his therapy. We stopped his physical therapy for a couple of years. He has taken swimming lessons, karate, and rock climbing classes at different times, and has generally run and played like any other kid does. When it became apparent this spring that he was ready for the next level of activity but lacked the coordination to move forward, we found a great private physical therapist who is respectful of his needs. He now runs, jumps (on the bed), and can hike uneven terrain without holding our hands. By waiting instead of forcing him to try to learn skills before he was ready to do so, he is a happy and enthusiastic participant in his therapy. His abilities have improved rapidly and he feels great about himself.

This is not to imply that our life is some sort of utopian existence. After all, we have kids with developmental challenges and this adds a different dimension to how we live and what we are able to do. We have a binder with a calendar of doctors' numbers, appointments, receipts, and insurance information that needs to be kept organized. Our family moved to a new state a year ago and our middle son fell to pieces. Weeping for hours on end, up until four in the morning screaming, with no communication or awareness of anything around him. It was as if we suddenly had a severely autistic child, behaviors that he had never displayed before.

As he has always been the most easygoing of our boys, this was a bit of a shock. After multiple tests and doctors, we are still working to help him find his way as he struggles to recover from a deep depression. He has extreme drops in blood sugar when he doesn't eat regularly and he is not able to recognize when he is hungry. This means that we have to regulate what he eats and when, even if he would rather be doing something else. If we don't, he has a major meltdown, screaming, sobbing, and slamming doors, at which point it is even more difficult to get him to eat and it can be hours before he feels balanced. This goes for anything having to do his body, such as sleeping or using the bathroom; it all must be monitored as we try to help him recognize his physical signals. We cannot participate fully in certain community activities and classes because he can't handle crowds for any length of time without becoming overwhelmed. A babysitter is not an option because he does not like to be left behind, left out of family activities. It takes some work to balance the needs of our oldest and youngest, who do enjoy classes and events, and our middle boy who does not. I am not embarrassed or ashamed of our son, but I do believe that we have an obligation not to let him be the local freak show. In other words, don't put him in a situation where he will not be able to be his best self, and be ready to leave without being punitive if it is no longer working for him.

It can also be challenging to connect with other families. Families of kids with special needs I have met all send their kids to school and often have hours of therapy as well. There is not much common ground because we don't believe in scheduling our boys so heavily. Perhaps it is not a belief for some parents as much as a lack of knowledge about other options for learning. Perhaps there are families who wish they could do things differently for their children, but are hindered by life circumstances. I realize that my family is fortunate in many ways. I am not a single parent, my husband shares the belief that our kids are better off at home, and our boys do not have overwhelming behavioral or medical challenges.

The local unschooling group includes parents and kids who are supportive, accepting, and a lot of fun to be around, but there is a lack of common ground here as well. When talk turns to the fun projects and interests that their kids are pursuing, I feel a bit of a disconnect as the big news in our house for the week is the fact that our seven-year-old can now dress himself. Don't get me wrong, this is an unbelievable accomplishment and is treated as such by us, it's just that people who don't live with kids like ours don't have similar experiences to relate. Trying to find resources at bookstores or online about unschooling kids with developmental disabilities leaves a lot to be desired. What little I have found focuses on schedules, curriculum, or is heavily slanted towards information on autism and ADHD. We are willing and able to find our own way with our boys, but it would be nice to have some connections with people who understand what we are doing and are on a similar journey. I haven't given up my search, yet.

We don't know where our kids will end up in life or what knowledge they will require. The schools and therapists don't know either. We no longer worry about what our boys should learn because they are five, seven, or eleven. We are raising our sons with an eye to what they will need to be good men, which has nothing to do with an ability to answer questions on a test or learn information at predetermined ages. I do know that we are closer as a family than we ever were when they attended school. Our oldest son invents games that will help his brothers learn to communicate and he is now much more patient with their needs. He has also gained an understanding of how life isn't always fair, but you move forward and do the best that you can with what you have, not fall to pieces crying "why me." Our middle son has recovered confidence that was lost to him, his joyful smile, and loving attitude. Our youngest is willing to try anything because he hasn't always heard that he isn't ready or that what he wants to learn isn't on the schedule. I know that they are all happy, both with their lives and with who they are. Do I regret the years that we missed out on this life of freedom? No, but I do wish that I had the confidence and information to forge our own path from the beginning. Now that we have found it, I can't imagine living any other way.

An Inadvertently Compelling Argument
for National Health Care
in Five Mutually Incriminating Scenes
by Ayun Halliday

Scene One

HEARTY AUTOMATED WHITE MALE: Good morning! Thank you for calling Sunspire. If you are a health care provider, press pound now. For information on becoming a Sunspire Child Health Plus member, press pound three.

LESS HEARTY AUTOMATED SPANISH-SPEAKING FEMALE: *(translation of the above)*

HEARTY AUTOMATED WHITE MALE: Members, enter your identification number followed by the pound sign. Enter only the numbers. Skip any letters or symbols.

(The Conflict-Avoiding, Procrastination-Prone Artist Mother of Epileptic Child, otherwise known as OUR HEROINE, squints through an obsolete contact lens prescription at a plastic card she fishes from her battered wallet.)

HEARTY AUTOMATED WHITE MALE: Please hold while we check our eligibility records. *(Pause)* Enter the patient's date of birth as an eight digit number, month-month, day-day, year-year-year-year, followed by the pound sign.

(OUR HEROINE, one eye twitching involuntarily, does so.)

HEARTY AUTOMATED WHITE MALE: For claims, press one. Coverage, benefits, and premiums, two. Precertification, three. All other services and information, four.

(OUR HEROINE hesitates, before hastily stabbing one of the aforementioned numerals.)

Pause

FEMALE REPRESENTATIVE NUMBER 1: Good morning, thank you for calling Sunspire. My name is Mrs. Drrwsschkx. May I—

OUR HEROINE: Hi, yes, my daughter's got epilepsy and—

FEMALE REPRESENTATIVE NUMBER 1: May I have your name, Ma'am?

OUR HEROINE: Oh, uh, sure, my first name is A as in apple, y as in yellow, u as in umbrella, n as in Nancy. The last name's H-a-l-l-i-d-as-in-David-a-y, but my daughter's got her father's last name, which is K-as-in-kitten-o-t-i-s-as-in-Sam.

(Pause. Audible tapping on a computer keyboard.)

FEMALE REPRESENTATIVE NUMBER: Would that be Milo?

OUR HEROINE: No, India. Milo's her brother.

FEMALE REPRESENTATIVE NUMBER: India, huh. That's real unique.

OUR HEROINE: Oh, uh, thanks.

FEMALE REPRESENTATIVE NUMBER 1: Different. May I get India's date of birth?

OUR HEROINE, suppressing irritation at having to resupply this information and resupplies this information.

FEMALE REPRESENTATIVE NUMBER 1: Thank you, Mrs. Kotis. And Mrs. Kotis, can I get you to verify your home address for me?

(OUR HEROINE overlooks the surname error and states her home address. Pause. Then...)

FEMALE REPRESENTATIVE NUMBER 1: Thank you for calling Sunspire, Mrs. Kotis. How may I assist you today?

OUR HEROINE: Uh, well, my daughter has epilepsy and her seizures have been increasing so her doctor had us do an EK—, I mean, an EEG, and we did it, except now I just got a bill from Sunspire for a thousand dollars saying it wasn't covered?

FEMALE REPRESENTATIVE NUMBER 1: Can you give me the date the service was performed?

(OUR HEROINE'S hands shake as she supplies the date printed on a statement received two months prior.)

FEMALE REPRESENTATIVE NUMBER 1: Thank you. Just one moment while my computer searches for … okay, thank you for waiting. I'm seeing here that Dr. Neurospikowski is not one of our participating providers—

OUR HEROINE: Dr. Neurospin … I don't know who that is.

FEMALE REPRESENTATIVE NUMBER 1: He doesn't participate, so any services provided by him wouldn't be covered. To qualify for coverage, you'd have to see a participating provider.

OUR HEROINE: I don't know who that is, though.

FEMALE REPRESENTATIVE NUMBER 1: Our records show that this service was performed by Dr. Neurospikowsky.

OUR HEROINE: Yeah, except that can't be right because our neurologist's name is Dr. Head.

FEMALE REPRESENTATIVE NUMBER 1: This claim was submitted by a Dr. Neurospikowsky.

OUR HEROINE: Except how can that be, our doctor's name is Dr. Head?

FEMALE REPRESENTATIVE NUMBER: Is he the one who performed the service?

OUR HEROINE: *(Uncertainly)* A technician performed the service. There wasn't any doctor.

FEMALE REPRESENTATIVE NUMBER 1: Then what I would suggest is call the doctor and ask him to resubmit the claim.

OUR HEROINE: *(defeated and submissive, wishing a good fairy would appear at the window to relieve her of this burden)* Oh … okay.

Scene Two

Many months, possibly as much as two years, later.

*The HEARTY AUTOMATED WHITE MALE and LESS HEARTY
AUTOMATED SPANISH-SPEAKING FEMALE offer OUR HEROINE the
Conflict-Avoiding, Procrastination-Prone Artist Mother of the Epileptic
Child their standard greetings. Allowing her mind to wander, she inad-
vertently selects the incorrect numeric prompt, and after some telephonic
thrashing about, finds herself disconnected. Muttering venomously, she
redials the number on the back of the epileptic child's membership card,
and is subjected to identical automated greetings. Listening more actively,
she succeeds in pushing all the requisite buttons. There follows an intermi-
nable ten minute interval, after which OUR HEROINE is patched through
to FEMALE REPRESENTATIVE NUMBER 43.*

OUR HEROINE: Hi, my daughter's got epilepsy and—

FEMALE REPRESENTATIVE NUMBER 43: Can I get your name, ma'am?

OUR HEROINE: A as in apple, y as in yellow, u as in umbrella, n as in
Nancy, last name H-a-l-l-i-d-as-in-David-a-y, my daughter's name is
India, like the country—

FEMALE REPRESENTATIVE NUMBER 43: That's real pretty—

OUR HEROINE: *(smelling a rat, but masking it with involuntary
Midwestern politeness)* Thanks.

FEMALE REPRESENTATIVE NUMBER 43: Different. Can I get India's date
of birth?

*OUR HEROINE erroneously supplies her non-epileptic male child's date of
birth, then scrambles to correct herself before her credibility is irreparably
damaged in the eyes of her children's insurer.*

FEMALE REPRESENTATIVE NUMBER 43: And if you'd just please verify
your home address.

OUR HEROINE, teeth grinding, verifies her home address.

FEMALE REPRESENTATIVE NUMBER 43: Thank you for calling Sunspire. How may I assist you today?

OUR HEROINE: Okay, well, my daughter has this neurologist she sees regularly, and I just received this bill for seven hundred dollars—

FEMALE REPRESENTATIVE NUMBER 43: Can I get the physician's provider number?

OUR HEROINE: I don't have the number, but I know he participates with you guys. He's her regular neurolo—

FEMALE REPRESENTATIVE NUMBER 43: (*disproportionately merry*) Ha, ha, that's okay! I can find it using his name.

OUR HEROINE: Great. It's Head, Franklin Head; he used to be at Beth Elohim, now he's at—

FEMALE REPRESENTATIVE NUMBER 43: May I have the date the services were provided?

OUR HEROINE: (*Guiltily scans the top statement in a collection of four, three of which have yet to be removed from their still-sealed envelopes*) Uh, last February?

FEMALE REPRESENTATIVE NUMBER 43: (*betraying no particular emotion*) All right, let's take a look at our records … hmm, okay, okay; I'm seeing that Monkeypants Pediatrics faxed a preauthorization request for India to see Dr. Head on December 14 of 2005, but that expired.

OUR HEROINE: But he's her regular guy. She's been seeing him since she was four!

FEMALE REPRESENTATIVE NUMBER 43: Unfortunately, in order for Sunspire to honor that claim, we would need for her primary provider, which in this case would be Monkeypants Pediatrics, to have faxed through a new preauthorization request in advance of the appointment.

Simultaneously:
OUR HEROINE: Oh, hmm, see, the thing is, though, I, I think they did. I mean, they're usually really on top of that sort of thing.

OUR HEROINE'S INTERIOR MONOLOGUE: Fuck, fuck, shit, shit, fuck me, she's right! I forgot about preauthorization! I probably forgot on purpose, because Dr. Monkeypants's receptionist gets so pissed when people leave it to the last minute instead of giving her a minimum of five days lead time! I hate talking on the phone! I hate myself!

FEMALE REPRESENTATIVE NUMBER 43: Okay, let's take a look. Yeah, hmm, all I'm seeing is that request from 2005.

OUR HEROINE: Oh … okay … uh …

FEMALE REPRESENTATIVE NUMBER 43: *(brightly)* The good thing is, once we do receive a request, it's good for three visits within one calendar year, so you don't have to call your pediatrician every time your daughter has got an appointment coming up.

OUR HEROINE: Yeah. Great. As far as this one goes, though, I'm still not sure what could've happened. I definitely remember calling and talking to the receptionist … do you think maybe she faxed it to the wrong number?

FEMALE REPRESENTATIVE NUMBER 43: *(dryly)* I suppose that's possible.

OUR HEROINE: Is that the sort of thing that could happen, in your experience?

FEMALE REPRESENTATIVE NUMBER 43: I'd recommend calling your pediatrician. Maybe they have some sort of record they could fax over.

OUR HEROINE: *(fatigued, two minutes shy of needing to leave to pick the children up from school)* Okay. And then should I call you, right?

Scene Three

Enough time has elapsed that OUR HEROINE, the Conflict-Avoiding, Procrastination-Prone Artist Mother of the Epileptic Child, considers herself something of a hoary old vet, the type of person who conceivably could handle this sort of thing in her sleep.

We find her in a royal snit. The pharmacist she bakes cookies for every

Christmas has made repeated attempts to refill the not-entirely-effective prescription drugs the epileptic child takes three times a day, but the stone-walling insurance company will not approve the transaction. According to the labels on the now-nearly-empty bottles, the epileptic child is en-titled to four more refills before her mother must go against her nature and bug the neurologist for another six-month prescription. The greetings of the HEARTY AUTOMATED WHITE MALE and LESS-HEARTY, AUTOMATED, SPANISH-SPEAKING FEMALE are by now so familiar that OUR HEROINE barely registers them, reflexively stabbing the appro-priate buttons on her telephone when asked. Then...

HEARTY AUTOMATED WHITE MALE: According to our records that policy has been canceled.

OUR HEROINE: *(((silent scream)))*

Scene Four

Some fifteen seconds after Scene Three

Majorly freaking, OUR HEROINE immediately redials. Frantic in her de-sire to muscle past the prompts of HEARTY AUTOMATED WHITE MALE and LESS-HEARTY, AUTOMATED, SPANISH-SPEAKING FEMALE, she rasps "Representative!" every time she is asked to enter make a selection or enter personal information. Finally...

FEMALE REPRESENTATIVE NUMBER 207: Hello, thank you for calling Sunspire Child Health Plus, my name is Debbie, may I—

OUR HEROINE, on the verge of having a seizure herself, verifies her iden-tity, then gabbles incoherently about a policy she claims has been canceled in error. She invokes epilepsy, as in serious we-ain't-playing epilepsy for which three different types of seizure suppressing medications must be taken three times a day. Apparently those medications have run out, and without insurance, she is incapable of procuring them in such quantities as will keep her daughter from suffering a mind-blowing, game-over seizure. OUR HEROINE leans heavily on her theatrical training, suspecting it to be the last, best option for someone like her, who, despite a fairly privileged upbringing and a college degree, has no idea how the system works!!! Fuck fuck fuck fuck fuck!!!

FEMALE REPRESENTATIVE NUMBER 207: Mrs. Halliday, if it's all right with you, I'm just going to put you on hold for one moment while I check our records, see if we can figure out what's going on here.

OUR HEROINE: *(gratefully)* Yes, yes, please!

SOULLESS CAUCASIAN SINGERS: Do you know the way to San Jo—

FEMALE REPRESENTATIVE NUMBER 207: Okay, Mrs. Halliday, I pulled up your daughter's file, and unfortunately, I am seeing that that policy was canceled due to non-payment on—

OUR HEROINE: *(sinking to her knees a la Willem Dafoe at the end of* Platoon *... Her college acting teacher would have no doubt objected to such untempered ham-handedness, but he is in Evanston, Illinois, with a new crop of students, and she is alone in a New York City apartment, attempting to flounder her way out of the worst pickle of her life, a pickle that could have been avoided entirely by simple bill payment.)* But, but, but, oh my god. Oh god.

FEMALE REPRESENTATIVE NUMBER 207: *(stoic, but possibly seething with offense at hearing the Lord's name taken in vain)* I can send you an application if you'd like to reenroll—

OUR HEROINE: *(quickly)* Can we do that over the phone now?

FEMALE REPRESENTATIVE NUMBER 207: I'm afraid that's not possible, Mrs. Halliday.

OUR HEROINE: I can give you my Visa!

FEMALE REPRESENTATIVE NUMBER 207: I'm sorry, Mrs. Halliday, but our system is set up in such a way that even if I tried to reenroll you right now, the computer wouldn't let me. The best I can do is send you the application and have you return it to us in time for the beginning of the next billing cycle.

OUR HEROINE: *(assuming the prawn position)* Oh god. Oh god.

FEMALE REPRESENTATIVE NUMBER 207: Now, you should know that along with that application, we'll also be require a check for the overdue balance on the canceled account, plus two months' payment on the new account, at whatever the current premium happens to be.

OUR HEROINE: But what are we supposed to do until then? She's got to have this medicine! Even with it, she has like five or six little seizures a day! She falls off the jungle gym at school! If she doesn't get it, she could—

FEMALE REPRESENTATIVE NUMBER 207: Mm, yes, that's why we recommend paying your statements as soon as you receive them.

Simultaneously:

OUR HEROINE: I know, I'm so sorry I fell behind, it's just I've had a lot on my plate recently and we were on vacation, and then, I, I, I ... wait, do you think maybe if I came by with a check?

OUR HEROINE'S INTERIOR MONOLOGUE: Fuck you, lady! If my kid has a seizure and dies it's your fault! No! Take that back! Don't jinx yourself! Oh my god, I'm so fucked. I'm a danger to my own child. I'm a horrible, selfish moron! This nightmare is entirely my fault!

FEMALE REPRESENTATIVE NUMBER 207: We're in Blue Bonnet Shoals. That's right outside Albany.

OUR HEROINE: There's not some office in the city where I could—

FEMALE REPRESENTATIVE NUMBER 207: No.

Simultaneously:

OUR HEROINE'S INTERIOR MONOLOGUE: Fuck fuck shit fuck shit!!!

OUR HEROINE: Please! She's only got two pills left before she runs out!

Long, long pause.

FEMALE REPRESENTATIVE NUMBER 207: Let me speak to my supervisor.

Scene Five

Three-and-a-half days and several dozen phone calls after Scene Four

HEARTY AUTOMATED WHITE MALE and LESS-HEARTY, AUTOMATED, SPANISH-SPEAKING FEMALE run through their customary spiels. OUR HEROINE, the Conflict-Avoiding, Procrastination-Prone Artist Mother of the Epileptic Child, clings hollow-eyed to something resembling a yogic breathing regimen, wincing as HEARTY AUTOMATED WHITE MALE reiterates that according to his records, this policy has been canceled.

FEMALE REPRESENTATIVE NUMBER 214: Thank you for calling Sunspire. My name is Cheryl Case. May—

OUR HEROINE: I'm calling about my daughter. Her account was canceled because I screwed up the bill, but I spoke with Debbie on Thursday and she spoke with Mr. Toms and he said as long as I could get a check to you by today, the policy could be reinstated, which is really critical because she takes all this seizure medication for epilepsy. I was able to get the pharmacist to sell me a few pills to get us through the weekend, but—

FEMALE REPRESENTATIVE NUMBER 214 interrupts to have OUR HEROINE verify her identity. Dutifully supplied. The account remains canceled. Oh god. Oh no. Oh fuckfuckfuckfuck no!!!!

OUR HEROINE: *(wild-eyed, frothing)* But, but, I sent the check on Thursday, right after I got off the phone with Debbie!

FEMALE REPRESENTATIVE NUMBER 214: You sent it to the address in Blue Bonnet Shoals, not the P.O. Box on the bill?

OUR HEROINE: Yes! Yes!!!

FEMALE REPRESENTATIVE NUMBER 214: Okay, do you have the Fed Ex tracking number?

OUR HEROINE: *(bowels freezing with regret)* I didn't send it Fed Ex.

FEMALE REPRESENTATIVE NUMBER 214: According to Debbie's notes, you were told to Fed Ex a check for the full amount for overnight delivery, with the understanding that we needed to receive that check by today in order to reinstate the account?

OUR HEROINE: *(barely audible)* I know but the lady at the UPS store said that since we're both in New York, and the post office was just a block away, Priority Mail would be just as good.

FEMALE REPRESENTATIVE NUMBER 214: *(Pause.)* Let me get this straight. You were at a place where you could send it via Fed Ex, and then you decided to go to the post office instead?

OUR HEROINE: I know.

FEMALE REPRESENTATIVE NUMBER 214: So, you sent it via USPS, Priority Overnight?

OUR HEROINE: *(ashen)* No, just regular Priority.

FEMALE REPRESENTATIVE NUMBER 214: Even though you understood that that check absolutely, no exceptions, had to be in our hands by Friday.

OUR HEROINE: *(Childlike in her wretchedness)* She said it would be just as fast.

FEMALE REPRESENTATIVE NUMBER 214: Did you at least send it certified or request delivery confirmation?

OUR HEROINE: No, I ... I used the automated machine in the lobby.

FEMALE REPRESENTATIVE NUMBER 214: *(under her breath)* Incredible.

OUR HEROINE: *(sadly)* Believe me, I'm kicking myself for not sending it Fed Ex. I guess I was thinking it would be a good thing to save twenty bucks. Stupid.

Defeated, OUR HEROINE stares at the cheap, boob-shaped overhead fixture in her cramped, $1,400-a-month living room, agonized that she is so immature as to have lapses during which her responsibility for her child's health seems less of a priority than checking her e-mail, or pursuing some half-baked artsy whim. Would that the precious creature had never been stricken, that health was a thing that could be taken blissfully for granted until some day in the extremely far distant future when OUR HEROINE, herself, is painlessly and poignantly expiring, surrounded by loving family members and high-thread-count linens.

FEMALE REPRESENTATIVE NUMBER 214: You do understand that a huge exception was being made in your case?

OUR HEROINE: *(Lord Jesus, have pity on this miserable sinner… she knows not what she does…)* I know. It's my fault that I screwed it up.

FEMALE REPRESENTATIVE NUMBER 214: *(sighs, murderously sick of dealing with incompetents such as this hippie dippy ding-dong.)* All right. What did the envelope you mailed it in look like?

OUR HEROINE: *(arm hair prickling, alert)* What?

FEMALE REPRESENTATIVE NUMBER 214: There's a *chance* it might have been delivered this morning, but we get thousands of pieces of mail every day. Maybe it's sitting in a bin in the mailroom.

OUR HEROINE: It was one of those red, white, and blue Flat Rate envelopes.

FEMALE REPRESENTATIVE NUMBER 214: Great. I hope you don't have anywhere to be because this might take a while.

OUR HEROINE: I can hold!

FEMALE REPRESENTATIVE NUMBER 214: There's no guarantee that it's there.

OUR HEROINE: *(Experiencing the adrenalin rush of a woman wrenching the roof off a car to free her infant from a flaming wreck)* No, no, I know! Take all the time you need!

FEMALE REPRESENTATIVE NUMBER 214: *(no love in her voice)* All right. Please hold.

An interval of nearly twenty minutes. Cue string heavy instrumentals of various soft rock hits. OUR HEROINE psyches herself up. She must be like the mother puma, ready to hop a Greyhound bus four hours north to Albany in order to sort through the insurance company's mail for them! She hopes security clearance will not be a problem. She hopes another mother will volunteer to pick up her children from school for her, because no way will she be back in time. She cringes to imagine how much a cab to Blue Bonnet Shoals will run her, but whatever the cost, she has lost the privilege to bitch about it. Her heartbeat rivals that of a hummingbird's. At last:

FEMALE REPRESENTATIVE NUMBER 214: *(grudgingly)* Well, you're in luck. We found it in one of the last bins we looked in.

(Cue offstage celestial choir)

OUR HEROINE: OH MY GOD!!! Thank you!!!!

FEMALE REPRESENTATIVE NUMBER 214: You do understand that this was a one-time thing. If you fail to pay on time again, we won't be able to—

OUR HEROINE: *(determined to prove that she will do better, that she will never ever fuck up again, that from here on out all will be smooth sailing and conscious, timely effort, the margin for human error all used up, and thus, permanently eliminated)* I understand! It was my one get out of jail free card and after that no more. Thank you! And please, tell Debbie and Mr. Toms thank you from me too!

FEMALE REPRESENTATIVE NUMBER 214: I'll reinstate your daughter's account as of today. It may take a few hours to go through.

OUR HEROINE *(Scheming to mail cookies to the address in Blue Bonnet Shoals. For one reason and another, she will not get around to actually doing so for another week and a half, and will worry that they will arrive stale, but she sort of knows the recipients have cemented their opinion of her, and probably wouldn't be too grateful even if the unsolicited treat had been Fed-Exed straight out of the oven)* Oh my god, I can't thank you enough!

FEMALE REPRESENTATIVE NUMBER 214 disconnects without thanking OUR HEROINE for calling Sunspire.

OUR HEROINE collapses on the carpet and remains there until shortly before she is due to pick up her children from school. For once, she does not feel guilty about failing to use her child-free time in pursuit of some negligible artistic goal.

❖ ❖ ❖

Discussion Guide

¶ How does the author's tendency to avoid conflict, procrastinate, and preoccupy herself with artistic goals of no discernible impact influence her ongoing negotiations with her children's insurance provider?

¶ Why might someone in the author's position not sign up for automatic bill pay?

¶ Why might the children's father balk at stripping the author of all duties relating to the children's health insurance?

¶ How many times in the last year have you heard the word "seizure" used in a humorous, non-epileptic context?

¶ Did you know Mark Twain had an epileptic child who suffered a fatal seizure on Christmas Day?

¶ Did you know that the title character in *Carrie* was partially based on an epileptic girl Stephen King knew in high school, who died of a massive seizure in her twenties?

¶ The author has another character allude to her as a hippie "ding-dong," albeit nonverbally. Is this an apt description? If so, why do you think she is relying three different types of prescription medication to semi-control her child's seizures, as opposed to herbs, crystals, and creative visualization?

¶ How does the author's nationality influence or define her experience?

¶ How might these scenes have played out prior to the advent of the automated-phone-system?

¶ Why are all the female representatives female?

¶ Might the author's attitude be a chronic reflection of the fact that she doesn't like to talk on the phone?

❡ Do you think the author has "learned her lesson" by the end of this piece?

❡ Would the author seem more sympathetic had she majored in business administration or something less frivolous than an archaic art form that rarely translates to a living wage?

❡ What if the author's child had leukemia or cystic fibrosis? What about autism, asthma, or a severe peanut allergy?

❡ What will happen when the author's child is no longer eligible for "Sunspire Child Health Plus"? Is that eighteen or nineteen? It's not like a new insurer could deny her coverage based on a pre-existing condition, or could they? Do we trust the author to begin researching the answers to this question in a timely manner?

❡ Wouldn't it be totally awesome if the author's child's epilepsy spontaneously cured itself?

Watching
My Son Grow:
An Illustrated Timeline
from Birth
to Three Years Old
by Joe Dimino

Birth to Two Months

During this time, most children will lift head a little when lying on stomach, watch objects for a short time and make "noise in throat" sounds.

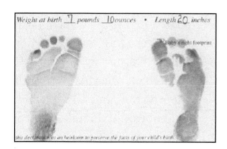

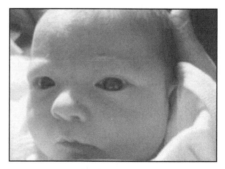

Actual milestones: After his first week he began latching on while breastfeeding.

The first real glimpse into my son's eyes was through the thick ointment they gave to him shortly after birth. I brimmed with a love I have never experienced before as I called his name and he tried like mad to open those new eyes to see his father's face and the voice he had heard through the womb for many months. In retrospect, it seems an apt metaphor for my little Miles Alfonso Dimino born a click before 5:00 pm. on the same day that Jim Morrison was born and John Lennon was shot—December 8—back in the year 2004. Why is this an apt metaphor?

Only four months after falling fervently in love with my wife, Carrie, we conceived Miles. We both knew that we had fallen in love forever; we felt ecstatic to marry in July and welcome our first child into the world about five months later. Things were moving at a quick clip at that point. My wife had a son from a previous marriage, then five-year-old Zen, and was well-versed in raising a young one. I was spending those anxious months leading to Miles' birth hearing a load of advice, congratulations, and stories about everyone else's experience in welcoming children into this world.

The birth of our boy was about as cautious as it gets. Carrie was very conscious of her eating habits and overall health. She even went as far as not eating sushi due to unsafe mercury levels. Additionally, the birth was to be natural without the use of any drugs. All of this was achieved when Miles was born. We felt highly relieved that it went as well as we had planned. To this day, the birth of Miles is one of the most amazing days of my entire life.

Miles had a hard time latching on while trying to breastfeed. We were assured by several nurses and our delivery doctor that this can be a fairly routine thing to happen. In full retrospect, this was the first sign that Miles was not going to fall into that category of "typical" baby.

As the months plodded forward and the excitement of fatherhood sank in, I began feeling the normal pangs of sleep deprivation and an extremely new life experience. Miles began breastfeeding, but would not take a bottle at all. It simply wasn't a part of his equation. He would not and could not latch onto the bottle as an alternative to breastfeeding. We only attempted to give him a bottle every once in a while. It was a sure sign of Miles' complete dependence on his mother for a very necessary ingredient of his growth and mental comfort.

◆ ◆ ◆

Three to Eight Months

During this time, most children will lift head and chest when lying on stomach, show active body movement, sit with little support, roll from back to stomach and change object from hand to hand and from hand to mouth.

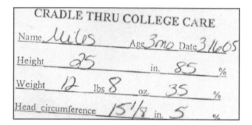

Actual milestones: He would start lifting his head some while on his stomach and sat on his own.

In the early stages of development, our family was getting a monthly check-up from a Parents as Teachers coordinator. Over this time, we had a helpful case worker who would visit our home and give us solid child-rearing advice. Even in the early stages of her visits, we voiced some concerns: first it was about his refusal to use a bottle. Later, Carrie would have her suspicions about his overall development. I, on the other hand, was blissfully oblivious to any glitches regarding milestones. But as time marched forward, both of us began to realize that Miles was going to have his own growth chart.

During routine visits and vaccination sessions with our pediatrician we mentioned some mild concerns to Miles' doctor. By seven months he wasn't rolling over. Our optimistic pediatrician would always assure us that everything was moving along just fine and some of these things simply take time. The doctor would always challenge the notion of the bell curve and say, "When he gets to college, no one is going to ask him when he started walking." Or, "Each child develops at their own unique pace." I cannot remember how many times we heard that throughout the first year and a half of Miles's short life.

Both our Parents as Teachers coordinator and pediatrician continued to tell us that it was way too soon to know if there was indeed something slow in Miles' development. They were genuinely unsure if there were any issues going on or not. Putting insurance concerns aside, I believe it's a very difficult task for a health professional to not only confirm, but also to disclose the fact that a child has developmental delays worthy of serious concern. My wife always felt there was an unspoken philosophy to allow parents time to bond without worry.

◆ ◆ ◆

Nine to Seventeen Months

During this time most children will pull themselves to stand and may step with support, nod their head to signal yes, pick things up with thumb and one finger, say two or three words, walk without support, speak and make their voice go up and down, drink from a cup held by someone, and use four or five words.

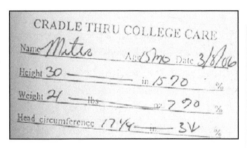

Actual milestones: He started to crawl and was beginning to pick up some things with his hands without precision.

Through the first twelve months of his life, I remained a determined optimist, believing that everything would be fine. This was also a mantra that our families and friends would reiterate to both Carrie and I when Miles would be crawling around shortly after year one without any hint that walking or talking would be in his future. Carrie knew better than everyone else that something was not right in his development. I can see how alone she felt with this knowledge, but hope kept everyone sane. It still does.

I began taking all these issues into heavy consideration when we hit the fourteenth or fifteenth month and he was still not crawling. As the months kept slipping away and there were neither words nor walking, we began to inch closer to the notion that things were different from what we were expecting; we concluded that some preventative steps needed to take place. Our Parents as Teachers coordinator mentioned that we should start to think about getting an in-home evaluation from First Steps to see if he qualified for their set of services.

◆ ◆ ◆

Eighteen to Nineteen Months

During this time, most children will walk without help, climb up and down on things, stand up and sit down without holding on, understand simple one-step directions, use more meaningful single words, gesture and use words together, hold out arms and legs while being dressed by others, and point to objects they want.

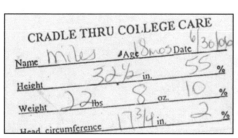

Actual milestones: He finally started walking on his own, but not too well. Also, he began using sign language more frequently to get things that he needed.

During the nineteenth month, we made an appointment with First Steps and had an evaluation done in our home. Ironically, this was the month that Miles finally started to walk. I remember that day as clear as anything that has happened in my life. We had stopped by Grandma Judy and Grandpa Austin's home for our regular Sunday afternoon visit. Shortly after entering the home, I told Miles to *walk to Gigi*. It happened. He quickly traversed about ten paces over the floor and collapsed in a giggle into Grandma Judy's arms. Carrie, Zen, and I looked in slow motion silence at each other not quite believing what we had seen. Both Judy and Austin looked at us with that *what's going on?* look and we said that this was the first time he had ever walked that far. We were all ecstatic, and for a brief moment I looked into Miles's happy eyes wondering if he waited all those months for some secret reason he would tell us some day far into the future.

During the initial First Steps evaluation, we told them that he had only recently started walking. We wanted to make certain that we conveyed to them that his balance and skill level was in its initial stages and didn't want his new skill to rule us out of getting much needed services. After a thorough evaluation and several weeks of waiting, we found out that he qualified for physical, occupational, and speech therapies. It was both a relief and shock. Our fears had been validated.

◆ ◆ ◆

Twentieth Month—Testing Phase

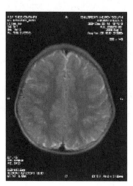 

With a sense of relief and fear for the future, we were thrust into a world of tests—genetics, MRIs, and an amazing range of pediatric specialists came at us. We were introduced to a medical community we had hoped never to know. At the same time, we were trying to figure out how to add twelve hours of therapy to our lives and how to keep our jobs and how to go to soccer practice. Forget maintaining friendships or the long forgotten honeymoon; we were in full survival mode.

Leading up to these tests, Carrie had done extensive research on the Internet to find out more about autism, Angelman syndrome, and other developmental delays that seemed similar to Miles's. Our first order was to go get blood and urine samples. Then, we were going to have to meet with an orthopedic surgeon to see what his recommendations were for Miles getting his gait and general walking straightened out. Finally, we were to have him sedated so that they could perform an MRI to see if he had brain tumors that might affect his language development and make walking difficult.

◆ ◆ ◆

Twenty-First to Twenty-Second Months—Results

Several months later, after countless hours in waiting rooms, we were told that he had no tumors and that all genetics could find was an extra long arm on his fifteenth chromosome. Since Miles has some facial features similar to children with Down's syndrome, such as epicanthic folds, a flat nasal bridge, and lowered ears, the overall consensus was a flaw in his genetic code.

◆ ◆ ◆

Pre & Post Two Years Old—Intense Therapy

During this time most children will give toys when asked, recognize a familiar picture and know if it is upside down, kick a large ball, turn pages in a book (two or three at a time) and use two or three words together, such as "more juice".

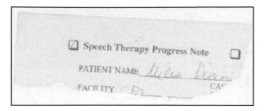

Actual milestones: He began to recognize toys and interacted with them for the first time. Also, he was trying hard to begin kicking balls, and trying to catch them.

After six months of therapy with First Steps, we had our first full evaluation of where Miles was developmentally. The synopsis was that he had made some solid strides, but there was still a need for all three therapy services and more collaboration on the therapeutic front. Furthermore, he had been diagnosed with SID (sensory integration disorder). In essence, he was feeling everything in his world differently. He needed our help and therapeutic assistance to cope with those differences.

We had another solid six-month stint of therapies, and both Miles and the family were getting more comfortable with strangers in our home and the more permanent ritual of therapy in our daily lives. In fact, we made some good friends in several of the therapists that worked with Miles. The therapists were always very encouraged by our participation and desire to see Miles improve through the therapy in which Carrie and I both believed.

Over the course of these therapy sessions, our son Zen was very involved in trying to understand what Miles was doing and how he could help. Zen has been the best big brother ever under very stressful circumstances. Carrie and I couldn't laude Zen enough for the love, strength, courage, and understanding of having to dole out the extreme time and attention that Miles needs.

◆ ◆ ◆

Two-and-a Half to Three Years Old—More Therapy & Growth

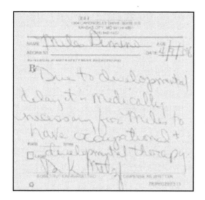 

During our one-year evaluation with First Steps, we accepted an invitation to include behavioral therapy as a part of our services. This was something that Carrie and I were wholly uniformed about. We had one of the area's foremost experts in autism therapy visit our home to evaluate what Miles's needs were going to be. About three minutes into her visit, she looked up at us and said, "Please don't get him tested for autism. He simply doesn't have it." Along with the relief of having an expert in the autism spectrum tell us that, we were conversely concerned about what she witnessed during her visit. Aside from our parenting skills, this evaluator said that we would have a huge problem on our hands if we didn't act immediately and start modifying his behavior patters. At the end of a very thorough and effective visit, it was decided that we would spend four days a week both in the office and at home giving Miles behavioral therapy services.

Neither Carrie nor I had any idea what to expect from behavioral therapy, and were again anxious for what was to come. The fact that a trained therapist with her experience level said he would be a big problem if behaviors weren't curbed put a fright into our bones.

This is really when the rubber hit the road. To this day, the behavioral therapy has been a triumph and contributes to Miles flourishing in his daily life. These dedicated and patient behavioral therapists showed Miles and us how to temper the tempest of his sensory integration issues, lack of language, poor balance, and general difficulty paying attention.

Again, Carrie and I were very involved in charting, giving him treats when he did a task successfully, and giving high fives. Now, it was very clear that Miles had several issues that were a part of the autism spectrum and that the spectrum is rather large. So, from his inability to speak and sensory integration issues, he was firmly in a spectrum that simply became a "special needs" label. We began to wonder if labels even apply in this emerging, mysterious, and confusing condition.

Carrie and I were introduced to a host of parents and children who are in the autism world. It didn't take long for me to understand that the spectrum is vastly different from having autism. Sometimes when I would see tantrums that wouldn't stop or classic autism behaviors that were quite loud, I would peer over at Miles and study his reaction. Usually he would keep doing what he was doing, but then he would stop every once a while to peer over and see what was going on. It was a frightening environment. Keep in mind, this was a facility that was in a strip mall, and they charged regular paying folks almost $4,000 a month for services. If it wasn't for the intervention of First Steps, I'm not sure how Carrie and I would have participated.

As we barreled through his year of behavioral therapy, he was two and a half and making great strides in all areas of his development. Over this year, he was finally exhibiting an interest in toys and general kid's stuff that had held little interest for him during the first two years of his life. We were starting to see him break out of this thick shell of developmental delay and start exhibiting typical infant/kid behaviors we hadn't seen before. The staff at the clinic loved Miles and again lauded him for how well he picked up concepts and tried so hard.

Those days of driving to the clinic and working rigorously with him for an hour of therapy were some of the most important moments in his growth. He was out of the house, interacting with other kids, getting good therapy and giving the world his mix of romantic happiness. I was really blown away to see my kid taking to learning and growing with such voracity. Sometimes I would see Miles leave thoughts of me being in the room and just thrive at what he was doing. It was during those moments that I would bite my lip as longing and expectations slipped away. I could just enjoy the coolness that was taking place. But after a moment, he would always return and look up at me for a good, wide smile.

During the summer when Miles was two and therapy was really heating up, Carrie and I decided to establish a cathartic blog (http://milesalfonsodiminotherapy.blogspot.com) that would be a good forum for us to communicate what was going to family, friends, and the world. We agreed that this would be an honest and frank forum to let those around us know exactly what Miles was going through and how we were coping. This blog was to include frank testimonials, tips, photos, videos, and any other bits that would better expose what kind of progress Miles was making. Overall, we wanted this to be a soothing mechanism to provide hope and healing for everyone who decided to stop by on a regular basis. Our ability to explain what was going on with Miles and why we simply weren't getting out seeing folks as much as we wanted to made it a bit clearer. We could let people in to get our honest take on our evolving lives with Miles.

I vividly remember the summer he was two because First Steps was going to give us a huge chunk of time for behavioral therapy. Carrie and I were pretty focused on assisting Miles in an emotional and physical growth spurt. In addition to the ABA clinical therapy in the office and in our home, he was still getting occupational, speech, and physical therapy services. This summer was interrupted quite a bit by a move. Our home had been on the meager housing market for about nineteen months. Our primary aim for moving was to get into a better school district for Miles. Our eyes were set on leaving South Kansas City for the more southern suburb of Belton, Missouri.

During July, the sale of our home was finalized and we scrambled to find a place in Belton. The stars aligned and we were able to find the home we wanted. We were going to get Miles ready to transition out of the First Steps services into Grace Early Childhood Center. This center was lauded in the Kansas City metro as one of the best facilities for dealing with children who are in the autism spectrum and have developmental delays. We were ecstatic with the life change that was finally going to afford us the opportunity to give Miles his own room. In addition, our break from a two-bedroom ranch home to a multi-level home with much more room and a finished basement was going to allow us a dedicated therapy space for Miles. In the old home, we had to endure the arduous task of converting our living room into a therapy room twelve times a week for every therapy session.

After the move and the intensity of summer wound down, we began getting ready to go through the scary step of getting Miles into an actual school. The months leading up to our move and after our move were quite stressful; we contemplated how life would be without an intense therapy schedule and with a transition into a public school program. Both Carrie and I had quite a bit to chew on as we moved into the last months of Miles' second year and his new journey into a big school environment.

◆ ◆ ◆

Three Years Old—Starting School

During this time most children will follow two- or three-phrase commands, sort objects by shape and color, imitate the actions of adults and playmates, and express a wide range of emotions.

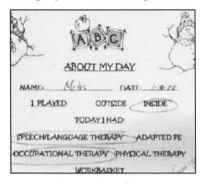 

Actual milestones: He started recognizing colors and shapes, along with following simple one-step commands. His ability to express a wide range of emotions, especially affection, continued to blossom. He started to have an active interest in being with other children on a limited basis.

This was another time of intense research that Carrie did to figure out what an IEP (Individualized Education Program) was and how we would help the school district develop the best plan to meet Miles's needs. The other key component came after Miles turned three and transitioned into Grace Early Childhood; he received an official screening at Children's Mercy Hospital to get an official diagnosis.

Miles was starting to get quite a bit taller and more mature in his overall look. Miles continued to refine that rare ability to light up any room or public place he walked into. From his infectious smiles to waving hands, he melted every heart he came across.

Leading up to our IEP meetings with Grace, we found ourselves against the wall because time was slipping away. Some administrative hurdles got in our way, and we had to rush in late November to get an IEP developed with the staff before Miles' third birthday on December 8.

We got exactly what we wanted when his final IEP was drafted and set in stone. He was to receive speech, occupational, and physical therapy, and also was to have a one to one paraeducator to ensure his safety. The other golden nugget exposed during this initial meeting was the possibility of Miles riding the bus on his own. Carrie and I were in such shock that Miles was even going to enter an environment where neither of us needed to participate full time, that a bus seemed far out of the equation. This thought spooked both of us. The staff assured us that there had never been a student in their school's history who either refused riding a bus or got so terrified that they never rode the bus.

We nodded and agreed to take Miles to school for the first several weeks and then give the bus a shot. Carrie, Zen, and I took Miles into Grace on his first day. I felt numbed by the enormity of my little boy actually going into such a grown environment. That first day of tears was tough, but the culmination of our love, the new move, and getting into the school we wanted let us see the growth our boy had made and made it all a cool experience.

When we picked Miles up that first day, he was in good spirits. As the days turned into a week and a week turned into weeks, he flourished. They kept thinking that he was going to slip out of his honeymoon phase, but it simply wasn't in the cards. Our Miles boy was a little learner and he was thriving in his new environment. The teachers loved having him in class and he was picking up a variety of new concepts.

Our next big school moment came when we took him reluctantly to the bus for the first time. I had it fixed in my brain that it wasn't likely going to work out, and that we were going to have to make new arrangements. The tears on that first day were flowing as his little yellow bus shuttled his scared bones from my grasp and around the corner into invisibility. It was another culmination of many *what ifs* as Miles took another brave, bold step into being an independent three-year old boy.

His transition into bus riding was much easier after the first week. In fact, it became the highlight of his whole day to do the rotating arms in sign language for the wheels on the bus. He loved the bus and his driver loved him. Everything was falling into step.

◆ ◆ ◆

Three Years & Three months—The Diagnosis

During February, we finally got our appointment with the hospital to see if we couldn't get him a diagnosis. The first day was a whole battery of tests, evaluations, and discussions with staff about Miles and how he was doing. At this point, Carrie and I were old pros at dealing with medical environments, an assault of questions, and investigations into who Miles is. Miles was also becoming quite oblivious to the line of testing and questioning. Again, either Carrie or I needed to be present in the room for testing to take place. We were always in the room during testing; we were always at a safe distance, but if we weren't, Miles wouldn't do much.

At the end of an intense three and a half hours of testing and evaluation, Carrie and I were unimpressed with this staff and their general grasp of his condition. We took it on the chin and had a follow-up session with just the two of us to discuss what label Miles was going to initially get in this long journey to ultimately find out what we had been waiting for these three long years. The final diagnosis was an *impulsive disorder*. In essence, they said Miles couldn't control himself and had a hard time dealing with impulses. They also ruled out autism and spoke with us about medicating options. They recommended that we think it over and try a medication to see how it might work.

Leaving this meeting, Carrie and I were frustrated at what we saw as a rather harsh diagnosis. There's no real way to understand a creature like Miles after a four-hour session.

On the drug/medication front, Carrie and I accepted this as something we might try. To put it to the real test, we asked his homeroom teacher what she thought, and she refused the notion strongly. Her stance was that he is an avid learner that can have behaviors modified by an educational environment. We have seen his ability to modify his behaviors repeatedly at home and couldn't agree more. On the heels of his diagnosis, it was a great relief to think that we could live a drug-free existence.

◆ ◆ ◆

Three Years, Eight months—Current Day

 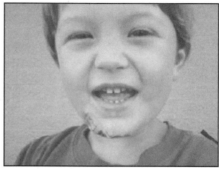

Miles just finished his last day of summer school. Over his eight months of schooling and therapy, he has continued to amaze us. After his six months, he has met a handful of IEP goals and is getting some new ones introduced to keep him evolving along a progressive path. He has little friends in school and generally becomes more open to new things on a daily basis.

I have always thought the real issue with Miles is that he is behind other three-year-olds by about a year. Sure, there are some other distinct issues that are very different from other kids, but his maturation is going to take longer. From a parenting perspective, it's almost sweeter. When little things like riding a bike and putting on his own shoes happen, they are victories that raise the hair on my neck. Since Miles entered my life, I have embraced the notion that it's no fun to rush the hand of time. I get a bit more time with my son to watch all of these little moments of life happen at a slower rate. This is how I stay sane and keep the laughter rolling.

The key to watching a boy like Miles grow is that he is the happiest creature I know. His infectious personality and zest for small things like water slides and frozen yogurts has enriched my life in ways that are hard to etch into the squiggles of ink on this page. I marvel each passing day to see how

Miles will grow that much more, from the shoes he will outgrow to the few new words that arrive here and there.

When you have a child with special needs, you can either break down or open the floodgates to what is amazing about life. I believe I have done the latter. I knew early on that I was going to embark on something that was going to be the complete opposite of what I envisioned parenthood to be. Even so, I wouldn't change one moment I have lived. Through the pain, exhaustion, and confusion, I decide each day to savor the joy that is within my family and this life. It's there—and when an opportunity as I have arrives I can do nothing more than charge hard with a smile, knowing that this is my life and I'm going to damn well live it to the sweetest limits.

Each time Miles grows a bit more, I imagine those tiny eyes rising up for the first time, seeing his dad peering down. What I see is a life that has made us understand that being alive is much, much more than walking, talking, and bell curves.

Authentic Activism
by Maria June

As far as I can tell, "disability" activism is not about having figured it all out. It isn't about agreeing with other disability activists point-by-point. It isn't about being beyond grieving, if you were ever grieving. It is not about having reached some kind of enlightenment, or feeling confident you have all the answers, or being an expert in all kinds of diagnoses, or never getting frustrated with a child or adult who has a disability, including perhaps yourself. It isn't about having the correct language (and believe me that once you think you've got that figured out you'll probably learn something to flip it all upside down again). It isn't about devoting every moment of your life to *the cause*, and it may or may not involve writing to lawmakers. It can be grassroots or legal, local or national, almost entirely public or semi-private. The success of activism depends primarily on the authenticity with which we approach our own experiences with disability. My experiences have come in two distinct parts.

Part One

At twenty-three, I became the mother of a fifteen-year-old who had multiple disabilities. My education in activism had begun.

It all started with a phone call. I was at work, and when the woman on the phone identified herself as an employee of a local foster care agency. I thought perhaps she was calling me about a potential collaborative project, or the need for volunteers, or maybe a youth with whom I worked.

Instead, she said, "I am calling you about a child. His name is Blake. I want to know if you would like to be his mother?"

She paused, and I began to shake. To physically shake. My hands were weak, so I pressed the phone against my ear with my right shoulder and put both hands on the phone to form a tripod with which to hold it. I smiled with joy, but also out of nervousness, fear, and confusion. Within a split second I knew why she had called *me*.

Several months before, someone I knew who is employed at this same foster agency asked my wife, Laura, and me about our desire to be foster parents. We discussed our interest with her, thinking little of it at the time. A month later, she called and told us that her agency was in need of more foster parents. She asked if she could have the foster home licensor give us a call, and we had agreed, but after speaking with the licensor briefly, we decided to put on hold our hopes of becoming licensed. The process of licensing itself was a lengthy and complex one, and the agency was an organization involved in the therapeutic care of many of our county's "highest needs" children.

We had a new puppy in our home, and both Laura and I were adjusting to new jobs. Because we hadn't pursued foster home licensing, we hadn't imagined the possibility of being called about a child. This call wasn't entirely out of the blue, but it was far from expected.

I held my breath as the director at the agency described the very special situation and why *we* specifically had been chosen as a potential family for Blake. Most of those details are too sensitive to share in a book even with the anonymity of pseudonyms, which I've used in this essay for the benefit of my children's privacy.

I wrote little notes on a Post-it pad.

Blake's needs were great. Though he was a teenager, due to developmental delays, his needs were also long-term, extending far beyond his anticipated years in foster care. The agency did not facilitate adoptions, but sadly there was no chance that Blake would return home to his family. He needed another family that could care for him permanently, even if this meant he would be living with his foster family at twenty, at thirty, at forty, or fifty. He needed strong advocates who could secure for him— over the long term—the necessary social, daily living, and educational services.

However, we were told living with him could be difficult. He had experienced a great deal of trauma in his life, and this caused some behaviors that were hard even for experienced therapeutic foster parents to manage. Yet even as the director explained this, she told me, "I think you two can do this. I really do, or I wouldn't be calling you." Of course, she also told us all the many things we would likely come to love about Blake. If we accepted the placement, he would become our son, and we would be hand-held through the licensing and training process so that Blake could come home as soon as possible.

Though a decision was needed in short order, Laura and I took all the time we were afforded to evaluate whether being Blake's parents was something we felt we could do. We spent two half-days with Blake. We hardly slept during those few days we were given to discern what was right for all of us. Everything was at stake, for Blake and for us. Finally, it became clear what we needed to do: we needed to say YES to this child. Love had become my driving force.

Blake arrived bravely. Moving from home to home—in other words, family to family—had been his life experience for over ten years and almost twenty-five families. While we had agreed to be Blake's "forever family," Blake figured we were just as likely to be another empty promise. Blake chose on his own initiative to call us by parental terms, but we later learned how comforting it had been for him to think of our relationship as being short-term. Not investing in his relationship with us made it low-risk for Blake.

Laura and I were brave, too. In our deliberations, we had taken a careful inventory of our skills and weaknesses. We knew exactly where we stood as parents, and we were prepared. In the months it took to get licensed, we attended trainings in everything from the history of foster care to advocating for children in the school system. We fell in love with Blake for the child he was, and our hesitations diminished.

I was quickly knee-deep in Individualized Education Plans, behavioral management strategies, and therapy appointments of various types. I changed urine-soaked bed linens when sleep was deep and responded to terrified cries in the night when sleep was fitful. I learned to read Blake's cues to keep our pets protected from his rage. I cleaned up possible fecal stains on the bathroom walls, created a food-hoarding drawer in the kitchen ("Blake's Drawer") where Blake stored enough to keep himself from panicking when memories of hunger were triggered by things that most folks don't notice, like the mayonnaise jar being less than half full.

I homeschooled during school suspensions and got to know my local police officers by first name during Blake's periodic psychiatric episodes that eventually became an accepted rather than frightening aspect of life. I learned to translate all kinds of subject matter, even grief, into concrete terms. After many months of trying many other ways to help Blake feel secure, I accepted the need for a sanity-saving "sticker chart" that I swore

I would never use when I became a mom.

I also learned how to shop with a fifteen-year-old who couldn't handle the emotional and sensory experience of shopping above the functional level thought typical of a three- or four-year-old. Blake once threw himself on the floor and had a full on kicking and screaming temper tantrum when I told him we were not at the store to buy a CD and that he was welcome to save up his allowance money for another week so that we could come back for it. How we made it out of the store without security being called on us, I'll never know. I will always remember the puzzled and horrified looks on the faces of older women, pushing their carts past our aisle shaking their heads while my strikingly tall adolescent threw himself on the floor stomping and wailing "But Mooooooommy! I want it!"

I looked so young. He looked so old. I wondered if they thought we were part of some twisted role play, or if they were instead thinking "Tsk! Tsk! See how young mothers go about ruining their children." Perhaps they couldn't make heads or tails of us at all. I soon learned to ignore the stares, and repeat in my head the mantra, "Just take care of your kid. No one else exists right now." This mantra was key in getting me through the dark day when I chaperoned a field trip out of town during which Blake got angry at his classmates, then his teacher, and finally at me. My child who couldn't manage walking through a grocery store took off running in a busy city. I reached out to touch his shoulder to get his attention so I could talk him off this ledge, and he screamed at the top of his lungs, "Assault! Assault! You touched me! You can't touch me! Don't touch me! Someone call the police! She's after me! She's assaulted me!"

I loved Blake even then, even in the earliest days of our relationship. I decided he didn't need my pity. He needed my love and support. He needed me to hold him accountable for his actions and *still* keep loving him. He needed me to respect him as an individual and a human being with human needs. He needed me to get to know him. He needed me to grieve with him. But he didn't need me to feel sorry for him. Love was not only my driving force, but my soulful educator.

My first opportunities for advocacy came in the school setting, but soon they began to spread into our family experiences in the larger community. The very first time I was an advocate outside of school, Blake was in the hospital, and in a way I was being my own advocate more than Blake's. It was only a few weeks after Blake's arrival, and we were at the ER after Blake had pulled a knife on us and finally on himself, threatening suicide.

We called 911, and after the arrival of some kind and helpful police officers who genuinely seemed to care about Blake's well-being, Blake was empowered to make the difficult decision on his own to allow us to take him to the emergency room. The intake nurse was gruff, and not at all impressed that we had all made it through our ordeal safely and that Laura and I were doing such a good job meeting Blake's need throughout (*I* was certainly impressed). Blake held his baby doll close to his chest as the nurse finished vitals and ran through her litany of questions. It was obvious she didn't feel it necessary to even try to understand Blake, and I felt my cheeks rush with fury about that as my child clung to me and to his doll. As she was taking the last of her notes, this nurse decided to go off-script. "How old are you?" she asked Laura and me. Laura stated her age.

I could feel how my whole face flushed. What did this have to do with Blake's care? None of the questions the nurse had asked thus far had provided her with any particularly useful insight into the type of care Blake was going to need. She hadn't asked what events preceded the episode, whether this had happened before, what type of treatment Blake had received in the past, or whether any special considerations needed to be made in Blake's care because of his developmental delays or other special needs. If anything, this nurse seemed to be ignoring all signals all together that would assist her in understanding what would be helpful to him throughout their interactions. She ignored his doll completely, though she could plainly see the success we were having in calming Blake down through doll play. It was setting in. This was not going to be high-quality care.

"Like I said, we're his foster parents. That's all you need to know. I've submitted the proper paperwork to you for medical decisions," I said off the cuff. "No, that's not all I need to know," she shot back. She leaned in toward me, placing her knuckles against the outer side of her thigh. "What is your age?!" she demanded again loudly. She was probably nearing three times my age, was twice my size, and she didn't seem particularly attached to her job and thus any evaluations she might receive. I was intimidated, but I pushed back again.

"I feel that this is really irrelevant." I could tell by this time that I was not advocating effectively. I was acting out of frustration, and was too taken off guard by the unexpected question to clearly understand what was causing my frustration. This was only stirring up the nurse's own frustration from God-knows-what other experiences she'd had that day, and her frustration with my unashamed questioning of her authority.

Looking back, this was only the ER, and all we needed to do was get through intake. I can now see that fact from two distinct angles. On one hand, she couldn't deny my child medical care because I refused to tell her my age. On the other hand, other nurses and a doctor would soon be caring for Blake, so the benefits of fighting were minimal. Besides, the real issue wasn't that she was asking for my age. It was the questions she *wasn't* asking, the lack of any sign of interest in the answers we gave her, and her cold demeanor toward a child whose life had brought him to hell and back. It was almost as if she was treating Blake like a pathology in and of himself, not as an individual with a complex and unique set of very human needs, the first of which was compassion. I wouldn't have been able to sort that out in that short, frustrated couple of minutes, so in retrospect, I feel at peace with my decision at that time to give in and tell her my age. "I am twenty-three" I said (the first Blake had heard of my age).

Later as I grew through my experiences as Blake's mother, I learned some of the most basic skills of successful advocacy:

Be clear about the core issues at stake. Whatever the issue, for me it usually comes down to two things. Are the needs of people with disabilities—*as they identify their own needs*—being served, or only the needs of others? And are the underlying assumptions humanizing or dehumanizing?

- ⁋ Choose priorities and work one step at a time. Educating small populations of people about even just one issue, such as a group of doctors about helping children advocate for themselves within the foster care system, is an enormous step not to be underestimated.

- ⁋ Know your rights. One of the most helpful things I did in order to advocate for Blake was to take a class about Individualized Education Plans that covered the role and rights of parents.

- ⁋ Demand nothing less than respect. I learned quickly that if I said the things I needed to say with confidence, and completely ignored all attempts to knock me down, it was much more difficult for others to treat me disrespectfully. In turn, my demands for how the world treated Blake included not talking about him like he wasn't there, humanizing his struggles as normal responses to abnormal life experiences rather than the other way around, and using Blake's own language to describe his disabilities.

❡ If cornered into being an antagonist, step back to allow room for a more proactive return. One effective sentence is, "Can you help me think of some ways to…" People generally want to be of help, and framing the goal can encourage the right kind of participation.

❡ Speak firmly but always out of and with compassion. Recognizing how difficult a teacher finds his position doesn't mean that I back down in asserting the standards he must meet. It only means saying, "That sounds really difficult."

❡ Assume everyone has human needs to love, to be loved, and to be of use. Fear and vulnerability are tremendous obstacles in cooperative problem-solving.

❡ Call out ignorance in the personal setting but save energy also for systemic work. I learned to have a few "one liners" in my head to stop verbal attacks on Blake in public so that I wouldn't go over potential responses in my head for days on end. I could focus instead on advocating for larger systemic change in our attitudes and policies regarding people with special needs.

❡ Approach all systems as structures made up of human beings. When we attack systems, there is always a personal investment behind that system. It helps to know in advance who is made vulnerable by attacks, and sometimes the best thing to do is to invite their leadership in problem-solving.

❡ I learned about the importance of self-honesty as well as honest dialogue between myself and Blake to the extent he was willing to give me that gift. I learned about the significance of teaching Blake skills for self-advocacy and empowering him to use them. I learned about the necessity of finding ways to cope with my inability to control the world and other's reactions to Blake. For me, authentic activism is on a person-to-person level. But I couldn't truly be effective at that work until I worked through some of my own hang-ups.

Part Two

A couple of years after Blake chose to move to a small group home, my son Mitchell was born. I had no idea that week that I was going to have a baby. At least, I had no idea what age child I was going to have and when. By that time, we had transferred our foster care license from our former agency directly to the state, and we applied for an adoptive home study during the transfer so that we could provide permanency for a foster child if it turned out in the end that it was in the child's best interests.

It took us about nine months to get our new license and adoptive home study completed, and then we began our wait. A nine-year old came to us for a short time and then happily reunited with her mother. Two weeks after she left, we received the call about Mitchell. He was just one and a half days old.

When I went to meet Mitchell at the hospital, I knew virtually nothing about him. I knew he was a boy. I knew some basic facts about why his birthparents could not care for him, and why history showed that the situation wouldn't likely improve. I knew his extended family members had been asked to take in Mitchell, but that these folks had been unable to do so. I knew he was having some difficulty eating and that he was jaundiced and in the special care nursery. I knew his birth weight.

This sounds like a lot to know, but the information was so watered down and I had a hundred questions. By the time Laura and I told the social worker that of course we would love to be Mitchell's foster-adopt placement, I was more interested in racing to the hospital than in taking notes.

I walked into the special care nursery and my eyes scanned each solitary bassinet looking for a blue name card. I would not be able to pick out my baby by distinguishing family marks, resemblance to me, eye, skin, or hair color about which I had no information, or even his resemblance to ultrasound images. I needed a name card, but I couldn't see the names from where I was standing. Within a moment, a cheerful nurse came to me and inquired about my identity. Then she said, "Let me introduce you to your baby."

"Let me introduce you to your baby." Those are joyful words I will never forget.

She led me to a bassinet, where Mitchell was wrapped from head to toe. His eyes were closed (as they would be for seven full days, like a little kitten). He was wrapped up so tightly, that I simultaneously wanted to let him be and scoop him up in my arms. The nurse immediately sensed my hesitation, and thinking that it was about all the machines to which he was attached, she said, "you can pick him up you know," and she brushed the cords and wires off to the side of Mitchell's body. Then I scooped him up, and drew him into my chest, taking him in.

In my former vocational life, I was involved in maternal-child health and had seen a number of real-life and video recordings of births. I remember wishing Mitchell would open his eyes so I could *really* see him. I needed us to look at one another the way newborns and their moms I had observed did. Looking back, I think the overwhelmingly sterile smell of the special care nursery contributed to my feelings. I couldn't catch a whiff of my baby, and the bright lights and scratchy starched blankets wrapped up to his chin seemed to discourage touch.

I pulled him closer to my body, hoping that even in his sleep he could smell me, however faintly. I rocked him and whispered sweet nothings in his ear. I wrapped his fingers around my own. He was (and is) so beautiful. My heart swelled.

Once upon a time, and this is *extremely* difficult to admit, I didn't think I had it in me to parent a child with a cognitive or neurological divergence. I can be impatient and am super intellectual. I worried I would snap at my child for not "keeping up with me" as I taught him about the world. I worried I would find it unfulfilling to parent a child who "wouldn't develop typically." I was ignorant. I didn't put two and two together—that *everyone* is learning all the time. I didn't realize I would find it fulfilling, including on an intellectual level, to find ways we could reach one another—to really connect and learn *together*—in both "typical" and "atypical" ways. I didn't think *I* would be the one having trouble keeping up with my kids as they taught me. I didn't realize my heart's capacity.

Motherhood meets us where we lack imagination.

It met me in my own fears about the unknown future, in my need to control outcomes to feel safe, in stories I told myself of scarcity: that the world is a place where we need to fight constantly to make sure our needs are met. From those first moments together in the special care nursery, Mitchell has been the apple of my eye. I adore him. The wholeness of who he is has been incorporated almost seamlessly into the spirit of my being.

Mitchell grew into a delightful young boy. He brings his gifts to the world and works to meet the daily challenges the world brings to him. It is funny how when it all gets boiled down, the same thing is true for every human being. During his first year, Mitchell managed a slew of health challenges. There were times I feared he didn't have the will to live. His health obstacles were beatable, but he was very sick. Being the subtle kid he has always been, I never saw him as a "fighter"; he sometimes struck me as a baby who was waiting to see where the chips might fall before deciding if he wanted to fully commit to life.

Thankfully, medical difficulties waned significantly during his second year. Our focus shifted to how Mitchell was getting on in the world. It was during that second year I attended a workshop with the HANDLE Institute. It was founded by an autistic individual who works with people with autism and other types of neurological differences from their peers. Mitchell hasn't been diagnosed on the autism spectrum. Still, I read with interest some of the differing viewpoints on autism, from the perspective that it's a biological disorder curable by biomedical interventions to the perspective that it is simply a different way of "being" in the world—not something that should be cured.

I was encouraged by the fact that the HANDLE Institute does not make a claim on either end, but rather is interested in decoding neurological behavior so that everyone—regardless of neurology—can understand their own behavior better. I came home with many tools that helped Mitchell (and me) cope with some of the abrasiveness of life and also with a new mantra: "All behavior is communication."

I began to decode my own patterns of behavior. In spite of having had a chronic illness since childhood that significantly impacted my life, I had always thought of the label "disability" as something having to do with someone else. Eventually those "someone elses" became my children, but I stayed detached from the notion of disability. Never mind that I really struggled in many ways through my childhood. Never mind that I now drive my wife up the wall with my idiosyncrasies.

Over the last year this has all shifted. I've begun saying to others that I am "not quite neurotypical." I've begun forgiving myself for many things I once thought of as "character flaws." I saw a neurologist to help me deal with memory loss and cognitive processing challenges. I learned I had been having seizures all these years! I learned that my patterns of thinking and communicating are indeed different than others. I finally realized that I, too, need to develop strategies that will help me survive the world in which I live.

Mitchell received a language pathology diagnosis (and the suggestion that if I sought further diagnoses, the list might get long). That doesn't scare me anymore. Each day the creative, loving exchanges between myself and my son are the source of new imaginings. I am braver now, venturing into the future with a sense of optimism that perhaps only parents of young children can have. I also worry and fret and feel the weight of the world on my shoulders on one hand, but on the other hand, I have found a new grace.

Mitchell does not know that we adults have lost so much of our ability to imagine. He is not self-limiting. He *can not be.* He is still blessed with the concentrated creativity of childhood. Mitchell has self-trust. And when I follow his lead, he teaches me to trust both of us.

The gift of witness I have been given is a precious and fleeting one. To glimpse the infinite, the ultimate; to feel God. I cannot explain this creative synergy, this most delicious spark, any other way except to say it is the closest I have come to living in full relationship with all that is holy.

Especially when Mitchell was younger and I was a newborn to this treasured space in my spirit, I worshiped the idols of limited imaginings, of futures defined by concepts of limited spiritual value. I grieved for possibilities of college and marriage as I have scripted them, fearful that because Mitchell has this or that neurological and cognitive challenge, he would miss out on something I deem necessary for a "good life." James Fowler wrote: "Real idolatry in the Jewish and Christian tradition does not have to do with the worship of statues or pagan altars. Idolatry is rather the profoundly serious business of committing oneself, or betting one's life, on finite centers of value and power as the source of one's confirmation of worth and meaning, and as the guarantor of survival with quality." Mitchell is teaching me to stop worshiping idols.

I am learning now that my job as an activist is largely to trust who Mitchell is so that others are called to do the same for him, and for others. I am now advocating, teaching really, *through love.*

When Mitchell was seventeen months old, a six-month-old girl, Reina, joined our family. Reina has a set of "special needs" that are so different from Mitchell's needs. Reina is blowing my mind! Though she has difficulty forming secure attachments due to a traumatic history, she is highly social and very overtly engaged with her world. She picks up information rapidly, but isn't always able to problem-solve when something is "off" (like me, and completely opposite of Mitchell). Reina is teaching me, too. I look forward to growing into "Act Three."

My activism is almost always on a person-to-person level. I recently conducted a training for colleagues working with families who have "special needs." I approach people with the honesty of my experience and work to dispel myths and frame the issues:

- None of us get to define what a "good life" is for anyone else. *All* people are learning throughout the course of life. Brain studies prove it. We tend to have a narrow definition of learning.

- All of us, neurotypical or not, disabled or not, have better ability to function (a.k.a. to survive or thrive in our society) at certain times, lesser ability at others.

- We have a moral obligation to make life easier on others when possible. "Universal accommodation" is a valuable concept.

- All behavior is communication. We can help one another function better by approaching each other with that understanding.

- People have a right to define and frame their identities. We can honor this by referring to others as they self-refer, whether using "people-first language" (for example, "person with autism") or identity-oriented language (for example, "autistic person").

- We each deserve to own our own stories, to maintain privacy when we feel we need it, and to expect respectful listening when we open up about our challenges and strengths.

Interpreting the Signs

by Andrea Winninghoff

There came a certain point in Jonah's life when he finally realized his isolation. The arrival of this awareness thankfully took many years of his early childhood, years he needed in order to develop the self-esteem and inner strength to navigate a world that is closed off to him. As a toddler, he was not clear on the fact that no one spoke his language. That they did not pick up their hands and respond to his endless questions or funny stories was of no concern to him. The beauty of being a very little person was that he, like many, believed that the world had been waiting for him to arrive and now that he was here, they were anxious to sit back and absorb everything he had to say. When he was a little boy, about seven, he continued to chat easily to non-signing family, friends, and strangers on the bus, whoever was willing to watch. He realized that they might not understand him but the act of engaging with a person, holding eye contact, and the drive to be understood was enough to keep him talking. It wasn't even until adolescence that he fully realized why no one was talking back. Not only did they not understand, but in most cases, they simply didn't care enough to try.

I am Jonah's mother but sometimes more importantly, I am the language conduit between him and the hearing world. Every social interaction, in fact, every single word, goes through me. I have a chance to freeze conversations and explain to my son why what he just said might embarrass someone or hurt their feelings. I can prevent painful or ignorant messages from reaching my son. I have a chance to simplify, steer, or end interactions as I please. I have the burden, luxury, and ethical dilemma of deciding if and how I will filter and manipulate communication. The responsibility is great and sometimes, as I limit my son's chances of being truly known, dangerous.

Internally, I do constant battle with my roles in Jonah's life while trying to protect him from that reality. If I am being the best mother I can be, I must be loving, protective and present for him. If I am being a good interpreter, I have to exercise distance and an unbiased perspective. These positions are equally important but often in direct opposition. If there is a solution to this riddle, a way to be more integrated, I have not found the answer. What is clear is that Jonah deserves a place in life where he doesn't *need* me to be his interpreter. Like everyone, he has a right to direct relationships with people who identify with him in his language.

Our inability to find a community that is open to both my son and me has always been at the core of our struggles. By the time he was three and ready to start preschool, I was very familiar with the politics and divisions within the deaf community. There are parents and school programs that insist on kids communicating in spoken English at the sacrifice of sign language. There are families and classes that used S.E.E.—"Signed Exact English"—a manual representation of word-for-word English that was developed by teachers. S.E.E. is not a complete language in and of itself and is never used conversationally. It is intended as a tool in academic environments. Because it is cumbersome and difficult to read, using it in place of ASL isolates deaf kids socially, both in the hearing world as well as the Deaf community. The intention of these methods as I see it is to "help" deaf kids conform to hearing society. The consequence is that they are often socially behind their ASL signing peers. The ability to conform has never been a family value of ours, quite the contrary. I was more concerned with providing Jonah as many ways to express himself as possible.

After exploring several deaf/hard-of-hearing or "hearing impaired" school programs, I was worried that I wouldn't be able to find a community or program that affirmed my son's culturally Deaf identity in a healthy and supportive way. The only program I hadn't visited yet was within a public school system that was notorious for its inadequate funding and lack of "special education" support so when I arrived, I was ready for the worst. I first met the teacher, Gary, during his morning class. He had become a teacher of the Deaf after having been an ASL interpreter for over twenty years. By the time I reached him, I already mistrusted "experts" and educators, who acted as though they knew more about my child than I, a teenage single mom, could possibly know. I knew Gary and I shared a similar philosophy about how to educate Deaf kids, but I remained suspicious and guarded. During my first visit at his program, I asked him a long series of questions and he responded with obvious irritation. I was sure that he and I wouldn't get along. His know-it-all, abrasive attitude toward me was, to put it mildly, unsettling. What I learned quickly though, was that after spending his career watching parents opt out of learning ASL, after watching kids fail in other programs and struggle socially, he was equally suspicious of me—another hearing parent who thought they had the answers. All of that aside, his classroom was alive, happy, and had pictures of signing hands everywhere. It was the perfect place for my son to develop and feel good about his identity.

I enrolled Jonah and after a couple months, I even started volunteering in the class as a room mom. Gary and I steered clear of each other for the most part—keeping our exchanges minimal and businesslike. I watched everything, though, and learned much more than advanced sign language from Gary. To say he was brilliant in his care, attention, and ability to draw kids out is an understatement and I couldn't help but love him for loving my son so well. Eventually, during recess breaks, Gary and I started to get to know each other over coffee. We learned that we had a lot in common both personally and in our intentions to raise Jonah with pride in his deafness and academic abilities. We became unlikely friends over the seven years that my son was in his program.

In Jonah's fourth-grade year, Gary took me out in the hallway and told me he was being laid off—the budget for the deaf education classes were going to be cut. Next year, my son would be limited to one all-ages, all-abilities, financially unstable program. Despite the fight put forth by myself and several other parents, the district was larger than us and the fight was over before it began. The summer came and Jonah, Gary and I cried our way through a hard goodbye. I had no idea what to do next with my limited options. I could place him in a mainstream program in a hearing classroom. He would have to adjust to a curriculum for hearing children and an inadequate interpreter. His social life with the other kids and his relationship with his teacher would go through another adult, just as I was originally trying to avoid. Square one. Once again, he would be isolated.

The second option was also out of the question—the residential state school for the deaf.

There was no way I would be willing to send my son three hours away every week, only to see him on the weekends. I certainly had no money to move. The school, like most state schools, is in a small town with no job opportunities, no college programs where I could work on my education and finally get us out of poverty, and no tolerance for a non-conformist, obviously gay butch mom like myself. In short, there was no place where both of our identities could safely exist in the same place.

Jonah begged me to take him to the school "just to check it out" and I begrudgingly agreed. On a midweek morning, we woke up at 5:00 am to make the long drive down a gray, bleak stretch of freeway. With each mile behind us, my heart ached more at the idea of Jonah liking it and feeling more at home there than he did with me. When we finally arrived, he poured out of the car and skipped ahead of me up the walkway like Dorothy in search of a wizard who would finally take her home. I couldn't hold back tears. I cleared my throat and wiped my eyes as I talked to teachers, principals, and school psychologists. Jonah forgot about my presence behind him as he talked to everyone with complete ease. I tried to stay on track with the staff, asking about curriculum, testing, after school sports and activities, but every time I opened my mouth I heard myself ask questions like "What if he feels lonely without me" or "who will sit at the edge of his bed and hold his hand when he has his first broken heart?" Quietly, I wondered who would mend mine if I let him go.

Jonah glowed as he talked to a group of ten kids, all his age. Their hands were flying faster than I could read but he didn't miss a beat. He turned to me and asked "Do you promise me that you'll let me go to school here?"

"I promise you we will talk about it when we get home," I said. An hour passed and Jonah and I met the principal in her office. Forgetting for a moment where he was, Jonah turned to me and asked me to interpret to the principal that he really loved it here and wanted to start as soon as possible.

She laughed, lifted her hands and said "You can tell me yourself because I can sign just like everyone else here." I was obsolete.

I was handed the school application packet. When we returned home, I placed it high on a shelf for six months and continued Jonah's enrollment in the public school—a small class full of Deaf and hard-of-hearing kids ages five to thirteen. The teachers and assistants were overworked and under-supported, and everyone knew it was a matter of short time before it was also closed down. Jonah's grades began to slip and he had no one to relate to. He became lonelier than ever. When he again begged me to enroll him at the residential school, I knew what I had to do. Late after his bedtime, I stayed awake, feeling angry and devastated over a thick pile of paper-work.

When Jonah was a baby, I was told by a Deaf man that someday, I would have to stop speaking for Jonah. I would have to be strong and loving enough to give my son up to his culture where he would be able to find and share himself with people who understood him in a way that I never would. Being a teen mother at the time, I had already faced a world that expected me to give him up before he was born. My decision to keep him was made and I resented that I was being asked again to revisit letting him go.

Within the Deaf community, whenever the topic of my resistance to send Jonah away came up, I was all but called selfish for keeping him from his culture. When I talked to hearing parents with hearing children and told them that I was considering residential school, I was met with a shock and cruel statements about how they could never do that to *their* family. These were painful remarks not only because they emphasized blatant judgment, but because they also pointed out that families with privilege like theirs would never have to make such a choice.

It has now been thirteen years since his deafness was discovered, and every Sunday night I help my son pack his things and get ready for the next week of school. Like many mothers, I sign permission slips, check his homework, and tell him to put his coat on before he leaves. Unlike most other mothers, I hold him especially tight for a little too long before I put him on a bus that takes him three hours and worlds away from me. For the first time in this, the third year he has gone away to school, I can hold back tears when we say goodbye. I keep a busy life to pass the time until Friday afternoon when he returns.

There came a certain point in my life when I finally realized my own isolation. This uncommon little family made up of the two of us, a culture's width apart from each other, has changed. Jonah has arrived in a place now where he can finally be his whole self. I still hope I find my place. In a community of parents with Deaf kids, I will always be the single, young, gay mom. Among gay parents, I will always be the one with the Deaf kid that they can't speak to. Being hearing, I will never be fully accepted into the tight inner circle of the Deaf community. Jonah's culture is his. It is large, vibrant, and as he rightly believed, they have always had a place waiting just for him, and they are anxious to absorb everything he has to say.

This is a sacrifice I have made—giving Jonah up to his culture—so that he can finally be known freely, without the filter of his mother. As I watch him become more independent, have friends and crushes, a life of his very own, I am confident that my decision was the right one for him. I don't fear that I will accidentally misrepresent who he is to the hearing world anymore. I don't worry that he will be constantly lonely. These days my fear is much more selfish. I am afraid that the physical and cultural distance between us will grow into emotional distance. There are times where we miss each other's meaning. Occasionally my intention and vocabulary misalign. They slip through my fingers and as they do, I fear he loses important pieces of me. As he becomes an older and more complex person, I am afraid that the nuances of his culture will escape me. The fear that breaks my heart is that because I found the strength to love him enough to let him go find himself in the freedom of his own world, he may never come back home to mine.

CHAPTER 3
Seen, Heard, Respected, and Believed

Ever have those times when something about your day stops you in your tracks and you wonder how you got here, into this life, this reality? It is as though you are seeing your interactions through a looking glass and the brief pause conjures questions like, How did I get from my past hopes to this reality? Were those actions mine? Did I use those words? Did I see a stranger's eyes catch and linger on the last interaction I had with my daughter or son?

Closer to home our realities, as special needs parents, seem normal and ordinary; these are our lives: it is the real deal, no bells or flashing disco balls. However, for many children and parents, when we walk into the world, the subtleness of our differences crumbles. We have become experts about our children and their various diagnoses. We are isolated from our parenting communities. Our families have been stared at, pointed out, and sometimes purposefully ignored. As parents, to be in the public eye means we must have our shields up and advocacy hats on. We have been asked every question in the book, from "Is he sign language?" to "What's she got?" Our children have played on playgrounds and we have watched as strangers corralled their children away from our children's awkward gait or their inexplicable vocalizations. Our babies have received apologetic looks. They have been patted on the head, cooed over, and, at times, they have balanced their own shades of activism in order to gain access to opportunities and resources that are their due.

The authors in this chapter reflect on the work and amusement of their daily lives. They ask what it has meant to be in these moments and wonder over the ways their perceptions of self have changed. Who are these men and women they have become as a result of their parenting experiences? How have the intimate struggles and public fights altered how they know themselves? Sometimes these bouts of contemplation are brought to fruition by unexpected interactions and sudden jolts of reality, and other times the authors find hidden answers as they watch their children maneuver uneven pathways or explore the cherished worlds of their imaginations.

What I Said, and What I Didn't Say
by Sharis Ingram

A few months back, my next-door neighbor, Ana, mentioned that she was co-teaching a graduate level class in social work at Hunter College on Autistic Spectrum Disorders. The class is cross-listed, so some students were on the therapeutic track, some were on the counseling track, and some were taking it as a psychology course. Since she felt it was important for them to understand what kind of impact their work will eventually have from the other end, the client end, would I be interested in speaking to them for maybe forty-five minutes one evening?

Oh, would I ever.

One evening a few weeks later, my husband came home a bit early and I went downtown to talk to the class. I talked and talked and talked. And then I talked some more. I ran over my allotted time. I ran over by at least twenty minutes, probably a good deal more, I don't know, yet I still could not squeeze in all the things I so desperately wanted them to know. But I think I got most of it in there. Things like how dismissive it feels to have introduced yourself by name to the service coordinator or the social worker or the therapist or what have you, and still be referred to as "Mom" throughout the meeting. Like how people look at my family and the assumptions and projections begin, yet when we start talking and demonstrate that we know what we're talking about with regard to our children's diagnosis and care, we can literally *see* them reassess us. Like how hard it is for us to get to all these appointments, and yet in all these years no one has ever mentioned that we might qualify for transportation. Or respite care. Or who knows what else. And how even though it felt like a big relief rather than bad news to finally get an accurate diagnosis of Asperger's syndrome for my daughter three years ago, it was really, really hard to deal with the possibility of having not one but two special needs children after my son was referred for an evaluation this past winter, even though at this point it would seem that my son's issues are likely to be less severe.

I talked about how, because their issues are not things that show up on genetic screenings or any sort of prenatal testing, I was unprepared, but even preparation can only take you so far. Just like parenting neurotypical kids. You may think you know what's coming, but you don't really know—no one does. I talked about how this is my job now. How even as annoying as it is to have people tell me all the time, *I don't know how you do it!* as though I have the option to stop, I know that we are lucky that I am able to stay home and have this be my 24/7, full-time, completely unpaid, no benefits job. Never mind how I do it, how do families where both parents need to work do this? How do single parents do it? I am completely overwhelmed nearly all the time, yet other than the same household responsibilities everyone has, this is all I have to take care of. I cannot imagine how much falls through the cracks for other folks, because it is always just one more detail to follow up after another, on top of all the other things that have to be done, and it is a child's welfare that's at stake. Yet, what are our options? Not to do it?

I talked a tiny bit about culture and class and about how I do not bother with any of the support groups in the city, because they tend to be full of upper-middle-class white families in Manhattan, with whom beyond the facts of our children's diagnosis we have little in common. I talked about how my experience with parenting choices in general is the complete opposite of my experience with dealing with my kids' issues. Because of the whole semi-bohemian—breastfeeding, cloth diapering, willingness to let a toddler get down and dirty and really explore a playground—set of values we embrace, we were outsiders, culturally speaking, compared to our parenting peers in our Harlem neighborhood when my daughter first started receiving services. Yet, the further downtown into white upper-middle-class Manhattan we went, the more mainstream our parenting style seemed despite the fact that my husband and I are Puerto Rican and black, not white, nor are we upper-middle-class. And yet it is the complete opposite when dealing with services. I simply have not got the resources those women have, and due to differences in race, class, and culture, my frame of reference is not theirs. We may have similar kids, but it seems to mean dissimilar things for us.

Then I talked and talked about food and homeopathic remedies, and what an impact those things have had on my children's lives. I talked about my daughter's food intolerances and her sensory issues and how finally last summer I stopped fighting her every single night and just allowed her to have the same two dinners over and over and over, because I couldn't stand it anymore. I explained that this made dinnertime somewhat easier, even though I was cooking two different meals almost every night, a thing my childless self swore I would never, ever do. I talked about my son's ears and how he had tubes surgically inserted to relieve constant ear infections. Still, every time I slack on the homeopathic remedies, he builds up a head full of mucous and starts pulling his ears again, at which point I remind myself to be grateful that at least he can hear us now and restart the remedies. I talked about how even though I am 99 percent certain that they both, but particularly my son, would be greatly improved by going wheat-free, right now, I simply cannot face it. Given my daughter's intolerances to any form of corn, rice, or artificial food coloring, to have one more staple ingredient eliminated from our diet is just more than I can do, even if it means no more eczema for her or ear infections for him. And then there is the question of whether my kids would even be willing to eat the alternatives, given their extreme sensitivities to taste and texture.

One of the other professors, not my neighbor, was very severe: *You don't get respite care?!* (Apparently she literally wrote the book on respite care, at least the first one) *You don't get transportation?! Your daughter doesn't get her mandated CSE services as outlined in her IEP and you never followed up?!* It felt very accusatory, like, *what kind of slacker mother are you?* But I carefully chose not to hear it that way, even though it came uncomfortably close to what that mean, whispery voice in my own head tells me all the damn time. Instead, each time she said something like this, I would take a breath and turn my attention back to the class at large and tell them, *Hey, I am not a social worker, I am just a parent feeling her way through the system.* This is not stuff I ever knew about in my life before kids. I have no formal training. I have done a great deal of reading on my own, but in the end it's all a trial by fire. The first time I heard about the availability of respite care or transportation was through other parents who are going through similar things. So every time I hear about something new, what I have to do is either find out about it on my own and hope I can figure out how to get it myself, or go back to my service coordinator and say, "Hey, I heard about this respite care thing, do we qualify for it?" and hope she can get accurate information for me about it (and it can be so damn hard to know when the "experts" have it wrong) or figure out how to sign us up for it, and hope that the change is not going to overset our already delicate balancing act.

I talked about how there is no aspect of our lives this doesn't affect, how I don't even think about certain aspects of the accommodations we've made anymore. *Of course* there are certain clothes that I simply don't even think about buying for my daughter because they'll be scratchy or distracting. *Of course* it takes two people to brush my son's teeth because he has such extreme oral defensiveness. *Of course* we try to keep spontaneous changes to our daily routine to a minimum because any variation from our usual schedule without a whole lot of lead time and coaching makes both my kids incredibly anxious and nearly always leads to tears. *Of course* I don't bring my kids into supermarkets or any other large store if I can possibly avoid it because between the fluorescent lighting and the "too many things that are all different," each one brighter and shinier than the last and all of them all crammed in together, my kids are almost guaranteed to flip out and tantrum. There are a million and one other things that we just do without even thinking about it, because that's how life is for us now. I told them, *I didn't sign up for any of this when I got pregnant. I thought I was just having a baby.*

Then I talked about how this was a big night out for me, because my husband and I rarely get to go anywhere because my kids are too much for the average teen babysitter to handle, our families are not really available for sitting very often, and most adult sitters in this neighborhood are looking for full-time or at least consistent part-time jobs and are not interested in my little bit here, little bit there, needs. The third professor pulled me aside afterward and suggested that I call a friend of his, who is the head of the speech pathology department at the college nearest me, and ask if there were any likely students who might want the gig, which was helpful and kind, and I deeply appreciated it. Sometimes just the offer of help is enough to stave off the deep feelings of isolation that this kind of parenting can cause, but that's rare.

Increasingly, I feel as though I am drowning, not waving. Burnout— becoming depressed and unable to do what must be done, and failing my kids frightens me so terribly I cannot allow myself to even think about it. Part of maintaining the balancing act is never, ever, ever looking down.

Then I took questions. Which, I have to say, although I was very clear I was willing to answer anything whatever that they might ask—*Please ask! Don't be shy!*—were very surface-y. It was like there was so much they didn't know, they couldn't ask good questions. Yes, I do have to explain my kids to other people a lot, however because Asperger's syndrome doesn't have any obvious physical hallmarks, it's not in the way one might expect. Instead of *What's wrong with her?* I get a lot of questions about why we're even bothering with all these appointments and services, since "[their] kids do that too!" and "But your daughter is so smart!" and "She seems fine!" Yeah, she seems fine. She is fine, in fact. At first glance, she certainly seems like a regular kid, a little quirky, maybe, until she drops trou and pisses in the grass "like a puppy" in middle of your wedding reception. Just like any other kid you know, until she will not stop talking about comic books or birthday parties or asking the same three questions over and over and over for hours on end despite your best efforts to change the subject or distract her and you find out what discussing something ad nauseam really means. Completely normal, until you discover the hard way that the majority of movies and television shows marketed to kids are so over-stimulating for her given her hypersensitivity to any kind of dramatic tension or conflict that trying to watch them will nearly always result in her huddled in a ball terrified and weeping, and/or a week of screaming nightmares. She seems fine, until something happens and you realize *she really isn't a neurotypical kid*, just like I've been telling you. Her brother seems fine too, until you realize the various routines that he has organized his days around have locked you in as well, unless you're willing to deal with the shrieking tantrums he throws when they are disrupted in any way.

Besides, at six and under, oddness can be kind of cute. After that these kinds of quirks can be a problem, and I'm not willing to wait and see if it "goes away on its own," as so many people seem to think we should. "Maybe she'll outgrow it!" Yeah, right. It is possible to learn how to navigate the social situations that are so hard for my daughter, or relax the rigid adherence to routines they both cling to, but they will never find it natural or easy. Despite the services they receive to help with these very issues, already other kids are starting to notice my daughter's differences; there are some who are beginning to shun her. Difference can be good. Ostracism is not.

The last student to raise her hand said, "This is very overwhelming." "Yes. It is," I answered. "I hadn't ever realized quite how much so until just now, telling all of you about it." I told them how hopeful I was for the future with them coming into the field. I gave them my e-mail address in case they had questions later on, because I know it's hard to think of everything in the time allotted, and we'd already run over. I thanked them for the opportunity to speak with them and their attention, and I went home. The bus ride home was very peaceful, but I was keyed up almost to the point of mania for nearly a week afterwards.

That night I woke up somewhere between two and three in the morning and lay there for a long, long time, thinking about all the things I didn't get a chance to tell them. Like how other parents of kids with spectrum disorders can sometimes be all *My kid's a misunderstood genius; your kid's just plain autistic.* Or how there are days when I feel the strengths that come with this kind of diagnosis are so spectacular that they are worth all the tantrums and wet pants and stigma. Or how fantastic it is when your kid connects, because so often they don't. I didn't get to talk about how scared I am for my daughter because she is so deeply naïve and unsophisticated; no matter how careful and mindful we are in our parenting, she could so easily grow into just the kind of prey on which certain sorts of human predators love to feed. I didn't tell them about how hard it is to be the one who has to show my child how to make and keep friends, given my own social anxiety. I didn't tell them that my project this spring is to schedule some play dates for her with the kids she would most like to be friends with, and do everything I can think of to help her maintain the friendships because left to herself, she simply doesn't know how. This sort of thing is not my strength at all, but it's not for me; for my kids I will do what needs doing.

I didn't spell out the economics of having high-needs kids, and how the never-ending appointments can become so expensive so quickly, and how there is always that nagging worry of *Is our insurance going to cover this? Will Early Intervention pay for it? Will CSE pay? Are we going to have to pay? Again? More? Will they even see us when our outstanding balance is already so high? Do I have cab fare, the co-pay, bus fare?* Since I am not earning any money and it would appear that I will never receive another W-2, what does that mean for the future? I don't make Social Security payments any more. After all these years of caring for my children, am I going to end up an old lady who lives on cat food, dented cans, and bruised produce? My kids are high-functioning, but will they be able to live independently? Balancing is not the only thing that requires a well-maintained safety net.

I didn't tell them that I have spent the wee hours of more than one morning lying in bed wondering how and when to tell my daughter about her diagnosis, what to say, what not to say, how to say it, what it means. She's not yet seven. Will she even understand? I don't know. The results of my son's evaluation should be arriving in the mail any day along with the card informing me of the appointment to go discuss the results. More than likely I'll have to have a similar conversation with him one day. Is practice going to make it any easier?

It was only supposed to be a forty-five minute talk. I didn't have the time or the words to tell these students even the tiniest fraction of what it's like to be the mother of special needs kids. The closest I could come was to say it's a lot like parenting neurotypical kids, only more so, much more. Really, what my husband and I do is not so different than parenting any child—you learn how they function best and you make it happen as well as you can. However, as with so many aspects of parenting special needs kids, you're doing the same things but to the most extreme degree imaginable, and sometimes way beyond what you could ever have imagined until one day there you are, balancing.

Jackpot!

by Amy Saxon Bosworth

Every parent with a "special (gag) child" knows what I'm talking about when someone tells them again what a present they've received, what a strong person they must be to be to have been given such a magnificent gift, like you won some disabled kid lotto. Wait a second; I didn't even buy a ticket! And who the hell wins three times in a row?

We are a mixed family, we confuse people. We confuse ourselves. I, the great mother of it all—am deaf. I have probably always had a hearing loss. I began using hearing aids in my late teens and lost it all (my hearing) in my twenties. After living in silence and denial for a decade, I eventually got bilateral cochlear implants. I am still very much a deaf woman, my implants help in some situations, but let's just break a stereotype from the get-go: CIs are not a cure for deafness, at least not for me. My children's father is hearing. He has loads of other imperfections. I could start listing them in alphabetical order, it would be very easy, but I'll bite my tongue and end the sentence now.

My oldest son, J. B., is a tad (understatement alert) on the freakish—so smart it's scary—spectrum. We have always known he did things differently, *little stuff* like reading the theological works of C. S. Lewis at age five and debating them with the bishop of the diocese. Stuff like having to stand on one foot and rock counter-clockwise while doing high school math in the first grade or reading the entire elementary campus library in the first six weeks of school. You know, *little things*. Testing showed nothing glaring except for an extremely high IQ and a pre-disposition for auditory processing disorder. We let him be himself, found a school that would make classroom accommodations, one that rewarded him for discovering new logarithms, gave him extra credit points for finding flaws in the textbooks, and didn't make him sit at his desk. He got thank you notes from textbook publishers, plenty of credits, and will be graduating from high school just a couple of years early this spring. I worry about other *little things* like keeping his shoes tied, his fly zipped, and remembering to eat. Otherwise I think he will be fine. His last batch of testing has revealed he has a hearing loss that has begun to progress and a rather severe central auditory processing disorder.

Kidlet number two we were told to abort! Abandon ship! Something ain't right. At five months gestation her triple screen was positive first for Down's syndrome, then we were told she was fine, then we were told, "wait, maybe dwarfism but the test is inconclusive." Anna was born happy and healthy until her onset of a mild hearing loss, at age six. But—big but—her audiogram didn't match what she was experiencing: extreme ringing, dizziness, and poor speech discrimination. Further testing showed that like her older brother she, too, has a severe auditory processing disorder. Their ears work so-so, but the brain can't understand. It's like getting a radio station not quite tuned in. Turn up the volume up and the static is going to drive her and in turn everyone in a half-mile radius nuts. It makes for one cranky, pissed-off little nine-year-old. (I really need an acronym for understatement alerts.)

Now Anna's biggest issues are people problems. She'll be fine as long as she's left alone. I may end up being arrested before the school year is over. I'm not saying its okay to play with matches but if that school burns to the ground I better have a good alibi. So far this year she has had a wonderful teacher who totally gets it, but a handful of assholes who totally don't. First there was a substitute, who when Anna didn't respond, thought she was being disobedient and threatened to discipline her. Anna wanted to go to the principal to seek refuge as she had been taught, but wasn't allowed to leave the room. As soon as I picked the sobbing mass of a third grader up, off we went to front office to have a little chat. The principal swore the sub would never have any interaction with Anna again, yet four days later she was back in the classroom.

We had it written in Anna's 504 and then again in her IEP that all district employees would be trained in how to deal with hearing impaired students, i.e. they may not be ignoring you—they may not be hearing you! Does that really take an in-service training? Do we need to have a lesson on how not to be a dumb ass? She has also gotten her hearing aid remote taken away by more than one clueless school staff member thinking it was a toy, iPod, or cell phone. They have a "zero tolerance" policy, they keep telling us. I have a zero tolerance policy on stupidity and I'm getting pretty damn sick of having to educate the whole fucking world or at least this little corner. Last week took the cake when the class photographer told her to remove her remote and hearing aids for the picture. Excuse me? It's the equivalent of saying "Hey you gimp in the wheelchair, that's not aesthetically pleasing, hobble over here." The company has offered to buy me off with a lifetime of school photos, they said the photographer was new and hadn't had sensitivity training yet. Could have fooled me! Try to take back that memory from my little girl's head.

Bambino number three was in utero just as all this was coming to light. I'm late deafened; the other two were big kids when they started having problems, so when a nurse tells me I'm holding a deaf baby as they are rolling me out of the hospital, I think she's a freaking idiot. "Go back and check your machine," I told her. "Run some other kids." She looked at me like I was nuts. Here I was, a deaf mom, and I was in total denial. You can't imagine how many times I banged that damn metal trash-can lid while we waited for the results. Three weeks later it was confirmed by auditory brainstem response that *yes*, Whit was moderately hearing impaired. At nine weeks, he was aided and now, at age three, he's hearing and voicing and signing but, he also has other … dum, de, dum, dum, *issues*. He hums, screeches, and refuses to talk or sign for weeks at a time. He is ultra-sensitive to drugs and chemicals and has had extreme reactions on several occasions. And then there is that rainbow spectrum in the sky no one can quite seem to nail down for me that just doesn't explain why he can focus so intently on some things like red cowboy hats or pirates with blue pants, while he's not with us here at the breakfast table some days, or even some times for days and days and days on end.

Genetics—the gift that keeps on giving. We have seen every doctor and specialist remotely associated with any and every body part any of my kids have that's slightly abnormal. My insurance company hates us. If they go into bankruptcy, I might feel just a twinge of guilt until I remember the premiums we pay are huge. Each doctor refers us to two more; it's like a pyramid scheme. It's not just their ears, it's not just their brains, it's in their blood! I have notebooks, volumes devoted to my kids flaws. I know what it's not. I have lists of behaviors, boxes checked in different colored ink. The only really cool diagnosis we have gotten has a page dedicated to it in the family scrapbook. One geneticist pointed out what I thought was a mole on J.B.'s chest. All three kids were in the room. He doesn't have three pimples like Anna thought she heard—he has three nipples! He immediately went back to school that afternoon and showed it off in Biology for extra credit.

So the Brady Bunch we are not. We live in a rural town—get those barf bags out—called Comfort, where we are truly the town misfits. We are not a nice quiet family, we are freaking loud. We don't mean to be; we try to control ourselves (okay, well, I do, sometimes). People don't get it. Just because we are deaf does not mean we are quiet. Our tongues are not connected to our ears. The inability to hear includes the inability to hear our own voice, therefore creating some nasty situations. You can't moderate, there is no volume control dial on yourself, you just have to watch to see when people start flinching or wait to see if they look confused so you will you know if you are talking too softly. I carry a laminated card in my wallet and was at the post office the other day trying very hard just to finish my transaction and get out before we were thrown out. I had Whit by the waist and he was humming and screeching to his own inner symphony showing everyone who would look at the card "I AM DEAF—PLEASE HELP ME UNDERSTAND BY...." Then, as I had him by one arm and a belt loop trying to juggle my packages and unlock the car, the entire lobby watched as he ever so deftly peed on the truck tire.

Like I said, we have been told he has *issues*. Really, you think? How exactly do you diagnose toe licking? Is that on the pervasive developmental disorder spectrum, the autism spectrum, or the going to grow up into a weird fetish spectrum? The kid sees anybody with bright shiny enamelled toes and it's all over. We go shopping and he has to be strapped in the basket and have something to distract him. He wants to lick toes. Do they look like candy? PTA moms don't think this is cute, nor does the librarian at the Comfort Public Library, nor the girl my son was trying to get a date with. I think she may have puked a little in her mouth. People do that a lot around us, maybe I should have little bags made with my monogram on them, you know, instead of Delta or American Airlines. Maybe I'll do that in my spare time and carry them around with us. That would make a good segment for Martha Stewart. "Today, Amy, and her three *special* children will be showing us how to craft lovely homemade vomit bags. They are just perfect for when the general public is repulsed by your handicapped children and can be customized to educate, advocate, and accommodate emesis at the same time. It's a good thing!"

Whit went to an oral school for speech therapy for a while and the other parents could not believe I actually "signed out loud"; they signed in the closet and sat on their hands at school. Give me a break! It's a rainbow world, people: it's 2008. We may not know exactly where we fit in but we aren't going to lie about it either. We sign and voice, we also flash lights, jump up and down so the floor shakes, slam doors, and throw things to get each other's attention. I have mirrors and cameras all over the house so what I can't hear, I can see. My kids absolutely take advantage of the fact that I can't hear them and they can't hear each other. I'm deaf, not dumb.

I've been deaf for a long time, even before the kids started to lose their hearing or Whit was born, so there are times when that just confuses things even more. Communication in our house is funny. Whatever works—you can sign it, voice it, take me to it, write it, or draw it on the magna doodle. One time I told Whit to grab his boots and he grabbed a-hold of my boobs, real nice in front of company. Sometimes I'll ask someone to rephrase if I don't understand them. Whit was trying to tell me something hurt and was signing but refused to show me where, what hurt. He finally voiced but I couldn't understand "finger" or "wiener" and asked him to use a different word, knowing he was in a non-verbal, fat-chance phase, he surprised me by very clearly saying "dick." When I asked where he had heard that word, he signed "brother." Wow, should I put that one in his speech journal for his therapist? "Now remember, mommy, every word counts!" Anna and J.B. will sign and write stuff down for me. They both sign well but prefer CART (real time captioning) over interpreters since English is their first language and they are both such fast, strong readers. Both have and will use the miscommunication card to try to pull one over on me. So we have important things like curfews and groundings written down and posted on the family bulletin board. Can you sign "don't pee on my leg and tell me it's raining?"

Nobody talks about this stuff. It's too uncomfortable. We are not some alien race. We are just your everyday mutants. People (there I go stereotyping again—boy, the hate mail I'm going to get) expect us to be quiet. I've seen it so many times at events, parties, workshops, restaurants. We scare you. My son gets the look out shopping, the "get that kid under control, make him shut up look," when he's just humming to himself. For as obnoxious and rude as we can seem, talking loudly, scraping chairs unknowingly, the general public is pretty rude and clueless themselves.

Most people need a little lesson in basic humanity. First of all, we are human. Don't touch us. We are not science projects. I'll be happy to explain and demonstrate but I have holes drilled in my skull and my equipment is held to the back of my head by magnets; if you come up behind me and touch my implants I may take you down. The same goes for my kids, their hearing aids are like a body parts, keep your hands to yourself. Would you walk up to an amputee and twiddle with his prosthetic? I didn't think so. Hearing aids and cochlear implants are looking less like medical devices and more cool and high tech, but please get our attention somehow before you put your hands on us. And to the lady who chewed my ass for letting my baby have an iPod, get a freaking life. Please be aware we are not being rude when we sign, we are not talking about you—probably. I would much rather have someone ask me a question than stare or mock me or my kids. It's cool if you want to learn a sign or two, or are curious about what's poking out of our heads, just ask. Talk to us, not about us. Guess what? We read lips.

When I walk into a room, whether it's a doctor's office or the school, most professionals don't know that I know what I'm doing. I've been advocating for special needs kids before I had any of my own. I lobbied for newborn hearing screening legislation years before my own son was a flunky. I never thought this was a system I would need to navigate but I'm in a boat alone with three oars. I know my rights and I know what my kids are entitled to. I know exactly what I'm seeing and I do not hesitate to call someone out on it. It scares the hell out of people when you know what those acronyms actually stand for. When they tell you to sign here, and here, and here, and you stop and actually read what you are signing or ask that something be changed before you agree to it, their poor little hearts stop beating for a second and they make little sideways glances at each other like scared woodland animals. That's okay, do what's right for your kids, the next kid that comes along will benefit from it too. I have had the school refuse to pay for my interpreter at IEP meetings, not inform us of changes in meeting times, test my child without consent, and I have been asked to have a doctor predate a form so that their records would be in compliance. When she was first diagnosed I had one teacher tell a relative before I could. "I'm so sorry, Anna's going to be deaf like her mother." I may be deaf but I have a voice and you will not shut me up.

Relatives and religion, the biggest one-two jerk-off I've dealt with so far. It might as well be a combo meal here in the Deep South. Hopefully you just have the junior size but some of us get the supersized bucket with all the extra sides of opinions, guilt, and condemnations. Don't try to heal me, don't pray for me, and for God's sake don't tell my kid if she prays hard enough her hearing is going to get better. It's obvious this is a progressive thing. Anna will buy sand at the beach and we have one relative in particular that has her more than convinced that Jesus unstops the ears of the deaf and opens the eyes of the blind. I have spent more than one night by my beautiful redheaded daughter's bedside drying her tears, trying to convince her that God loves everyone and that she has done nothing wrong. She is not paying for the sins of her parents—um, obviously me, since I'm the great amazingly fucked-up freak. If there is a heaven, she will most certainly be there, and in my heart I hate myself for fantasizing about sending people who give little innocent children nightmares, a hot, fast, one-way ticket in the opposite direction. *Many paths, one God—judge not*, is the example I try so hard to show my children, but boy that single-minded bitch pisses me off.

The best advice I have ever gotten was from Dr. Charles Berlin who consulted with me by phone through deaf relay, no small feat, my family would rarely even call me on the phone—too much trouble. He told me to get a mirror, because we were doing a genetic pedigree. I had the computer and my phone lines all tangled up so I tripped and ran and grabbed a mirror and rushed back to this great scientific giant of a man I had left on hold. "Okay Dr. Berlin, I'm back." I thought he would ask me about my eye spacing, or the placement of my gray hair. He asked me what I saw. Huh? He told me to look closely because I was looking at everything I needed for my children. "Amy," he said, "You are the expert. You are all those kids will ever need." I think he might have been right.

The second best advice was from son's senior advisor. J. B. is graduating early. I was trying to understand just basic information, and being blown off, asking for things in writing at parent meetings, wanting very much to be a part of his senior year, not understanding how to order invitations, his cap and gown. The other mothers marginalized both myself and his right to even be in the senior class. J. B. had no trouble in school but over and over I was being shot down when I tried to get information, help, and ridiculously even donate money to his class. Very upset, I asked his advisor what I needed to do, she gave the bird and said "Amy, screw 'em." As Henry Kisor said, "Deafness often still frightens away the ignorant and the self-regarding, and that in itself can be a blessing." She made sure I got the information I needed but reminded me that there are times when you just don't need to waste your time on people.

I get told a lot, "I just don't know how you do it." The truth is, I call a good friend at least once a week and say "Tell me again why I don't beat my children." I do it with a text phone, a vibrating alarm clock, a color-coded calendar, and hearing alert dog named Holiday. I do it with my kid's dad's support, a man who also still happens to be my best friend. The truth is, it sucks. It feels like you are fighting a war for the people you love most and you don't know who you are fighting against or when the end is in sight. Some days I don't shower. I don't cry anymore. I've lost a lot of weight. People hardly recognize me, and they want to know what kind of diet I'm on. Honestly? Well, I really don't have much money for food with all the co-pays and the gas traveling back and forth and when I do, I don't have time to eat. I can't count the number of times I've fallen asleep in my plate close to midnight. You just sort of lose track of yourself. But I open my eyes at five in the morning and slip my magnets back on and Whit is screaming, "I need to pee" and catapulting over his Dutch door, and Anna's bitching because someone ate all the dates out of the granola. J. B. hogs the bathroom like any normal teenager. Somehow we manage to get six hearing aids in, two remotes on, two headpieces affixed, two processors on, one FM system looped around the neck, check everyone's batteries, and get out the door by seven just like all the other families on the street.

Sometimes I feel normal, but sometimes I imagine us like old-fashioned *Saturday Night Live* coneheads, obvious freaks, piling into our SUV, trying to blend in but never really able to be real people. So I fall asleep in my plate and I wake up vibrating and I apparently breathe and function on some level because I do love my children. I smile when I see their faces. I rejoice at their progress and their success. The truth is that if you stepped back and looked at the big picture you would walk right over the edge, close your eyes, and fall blissfully into nothingness, which sounds pretty damn good most days.

What Should Have Been...

by Megan Raines Wingert

It is taking time to accept that my child has a disability, or several. We knew when we adopted him that given his prenatal and birth history, he would certainly be at risk. Unfortunately, knowing of the possibility and coping with the reality are two somewhat different things. We are moving in fits and starts towards acceptance of the situation, as most parents seem to do. What surprises me more is the difficulty I have in coming to terms with myself.

Like many mothers and fathers I had visions of the type of parent I would be. I would have a home-birth and would breastfeed for several years. I'd answer questions patiently and encourage exploration and play. I could envision joining my children in fantasy games incorporating all sorts of toys and furniture props. I'd be respectful to them and of their need to be children and use gentle, loving discipline techniques to guide their behavior. Most of all, I'd enjoy spending time with them and look forward to our interactions. It was a lovely fantasy, and as seems to happen to many parents, fate was to provide plenty of opportunity for us to reflect back upon it ruefully.

My son came to us through the foster care system, which quashed certain parenting options from the get-go. My husband was also unemployed and soon to return to school full-time, so staying at home was not an option for my son's first two years of life. I knew the first few months would be hard—that it would take time for the drugs (and alcohol?) to leave his system and for him to heal. We'd been through it before with our first foster son and watched him develop into a wonderfully easy older infant before he returned to extended family. Ah, the delusions of baby lust. Instead of the gentle child I was imagining, we were gifted with an incredibly intense and complex little boy whose needs were not particularly well suited to my flights of parenting fancy.

I never anticipated the guilt I would feel over the days I dreaded hearing his voice in the morning, signaling a new day of struggling to retain my sanity and not ruin this little boy. The harsh methods I've tried (prescribed by the "experts") in an attempt to change certain behaviors when nothing else worked. The shame of knowing that, at times, my son has looked at me with fear. The fear that he may be aware of the emotional distance in which I have sometimes sought shelter. The times I see him searching for praise, love, approbation, validation—and I have nothing genuine left to offer. There are times when frustration, anger, sadness, and fear blind me to the wonderful aspects of who he is, prevent me from seeing him for the small child he truly is, causing me to respond to him without empathy, respect, or kindness. How awful that this child, already so irrevocably altered by one mother, has so often felt the sting of rejection from another.

In truth, he is frequently a real handful. I'm curious, for instance, what my neighbors thought if they happened to have been watching out the window during a particularly bad moment a few months back. Did they hear me raise my voice and judge me harshly for yelling at my preschool-aged twins to "get their bottoms over here *now* or face a time-out"? Did they see me hanging on to my five-year-old son's wrist with a death-grip, holding the baby on my hip, using my legs to prod my confused and uncooperative twins into the house? Did they call me a "screeching harpy"? Did they contemplate calling protective services? I'm sure it wouldn't be the first time it's crossed somebody's mind.

It doesn't ever seem to occur to strangers to offer a hand when they stop and stare at us as my kid loses his cool. One neighbor was initially friendly but now keeps her distance—I always wonder if it has something to do with the amount of screaming and crying she has heard from the two of us. If she had offered a hand as I desperately tried to herd the twins into the house, she might have realized that something, perhaps my requests for the kids to clean up their toys and go in for lunch, had triggered my older son's temper and he had begun to throw, smash, and destroy toys. I was holding his wrist to try to keep him from damaging anything or anyone else en route to his room, where he could cool off and regain control.

I'm sure I seemed like the Wicked Witch of the West, but I was trying to act quickly enough to prevent further escalation and unable to leave any of the other three alone in an unfenced front yard with cars whizzing by.

Perhaps she could have offered a hand to one of the twins who, it turned out, was trying to respond to my previous request to clean up, and when challenged by a stuck toy that he couldn't separate to put away, just froze in confusion. She could have held the infant, who had been frightened by his brother's screaming and began to howl himself, adding his perfectly reasonable request for a nap to the already overwhelming din.

On another day recently, our house was hit with a particularly bad case of contagious howling during the "witching hour," and in seeking a moment of mental refuge I glanced somewhat vacantly out the front window, only to see a man standing on the edge of my front lawn, staring up at my house. He stood there for quite a while. In fact, my husband had to walk past him as he entered the house upon returning from work, joking that I was lucky he hadn't just turned around and headed back considering the noise level and, by the way, did I know that there was a man standing on the road staring at us? For some reason, that incident still makes laugh.

Not all of our interactions with curious strangers have been so benign. There was the woman who followed me out of the supermarket a couple of years ago and stood and stared at me as I loaded my infant twins into the car, and then tried to buckle my kicking, screaming, howling preschooler into the back. She noted that he had been screaming throughout the store. "Yes, I know, lady, I was *there*." She wanted to know if he was mine. "Yes, he's adopted. If you need to, look in the car and see his car seat, all properly sized for him" (and then, please, go away!). As if someone would *want* to kidnap a raging three year old. "He's really very upset." "Yes, he is. He'll calm down now that's he in his seat—it's quiet and darkened back there. He'll be fine." "I don't know" "OK, well, he has developmental and behavioral problems—this isn't all that unusual for him."

Lady, what do you want me to tell you? He was angry because he kept trying to lean all the way over the side of the cart and had just missed being swiped by another cart and then immediately did it again. He lost the opportunity for his desired reward for good behavior—a bagel. It made him mad, even madder than not being allowed to lean way, way over the side of the cart. He began to hit me and tried to hit his infant brothers. I had to hold his hands and that made him angrier. If I hadn't really, really needed one or two of those items in the cart, I would have abandoned it and taken him out. As it was, I made it through the self-checkout as fast as I could, leaving behind many food items I would need in the week to come. By this time, I'd had to take him out of the cart to keep the twins safe and was holding onto him for dear life, as he pinched and hit and kicked and screamed. I knew that if I could just get all three safely belted into their seats, the motion of the car would quickly soothe him and a tenuous equilibrium could be restored. Not only was it humiliating to have someone watching me from just a few feet away, contemplating whether or not she should call the cops, but by preventing me from starting the car, she was keeping me from doing what I needed to in order to calm things down.

It's a repeating theme in our lives, this being judged, this threat of being reported to CPS or to the police. My husband found himself being followed by a truck a few years back. The truck forced him to the side and rolled down the window asking, "Is that your kid?" "Yeah." "Are you sure?" "Yes." (And again, who the hell would *want* a screaming, raging two-year-old?) "Well, you need to go back to the store—the cops have been called." So he did, followed closely by this "kidnapping-foiler." When he got there, he pulled in, opened the door and encouraged the man to see for himself that our son was unharmed and, in fact, our son. He reports that the man was somewhat chagrined when he asked our son what was wrong, only to hear "Daddy said no French fries! I want French fries!" McDonald's had been closed, and that pissed little guy off. However, I'm sure it provided Security the most excitement they'd had that week.

It's hard to know which is more difficult to take—the comments from strangers who see me in a very different way than I see myself, or the comments from the professionals who are supposed to be our path toward help. There was the developmental pediatrician who told me flat-out that I was preventing my son's behavior from improving by keeping him at home with me. She stated that my desire not to have my three-year-old in an all-day program, five days a week, reflected something wrong with me, an inappropriate inability to separate from my child. An inability that was harming my child, preventing him from developing normally, and from improving his behavior.

There is always the school district, with its belief that no child can be best served without its intervention. This is a panel of people who will not provide the recommended play therapy to help my son learn to cope better with his anger, because "since he isn't in school, his poor behavior isn't hindering his academic progress." They demanded that I put my son in a program that we all agreed was inappropriate, for the sole purpose of having him fail, and thus, in their eyes, establishing the necessary paper trail for the provision of the thrice-recommended services. I was chided, relentlessly, for my unwillingness to set my son up to fail, even if it was to obtain a needed service. Again, I was told that I was preventing him from later school success. I was asked over and over why, since he is such an intense child, I wasn't happy to ship him out for the day and have a little break? A little time with my other children?

I've been trying to get help with my son for five years now. It's been an endlessly demoralizing process. It also makes me feel like I'm living two separate parenting lives. In one, I follow my instincts as much as possible. I've breastfed my younger kids for as long as they've needed, I've co-slept with them, and rarely separated from them for more than a few minutes until they were ready to leave without looking back. I've respected their need to be with mommy, as all-consuming as it can be, and I've taken pride in myself and my ability to nurture them. I've helped other moms to do the same, encouraging them to follow their children's lead and to value the time they have with their little ones, for it is fleeting, even if it doesn't seem so at the time.

In my other life, however, I'm told that that the longer my son stays with me during the day, the more harm I do to him. Never mind the unmitigated disaster that his day-care experience was, somehow that was "different." I'm told that I am incapable of "fixing" him—he must be handed off to others who have more "know-how", even if they know nothing of my son himself. That I should be relieved and grateful that someone is offering to absolve me of my responsibility to him—"put him in their hands and they will take the reigns." They have the "one size fits all magic cure," if only I'll sign him over. They focus on fixing his weaknesses, with no care for encouraging his strengths. And navigating their labyrinth is a particularly tricky task. In one sense, they are right. Sometimes they do have things to offer that would benefit my son, things that I'm not sure I could provide quite as well. How then to get what we need without selling my soul to the devil? How to "take what works for us and leave the rest," when the power only goes in one direction?

The truth is that I spend plenty of time doing things right with both him and the other kids. I spend hours following their lead as they play, I listen to their stories, try my best to answer their questions, and try to make them happy when I can think of a little surprise that will delight them. But, when something goes awry, it's my son's rages and the awful way they make me feel that stick with me at the end of the day, magically erasing all the positive things that have transpired in our day. Perhaps that is why the comments from strangers, the endless criticism from those who are *supposed* to be providing services to help my son, the offhand and innocent comments from friends who would never put *their* child on medication, sting so much. When they judge me and find me wanting, they are only reflecting what I feel in that darkest of places in my heart—that they are right, that I *am* failing at raising my son.

Would I feel the same degree of insecurity if he had been born to me? I don't know. If he had, he wouldn't have suffered brain damage from prenatal drug and alcohol exposure and this would probably have made him a lot easier to parent. But would I have advocated for him differently if I had known for sure when he arrived that he'd be staying? I don't think so. I fought hard to get him good medical care, access to therapeutic services, and to keep DSS on its toes. I failed, most of the time, but I gave it my all. And yet, while I don't think being an adoptive parent adds much to the insecurity issue, I think the fact that I fostered him first does. I didn't bond with him in the same way I bonded with my first foster son (back when I foolishly believed he would be mine forever) or the way I did later with the ones I fed at my breast. I was still grieving for the child I had "given back" to his birth family and I feared I would eventually lose this baby, too. It made it hard to fully give my heart when for two years I knew he could be yanked from my home without any notice on the slightest whim of DSS.

It wasn't that I didn't care for him well—I did. I swaddled him and cradled him to my chest, spending long night rocking his stiff body as his addled neurological system fought sleep. I couldn't feed him my milk, but I always held in my arms to feed him, singing and talking to him. I spent as much time as I could playing with him. But, I didn't insist that my husband, who was out of work and suffering from depression, care for him during the day. I didn't necessarily think it would be good for either of them. Instead, after being abandoned by his birth mom, and then shuttled between a few strangers, culminating in short hospital stay, and followed by two-week-long stay with a different set of foster parents, I put him into day-care full-time a mere week after he had arrived with us. A day-care situation that was certainly reputable, but didn't meet his needs well at all. Can you imagine all of that in the first eight weeks of life?

Not surprisingly, I think he developed mild attachment issues. The truth is, I shouldn't have taken an infant in if I wasn't going to be able to be home. I was taken in by the logic endemic in the foster care system—"it might not be ideal, but it's better than what they'd get if you don't." Even more fundamentally, I was being selfish. I wanted to be a mom again and I didn't want to wait for some indefinite time when I could stay home.

I know, deep down, that I haven't done as well by my oldest as I have by my others. We, who had never been separated, were much more securely attached much earlier on, and it buffeted us through the tempestuous early years in a way that my eldest and I sorely lacked. There was always the knowledge in the back of my head that it didn't have to be permanent, that my life didn't *have* to be filled with this constant destruction and rage and exhaustion. I could call DSS and find him a new placement. I never would have actually done it, but I did fantasize about it sometimes.

Things are better now, a few years down the road. My bond with and love for him feels much more like the bonds I share with my younger children, but I doubt it will ever be the same. The fact is that I failed to mother him during his early years the way I mothered his younger siblings, which leaves me to dwell, guiltily, on my fantasy of "what could have been."

Building Bridges into Ordinariness

by Ziva Mann

In my (medical) neighborhood, the kids walk to school. Uphill, if need be—both ways. In the snow. Short bus? Never heard of it.

As the parent of a child with multiple diagnoses, my favorite one is his bleeding disorder. Shai has severe hemophilia, which means that left to his own devices, his body does not create a clot. Children like him can bleed into their muscles, their joints, and most scarily, into their brains. Except that by and large, they don't. Hemophilia is typically controllable, managed at home by loving parents wielding tiny, sharp needles and hunting for veins. Any junkie can find a vein, we say, and turn our little guy into a pincushion. Needles are love in my neighborhood. And, pumped full of this sharp-edged love, off my boy goes to do the astonishing, idiotic things that boys seem wired to do.

When Shai was tiny, the world looked dangerous to me. It just didn't fit him, I decided, and did my best to wrap him in a bubble. But too many boys with hemophilia are developmentally delayed, the doctors told me. It's common to see them held back from walking until they are sixteen, eighteen months. Love holds them back, the doctors warned, soft caring arms that keep that small body from falling and bleeding. I listened politely, and then went home and got down on my knees, looking for sharp edges and places to pad. I worked to make his world safe, but Shai didn't care about my protections. He learned to walk at ten months old, pushing his way past the safety I'd built for him. Inevitably, his right knee bled, swelling and forcing him to stand on one leg, like a lopsided stork. Standing in his crib with his knee looking like a reddened grapefruit, he grinned at me. Holy crap, I thought, he's grinning—with a bleed that must hurt like hell. Stumped, I sat down to think this parenting thing over. Maybe, just maybe, the kid's the one in charge, and not me.

We struggled with this idea for a couple of years—Shai, his dad, doctors, my abused maternal fantasies, and I. Eventually, we cobbled together a rough sort of plan: balance. Pre-medicate, weigh the risks, and accept that sometimes we just have to let the kid fall. So, I pump Shai up with his clotting meds and then send him off to play soccer, hike, or climb really just that high on the playground. There he goes, I think, and slap on my best poker face. "Lookit me, mom!" he yells down. (*I can't reach him if he falls from there, I have to trust him—I hate that part—did I pack the emergency kit in my bag today? Crap, I can't remember.*) "Looking good, honey!" I call and lean back, deliberately, against the park bench.

Yep, we're a bus-free normal around here. It might be a sharpish, teeth-gritted kind of normal on some days, but we're normal folks, who happen to have elaborate emergency kits in our cars and diaper bags, and have our hematology team on speed dial. Normal, with MedicAlert bracelets. Normal, normal, normal, normal, normal, normal, normal, normal, normal, normal, normal—has the word lost all meaning for you yet? It has for me. What's normal? We clotting moms ask each other. Is there a real, standardized concept that we can point to, and measure ourselves against? And if we can find this normal on a map, can we drive over and throw a brick through its window? I simply cannot understand how this "normal" is a useful concept for anything other than exaggerating how difficult difference can be.

Ah, well, I tell myself. I never really liked the old normal, anyway. Now, this—this is real, in-the-trenches parenting! I am a tough as nails, unflappable mama with skills. Mostly.

When Shai was four, he whacked his head on a sharp corner. "Oh, no," said I, "we're experienced hemo-parents now. We won't overreact." To prove the point, I called a friend and invited her to be insouciant with me. I told her about the time that I rushed a baby Shai to the ER after a head bonk. "I tried to start the car—with the kid's toy keys!" I told her, and we laughed. Yep, we agreed, with some experience under my belt, I was a calm, sensible person. Until the following day, when Shai threw a tantrum (*Symptoms of a bleed into the brain*, my mama-MD informed me: *change in personality*).

Shai screeched at me, using language I'd never heard before. Change in personality: check (*Gross motor skills affected*, the mama-MD continued). Shai tripped over his own feet, still roaring. Gross motor: check. (*Potential nausea, loss of appetite.*) Shai threw raspberries at me, refusing to eat them. Appetite: check. All systems go for head-bleed maneuvers, I thought grimly, and strapped the infuriated child into the car, his head now revolving on his shoulders.

I took him to the ER, where a worried team of doctors did a whole lot of medicine. "I'm glad to tell you that he's perfectly fine," a nice ER doctor told me. Horrified, my husband and I looked at each other. Fine? Does that mean that there's no medicine for the screeching horribles? "Normalcy," my husband informed me, "bites." I sat back down on the floor. Time to rethink this parenting thing again, I told myself. Am I still not in charge?

Reality holds sway, and it makes no apologies for what it needs to be. Got a bleed? Reality dictates the new patterns of the next two or three days, with Shai on the couch with ice on his leg, and me mixing up the clotting meds and debating pain control while Shai argues. "It's not that bad," he lies, and tries to walk on it. (*Significant swelling of the calf, redness and heat indicating bleeding into the muscle,* says the mama-MD, unmoved.) "Put your butt back on that couch," I snarl at my child, and hunker down for a few days of that as a refrain. Got an ER run? Oy. Time to pack a bag and write off that early-morning conference call—this will take a while.

Reality scoffs at what I thought normal would be, and embarrassed, normal slinks off into a corner. Self-pity becomes the thing I do after the crisis is over, and fear becomes the feeling that I kick aside to get the job done. Skills emerge, developing and bolstering, and I relax, feeling less helpless. I know this gig. It's not normal, but it becomes . . . ordinary. Shai-driven ordinary, whose shifting routines are recognizable. Caught up in meeting the day's challenge and backed up by my medical team, and my fellow hemo-parents, I can feel pretty kickass. Short buses? Bah. Who needs them?

When reality hits you in the face, you might argue that there's no choice but to accept it. You'd be wrong. I can hide from all sorts of realities, clinging to fantasies of normalcy. It took some strength for me to look at the new, non-clotting reality, and to step into it. Shai needed me to do this, which stripped the matter right down to a non-option: step into Shai's world, because that's where he lives. But where he lives isn't where I grew up, and all of my ideas of boyhood had to be rewritten for a kid who plays soccer with pads and care and meds. My husband found it easier. A short, slim Jew who loves baseball, his idea of manliness is to read bedtime stories and play catch with his son. I congratulated myself when Shai was diagnosed: unlike my family, who mourns the loss of a potential hockey player, my husband has a sense of manhood that will suit his son's physical limitations well. But perhaps I should have explained that to Shai.

My lovely, gentle man was shocked first to see his son refuse to clot, and then again to see his son swing a bat. Damn, the kid's good. He's got an eye for the ball and power behind his bat, and a Medic Alert bracelet. He wants to play for the Red Sox, he tells us, and when he hits the ball, "Hey—you know, he's got quite a swing," says some random dad, holding out our ball. "He's a natural." Yep, he is, and we have absolutely no idea what he'll do with it. Can Shai's shoulders handle the stress of baseball? We just don't know. There are no rules in place for Shai, and blessed few expectations. And there's just no translating his ordinariness for people who don't live in a shifting, unexpectedly ordinary landscape of their own.

That's not to say that I cannot build bridges from that other world to where we live. Some days I feel that I am permanently an ambassador, an uber-chipper tour guide explaining Shai's medical stuff. I talk to friends and family, and many shyly ask to watch the kid get his clotting medication. Shai himself loves to do presentations on hemophilia at school, and insists that I give him a dose at the end of the show. "Look!" he says with a needle in his vein. "It really doesn't hurt." Awed, the other kids watch, and disability becomes heroism. But sometimes I run into someone who doesn't—quite—want to cross the bridge with me. My father, a doctor with a gift for needles, is a quiet but forceful advocate for his grandson. Still, he will not give Shai his medication. "I don't want him to associate me with needles," he explained. "And if needles are love?" "Well, even so," said the grandfather, backing away from our kind of ordinariness. I hugged my dad, and let him retreat. I don't need to make him live in our world, I told myself, so long as he's happy to be a visitor. Besides, sometimes even the perkiest of tour guides just wants to go home and put her feet up.

Of all my audiences and bridge-crossers, I have the most fun with the schools. A student myself when Shai was born, I had to send him to a day-care center. My first presentation to teachers and directors required a lot of tissues (for me), but eventually I learned how to do a decent dog-and-pony show, complete with jokes. With so many children with asthma, allergies, and diabetes coming to schools, kids with medical stuff are nearly commonplace. I walk into these meetings with Shai's diagnosis whining in my ear. *Use me*, it begs. *Label him.* But no—if he's the kid with the clotting thing, then he's all too easily not the kid swinging the bat, or shrieking from the top of the climbing structure. Ordinary, I tell myself. He's got to be ordinary. But there's a room full of serious faces and papers, waiting to talk about the way that he's deficient. Oy.

Oh yes, an embattled mama am I, valiantly trying to raise a non-disabled, medically challenged child. Truly, I am a martyr fighting the system—all hail me! Except, of course, that I called that meeting, and to call it, I waved the ADA (Americans with Disabilities Act) flag. Ordinariness and pragmatism are all very well, but every so often, the gimp card has just got to be played. Pay attention to me, says the gimp card, I have legal rights because I am disabled. The strategy gets attention, but it also carries risks. How can you be ordinary, if you are also disabled?

If I were the kind of person who mixed drinks, I'd tell you that meetings like this are like mixing a cocktail. A splash of disability to get the administration's attention, and a dollop of fear to make sure that they take this seriously. Finally, a whisper of humor and normalcy, to remind people that there's a child involved, and not just a diagnosis. Swirl gently and serve, with a slice of lime. Nice imagery, no? But it absolutely does not work.

The people I talk to all have their own ideas of how Shai's world works. They assume that I am a martyr, that Shai is a fragile child, and that there are bubbles to be built around him. Or, they assume that I'm an overanxious parent and that Shai is really just fine, and they resent the ADA making them do things for me. Depending on who I'm serving that day, the drink has to be different. More humor for the scowling skeptics, persuading them that I'm a sensible, likeable person. Less gimp for the people afraid that Shai—and I—will crack and fall apart on them. And lots of emphasis on Shai himself. He's a great kid, I tell people earnestly (except when he's whacking his little brother on the head). He's generous and empathic (except when he's being whiny and selfish), and you can trust him. He knows his body, and he'll tell you when something is wrong (unless he decides to lie). We look at each other over our drinks and consider. Um, I admit, I should say that he's also an ordinary kid, with ordinary kid issues. The teachers look at me knowingly, hearing in the admission all of my parentheses. Okay, say the teachers and administrators, astonishing me. We'll give it a try.

Recently, I thought of a brilliant idea: instead of pestering me all summer, Shai could go to camp. Another mom tossed a pamphlet at me: farm camp! Send your child every morning, let him dig in the dirt, catch toads, and hike through the forest. He'll come home muddy, stinking, and happy. Sounds perfect, no? So, I sent out the application, added an alarmingly large check, and Shai was in. But before he started, we needed to have the meeting. Cocktails, anyone?

The farm, when I drove up, was wonderful. Big, old trees. Flowers. A farmstand with locally grown produce and grapevines threading through an arbor. A sign that read: WARNING (smelly) CHILDREN. I grinned at the sign, and went to the office. In the conference room, I found three people. Three very tense, worried looking people. Aha, thought I, these folks are going to be tough. But I was prepared: I know my child and his diagnosis. I know our rights: as long as I sound fairly reasonable, he should be accommodated. And I do a great Miss Marple imitation.

Miss Marple is an Agatha Christie character, a fragile elderly lady who should have no business mucking around with police stuff. But she's so sweet and lovely and insistent that she gets her way. People want to be nice to Miss Marple, because she herself is so lovely and nice. Nice plus persistence, with a determinedly reasonable air—it never fails. Shrill and worried, however, lets me down every time. Need the best IV nurse in a busy ER? Use Miss Marple. Be polite, firm, and understanding ("oh, I'm so sorry to bother you—I can see you are busy—but he's got really tricky veins, and I'd hate to waste time with anyone other than Vicky. Is she on tonight?"), and hello! There is Vicky, standing before you.

Miss Marple can handle the farm people, I told myself. Just smile, take a deep breath and Marple it. I sucked in some air, and sat down at the table, wearing my best Miss M face. "So, shall we talk about how this is going to work?" I asked them. They looked worriedly at me, so I kept going. "Or shall I start by introducing you to Shai?" I suggested, and pulled some photos of Shai out of my bag. The previous summer, I'd watched a school principal melt over pictures of Shai, finally seeing the child instead of his medical diagnoses. But the farm director pushed the photos aside. "I can't look at these," he told me, and hunched his shoulders. I watched this man trying to back away from my son, and took a deep breath. "Okay," I said. "I can see that the diagnoses are looming larger than Shai himself. So, let's start there: tell me what you are worried about."

Over the next hour and a half, I listened.

"Kids get scraped up here!" they told me. I looked politely encouraging.

"Kids can get cut—or poked—or fall down," they implored. I nodded calmly.

"Kids can get bruised!" they begged. I looked unconcerned but respectful.

"Kids can get poison ivy!" they wailed, and I grinned, and dropped Miss Marple. "What—do you throw them into patches of the stuff?" There was a pause while the others realized that I was making a joke. "Um, no. But it's there." Miss Marple back in place, I promised that I wasn't worried.

Deflating rapidly, the farm folk offered a last plea: "The kids do get dirty, you know." I leaned forward. "That," I said, "is exactly what I'm hoping for." And I took a deep breath.

"Look," I told them. "Shai is an ordinary kid, for all of the medical hoo-ha. He climbs things, he loves baseball, and he digs in the dirt. If he isn't collecting bruises, then we're doing something wrong. And if he's clean and tidy, then I'm worried. It's simply a matter of working out where our risks are, and putting safeguards into place." We sat there, looking at each other. The farm folk were running out of reasons not to take Shai, and I had failed to fold on them. Still, one last reason hung in the air.

Reluctantly, the farm director spoke. "I can see that you want your son to be normal," he told me, and sighed. "And I can respect that." But don't make me do it, he begged, silently. Miss Marple smiled at him gently, firmly ignoring his plea. "Thank you," I said. "I appreciate your understanding." The farm director's shoulder slumped, and he looked resigned.

Two weeks later, Shai went with me to meet the farm's counselors. Miss Marple, I thought grimly, did not get stuck with a sidekick, still less a sidekick with a propensity for clowning in front of groups. At our last such meeting, I discussed abdominal bleeds with a group of teachers, while Shai stood on a chair and made faces behind my head. "Sit *down*," I hissed— and Shai started to improvise a pleasantly scatological ditty. I growled. He grinned. In the middle of explaining about joint bleeds, he spoke up. "Oooh, I thtuck the medicine in my butt!" he mugged, and demonstrated. The teachers laughed. I did not. Sensing a possible repeat performance, I lectured him all the way to the farm. Don't cost us any goodwill, I begged silently. Don't appear to be anything other than the sweet kid that you— occasionally—are, the kid who is worth going the extra mile, the kid that makes the effort all worthwhile.

And oh, but for once he was that kid. I breathed quietly as he explained to the counselors what it feels like to have a joint bleed. He earned their faith in him, the skinny little six-year-old who will be in charge of telling the adults when something is wrong. "It's his body," I said to the counselors, as I've said to teachers, administrators, and babysitters. "He'll tell you when something is wrong." And Shai, my improbably serious sidekick, made them believe it. We laid out the preventative plan, the backup plans, the emergency plans, and helped everyone believe that we'd thought of everything—that everything was going to be under control. "To be honest," I said wryly, "Shai usually bleeds on my watch. If something exciting is going to happen, he tends to save it for me. But we'll prepare just in case." I left them smiling, admiring the brave kid and his slightly cracked mama, and prepared to learn just how ordinary we really are. This, I thought, could really work.

On the way home, I grinned at the kid in the rearview mirror. "You did well, Shai," I told him. "Really well. I'm proud of you." He smiled back at me. "Thanks. But, Mom? My fingers feel funny." I mentally inventoried my bag. "Oh?" He nodded, ruefully. "Yep. They're swelling and they feel hot and tight." (*Bleeding in the finger, muscle more likely than joint as the site for the bleed, the location creating risk for compartment syndrome and lasting nerve damage*, the mama-MD informed me.) I cracked an instant ice pack and tossed it into the backseat. "Slap that on, kid, and get back to me in ten minutes."

Hands firmly on the wheel, I drove us home, just one more car on the road. And if I took a couple of turns too fast, well, I'm almost sure that nobody but me noticed. I'm still not in charge of this parenting gig, I admitted to myself. But damn if those aren't *my* hands on the wheel.

Diagnosis Invisible
by Stephanie Sleeper

If I think about my son's third open-heart surgery for more than about three seconds my chest seizes and I can't breathe. I feel like my body is collapsing on itself, and I start to howl but I can't draw a breath. Somewhere inside, I consider calling my therapist to request that Xanax be added to my daily cocktail but I never go to the phone. Maybe it's because no amount of prescription meds can make the surgery go away, or maybe it's because I somehow want to feel it in all its glory, kind of like unmedicated childbirth. And I can't numb my own suffering while my kid can't escape his. I feel guilty enough as it is.

I haven't ruled out the Xanax.

My son was born with a congenital heart defect called tetralogy of Fallot, which is a complex defect involving a large hole in the heart, a defective valve, and constricted blood flow to the lungs, also ignominiously called "blue baby" syndrome. He was taken immediately to the NICU after birth and diagnosed about eight hours later, on Christmas morning. Later that day, one of his nurses chirped that tetralogy of Fallot is the "most common heart defect!" Thanks, I feel so much better now. I can't remember if that was before or after she told me that his heart murmur was so loud it sounded like a train driving through his chest. She announced that you could hear it just as clearly through his back! Though I realize that she was excited about the medical marvel of a heart that sounds like a train, her comment stung. We were still in shock that our baby was not healthy. That's the refrain you repeat over and over throughout a pregnancy, "I don't care if it's a boy or girl, as long as the baby is healthy!" We didn't need her to remind us that he was *not* healthy. However, the award for most insensitive comment goes to the neonatal resident who told us that he might turn "as blue as a popsicle stick" while waiting for his first surgery, followed by a litany of increasingly terrifying things they might have to do to him if that happened.

A few days ago I called the child life specialist in the cardiac unit at the children's hospital to talk about how we can manage my son's hospitalization. I told her that he also has high-functioning autism and severe tactile sensitivity. She told me that they had treated autistic kids before and that offering them choices really seemed to help, for example, would he like to have the blood pressure cuff on his arm or his leg? I tried to be optimistic. "Hmmm, yes, that's a good idea," I said. But I knew she didn't really understand what I was saying. I knew we were going to be depending on her to make his experience less traumatizing, so I tried to frame my words carefully. She sounded very sincere and knowledgeable, but I knew she wasn't quite seeing the whole picture. "Well, what I'm *really* worried about is that he doesn't really tolerate any sensory stimulation at *all*. He won't even wear a band-aid. It takes him up to an hour to accept wearing clothes in the morning," I said. I didn't add that shirts that are three sizes too big are still "tight" and "bumpy," or that he often has extended meltdowns about how his car seat feels, or how he *thinks* it is going to feel, and about how upset he is that he has saliva in his mouth because it's so *wet*. We could not get an accurate blood pressure reading on him until this past year because he thrashed around like a wounded animal. In the hospital, he is going to have EKG wires stuck all over him, chest tubes draining blood that has leaked around his heart, a pulse ox monitor clamped to his finger, central line and regular IVs, and oxygen tubes taped to his face in addition to that blood pressure cuff.

My son was diagnosed with high-functioning autism about six months ago. It was only the confirmation of what we had known for about two years, though we had an impossible time getting people to believe us. He talks! He makes eye contact! He can't be autistic! I wanted to believe that the heart condition was the extent of his problems, and so I believed his doctors when they told me that his behavioral problems were related to his heart surgeries. But they weren't really concerned with his behavior at all. He was eating and growing, his liver wasn't enlarged (a sign of heart failure), and that was what mattered to them. I wasn't quite convinced, however. The first clue came from my communication with other moms of "heart babies" on an internet bulletin board. I read that many of their babies seemed to sleep more than twenty minutes at a time, and in a crib, no less. I consulted my trusty Dr. Sears baby book and learned that he was something called "high needs." Okay, that about sums it up. The book promised me it would get better. It didn't.

When he was still a baby, I mentioned his extreme "colicky" behavior to his cardiologist at one of his checkups, hoping to hear that it was indeed heart related, or *something* that would get better with time, and he suggested that I try letting my baby cry in his crib for a while so he could learn to fall asleep on his own. I just stared at him. "Um, are you cracked?" I wanted to shout, but didn't. "He turns blue when he cries! I'm supposed to leave him in there blue and screaming? I thought the point was to make sure he *doesn't* turn blue?!" Even professionals who have intimate knowledge of babies' medical needs seemed to always fall back on mainstream parenting techniques, no matter what the situation. It's like they have no other tricks in their bags to offer us.

This experience was emblematic of the kind of cognitive dissonance I've encountered in relating the medical and behavioral aspects of my son's diagnoses. The heart specialists look puzzled when I talk about his autism, and psychologists throw their hands up about heart issues. They don't really talk to each other. They send reports back and forth. They contribute to the file. They tend to blame his issues on the other diagnosis. Oh, he acts like that because of his surgeries! The body takes time to recover from that kind of trauma. No, he acts like that because of the autism! That's not heart related. His heart is doing fine. He should be fully recovered.

The truth is that he *was* fully recovered. His heart was working about as well as it possibly could. He grew, he hit milestones more or less on schedule. His regular cardiac checkups showed that his repair was holding up. I relaxed and blindly trusted the cardiologists' prognosis that he had a very small chance of needing further surgery. As far as we were concerned, he was a normal, healthy toddler, if a bit intense. But as he got older and his behaviors seemed to get worse, not better, I had to believe they were not heart related. His heart was fine, remember? If his behavior was heart related, that would mean his heart was not fine at all. So I smothered myself in research. I knew there was something wrong with him, but I had to believe it was not something that would kill him. But what was it? Sensory Integration Disorder? Anxiety disorder? ADHD? OCD? Definitely *not* autism. He makes eye contact, remember? My mom, who teaches kids with autism spectrum disorders, told me stories about her students, who seemed much "worse" than my son. I wanted to believe her. But the possibility still gnawed at me. I studied the *DSM (Diagnostic and Statistical Manual of Mental Disorders)* criteria, all kinds of autism scales, and parent stories, and decided that he was much too social to be autistic. Several years ago, another therapist told me that he had PTSD (post traumatic stress disorder). I'm sure she was right. I think all special needs kids and parents have PTSD.

The tipping point came when my son was just over three years old. After his sister was born, he completely broke down and stopped functioning. We could not leave the house. We could not even move off the couch. They both screamed all day long. He did not eat; he did not sleep. I was at the end. At my daughter's six-week checkup I bawled in my pediatrician's office, which was, frankly, not a novel occurrence. I had repeatedly asked for something, anything, that would help him stop screaming all the time, that would make him eat, sleep, ride in the car, go to a friend's house, wear clothes, or allow me to put him down to go to the bathroom without screaming. But this time, instead of shrugging her shoulders and saying he was too young for any medications, she finally referred us to a child psychologist. I was thrilled. Finally! What I did not realize was that the psychologist's version of therapy would consist of interrogating our parenting skills, summary judgment of "overprotective parenting," three visits for "play therapy," and her self-satisfied proclamation that he finally used the potty (after six months of our trying every trick in the book) because of her "therapy." I don't mean to disparage the many wonderful professionals that we have encountered. There are truly many talented and compassionate people out there. However, they seem to be rather few and far between. You always know when an individual or group is good, though, because they have a waiting list a mile long. If you find someone who can give you an appointment in the next month, don't bother.

A friend of mine finally convinced me that my son has high-functioning autism. She spoke in an endless loop about how her Asperger's son was *exactly* like mine at ages three and four. Exactly. Somehow she convinced me it was possible, and so I made the call to our regional center for children with disabilities for an evaluation. When I finally got through, the coordinator asked me a few questions, concluded that he was very high functioning, and informed me that "Asperger's is not a qualifying diagnosis." The system is overloaded, and only severely impaired kids can qualify for services.

I was told by friends to fight for services, but I thought that I could help him on my own. I thought that I could make up for all the powerlessness I felt about his heart defect by "fixing" his behavior. I was about to get a PhD in the humanities, which is basically an advanced degree in doing research. I can't do heart surgery, or make his heart magically whole, but if there's one thing I can do, it's research. I researched therapies and tried them out on him: Relationship Development Intervention, dietary changes, nutritional therapies, the Wilbarger technique. I fought unsuccessfully with my insurance company to have occupational therapy covered, and so I started him on a "sensory diet," as sensory integration was (and is) his main issue. I became "autism mom", not "heart mom." By focusing on the autism, I could forget all about his heart. It's not like autism is going to kill him.

Now that he is about to have that surgery he was never supposed to need, I am a "heart mom" again. I am powerless again. There is nothing I can do to fix his heart, to make his circulation better, to keep his lips from being blue when he runs. So I've decided to do what I'm good at: research and planning. I've researched everything, just like I did to prepare for his birth and every part of his life. I made a social story scrapbook of images from the hospital website to help him understand what's going to happen. I found my old online board for heart moms and pestered them with questions: what to expect for recovery, how to explain it to him, and what to say if he asks about dying. Instead of Xanax, I've decided to craft myself into oblivion. For my space-obsessed kid, I have made three pair of space-print boxer shorts, three solar-system painted T-shirts (three sizes too big, of course), a pair of orange knitted wrist-warmers with black rockets on them to wear over the IVs , and a space-print body pillow. I don't know if any of this will help, but at least I feel like I'm doing *something.*

I am caught between extremes: work/family, typical needs/special needs, "heart mom"/"autism mom", "mainstream"/"alternative." But I don't feel like I belong in any of these categories. I'm stumped about where I fit, or if I even care about these cliques of parenting. The most confusing is the spectrum between "mainstream" moms and "crunchy" moms, and between the crunchy special needs moms and the mainstream special needs moms. I'm generally not mainstream enough for most heart moms and not alternative enough for the crunchy moms—especially not for the crunchy special needs moms. My son had more meds in his first two hours of life than most alternative-parented kids have in their first eighteen years. I have fewer qualms about medicating his anxiety as a result. I have every belief that alternative remedies work for many kids on the spectrum. All I know is that he lost two pounds in one month on the gluten-free/casein-free diet,

171

and he could not afford to lose two pounds. We went back to chicken nuggets and quesadillas.

But there are no alternative remedies for heart defects, so the heart community is generally less accepting of alternative parenting. At the time my son was born, very few heart moms were able to breastfeed, mostly due to dictatorial NICU policies regarding feeding that further complicated the difficulties of their babies' medical issues. They had never seen a sling before. Why did I want to hold him all the time? Didn't I know he *needed his rest?* To keep the kids quiet and still when they had echocardiograms, which can take up to forty-five minutes, our cardiologist's office had a basket of lollipops. When my son was two months old, the tech tried to give him a lollipop. Two *months* old. Not two years. I said "No! He's never had sugar, and I don't want him to choke on it!" (Are you *crazy*, lady??? He's *two months* old!) Instead, I whipped out my breast, climbed on the table with him, and leaned over him so he could nurse while she did the scan. She kept bumping my breast with the echo wand, but I really didn't care. It worked. He calmed down, and she got the scan. I breastfed him during his echoes until it didn't keep him calm anymore, when he was around two and a half. But I could always tell that she disapproved. How could I possibly think that breastfeeding was better than a lollipop?

As so many people have told me over the past few years, my son doesn't "look" special needs. Yes, he makes eye contact. No, you can't see the scars unless you look closely. Both of his diagnoses are fairly invisible. If you saw him in a grocery store you'd think he was a pretty typical kid—average height, if skinny, and ravishingly cute if I do say so myself. Not blue, unless he gets cold or overexerted. And if it were a good day, you would probably tell me that he doesn't seem autistic at all to you, in fact, am I sure that he is autistic? You might think something was off if he decided to talk to you, but on a bad day you'd probably assume that his behavior was due to bad parenting. Everybody does. On one occasion, an older woman chastised my husband for letting our son leave the house without a jacket in sixty-degree weather. She advised him to watch "Supernanny" on TV in order to learn how to be a good parent.

The "invisibility" of his diagnoses is both his greatest misfortune and my greatest source of guilt. It may seem odd to say that having "invisible" diagnoses is a misfortune. After all, he can generally "pass" for "normal" in polite society. He usually doesn't experience the awkward glances and patronizing statements that many special needs children (and adults) receive. But I don't want him to "pass." I want everyone to know how hard he tries to say hello to his teacher when she says "good morning" to him, to take turns with his sister, to cope with an unexpected extra errand on the way home, to understand that when he pushes someone, it hurts them. When I told him that the doctors were going to "fix his heart some more" so that he would be able to jump really, really high and not be so tired, he responded, "Like in the bouncy house when I got tired and I had to stop and I was really mad? Okay." He has more resilience than half the adults I know. I don't want his struggles and his achievements, minor though they may seem to a lot of people, to be invisible. Being autistic and having a bum heart are part of who he is. I want everyone to see his scars.

As for the guilt, I'd think that's obvious. He could have been born with a much, much worse heart defect. He could have died. He could have needed more surgeries, a g-tube, a trach, years of physical therapy to learn to walk. He could not have been able to walk at all. He could be non-verbal, not able to feed himself or dress himself. There are other kids in the pages of this book whose lives will probably be more difficult than his. Thinking about these kids is supposed to make me feel blessed or lucky. It doesn't. It makes me feel rotten for thinking that life with him is so difficult, and it makes me feel angry that I'm supposed to believe that special needs is a "gift."

The Iraq war started the night before my son's second surgery. I had been vaguely aware of the buildup to the war as something I would probably be very angry about if I were living in the same world as everyone else. But we were waiting for more surgery. The night the war started, he had been admitted because his implanted shunt had effectively closed, requiring immediate surgery. His oxygen sats were down in the 60s and 70s after a pre-op catheterization test (100% is normal), and he had to be on oxygen and a heart-regulating med. He was three months old. We shared a room with another little girl who was in heart failure and on the transplant list. She was watching *Dora the Explorer* on her TV. We had the news on, but the sound turned down. I remember watching scenes of invasion, bombing, and destruction, but instead of the endless chatter about how short the war would be and how we were saving the Iraqi people from a terrible dictator, the soundtrack was the beep, beep of the machinery, with occasional alarms as his pulse ox dropped back into the 60s. I kept glancing over at Dora and her giant eyes, and at the little girl, staring wide-eyed herself as her mom curled up next to her in the bed.

This is not a "gift." It is not a "blessing."

I am not supposed to feel this way. I am supposed to believe that god only gives me what I can handle, and that god gave me this child because he knew I was the best parent for the job. And, somewhat contradictorily, that he gives me what I need, not what I want. I know religion is a great source of comfort to many families with special needs children. I do not make light of their beliefs any more than I want to negate the challenges that ordinary parents face. We special needs parents are always expected to put a happy face on our lives. "Oh, yes, the surgery went great! He had a bit of trouble with bleeding, but you know, it's okay *now.*" Or, "Oh, she is transferring schools again; we're sure this new one *that is over an hour away* will work out much better." People want to hear that we're dealing just fine. They want to know that we believe that having a special needs child is a gift, so they feel less guilty that their own children are healthy, able-bodied, and typical. There but for the grace of god, you know.

The guilt that parents of typical healthy children feel is my guilt too. When I read on the heart moms' Internet boards about another heart child who did not make it through a surgery, I know that I am no different from other parents of healthy kids.

My child lived.

If there is one thing I have learned from my experience, it's how to respond compassionately to parents of special needs children. I know never to say what a mom at a playgroup recently said to me, that her daughter was about to have dental surgery to save her front teeth and so she knew what I was going through. I'm sorry, but unless it involves heart-lung bypass, she does not. Other well-intentioned people have told me that he's going to be fine, that Children's in Boston is the best pediatric cardiac hospital in the world, and that they do this surgery every day. Intellectually I know this is true, but it's not what I need to hear. He might *not* be fine, though that isn't the way the mini-series usually ends. I always cringe when people tell me how strong or brave I am. My mom offers this praise regularly, saying that she could never have handled what I have been through. I always tell her that I'm no stronger or braver than she is. I just don't have a choice. We are moms, we do what needs to be done, and we try not to end up hospitalized ourselves in the process.

My helpful friends just listen. I seem to have a burning need to lay out the whole story in all its gory details because it somehow makes it both more real and less terrifying. They don't look too horrified or uncomfortable when I talk. They nod sympathetically. And when I'm done, they say,

"Wow, that is really shitty." (It helps when they swear. It adds gravity to the situation.) They say, "I'm so sorry. I brought you some chocolate." They bring meals. They take the kids outside in the yard so my husband and I can just sit on the couch together, alone. They don't wait for me to ask for help. And I feel like I can never repay them for their kindness.

Epilogue

I just dropped my son off at summer camp for the first time since his surgery exactly two weeks ago. That's right, two weeks. It appears that he channeled all of his rage over the insufferable sticky tape and tubes attached to his body into the fastest recovery his doctors had ever seen. He was out of the ICU within twenty-four hours and released from the hospital in four days. Four days! A bit premature, they said, but he was being "hostile" to the nurses and they felt he would recover better in a "safe" environment. (Their words, ha.) Though he will need to have another non-surgical procedure in a few months, the surgery itself went very well, and his heart, according to his cardiologist, is now "happy." I hope it stays happy. I hope my friends know that even though I can't repay them, and can't express how much their help means to me, I am grateful for it. And I hope that people who don't know what to say can realize that listening, and not saying anything at all, is the best thing they can do.

A View through the Woods
by Christy Everett

To the Woman Who Stares and Looks Away,

I want to tell you, "Don't be afraid"—but truthfully, I'm terrified too. Sometimes I want to be the one walking past, in your comfortable shoes, with no more than a twenty-second stare into this life of mine. This life that is not what you think it is, not even close, so don't feel sorry for me, just slow down, and listen for awhile.

◆ ◆ ◆

I'm crying by the second page, but I keep reading the book aloud. It's called *Nick Joins In*, by Joe Lasker, about a boy in a wheelchair who prepares to go to school for the first time and wonders if the other kids will like him. The boy's fears echo my own as I prepare to send my son to his first day of preschool.

Will they think he's a baby because he crawls? Will his walker and braces scare them? When Elias doesn't look into their eyes will they think he's ignoring them? Will they understand what he does and does not see? Will they grow impatient with his pauses, with his processing delay? Will they understand what he says or become frustrated when his words don't make sense? Will he be excluded from their games? Will they laugh at him? Will they point and stare? ... Will he learn that he's different and that different is not always "OK"?

Elias loses interest in the book and squirms from my lap to explore the basement where I sit in the gliding rocking chair that used to be in his room before we rearranged it to make more space for playing.

I stay seated in the wooden rocker and keep reading. Elias pulls playing cards out of the deck and spreads them across the green carpet, folding the Queen of Spades in half and chewing on the edge. I keep reading. The teacher in the book lets the class ask the boy questions. *Why are you in a chair? Why do you wear braces? Why can't you walk?* My voice breaks and I heave as I read but I can't stop. Can't stop reading it aloud. Can't stop crying. Not little tears but full body sobs. Alligator tears. Dinosaur drops.

As I read on, I wonder why the teacher doesn't let the boy ask the other kids questions when they are through interrogating him. It's only fair. As if any of this was fair.

"Mama's just a little sad," I tell Elias between sobs and he repeats my words. *Mama a yittle ad.* "Mommy's crying." *Mommy kying.*

I keep reading. Keep heaving.

Elias just smiles and cruises from the desk to the bookshelf with dusty books about glacier travel, long-distance hiking, and white-water rafting, the bookshelf to the desk with piles of insurance paperwork and therapy notes, the desk to the milk-stained rocking chair where he smiles at his Mama's tears.

◆ ◆ ◆

I want you to know that sometimes, you're right, it just sucks. I'm not a big fan of playgroups or clusters of moms. I hate hearing birth stories, especially the easy kind. The curious stare of a baby can make my stomach drop. I clench my jaw when I hear: "He just got up and started walking at nine months." It's not that I don't like women; I miss the camaraderie of a girls' night out. It's just that I can't play along anymore. I can't share anecdotes. Can't compare. And I don't want to hear how strong I am. How I'm the chosen one.

"Let me tell you what my son can't do," I want to say when the conversation turns to the accomplishments of our offspring, which it does, it always does. As if the moment we give birth or adopt we forget about our interest in art, literature, politics, relationships, sports, sex, or gossip, and resort to comparing our babies' bowel movements. We babble about head movement, tummy time, and noises that resemble words. We all do it, even those of us who still can't believe we're mothers.

But some of us can't keep up with the conversation—and its not that

we live in a different country, we live next door to you, in the house
you don't want to look at because you can't imagine living here. You
can't imagine being me, the mother of a boy with wheels, a boy who
can't fully see. You want to either pity me or place me in a tower. You
want to think this was God's plan. Or that my son chose me for my
natural parenting abilities. You want to find special traits about me
to put distance between us so that your next child could never have
special needs. Never. Not you. You couldn't do it—you think.

◆ ◆ ◆

"I'm sorry what did you just say?" I ask the school psychologist who in-terviews Nick and me during Elias's assessment by the Anchorage School District for special needs preschool. For almost two hours, we answer questions, as the evaluators—a physical therapist, occupational therapist, speech therapist, school psychologist, nurse, and vision educator—ask Elias to sort, match, color, roll, slide, string, drink, eat, and do a variety of other tasks to determine his level of need.

After we navigated down the long drab hallway with tight corners, and walked into the cramped windowless room, the psychologist ushered Nick and me to seats at the card table. The PT guided Elias over to a small wooden chair by a toy-filled table set up next to us. I wanted to sit down with him, in my own small chair, to explain that balance is an issue, that we aren't sure what he sees, but I didn't have a chance to say a thing to these strangers before they started silently interrogating my son.

My baby boy.

I understand why, it's a standardized assessment. He may be in diapers but he's entering the world of public school. The world of evaluations and tests. I know I won't be able to speak for him forever. I know all his life he'll be evaluated by people that don't know how precious his is, but it doesn't matter if your child is trying out for the Olympics or for special needs pre-school it hurts to watch others judge your kid.

"I'm sorry, can you ask me that again?" I ask the psychologist, and once again I try to listen to her question—*How old was he when he first sat up?*—to give her my focus, instead of eavesdropping on the therapists as they interact with my son.

It's not like any of this is new for us. Elias has undergone all kinds of evaluations and tests since his days in the NICU. Beginning with an Apgar score of 0,0,3, he has constantly been assessed. Even so, it's all I can do not to cry as I watch these professionals follow my son with their pens and pencils scribbling, their brows furrowed.

"Oh, you're all done with this toy." One of them says when Elias stops following their directions on how it should be played.

No, I think, *he just needs to turn it around, to touch every side, to see what happens if he puts it upside down, even if it's not supposed to work that way.*

"Um, can you repeat the question?" I'm trying to stay with the interview, to be a good parent, to comply—but Elias sits only a few feet from my lap, from my arms that want to scoop him up and hold him close as we escape from the over-crowded room. I want to run down the long hallway with its sharp turns, and leap through the front door into the crisp outside air, where we all squint when we face the sun.

◆ ◆ ◆

I'm no different from you, not really. I wasn't born to do this, not chosen because of my wealth of compassion, patience, or grace. I looked away once, just like you—and I still don't naturally embrace all differences. I still sigh with relief over what my son can do. I still compare him to other kids who are even less able and wonder about their Mama's days. What are their late-night worries? What do they dream?

I don't always embrace this life of therapy visits, doctor lists, and enough paperwork to wallpaper every house on my street. Sometimes all the pudgy toddlers running around the mall make me mad. I find myself hating pregnant women, and driving my nails into my palms to keep from crying when friends with able-bodied children try to compare their challenges to mine.

Instead of seeing Elias's repetitive way of communicating as cute, he frustrates me. I want him to answer a question straight. I want him to look at my face. I want him to connect but with his eyes, not his sticky hands. I don't want him to hold onto my pants to stand up.

I want space.

And I hate myself for being frustrated at him for things beyond his control. As if he planned any of this. Pummeled by my own son's brain. I'm scared about what it means to have this adorable little boy grow up into a man who may never be able to care for himself. I'm scared that he may not be able to communicate in a way that I need him to because god damn it why should one little guy be burdened with so many challenges: breath, vision, movement, growth, please no, not communication too.

I'm not just scared for Elias but sad for the little girl I used to be who sang into her bathroom mirror and was sure she'd be someone someday. For the young woman who moved to Alaska with money in the bank and nothing but possibilities ahead. For the woman, like you, who could choose to look away.

◆ ◆ ◆

Three teenage boys, dressed in black with chains, multiple facial piercings, and elongated ear holes, hold the doors to the mall open for Elias and me.

As they watch Elias, their faces change, and they stand there waiting as he maneuvers his walker not around but over every crack and bump in the sidewalk. Elias calls them speed bumps and will go out of his way to find uneven ground. Like the teens holding the doors, Elias will not take the straight path.

And by the way they smile, with not just their lips but their eyes, instead of the Goth exterior that usually frightens me, I see the little boy in each of them.

As we walk through the double doors they hold open, with arms outstretched, I thank them and head toward the elevator, our ritual ride after Elias's swim therapy in the mall's athletic club. We may be the only regular mall visitors who never come here to shop, or to cruise for companions, but to ride.

An athletic gray-haired man with one wooden crutch waits at the elevator with Elias and me. He smiles at Elias who bounces, locking and unlocking his knees, as he stands in front of the metal doors with his walker, and says "abater" over and over again.

"Is he yours or are you watching him?" the man asks.

"He's mine." I touch the top of Elias's head and run my fingers through his wispy blonde hair.

"He may have challenges, but he's awfully cute."

"Thanks." I smile.

And then this stranger gives me a gift, a way of asking Elias's story, which breaches the perceived distance between us all.

He says, "I know I have a lot of challenges. What are some of his?"

◆ ◆ ◆

I'm not telling you all this to be fixed or pitied, not even as a cry for help, but to tell you I'm not always strong. Not always over-flowing with love and kindness. And not so different from you.

And maybe I'm telling you this because I saw your freckled face, your doe eyes that darted south when you noticed me watching you watch my son. I can still see you and though I don't know you, I do. In you, I see my own reflection, and that of women everywhere who strive to live up to expectations we'll never reach. Who gauge our success based on where we fall in the pecking order of perfection, racing towards an icon of motherhood, of womanhood, that does not exist. That will never exist. And only promotes feelings of insecurity, jealousy, bitterness, and utter exhaustion.

I'm tired of feeling like a bad parent because I don't work on Elias's needs 24/7, because I don't have all his paperwork at my fingertips, because sometimes my disabled son annoys me, because I want him to nap longer, because I want time to myself, because I can't fix him, because I even want to, because I don't have all the answers, because I can't always understand him, because I need help sometimes.

Because I see him through your eyes and, just for a moment, I want to walk away.

◆ ◆ ◆

Two first-grade boys sit on a small wooden bench outside the office of Turnagain Elementary and watch Elias and me as we enter the hallway for his morning preschool class. One of them stares at Elias's walker with a quizzical look. The other one smiles.

The first boy, the skeptical one, asks, "Why does he use that?"

181

"To help him walk," I say.

"He can't walk?" the boy responds, in a tone reserved for shocking insights of the negative kind. *What do you mean there's no such thing as Santa Claus?*

"No, not yet." I say, channeling my inner yogi, the part of me that holds nothing but respect for curious judgmental boys.

The smiley one says: "When he's a kid, he'll probably be able to walk because he's just a preschooler."

I smile at him and say, "We hope so."

"Why can't he walk?" asks the other boy who has yet to smile but stares at my son with a wrinkled nose.

"Well," I pause. "It's kinda complicated... His brain has a hard time talking to his muscles."

As I say this, Elias wheels over to the boys, lets go of his walker, holds onto their thighs and says, "Hi!"

The smiley one leans his head down and says, "Hi! What's your name?" The other boy leans back, wide-eyed.

"Yia."

"His name is Elias," I clarify.

Leaning even closer to Elias and looking right at him, the friendly boy says, "My name is Jose and this is Willy." He points to his neighbor, the blonde boy with pursed lips.

"Can he walk without it?" asks Willy, as Elias cruises across their laps to the edge of the bench.

"He can do what he's doing now, hold onto things and cruise, but if he lets go, he loses his balance."

"Does he fall down?"

"Yeah, he falls down a lot—but he's pretty tough."

Still no smile from this boy who talks to me instead of my son.

"How does he get around at home? On his knees?" he asks.

"Yeah, he still crawls."

Jose smiles at Elias and asks in a singsong voice, "Can you show me how you crawl?"

Elias, as if we practiced this, moves to the floor and crawls around the corner of the hallway.

And Willy, the judging skeptic, finally smiles.

Both boys get up to follow my son who crawls towards his preschool classroom.

Jose reaches his hand down to Elias and says, "Here, I'll help you up."

As Elias stands and struggles to find his center of balance, almost falling, forcing Jose to pull him up with all his strength, Jose says to me: "I can tell he has a hard time walking."

I reach for Elias's other hand and he stands between us, steady—together the boy and I walk him to his classroom. Before we enter the doorway, I peek behind me and see Willy watching us, still smiling.

◆ ◆ ◆

And maybe if we didn't spend our lives comparing and competing we'd believe more in ourselves as mothers. If we didn't have growth charts, milestones, and test scores we'd never weigh Elias's differences as less than, never see him as damaged, never peek and look away. The truth is, I sometimes find the general tasks of parenthood—waking, feeding, changing, responding, comforting, teaching—more challenging than visual impairment, lung damage, and developmental delay. Sometimes preparing a healthy breakfast, every morning, without fail, the relentless routine of daily care, the drudgery of endless repetition, is worse than walking through a grocery store with a legally blind boy and his walker. There's delight in the abnormal, in the unexpected appearance of a little blonde boy with wheels.

Sometimes I think I'm the lucky one, because Elias teaches me to slow down, to jump out of the race, to be exactly where I am instead of running towards an elusive finish line of perfection. He gives me a Get Out Of Competition Free card. An "out" to the My Kids More Talented Than Yours game show we play. Because when you almost lose your child, but don't, the moment still matters—a flash of eye contact, the sound of the word "mama," a warm cheek with the familiar scent of buttered popcorn and honeysuckle.

◆ ◆ ◆

It's been one of those mornings. Can't find the car keys or Elias's snow pants, can't seem to walk out the door without walking right back in for my cell phone, his water bottle, the handicapped parking pass. We arrive at preschool forty minutes late. Ms. Robin stands by the door ushering the kids into a line to walk to the library. She smiles when she sees us.

"Who wants to walk with Elias?" she asks, as I hang Elias's blue coat in the cubby he shares with Logan.

A chorus of "meeee's" responds as hands race to be the tallest. His peers stand on their tippy toes, waving, as if she asked who wants ice cream, or who wants to meet Elmo.

Not every kid wants to trail behind the others, next to the smallest one who often just stands in the middle of the hallway with his walker, smiling and looking around, saying "big kids" and bouncing when a line of older kids trails past, but the enthusiasm of those who do, makes the frustrations of my botched morning disappear.

As I walk outside into the below-freezing February air, I find myself humming part of a familiar refrain, from a song I can't fully remember— *And in the morning when I rise, you bring a tear of joy to my eyes, and tell me, everything . . . is gonna be alright*—like a chant, a promise, a prayer.

◆ ◆ ◆

You can't really get it with a glimpse. You need to look longer, more deeply, to understand. I can hear you saying you don't want to be rude. You don't want to stare. But you were staring, until I looked your way, and then your eyes couldn't meet mine.

Maybe you want to reach out but you just don't know how to approach, what to say.

If you asked, "How old is he?"—because that's the first question we always ask, how old, as if a number can contain a child, as if age makes us understand—there was a time when I wouldn't have told you the truth anyways. I lied regularly when he was younger to avoid the look of surprise the questioner always failed to hide: "But he's so small?"

I lie less now that he's three, now that he's cognitively beginning to understand.

You could ask me his name—Elias—that's a start, a solid place to begin. Maybe if you asked me, I would tell you the whole truth, not

184

just his name or age, but his history. Maybe as we waited in line to empty the contents of our carts, I'd spill Elias's story.

I'd tell you he arrived breached, four months early, weighed one pound twelve ounces, and his heart stopped at birth. I'd tell you he spent seven weeks on a respirator and underwent heart and brain surgery before he weighed two pounds. I'd tell you the doctors didn't expect him to survive, call him my miracle baby, make you forget about the ice cream in your cart.

Maybe we'd continue to talk on our way to our cars. I'd tell you how happy he is, how adaptable, how funny, how brave. In response to your attempts to draw Elias's blue eyes towards yours, I'd tell you he has a condition called nystagmus that keeps him from communicating with his eyes. That he's considered legally blind but he sees. He knows colors, people's faces, the pictures in his books.

"He also has cerebral palsy which is just a broad term for damage to the brain that affects muscle control," I might say as Elias kicks his skinny legs in the cart by the back of our truck, excited to be outside, doing errands, with people, alive.

Maybe you'd work up the courage to ask, "Do they know if he'll ever walk?" and I'd tell you we don't know. That nobody can predict the pliability of a preemie's brain. I'd tell you we've lived in the waiting room since his birth, our pockets loaded with questions, and nothing but time to give us a response.

You might smile and say, "He sure is cute." Or if I pulled him out of the cart to cruise around with his walker and you saw him navigate parked cars, potholes and curbs, you'd say, "Wow, he's really good with that thing!"

And I'd say, "You should see him lead me through the woods."

My Friend Christine

by Marcy Sheiner

In May of 2007, the U.S. Supreme Court ruled in a case related to the education of children with disabilities (*Winkelman v. Parma*), that parents contesting their child's IEP (Individualized Educational Program) can advocate for their children in a court of law rather than having to hire an attorney.

Jacob Winkleman is a student with autism whose parents disagreed with their district's IEP for their son, and chose to place him in a private school. They petitioned a federal district court to get reimbursed for tuition, and lost. In appealing the decision, the Winklemans chose to act as their own attorneys, having already spent three years and $30,000 in legal fees on a household income of less than $40,000 per year.

The U.S. Court of Appeals for the Sixth Circuit dismissed their appeal, finding that IDEA (the Individuals with Disabilities Education Act) does not expressly provide for the right of a parent to represent the interests of his/her child in federal court. Neither could they represent themselves, because IDEA provides for the rights of the child, not the parents.

Because my son didn't receive the benefit of the IDEA until his senior year of high school, which is when it was passed, I myself managed to escape this particular aspect of parenting a child with a disability—about which I'm not entirely unhappy. I did enough fighting with doctors, social workers, and everyone else who tried to take charge of his life, so I know what it's like to be treated as if I'm his adversary rather than his advocate.

Assisted by Legal Rights Services in Ohio, the Winklemans took their case to the Supreme Court, which ruled in their favor. The Court recognized that the whole purpose of IDEA would be undermined if those who couldn't afford legal fees were unable to appeal such decisions. Whereas the circuit court had ruled that in special education cases the injured party is the child, not the parents, the Supreme Court stated that the rights of the children and parents in these cases are "inextricably interwoven." The wording of the decision alone is itself cause for celebration. Considering the abuse that parents have suffered at the hands of professionals, the Court's acknowledgement that our interests are congruent with those of our kids is quite a sea change. Far too often parents, especially mothers, were and *still* are seen by doctors, social workers and shrinks as an obstacle to be overcome rather than advocates for the child's welfare. Because we demand the best for our kids, some of the people who work with them view us as impediments. There's no denying that with a parent on alert, the jobs of these people can become more difficult: they have to do more than the bare minimum. Disability advocates expect the Winkleman decision to have far-reaching affects on parents and children with disabilities. At this point, it's too soon to tell exactly how and how many.

As soon as I heard about the decision, I couldn't wait to talk to my friend Christine. I was eager to hear her reaction to the news that the Supreme Court of the United States officially pronounced our needs and the needs of our children to be *inextricably interwoven.*

While I didn't know Christine back when her son Billy started having seizures, from her description I feel like I was there. She was living in Greenwich Village, a single mother of two—Billy was two, his older sister five or six—a beatnik morphing into a hippie. They were walking down the street, and Billy, like any two-year-old insistent on walking by himself, lagged behind. Christine turned around to check on him and saw him lying on the sidewalk having a grand mal seizure.

Theoretically, seizures themselves are not harmful. Theoretically, a person can have a grand mal seizure and get up in a few minutes dazed and confused, but functional. To anyone watching, however, a grand mal seizure is terrifying: in a typical incident the body jackknifes repeatedly, stiff arms and legs scissoring. The person loses consciousness; the eyes close, the mouth opens, the tongue sometimes hangs out. Many moons ago, the big fear was of the tongue falling back and blocking the airways, so people used to stick things into the seizing person's mouth as a preventative. After several decades of broken teeth, bitten fingers, and near strangulation from pieces of cloth or wooden spoons, medical advice changed: now we're supposed to gently move the seizing person onto his or her side so gravity can do the job by allowing the tongue to hang loosely.

On that day of Billy's first seizure, Christine wasn't aware of any of this. It must have looked like her baby boy, lying in the middle of a Manhattan sidewalk violently shaking, was dying. The event marked the first day of a life spent among doctors, social workers, physical therapists, speech therapists, emergency rooms, and special educators. Most people take family privacy for granted, but when you have a child with so many needs, your life is open to the kind of scrutiny that few lives can withstand. Your habits and parenting practices, from diet to discipline, are poked and prodded by strangers with PhDs. Parents of disabled kids are subject to an inordinate amount of criticism and advice, much of it contradictory. The effect on many parents is an erosion of self-confidence, insecurity about parenting skills, and free-floating paranoia. I know that's the way I felt every time some hospital nurse grilled me about my infant son's diet, a perpetual frown on her face, or, later on, when a school guidance counselor questioned my disciplinary methods. "What are the consequences of his actions?" I remember one particularly annoying counselor asking about my six-year-old. Truth be told, my son hadn't yet given me reason to discipline him, but to say so, I felt, was somehow an admission I'd fallen down on the job.

After Billy's first seizure, more kept coming. It sometimes happens that none of the many toxins devised to control seizures do the job; unfortunately, Billy was one such case. Medications were tried and their side effects endured without success. Throughout his life Billy, went through periods of greater or lesser seizure activity—but he was never seizure-free for any length of time. While an occasional seizure might not do harm, relentless shocks to the brain exert a heavy toll: Billy lost whatever speech he'd developed, and eventually he lost the ability to walk unassisted, to care for himself on a basic level; he was diagnosed as having a little-known disorder called Sturges Weber syndrome, and became mentally retarded (the current P.C. term is "developmentally disabled").

Christine tried everything. She investigated expensive schools, alternative teaching methods, biofeedback, and nutrition. For several years, Billy was placed on a rigorous daily schedule of physical therapy assisted by a team of volunteers, most of them friends and family. Short of lobotomy—which *is* one treatment still used for seizures—she considered everything. She saw improvements when nobody else did, and spoke of a future for Billy that nobody else thought possible. While the rest of us found alternate ways to communicate with Billy, Christine claimed to understand his sounds. He'd say something like "L'Ha!" and she'd reply, "No Billy, we can't go fishing today."

Fishing. Christine took Billy fishing in nearby streams and rivers; once, they even went out on a deep-sea fishing boat. She took him on beach vacations, city weekends, and to carnivals, street fairs, and festivals. In our small town, no community event would have been the same without the two of them: Billy in his football helmet, leaning on and eventually towering over Christine, who'd make sure nothing exciting or interesting escaped his attention. Under her tutelage he became a rock fan to rival Jack Black in *School of Rock*—he owns a staggering number of stereo components, and together they'd play the Rolling Stones or the Cars, the volume turned up full blast. Whenever we crossed the Tappan Zee Bridge on the drive into New York City, Christine would make sure something wonderful was on the tape deck. Crossing the bridge on a sunny morning with Billy, Rod Stewart singing "Maggie May" at maximum volume, was one of the peak experiences of my life. I loathe sentimentality about disability, but peak experiences do seem to occur around Billy. When the phenomenon *We Are the World* came out, I videotaped it, and sat with Billy cross-legged on the floor in front of my television to watch. As each performer appeared— Stevie Wonder, Bruce Springsteen, Bob Dylan—he let out an ecstatic howl, pointing at the screen, rocking back and forth, barely able to contain his pleasure. Another peak experience.

Back then, Christine was the only mother of a child with disabilities that I knew, and we became close friends. Most of the people in our circle were former hippies turned New Age-ish entrepreneurs—the issues in their lives were very different than ours. She was and is the only person for whom I would, and did, do anything, no questions asked. She's the only person I know intimately to whom I don't have to explain myself: she understands—no, she *knows*—me and our family's dynamics. She's the only one of my friends who's never once said anything insulting or offensive to me regarding parenthood or the way I raised my kids. Most importantly, whenever the shit hits the fan, I have only to think of Christine and my problems pale in comparison. When I feel like screaming at my son, or being less than loving towards him, I have only to picture Christine and Billy to change my mindset. Watching her all these years has shown me what real strength and courage look like.

I used to call her a saint—which made her crazy. She taught me it isn't saintly to take care of someone you love. I should have known better, considering I'd had similar experiences: when my son was an infant, other mothers would bounce their healthy babies on their laps and say, thinking it a compliment, "I could never do what you're doing." What I heard was: *I'm not like you. My baby isn't like yours. You're not normal.* I knew even then that any chance occurrence could push them into my situation, and that they'd endure, just as I had. Besides, what choice did I have?

Now forty-five, Billy no longer sits on the floor watching rock videos. He doesn't even sit. For the past few years, he's been confined to a hospital bed in Christine's living room, eating through tubes. After the events leading to his present condition, Christine had to fight the hospital administration for the right to take him home rather than put him into a nursing facility. She learned how to operate his ventilator and obtained round-the-clock nursing care, yet even when she fulfilled the requirements of these regulations, she had to go to court for the right to take Billy home. A lot of people, me included, might not have done all that: we might not have wanted someone requiring such a high level of care in our living rooms. Christine hardly gets a break these days; she rarely even leaves the house. Yet she'd rather have Billy home, where he can see family and friends and be mentally and emotionally stimulated, than shut away in a facility with sick people. She'd rather deal with the tedium and difficulty of caring for him than with the depression, guilt, and anxiety she'd feel if he lived in an institution.

It was the same during Billy's adolescence when, on the advice of professionals, he lived for a few years in a nearby group home. She worried about him constantly, and fought to get more flair and color into Billy's life than the home could or would provide. Christine's been insistent on getting Billy what she believes he needs rather than what the county or state deems adequate, and she has a reputation as a troublemaker (of which she's proud). During most of Billy's life, she was alone in this struggle, but in the 1980s, parents of children with disabilities rose up en masse and demanded rights for their kids, plus a few things that might be seen as privileges. This parents' rights movement—moving, unsentimental and assertive—is responsible for changes in legislation, education, attitude, and accommodations for children with disabilities.

When I told Christine about the *Winkleman* decision and its wording, she reacted exactly as I'd expected: she gasped and giggled—she has the most endearing giggle—when I said the phrase *inextricably interwoven*. With those words, the Supreme Court acknowledged an essential fact of life for families with disability, one previously ignored or maligned: the welfare of the parent of a child with a disability depends on the welfare of the child, and vice versa. That's why mothers of kids with disabilities aren't saints, or even particularly admirable for doing the things we do. That's why Christine puts so much energy into Billy's well-being. Ultimately it comes down to selfishness, or rather, self-preservation. To quote a character on *Law and Order*, "You're only as happy as your unhappiest kid."

Scout

by Robert Rummel-Hudson

When I was a kid, my heroes were always explorers. I had no use for sports figures or entertainers, and I wasn't sophisticated enough to idolize writers or composers just yet. (Turns out most of them were freaks anyway.) I only had space in my hero worship for those men and women who set out from their comfortable places and struck a path into the unknown. They didn't even have to be successful, either. They mostly weren't entirely successful, come to think of it. Captain James Cook was regarded as a living god by some of the South Pacific civilizations he found, but was killed by grumpy Hawaiians in the end. Amelia Earhart fearlessly took on the aerial circumnavigation of the globe but then mysteriously disappeared, probably eaten by the Pacific Ocean. And the South Pole gave us Robert Scott, who *almost* became the first to the pole and then *almost* got back without freezing to death, and Sir Ernest Shackleton, whose expedition never even made it to solid ground before his ship was crushed by the pack ice, but who managed to save his entire crew through skilled leadership and crazy good luck.

Success was never my yardstick for my explorer heroes. I simply admired them for setting out into unknown worlds, usually with only a vague idea of where they were going or how they might get back.

Turns out, I was destined to join them.

When my daughter Schuyler was born eight years ago, she inherited two significant things from me, at least one of which was genetic. That thing was the rare brain malformation called bilateral perisylvian polymicrogyria, now identified in maybe a thousand patients worldwide, which has robbed her of the ability to speak.

The other thing she got from me was a love of the unknown and an inchoate desire to explore it. For years, Schuyler has occupied an internal world mostly her own. Before she began to break through the walls that kept her from communicating with us; about three years ago, Schuyler spent most of her time in her lonely world. Now that she's using an electronic speech device and sign language, she walks in my world, too, more and more as time goes on. But when she plays and sings to herself and converses with her toys and dolls, and most of all when she dreams, she returns to that secret place.

Sometimes, she takes me with her. I don't understand most of what I experience there, but I try to keep up the best I can.

Fathers and daughters often have unique relationships.

Mine with Schuyler is very different from the one that she has with her mother. For Schuyler, Julie represents home and safety and security. My job is different. For Schuyler, I am a sidekick and a co-adventurer. My relationship with her is complicated. I often don't completely comprehend it myself, and yet it remains my most cherished enigma.

From what I can tell, three primary types of inhabitants live in Schuyler's internal world. There are mermaids, there are fairies, and there are monsters. Variations exist in that population, of course; dinosaurs are a subset of monsters after all, and pirates show up from time to time, just to keep things interesting. But for the most part, mermaids and fairies satisfy her need for girly friends (she hates being called a princess, I'm happy to say), and monsters are her best friends of all. She may have a figurative monster living in her brain, affecting her life in sobering, real-world ways, but when Schuyler imagines monsters, she thinks of them as her friends.

A few months ago, she saw a monster in a toy store, which caught her imagination and stayed with her. She asked about it every day for a week until I finally broke down and bought it for her. It wasn't a cute monster at all. It was, in fact, a large, snarly, drooling Rancor from the *Star Wars* movies, all claws and teeth and menace. She may have thought it was the monster from *Cloverfield*, a film that I had shown her in a moment of stellar parenting and whom she had also declared as her friend. (*"I love him!"* she told me on her device. *"He lives in New York!"*)

When she got her new monster, she named him Sam. She declared that *"Sam no eat friends,"* which was of course a relief to me. When she played with Sam at home, she stood one of her little Tinkerbell figures gently in the upturned palm of his monstrous clawed hand. *"She is girlfriend,"* she said.

The more time Schuyler and I spend together, particularly during the summer, the more conspiratorial we become, which is nice, at least for us.

When she brought Sam the Monster in the car with us, she asked for me to play the "monster mix" I'd made for her on my iPod, consisting of music from monster movies like *Cloverfield* and *King Kong* and *Jaws* and *War of the Worlds*. We drove along, pretending to devour the people we saw on the sidewalks.

"Daddy!" she said, not on her device but in her excited little girl's voice, which she prefers to use when she can. It comes out mostly in Martian, but many of her verbal words are often intelligible to those of us who spend the most time with her. "Eat that guy!"

Which of course I did. When she ate that guy, she only consumed half, handing me the rest. Schuyler is a very generous monster.

Schuyler often conjures up random questions, the same kind that I suppose most kids her age come up with. Because so much of her world is internal, however, I usually don't know what inspires her to ask them. Last fall, Schuyler began asking about death. She originally brought it up in a question about my father (whom she now believes resides in every cemetery we drive past), but after I answered her questions honestly, she became fascinated by the topic in general.

One night, while we were playing, Schuyler informed me that I was dead. She even made up a sign for it. Her hand touched her forehead, similar to the American Sign Language sign for sick, but then it flew off like, well, your soul, I guess. She instructed me to lie motionless on my bed while she concocted a ceremony of her very own, singing a jaunty little tune to herself as she went back and forth from her room to fetch supplies and mourners.

If you should attend my funeral in the hopefully distant future, here's what you might expect from Schuyler. First, she ritualistically waved various pieces of plastic jewelry over my head. The gesture seemed oddly Catholic to me, ignorant agnostic that I am. She then took a play fork and offered me invisible food. But if I tried to eat it, she gave me a stern "No!"

"Daddy, you're dead," she reminded me.

After I explained to her that at a funeral, someone gives a speech to say goodbye to the person and tell why they'll be missed, she wisely selected her teddy bear Jasper, the elder statesman of her toy animals, to put my life in perspective. He chose to deliver my eulogy in Martian, of course.

I know this all sounds wildly creepy, and I must admit, it wasn't my first choice of a game to play, especially not two weeks after my fortieth birthday. But I was proud of her for asking about such a rough concept, and for continuing to turn it over in her head as she tried to make sense of it. Like so many other things in her life, she didn't find it sad, only puzzling. At the end of our game, Schuyler decided she wanted to be dead, too, and joined me on my slab, giggling in a very uncorpselike manner. The concept of death was complicated, to be sure, but Schuyler's interpretation of it was clear and simple. She didn't need words to grapple with it, only play.

Sometimes Schuyler becomes upset, and our inability to always know why is both frustrating and a little scary. It's hard for her, I know. She doesn't express frustration with her situation very often, but sometimes she just can't say what needs to be said, even when she goes to her speech device. That's when Schuyler becomes angry at her condition.

We received a call one day from the teacher of her special class, the one filled with kids like her who use assistive technology to communicate. When Schuyler got off the bus at school that morning, her teacher said, she was in a bad mood already. Something was wrong, that much was clear, but she wasn't able to tell her teachers or the school nurse exactly what it was. She was able to express that she didn't feel well, but she was struggling to tell them exactly why. Finally, they determined that she had a headache. They figured it out because she told the school nurse, in her own way.

She had the nurse put a band-aid on her head.

I've seen it so many times, I've watched her work her way around communications obstacles in different ways, sometimes imaginative and sometimes crude but always effective. It's a wonder to watch, fascinating to see how her brain works.

One of the stories that I shared in my memoir but hadn't ever actually told anyone before took place on the evening that we got Schuyler's diagnosis, back in the summer of 2003, roughly a thousand years ago. I had to go straight from the doctor's office to a meeting at work, where I mostly just sat in the back and pretended to watch a PowerPoint presentation while my heart broke into jagged little shards. When the meeting was over, I stopped by my desk and Googled "polymicrogyria," and when I'd read quite enough, I left for home.

On the way, I saw an old Gothic-looking church that I passed every day, and something inside me just snapped. I pulled over, got out of the car and, in my anger and my hurt, I dropped to the ground and offered up to God what was perhaps the most sincere prayer I ever prayed in my life. It was a ridiculous prayer, but it was one that I meant with everything I was.

I asked God to take Schuyler's monster from her and give it to me instead. I probably didn't ask so much as demand it, really. I was thirty-five years old. I'd said enough in my lifetime. *Give it to me and let her walk away free of it.*

I know how silly that sounds now. But at that moment, I wanted it so much and meant it so sincerely that as soon as I said it, I sat quietly for a moment, waiting for it to happen, bracing myself for the transformation that I knew was coming, that *had* to come, because I wished for it so hard and because it was fair. It was an absolutely fair trade.

God said no. And so I cry for my lost faith when no one's looking, and I hold a grudge against God, because he was wrong to say no.

Now I dream of Schuyler, but not as she is. In my dreams, she speaks to me, always comforting me, telling me that everything's going to be okay. I've written about that before, but something has only recently occurred to me about these dreams, something that I never noticed before.

In my dreams, Schuyler speaks to me, but I almost never speak back to her.

Perhaps the Schuyler in my dreams is the little girl that she would be if God had said yes and had silenced me in exchange for her freedom. Some dreams deserve to come true; some prayers deserve to be answered. I still haven't made peace with the fact that they haven't, but I'm working on it, I suppose.

Schuyler's dreams have always fascinated me, mostly because of all the parts of her life that we are occasionally privy to, her dreams remain the most unreachable. She has never shared them with us in any meaningful way; I can only think of one time, after she was troubled by a bad dream about monsters of some kind. But even then, she didn't seem frightened, only very sad, and she wouldn't share any details.

That's how it is with Schuyler. As she gets older, some doors open up, and we can see parts of her world that were closed off to us before. But she can slam them closed whenever she wants, and sometimes she makes that choice, particularly when she's pissed off. She stops using her device, crosses her arms in frustration, and starts jabbering in a stream of Schuylerese that is two parts Martian and one part whine. Schuyler can be a pill when she chooses to be.

Even when she's happy, though, there are doors seemingly forever barred to us. Her dreams are her own, and so are her songs. She breaks into little melodies of her own creation, with lyrics that go forever untranslated. I'm learning not to ask her about her music, as that is the fastest way to make her stop singing. When Schuyler sings, you listen and you take the part

196

that is meant for you, the sweet and untethered melodies that flit around like moths, never landing, always moving. The lyrics we just have to live without. They are hers alone.

Sometimes when Schuyler and I are alone together, she'll cuddle up close to me and become very focused and serious, her face close to mine. These are the moments when she lets me in, and it's then that we talk to each other.

In one of these moments, I brought up a question that frankly, I'd never asked before. I'm not sure why it hadn't occurred to me before then.

"Schuyler," I asked. "Do you ever wish you could talk?"

She looked at me for a moment.

"Yeah," she said with only a touch of sadness. It's one of the handful of words she can speak fairly clearly.

But then she thought about it and changed her mind. "No," she said, and smiled. "You don't want to talk?" I asked.

"Huh uh."

"Really?"

"Noooooooo," she said with a little smirk and an eye roll, as if it was a silly question.

"You getting along okay like this?"

"Yeah!" she said with a laugh, and that was it. The serious talky window was closed and we were back to play time. Which was perfectly fine with me. I liked the answer I got.

Recently, Schuyler has begun to outwardly express her own awareness of her monster. She has this thing she does now to explain it, a whole story told in gestures and sign language. She gently touches her throat and shakes her head. She then touches her head with her finger (the sign for "think") and draws a line down to her mouth, signifying how the things she wants to say don't make the trip from her brain to her mouth. I like how she recognizes that her voice is broken, but her mind is working. It's important for her to know that her thoughts are there, and they are unbroken.

The significant thing about this little mimed explanation of Schuyler's condition, however, is that no one taught it to her. It's all hers. While some people worry about how to tell their broken children what's wrong with them and how to explain it in gentle terms that won't bruise their delicate little psyches, Schuyler has figured out her own harsh reality by herself and expresses it without a hint of self-pity or drama. Schuyler knows her monster better than any of us; it's presumptuous for anyone else, even me, to pretend we understand it, too, or to think that we can somehow tell her something about it that she doesn't already know on some visceral level.

Occasionally Schuyler balks in public at using her speech device to answer other people's questions, and the sense that I get from her is that she may be starting to feel, if not embarrassed, at least self-conscious about it. Schuyler may delight in being a weird little girl, but only when it is on her terms. A speech output device still represents her very best (and possibly only) chance of being able to spontaneously communicate any kind of real expressive thought, but it remains an unnatural way for a little girl to speak. I suspect the day is coming, and soon, when her desire to be "normal" is going to cause some serious heartbreak for her.

There's one literary figure with whom I have always associated Schuyler, although to even say it aloud breaks my oft-broken old father's heart right in two. In her own very unique way, Schuyler is Pinocchio.

Well, to be honest, that's not the only literary association I've ever made with her, and with our whole situation. I recently watched the film version of *To Kill a Mockingbird* again. I can't tell you how many times I've seen it, or how many times I've read the book, for that matter. They seem like two parts of one whole experience, so perfectly matched as they are, in a way that is rare for books and their film adaptations.

I've loved that book most of my life, ever since the first time I read it, back when I was probably about the same age as Jem Finch. And yet, in looking back on the years behind, it seems strange that I would have ever known that story without associating it with Schuyler. I watch the movie now and I am aware of the relationship between Atticus and Scout, the wise father and his wild and different little girl who is curious about a world that is meaner than she is but which is also full of mysteries to be explored. Now I find myself experiencing the story from the perspective of the father. Atticus tells Scout that you can never truly understand someone until you see the world from their perspective, to climb in their skin and walk around in it for a little while. In struggling to make my way in Schuyler's internal, solitary world, I think I finally understand what that really means.

It's an imperfect parallel, of course. In her secret world, that place I can visit alongside her but can never fully understand, Schuyler is herself equal parts Scout Finch and Boo Radley , an imperfect explorer in a world not entirely her own.

And as a father endeavoring to guide my little girl, even as I try to find the way myself, I'm no Atticus Finch, although God knows I do try.

CHAPTER 4

How Do We Do It?

Respite, Community Support, and Transitions

"I don't know how you do it." If each one of us with a special needs kid got a dime for each person that told us that we'd probably be rich—or at least have enough money to pay for a qualified care provider's salary to give us a little help. It seems like there are never enough resources or experienced respite providers. Parenting in and of itself is stressful, but add in the special needs and sometime we want to be banging our heads on the floor right next to our kids.

While we have more options for help with our kids now than forty years ago, as two writers in this chapter remind us, the demand outpaces the supply. Respite and caregiver work is woefully underpaid, social services are underfunded, and the number of kids needing these services seems to be skyrocketing. For those of us—most of us—that can't afford to hire caregivers on our own for our kids, we have to rely on getting off of mammoth waiting lists and into subsidized or free services, which came be months on up into years.

And in many ways, it's an impossible situation—those agency-provided care providers who are available are also mandated reporters, trained to look for signs of child abuse, putting us on edge for every scratch or bruise. When the system works, and kids are protected, it's an exceedingly valuable service. But it also serves to put us on constant display. Are our homes too messy? Our lifestyles too alternative? Our shelves filled with books that are too radical? Should we hide the things that make us different and try to appear cookie-cutter to the folks that invade our space? Alternately, should we dress down and hide our tattoos or fudge on our professions when we go to a support group or conference?

The writers in this chapter describe how their communities, support groups, and caregiver situations shape how they get through their days. Their stories span four decades of raising children with disabilities, and show us no matter how far we've come, progress is still needed.

My Mama Drove the Short Bus

by Sabrina Chapadjiev

My mom, Magdalena Bueno, came to the States in 1964 from Quito, Ecuador at the age of twenty-one. She had been working as the secretary for the embassy of Guatemala when she decided to visit her brother in Chicago for six months. Here, she met my father, Shefket Chapadjiev, a man who had only recently escaped Communist Bulgaria. Soon they were married, and my mom was pregnant with my brother, Sammy (Sadac) Chapadjiev. Sammy was born with brain damage.

I came into the story much later than all of this. Ten years younger than Sammy, I never really had to take care of him the way my sister, mom, and dad did. The bulk of this responsibility fell on my mom who had arrived in a country without the language, resources, or knowledge of what it meant to raise a handicapped child. Recently I interviewed my mom on her experiences.

◆ ◆ ◆

Q: *What were your first thoughts on coming to America?*

A: Oh my Gosh. I came from Quito where I never even saw a TV, to where my brother already had a TV. It was completely different—amazing. It was like a dream.

One of my first memories was when I was working very close to Marina City. It was my first winter here, and somebody said it was snowing outside. I was so excited! I went to the washroom, because I knew it had a small window near the ceiling, and stood on the toilet so I could see the snow falling. That was the first time I saw the snow.

Q: *How did you meet Dad?*

A: I met Dad when I was going to school for English. He was going with (his friend) Hamid, and I was going by myself at that time. Somehow, they started waiting for me outside. He must have just said "hi," because neither of us spoke English yet. Then he invited me to go out. We used to go out to a place called Café Berlin, a place for dancing and music.

Q: *How long before you and dad got married?*

A: Two years.

Q: *And next thing you know, you're married to this Bulgarian.*

A: I know. Jesus. At first I was thinking, what did I do? Different religion, different habits, different way of living, different food, everything was different. It was really difficult at first.

Q: *Were you planning on having a child?*

A: No! It was too soon—I didn't know what I was doing. At that time, we didn't plan like they plan now. Suddenly, I was pregnant, working, and living in this little apartment. Sammy was born on May 21, 1967.

Q: *What doctors did you go to while you were pregnant?*

A: Doctors? Oh, Sabrina! I still didn't speak the language! Daddy found this Yugoslavian "doctor," who didn't speak English either. I would tell Shefket what to tell him and then they would speak Bulgarian to each other. But this man wasn't a doctor. He was a butcher, honest to God. He had no idea what he was doing! He just pretended he was a doctor for all these people from other countries. One time, we went for an appointment and I saw him acting as a dentist for someone. He was people's dentist, or their doctor—he would pretend to be anything you needed him to be, but I really believe he didn't know anything about anything.

Q: *Did you go to him because you didn't speak English, or because you didn't have money?*

A: Probably both. What a mess!

Q: *Can you tell me about what happened when your water broke?*

A: I was working at home, and one old lady was going upstairs with a bucketful of wet clothes. I said, "No, I'll do it for you." I took the heavy bucket, went upstairs, and saw that my water broke in front of her steps. But I was only seven-and-a-half to eight months pregnant: it wasn't time yet. I called Shefket to call the doctor, and the doctor said, "Don't worry about it. Just go to bed and stay there. Don't move."

That was so stupid! If I knew better! Jesus, it makes me cry now. Daddy was working two jobs at that point, so he left me a sandwich and a glass of milk and went to work. And here I was with my contractions. I mean, you can't do that! Your water broke; you go and have the baby! I really believe that this is why Sammy is the way he is.

Q: *When did you realize something was wrong with Sammy?*

A: At the time I was pregnant, Martha was also expecting. Her son, Ivan was born a month after Sammy. When Martha and I would get together, I would see that Ivan, being one month younger than Sammy, was already doing things Sammy wasn't. If you gave Ivan toys, he would play with them—Sammy would just drop them. I went to a doctor and said, "I think something is wrong with Sammy," and he said, "You're comparing him with everyone else. Sammy's just different."

But then, Sammy started having asthma attacks. They had to give him oxygen in the hospital, and we ended up in the ER so many times. One time, he went to the hospital for asthma, he was probably six months old, and I asked the doctor, "As long as he's here, can you make him have some kind of tests?" These days, they do the tests the same day kids are born, but back then, they didn't. I had to leave him overnight. It was so hard to leave the hospital without him.

Soon they had the results of the test and called me to say, "You'd better come in to the office." It was a long drive, but Sammy and I went, and they told me, "He's mentally retarded, will never walk, never be toilet trained, and never be able to talk." They told me he would be just like a vegetable. When I started crying, the doctor said to me, "Don't cry. You can go give him to a state institution, go home, and have another one."

I took Sammy out from that office, and started walking on some street in Chicago, thinking, "They are stupid, they don't know what they're talking about! I will make him walk! I will make him talk! He will be okay!"

It was so confusing, because at that point, I had never seen a mentally retarded person. I never saw one in Ecuador. They probably hid them;

so I didn't even know what they meant by that. My mind was spinning, thinking, "What will I do? Maybe I can take him and myself to an island to live by ourselves so no one will make fun of him." I wanted to take him to an island because I was also thinking that if I went some place and they didn't accept Sammy, they wouldn't accept me. I didn't know what to do.

I went to buy a book. I was doing my best with English, but it was still hard to read. The main thing I understood in this book was that they said that the number one thing for kids like Sammy was to have a schedule. To give them a routine.

Well, I'll tell you—I made a big schedule that filled the wall. And this schedule wasn't by the hour—it was by every fifteen minutes! We did everything by this schedule. What time he washed his hands, what time he watched Sesame Street. What time he ate breakfast, went to bed, what time he gets up, what time he brush his teeth.

Then one time, I was feeding Sammy and suddenly it felt like he stopped breathing for a second. But I couldn't tell—was it Sammy, or was I imagining things? We'd already gone to the emergency room so many times, and with the doctor's constantly telling me that there was no hope, I almost started expecting something to go wrong.

I took him from his chair and started screaming, "My baby's dying!" and ran downstairs for help. My neighbor was a nurse. She came out, looked at Sammy and reassured me everything was alright. And it was. Nothing was wrong with him. At that time, I was going so nuts with this schedule, things had to be so perfect, so precise that I still wonder if that really did happen.

Q: *How was Daddy during all this?*

A: Daddy was working a lot. We really needed the money. We didn't have insurance, and there were a lot of hospital bills. Plus, he was thinking that, with Sammy, we needed a little place of our own so he wouldn't bother anybody. Sammy would be in his walker trying to walk, and the downstairs neighbors would pound on the ceiling because of the noise. So Daddy was always working, two full-time jobs, smaller jobs—whatever it took to pay all these bills, and to save money to eventually buy our little house.

Q: *When did Sammy start walking?*

A: Oh, I remember how I taught him to walk. He was so cute. Ivan was already walking, Sammy—forget about it. So every day, I would try and teach him. Sometimes, I got so frustrated I would shake him and say, "You've got to walk, you've got to walk!" One day, when he was thirteen-and-a-half months old, I sat down on the floor and he put his arms around my knees. I backed up slowly, with him still hanging onto me. Little by little I backed up more, until he started walking by himself. It was amazing. I was so happy I called Shefket at work, crying of happiness. Every time he accomplished anything, walking or talking, it was a big thing because they had told me he would never walk or talk.

Q: *How long did it take Sammy to talk?*

A: At home, he started talking at three or four years old. But when he finally did talk, he would only talk to me at home, never to anyone else. He entered Kirk Center (a school for the developmentally disabled), when he was four years old, and didn't speak there for three years. They labeled him mute. I said, "No! He can talk!" But they didn't believe me. Finally, I had to record him speaking for them to believe me.

Q: *Were you speaking in Spanish to Sammy?*

A: My mother, who sometimes came from Ecuador to help us with Sammy, always spoke Spanish to him. I used to speak Spanish to him too. But one time they told me it was too much for Sammy, that we couldn't speak Spanish at home anymore. I told my mother that, and she went back.

Q: *How long did it take you to toilet train him?*

A: Toilet train? Well, when Sammy was two years old when I decided—that's it, no more diapers! And you know what I did; I threw all the diapers away, and every hour or hour and a half, I would bring him to the bathroom.

Every once in awhile, Sammy would have an accident, and it would be a mess on the carpet. I hated cleaning it; it would make me so angry that I would shake. When I went to Ecuador, (my brother) Nandito said, "You're driving yourself crazy!" But I trained him. Hour by hour, I trained him. It took seven years.

Q: *By this time, you and dad had moved to the small house in Elk Grove, a suburb of Chicago. What was it like moving with Sammy there?*

A: I didn't know how the other families would react. I was nervous they wouldn't accept us. They would call to invite me over for breakfast or coffee, and I was always lying, saying, "My baby's in the bathroom, my baby's sleeping."

But, when I finally introduced them to Sammy, they helped me so much. Judy and Mike (our neighbors) were the ones that told me I should put Sammy in a school. I didn't know they had schools for people like Sammy. But Judy and Mike helped me to put Sammy in Kirk. Can you imagine? He was going on the bus and I could relax a little. It was a relief for me, and I could finally concentrate on Sophia a little bit, who was just a baby.

One time, somebody said that the kids in the school were being mistreated. Someone told me that the teacher was spanking them with a ping-pong paddle. I was so angry, I thought, "No way! I have to keep an eye on my boy! How can I do this, though?"

Then one day, the bus driver came by to drop off Sammy and it was a different bus driver than usual. I went on the bus to say hello to all of the kids, I high-fived them and I took Sammy out. I went back inside and a little bit later, I received a phone call from the bus company. It was Mrs. Davidsmeyer, the owner of the company. She had been driving the bus that day because the person who was supposed to had quit. She got on the phone and said, "Maggie, this is Mrs. Davidsmeyer, and we need people like you to drive this bus. You understand the kids; they like you. Would you be able to drive the bus to Sammy's school?"

I thought it was a great opportunity. If I drove the bus, I could keep an eye on Sammy's teacher to make sure Sammy wasn't being mistreated. But there was a problem. Sophia was not even one year old, and I couldn't leave her home alone. So I said to her, "Mrs. Davidsmeyer, I have a little girl…" She said, "That's okay, you can take her with you."

And can you believe it?! They made a special chair for Sophia. It was a wheelchair, but it had hooks in it so I could strap her in so she couldn't move. She wasn't even one year old! I remember that whenever I finished driving the bus route, I would put a blanket in the back of the bus and give her the bottle.

Q: *Weren't you afraid to drive a big bus full of handicapped kids?*

A: Oh my gosh! I was so scared. So scared! Of course, they trained me, but the first time I drove the bus was the worst. There was a kid in a wheelchair that would stay at a school far away for the week, and I would have to drive him there Monday, and pick him up Friday. So it was a Monday and it was windy and raining. I could hardly even see the street. Sophia's in the back and she's crying and I can hear her, and suddenly, I have to drive on this two-way street, where the cars are coming right at me. Sophia's crying and crying, and suddenly, the wheelchair that the kid is in somehow unhooks, and I felt him fall on me, right on my back. I'm crying, Sophia's crying, we're in this street and the wind and rain won't stop. I was so scared. But I slowly pushed the wheelchair back with my back, pulled off the side of the road, and locked his wheelchair back into place.

Q: *How was your English then?*

A: A little bit better. But they wanted me to speak over the radio, and I refused to do it, I was so nervous to talk. The only thing I would say was "10-4."

Q: *Did you like driving the bus?*

A: Yes. Yes. Because the kids, oh my gosh! Do you know, in the beginning, I thought nobody could talk. I thought they were just make noises. Then little by little, I began to understand them. They weren't making noises, they were all talking! Soon, I realized they were damaged more physically than mentally, because they were all in wheelchairs.

And they were smart too!! We had so much fun! I used to get up and say, "Okay, Ladies and Gentlemen! We are going to play Name … That … Tune!" I would sing a little, "La la la la laaaa…" and then right away, someone in the back would shout, "Stranger in the Night!" Oh, they were great! Some times I would say, "Okay, ladies and gentlemen. Today, we are not going to Kirk Center. Today we're going to NEW! YORK! CITY!" Oh, they would laugh. It was great to drive the kids.

Q: *It must have been hard to drive with so many wheelchairs.*

A: At that time, I had to drive seven kids, all wheelchairs. When I picked them up, I had to make sure I put the wheels on the right way so they didn't move while I was driving. Sometimes, the kids didn't want to leave the house, so I would be waiting for them. Eventually, I would go inside to help their mothers get them to the bus, so I became friends with their mothers too.

One day, they called me from the office and said, "What are you doing?! Your job is to drive the bus! To be behind the wheel!" I said, "If you want me to be that way, you can have my keys, because I won't drive anymore. How could anyone see a mother that's having a hard time and just sit there watching? If you want me to be that way, I won't do it." Finally, they told me that I could keep on doing what I was doing if I didn't tell anyone. And so I kept on driving.

Oh, the mothers loved me. If they were running late with their kids, I would open the doors and I would wait—no problem. Sometimes, they would send me with packages from one house to another, "Can you give this to Sue?" or "Can you give this to Mary?" Oh, all the mothers loved me.

Q: *Do you think this is why Sophia is so good with handicapped kids?*

A: Sophia was always good. She and Sammy—they were great. Sammy was great with her, too. I remember one time, Sophia had only been home a few days, and was in the crib, and I got up in the morning to find big, chubby Sammy on *top* of the crib, sitting down and playing with her. Can you imagine?! He could have killed her. We put a big hook up high that would keep the door closed, so Sammy wouldn't be able to reach to open the door. Another time, I got up and found him with a broom—trying to open the door. I still have no idea how he did it.

Q: *How long did you drive the short bus?*

A: I drove the bus for two to three years. I stopped when I was pregnant with you.

Q: *And you were pregnant with me for a long time, right?*

A: Forever, honest to God. When Sammy was about nine years old, I was pregnant and expecting you. At about that time, we took him to neurologist to have a chromosome test. The day after the test, a woman called me and said, "Miss Chapadjiev, I'm so excited to tell you that I know what's wrong with Sammy." I couldn't believe it. In all of those years, no one knew why Sammy was this way.

We had tried to find out. When he was little, I had taken him everywhere because I was going to find the doctor who was going to cure him. You have no idea how many places I took him. Most of them were paid for by the government. They took x-rays of every single bone of his and put them in a line to examine one by one—everything was perfect.

Everything! There was no diagnosis. I took him to the universities where they studied Sammy. We both would sit, quietly, not speaking English, while the students tried to ask me questions. "What does he eat, what doesn't he eat? Does he sleep? Does he this, does he that?" I did my best to answer, even when I couldn't understand them. One time they took him by the cheeks, and said, "This is what it's like to be handicapped," and I said, "No, all my family has cheeks like that!" I had taken him everywhere!

Anyways, this doctor was so excited that she was the one that would tell me what was wrong with Sammy. She said he had a little extra piece in one chromosome, that his brain damage had something to do with his chromosomes. I remember asking her on the telephone, "What chances do I have to have another child like this, because I'm pregnant right now. Six months." She said, "If I were you, I'd have an abortion, because you have a fifty/fifty chance." And I said, "You know what? That'd be murder." I didn't think about it for a second. I just hung up on her.

Of course, after that, I was afraid to give birth, and I'm telling you, I was pregnant with you forever. You were due at the end of October, and you came in December. The doctor understood that psychologically, I wasn't letting you go, and eventually was going to induce labor. When you were finally born, they took you for the chromosome test right away. It was a relief for me to know that you weren't handicapped.

Q: *You didn't have that pressure with Sophia, but you had that pressure with me?*

A: Oh yeah. When Sophia was born, I wasn't even thinking about the chromosome. I tested Sophia myself to see if she was normal. I drove her crazy testing her—clapping here, snapping there—looking for her reaction. My mother said, "Leave that baby alone!" But with you it was different, because from six months on, I was really scared I was going to have another baby like Sammy, or maybe even worse. So what did I do? I cried.

Q: *But if Sammy's the way he is because of chromosomes, then do you still blame the doctor that delivered him?*

A: I'm not sure about the chromosome test, because I never had one done again on him. What I do know is that my water broke, I phoned the doctor and he told me to stay in bed. I didn't go to the hospital for two days. That had to have an affect on him, because he probably didn't have enough oxygen going to his brain.

Q: *What was Sammy like when I was born?*

A: Well, of course, Sammy didn't care for you. Sophia was okay, but there was no room for one more according to him. He was pulling your hair since you were little. Ever since you had four hairs, he was already pulling them. I didn't know what to do to make him stop. You were always scared and crying. I would find you under the bed hiding from Sammy. I didn't know what to do.

Before you were born, I could hold Sophia in one hand and Sammy in the other. But then I had to hold you, and of course I had to have Sammy's hand, so Sophia would start to cry—"You don't love me anymore!" It was tough for her. I told her one time, "What's the best part of the sandwich? Bread is bread, but what makes a *really* good sandwich? What's in the middle! And you are in the middle." Oh my gosh, that was the best thing for her; she used to turn to me, smile and say "Mom, 'the sandwich.'"

Q: *When did you decide to send him to Clearbrook (a residential facility for the developmentally disabled)?*

A: For years, I had resisted having Sammy live in another facility. But it was hard. The social worker used to come and say, "You don't have to cry. Sammy can live someplace else and you can visit him." I always told her, "Do me a favor, don't call me anymore. When I need you, I'll call you. Until then, don't bother me."

Finally, Daddy had a little money that we could spend going to a better place than McDonald's, and I said, "I want to go for vacation," and I convinced him we should drive to Florida, the five of us. At that time, Sammy was swearing, "F- you!" to everybody. We would go to a restaurant, and he'd yell "F- you!!" to everyone. You'd start crying, I'd start crying. It was a mess! When I came back from that vacation, I called her.

Daddy had thought it was a good idea for many years, and I always said, "No and no and no!" Once, Sophia said, "Daddy, Sammy just doesn't belong just to you. He belongs to the family, to me, to mom, to Sabrina. So let's take a vote." Well, Sabrina voted no, Sophia voted no, and Mom voted no.

Q: *I bet I wanted to vote yes, but with Sophia staring at me, I wouldn't.*

A: (she laughs) Sophia was so little. One time, I saw that she was kind of sad and quiet. She asked me, "If there's a God, then why did he send

Sammy?" I said, "If everything was beautiful and the same, it wouldn't be life. There have to be good thing and bad things in life. To appreciate the good things, God has to show bad things too. He chose us, our family, because he knows we can help in this job. He sent Sammy to our house, because he knew our house would be the perfect house for Sammy. And we are helping him in his job." And I believe this.

Q: *They didn't expect Sammy to live so long.*

A: The doctors told me that nine years old would be enough. They told me the most they would make him would be nineteen. So stupid. He's forty-one now.

Q: *You think Sammy is your angel?*

A: Yes. Yes, he is.

Q: *Are you happy you had him?*

A: Yes. I feel blessed with him. I believe I have direct contact with God through Sammy, and I believe things happen for a reason. I completely avoid thinking "What if's," like "What if Sammy was okay?" I always took him exactly the way he is. And I really believe he's a special person. Sometimes I'm thankful that he's not a little bit better, because he's not conscious of the fact that he's handicapped. He just loves that song from Mister Rogers, *I'm Different*. The kitty cat's singing, "I'm different." It's a beautiful song.

Q: *What do you think is the biggest lesson you've learned from Sammy?*

A: To be patient, you know? I used to be so strict, so straight, so perfect. I found out that there are more important things than having a neat house and things in the right place. Sometimes I say God sent a professor to our house—to teach us patience and to not judge people, to just love and be happy. Sammy, he hugs everybody. He has no prejudice. It's like he see the souls of people, not the outside. Everybody is the same to him—he doesn't care, he just hugs. Everyday is love.

How I Met Jennyalice
by Shannon Des Roches Rosa

I was feeling justifiably grumpy on the day I met Jennyalice.

I carved a rare chunk of free time out of that ever-so-fateful morning, and was spending it in a local café, trying to illustrate a custom coloring book for my son Leelo's sixth birthday party. I write "trying," because I couldn't stop fuming and fretting over how badly kindergarten was going for my Leelo, my beautiful boy with autism. I felt helpless, betrayed by the school system that was supposed to help him, and isolated from his school's parent community. I didn't know where to turn, or what to do.

Leelo was in a brand new autism kindergarten class at an excellent local public school. The school district had created the class with the very best intentions: they had a half-dozen incoming kindergarteners diagnosed with autism, and decided to concentrate their resources on a classroom and curriculum just for these kids so they wouldn't have to scatter them and their aides throughout several schools. They recruited a special education teacher with more than twenty years' experience to teach the class. They gave this teacher three aides to help manage a class of six students. Looks good in print, no?

In reality, it was beyond problematic.

The teacher's twenty-plus years in special education did not include any skills or experience working with kids who have autism. And, for reasons I still cannot fathom, the teacher paid only lip service to acquiring those skills.

When the district became aware of the teacher's deficits, they hired my son's empathetic and experienced home learning program supervisor to train the teacher and aides in autism learning styles and teaching techniques. The teacher would participate in these training sessions, smile enthusiastically, and then return to setting up elaborate arts and crafts projects that were inappropriate for most students' abilities or attention span.

Thankfully, the one-to-one aide assigned to my son instinctively "got" Leelo. She soaked up his home supervisor's teachings, and independently developed a parallel, seditious, appropriately icon-based curriculum for my son. But Leelo was ultimately "taught" by his teacher, spending his entire school day under the control of a person who refused to learn how to communicate with him. Being in that class pushed too many of Leelo's overstimulation and confusion buttons.

He came home agitated almost every day.

The teacher was not the class's only problem. It would have taken a truly remarkable educator to give Leelo and his classmates appropriate instruction, because those children had almost nothing in common except their autism diagnoses. "Autism spectrum" is not a throwaway term, and this group of children illustrated the range within that spectrum, vividly.

Some of his classmates were perfectly conversational, but had social and behavioral quirks. Some were quiet and compliant but needed constant encouragement to engage with staff and students. Some could not sit still, some wouldn't move without a prompt. Some were hyperlexic and could read anything put in front of them, others had problems identifying their letters—at least, in the way they were being asked to demonstrate this knowledge. Some had the additional hurdle of being taught in English while having another primary language at home.

Many of the kids were compliant, and tolerated their educational setting well enough, but Leelo had an awful time just *being* in his classroom. He couldn't sit still in the uncomfortable, old-fashioned desks. The highly verbal, text-based, writing- and tracing-oriented curriculum was beyond his verbal abilities and motor skills—he was not conversational, though he spoke "fluent requesting," and his grasp had not developed to the point where he could hold a regular pencil properly, let alone write with one.

So, while he was constantly learning in his customized and visually based home learning program, he was set up for failure in the classroom. Understandably, Leelo spent much of his school day acting out, jumping out of his chair, obsessing about and chewing on straws, trying to bolt, humming, and vocalizing in random bursts. When really agitated or excited, he would punch or push. I was grateful that he seemed to bottle up any real aggression until he got home, where he took it out on me. My arms were a mess of scratches and scrapes, but that was tolerable as long as he was okay at school, as long as he didn't hurt one of the aides, or classmates.

And he was okay—until the day his wonderful aide went on her break while Leelo went out to recess. He ran across the playground and, using the force of his acceleration, pushed a girl from one of the regular kindergarten classes into her teacher.

If Leelo's behavior was unacceptable, the reactions were worse. Though neither the girl nor her teacher was injured, the girl's parents and that teacher were furious that my son had been "allowed" on the playground in the first place. They held a meeting with the principal that same day, demanding that Leelo be excluded from the recess that was one of few bright spots in his day. The principal, without even consulting me, agreed on the spot. And *then* I found out about the incident, when I arrived for pickup and was told by my son's teacher that Leelo was no longer welcome at recess, and why.

Somehow I took Leelo's hand and stumbled back to the car. I was enraged, but also paralyzed by the shock of blatant discrimination. I couldn't believe education professionals would punish a special needs child without consulting his family. If Leelo had been a typical child, they would have included his parents in the disciplinary meeting, and tried to work something out. What little faith I had left in that school sputtered out.

I was angry with the girl's parents, too. While I was very sorry that Leelo had scared their daughter so badly and understood their protective attitude, their actions were not forgivable. They demanded punishment for a child who lacked the verbal skills to join the discussion, without consulting that child's parents. I doubt they would have reacted so harshly to a child who was capable of talking with them, capable of apologizing.

Plus, I knew that a similar altercation had happened between two "typical" children during the previous year. That incident had resulted in one child's scalp needing stitches, but neither had been barred from the playground because they were "just kids being kids." It seemed the girl's parents couldn't see past the "special needs" part of "special needs child."

I suspect those parents were annoyed that the autism kindergarten was allowed on their daughter's campus in the first place. Leelo and his classmates had invaded the most coveted school in town, the one with the highest test scores and largest number of personal castles and sticks-up-asses in our otherwise laid-back and diverse town. A class full of special needs students did not fit with that school's image, and they were not welcome, not even in their separate portable classroom.

The other parents from the regular kindergarten classes—the classes whose doors opened into the same courtyard and shared playground as Leelo's class—were at best confused as to why kids like ours were going to school with kids like theirs, and at worst openly resentful. Even before the bias-exposing recess incident, no teachers or parents had attempted to include my son or his classmates in kindergarten activities, to integrate them, or to even talk about them.

We walked with those parents ever single day as we all went through identical routines to pick up and drop off our children, yet we were as unmentionable, as uncomfortable a presence as our children. I was at a loss for a way to identify with those other adults; Silicon Valley is famous for its herds of geeks-turned-multimillionaires, yet no other parents at Leelo's school had snarky t-shirts or funny-colored hair. If I hadn't occasionally chatted with two friendly parents from our former co-op nursery school, I might have suspected that Leelo and I were ghosts.

I hated that school. I hated those parents.

And, as I sat in that café on the morning I met Jennyalice, listening to angry music on my iPod and scribbling away at Leelo's coloring book, a woman who looked like she could have been of those parents appeared at the table next to me.

I bristled.

Her choppy blonde hair sparkled with highlights as she plopped her adorable baby girl in a high chair, then helped her grandmother to sit down. She chatted amiably, curling back perfectly lipsticked lips from perfectly white straight teeth into a perfectly beautiful smile whenever she laughed. She wore eye makeup, her clothes were neat and mall-fashionable, and her cheerful, easygoing attitude made her appear to have nothing better to do than idle over lunch.

I glowered in my scruffy "WTF?" t-shirt and clean but ratty jeans, trying to ignore her. But she was as audible as she was perky, and I became increasingly irritated. People like her made my son's unpleasant school days even worse, and now they were infiltrating my café—my sanctuary—and poisoning my precious chunk of child-free time. Couldn't she and her thoughtless friends leave me alone?

I stewed, savoring my resentment of her and everything she stood for, knowing that privileged parents like her could never understand my life.

Then I overheard her say, "and my six-year-old son has autism."

I gaped. I took one ear bud out of one ear and blurted, "Excuse me, but did you just say that you have a six-year-old son with autism?"

She looked at me quizzically but graciously, and said, "Yes, I did."

My eyes bulged, my reality shifted. Then I started gushing. "I have a six-year-old son with autism, too! Well, I mean, he will be six next week. I'm working on this coloring book for his birthday party because he likes rhymes and I hate goody bags. Where does your son go to school? What class is he in? How come he isn't in the same class as my son? Where do you live? How come I don't know you already? I'm Shannon, by the way."

She laughed past my jabbering, shook my hand, and introduced herself as Jennyalice. She also introduced me to the elderly woman with her, who was not her grandmother, but rather a friend she had met through her volunteer work delivering library books to the housebound. She pointed out her daughter Lucy (who was as perfect as she looked) and then started telling me about her son—at which point the last venomous thoughts left my head, and I realized the only asshole in the room was me.

Her son Jake is a boy with acronyms and "ics," autistic, ADHD, cerebral palsy (ataxic), and a little panic disorder, too. He gets horrible migraines. At one point, his sleep was so severely disregulated that he did not rest for more than ten minutes in a row for over fifty days.

Why? She had no idea. She drank no caffeine, ate no fish, and avoided all alcohol while pregnant. She had an uncomplicated pregnancy and birth. The explanations, she had even fewer of them than most parents of special needs kids. But instead of growling at the world from a dark café corner, she was out taking care or herself, her family, and other people.

My heart grew three sizes. I lost my grump. I latched onto her. And I have yet to let go.

Jennyalice has looked past this introductory incident, though she brings it up whenever I deserve a good cringe. She delights in my technicolor hair, and is usually polite enough to avoid wearing twinsets around me. She is bawdy and fun, kind and just, and thinks that the parents at my son's kindergarten were as big a bunch of dickheads as I do.

She is one of us. She just looks like one of them.

◆ ◆ ◆

Jennyalice and I have managed to do a world of good together since that day. Though I had always muttered, "Death before PTA," Jennyalice and I helped found a local special education chapter with a group of strong, knowledgeable, like-minded parents.

Several of our board members' children also survived Leelo's ill-fated kindergarten class, and went on to more appropriate placements for first grade. Leelo now loves school. We realized that forming a special education PTA was the most straightforward way to empower parents like us and children like ours, to give us the power and knowledge to protect our kids from being trapped in inappropriate educational environments.

We also provide a support network for the other special needs families in our district. No parent should feel as alone as I did the day Leelo was bounced from recess, and no parent should have to figure out the complicated steps of the special education cha-cha-cha when so many other parents are veteran dancers.

Not that we embody altruism. We are avenging Furies when our children are mistreated or misperceived. My friend Elaine says that our PTA slogan should be "Where angry women come together." Thankfully the PTA gives us a way to channel our ire into socially acceptable good deeds and projects.

We bring in special education professionals and advocates for parent education nights. We have ongoing support groups. We have social mixers. We always provide free babysitting and Spanish translation at our meetings, so that parents for whom those two items are barriers can participate. We work especially hard to foster inclusive environments, integrating special and regular education students in various projects and events. We've developed inclusive art programs, and plan to sponsor a district-wide Inclusive Schools Week, every year.

As individual parents of special needs children, we are not always taken seriously; we are too often handed a bucket of pity, patted on the head, and then avoided or ignored. Being a member of a special education PTA gives us, gives our work legitimacy.

◆ ◆ ◆

When Leelo first started kindergarten, I donated three books about children with autism to each regular kindergarten class: *Andy and His Yellow Frisbee*, *My Friend with Autism*, and *Ian's Walk*. On Leelo's last day of kindergarten—his last day at the school that had treated him so badly—Leelo's teacher handed me a bag containing every one of those donated books. Leelo's class wasn't going to be at the school any more, so the school no longer needed to educate its kindergarteners about autism.

With Jennyalice and the rest of our special education PTA, I will continue to wage war against this kind of ignorance and disrespect.

No Use in Crying

by Jennifer Byde Myers

It is 1:15 pm.

I know there's no use crying over spilled milk, but is there a caveat for spilled chocolate milk, a full nine ounces of it, streaming across the counter and onto the recently mopped and swept-only-five-minutes-ago floor? Do you think there is use in crying over that? Probably not, I suppose.

What about a few tears thinking about the aide for Jack who yesterday was so terrific, and on time and great with Jack; so comfortable and kind, and sweet with Katie too? And she cleaned the counters and the trash heap we had piling up next to the recycling. How is it that the same aide sent a text at 12:49 pm letting me know she can't make it at 1:00 pm? I am alone with two kids whom I cannot contain in the grocery store, and a near empty refrigerator. We have no fruit, and no milk, and now as I start looking, very little idea of what to make for dinner, which will inevitably come around again in a matter of hours. I had a plan. I was taking care of myself. I had help coming. And now I'm digging through the pantry with tears in my eyes.

I hate looking for a new aide.

Finding care for Jack makes me feel incapable, behind schedule, stupid, tired, angry, woeful, misfortunate, pitiable, and exhausted. I feel indulgent, lazy, spendthrift, and poor all at the same time. Because really, shouldn't I be able to do this by myself? It makes me question what kind of mother I am, what I do (or no longer do) for a living, and how I measure my worth in society. Finding the right care for a special needs child is, perhaps, more difficult than having the special needs kid in the first place.

We were lucky when Jack was young. He didn't walk until he was two, but people are more forgiving when special needs children are young. Perhaps the child who is behind physically or developmentally is viewed as a large baby who simply hasn't developed the skill, and not as a child who may never have the ability. It's still hard to tell that a kid like mine is that different. Well, I mean aside from not hitting a single one of his milestones on time, who could tell with that beautiful face and the soft curls framing his hazel eyes that he was so different from other kids?

Meche was our first aide for Jack. I have a friend who is older than I am, and I figured that if she had ten more years of life experience and was generally a more cautious person and had hired Meche, then perhaps I could trust her with my kid as well. Meche was precious and petite. Jack seemed to be half her size already. She spoke Brazilian Portuguese, and sang songs to Jack. And when he cried, sometimes for a week at a time (no really!), she would just say over and over, "No llores, Lindo. Lindo." She even patted my hand and chased me out the door when I lamented that he was too much and I should not expect others to care for him. Meche was the only Mary Poppins we've ever had. She had to move across the country after only six months.

Next we hired a woman who, we soon discovered, sat on the couch, reading the newspaper. The *entire* paper, while Jack hopped around the living room unable to get his own toys, hold his own cup, or express verbally anything he needed. She complained a lot and always ate two scoops of ice cream for every scoop she fed Jack. Clearly, I was desperate. I came home just one too many times with the crossword puzzle half done already, and the kitchen a mess with my cookbooks and dirty cutlery, with complex dishes simmering on the stove. I didn't need to pay someone to provide benign neglect and unasked-for mediocre cooking when I can do those things myself. I really, really wanted someone to take care of my child.

Somehow I thought I could have a job outside the home. You know, a forty-plus-hour-a-week job, and still have a child with special needs. I took jobs on contract, so I could make my own hours, but there were forty of them, at least, every week.

I tried Jack at a home day-care, a small, one-woman operation. I felt guilty because my child was a lot of work, so I paid for a full five-day slot even though I only used twelve hours over two or three days. He was there for less than two months. Jack got kicked out because he "needed as much help as an infant." She added, with disdain, "Have you considered that your son might need a more developmental program?" And while I didn't say any of it out loud, I thought, "Hmm? Thanks. Thanks a lot. Yeah, bitch, I have. He's enrolled. We have our early intervention program on

Thursdays ... you know, Thursdays, when I am still paying you even when we're not here?"

Those early intervention classes were terrific and we never wanted to miss them, but they were once a week for two and a half hours in the middle of the morning, which meant that I still needed afternoon coverage. To get help in the afternoon meant that I had to pay for the whole day. There seemed to be a similar task nearly every day of the week. On Wednesdays, I would leave work, pick Jack up from day-care, take him to another city for physical therapy, then drive him back to day-care, and return to work. That's another two hours I paid to have my child watched when he wasn't even there, just trying to keep the damn space.

The one-woman operation suggested we hire a personal nanny. I stopped trying to ever work a full-time job.

Of course we still needed part-time help after school and over breaks. One summer we lucked out when I hired the high school valedictorian who has a brother with special needs. Amy is amazing, energetic, and trustworthy. I got Jack and Amy passes to the local amusement park, and they went a few times a week. One evening they stayed out two hours past their set time to come home, without calling. She simply lost track of time at the water park. She called me as soon as she figured it out so I wouldn't worry, and to let me know that Jack had already eaten dinner: one super size order of french fries and a sixty-four-ounce lemonade. Fantastic! I still counted myself lucky, and I cried when she went away to college.

We borrowed a German nanny from a friend once. We became close with her. She ended up finishing her studies as a child development major specializing in children with autism, so clearly my son had an impact on her life. She was mostly great, except when her childhood sweetheart decided to break up with her in long distance phone call. Her heart shattered and so did most of her child-care skills. Ah, to be young and in love.

Whatever.

And then there was Chevelle. Oh yes, Chevelle—we changed the locks after her. She started out as an aide in Jack's classroom. She ended up a meth-head with a mouth full of lies. Slowly but surely she began down the path of "Can I get paid for the week, today?" which of course just put her in a bind at the end of the week, and made it hard for me to budget my money over the course of the month. She flaked on us right as our second child was due. Her cell phone got turned off. Her car broke down. She got carpal tunnel. We are also fairly certain that she is the person who passed along methicillin-resistant *Staphylococcus aureus* to my son. MRSA is that nasty infection impervious to most antibiotics. People die from MRSA infections. Our brush with the infamous ick landed Jack in a hospital for three days when Katie was only two weeks old. Jack didn't have a diaper rash apparently, and those boils on Chevelle's arms were not, as it turns out "giant spider bites."

It was about this time that I posted an ad on Craigslist. Everyone else does it; I had heard the chatter at the park, "I found the perfect nanny." Why shouldn't I have that luck? Well apparently my ad was a bit too much for some people.

CARE NEEDED FOR MY CRAZY MONKEY BOY—
NANNY, BABYSITTER, SOMEONE!

We are a fun-loving family with a special needs child. He has mild cerebral palsy ataxia (he walks like he's drunk, but he does walk, run, hop, skip, jump and climb). He is also on the autism spectrum (but hey, isn't everyone these days?). He is healthy, and strong... with an emphasis on strong. At just 5 1/2 he's already 3'11" and 59 pounds of pure muscle.

Our kid has a lot of energy, loves to eat and run around the park or play in our backyard. He is just beginning to talk, so he is a bit frustrated trying to communicate, but it is pretty easy to figure out what he wants once you get to know him. He is actually a very easy kid to watch as long as you don't ever let go of his hand in a parking lot.

So basically I need a bit of help. I am about to have a baby... any day now, and our boy's current caretaker needs to have surgery, and can't take care of the physical needs of children anymore (What a great surprise for me!). I am also still doing some consulting work, so we would like to find someone who wants to stay with us for awhile.

So we are looking for:—A part-time nanny (babysitter, caretaker, second mom, child care provider, girlfriend whatever you want to call it...).

Approximately 20 hours a week.

Fairly set schedule (say Tues, Wed, Thurs 1:00-6 pm and a date night? We can work it out).

Occasional additional hours possible if desired.

Our last three caretakers have been $10.00 an hour. This is somewhat negotiable. I know it's not a million bucks a year, but the pay will be consistent and the checks won't ever bounce. We also provide money for ice cream, zoo, gas money for trips and such ... of course.

Pick Monkey Boy up from the bus (in front of the house) during summer school and into the fall so timeliness is VERY IMPORTANT.

Prepare healthy snacks (or not so healthy trips to the ice cream parlor).

Light cooking (for the kiddo, not for me ... but you can unload the dishwasher for me if you really want to).

Take Tiny Man to the park, or zoo or something so you two don't die of boredom.

Get him ready for bed with bath, jammies etc. if necessary.

Provide consistency with kiddo's school and life goals (potty training, eating with a fork, walking and holding hands etc.).

Change diapers, wipe his nose when he catches a cold this winter, and all of those other things that I would do if I were watching him (like save him from a burning building).

Requirements: Male or female candidates only, excellent driving record, English speaking, experience with children and love of them, patience, valid California driver license, your own safe and insured car (although we do have a car which could be used. We can talk about this one), and references. Joie de vivre. Physical strength and energy is a must. Please be willing to make at least a bit of a commitment. May not bring your own children. No smokers (or at least you can't do it with the kid, or smell like smoke). We have two golden retrievers who can stay in another area of the house while you are here, but the kid loves the dogs, so probably being comfortable with dogs would be helpful. Oh, and you must be able to tolerate

*a dark sense of humor and a very frank family. Please email me
and we can figure out if we are right for each other. Thank you for
considering our family.*

I was honest about the job; wiping butts and noses is not a pretty thing.
Three years ago I was offering $10 cash per hour, which was the going rate
in our area for a babysitter. I know I was asking a lot, and I know watching
my kid can be hard work because I do it, but I could not offer to pay $20
or more an hour for those services. I just couldn't afford to. Ten dollars an
hour might not seem like a lot, but we always pay for the hours we book,
even if we don't use them, and I didn't want a therapist. Jack had enough
of those already. I wasn't asking for a degree in psychology or a masters in
political science either. I was also quite clear that they would need to have
a friggin' sense of humor because that was the only way we were making it
through our life with a special needs child.

Not surprisingly, I received several very mean comments both posted
online and sent to me directly. I deleted the most cruel, the ones that made
me cry. The anonymity of the Internet left people more bold and ready to
share their criticisms. Even the more mild responses left me feeling harshly
judged:

*Is it just me... or is this woman totally spun? Did anyone read
her posting? I mean I realize everyone is different but talk about
strange... Actually aside from her bizarre wording and "humor" in
her posting, I think the humor truly is what she is offering in terms of
salary. That little per hour for all of these expectations and demands
for a special needs child???!!! This lady truly has lost her marbles. I
feel sorry for this child...*

I received just a few responses that showed support:

*You want higher wages for babysitting/nanny work? Eliminate about
70% of the people trying to get these jobs, or create a whole bunch of
families that will need the services. That will inflate the wages. If the
job ad doesn't suit you, then move on to ads that have a higher dollar
pay and good luck getting and keeping them.*

*Also, it is PAINFULLY obvious that the mother has not lost her
sense of humor in dealing with life. She clearly loves her "little
man" or "monkey boy" and who the hell are any of you to judge the*

nicknames? Maybe this little boy named himself monkey boy after Curious George or who knows what book or story.

You'd all do to lighten up a bit. Her sense of humor was obvious throughout the ad, and spelled out at the end in plain English.

Live and let live, little man monkey boy probably feels as loved or more loved than most kids in America. Rock on, Monkey Boy's Mamma. Don't let them mess with you. Congrats on the new baby.

Of course the Craigslist thing never panned out. I tried. I scheduled an interview with one young woman who had to cancel at the last minute because her car got towed. I almost hired her over the phone because it sounded like she was the kind of "not helpful" we were used to having in our home.

So where does all of this leave me? I start to wonder why I hire anyone at all. I mean why shouldn't I be able to watch my own children all the time? What is wrong with me? And I know it's important for me to get a break from what most view as a challenging life, but it starts to feel like it's not really making my life easier. This doesn't feel like easy. I keep having "the talk" with Jack's current aide about timeliness, and she keeps being eighteen minutes late (the exact amount of time it takes for her to get from her house to mine). I get a text message at least twice a week "IM ON MY WAY K?" No! It's not okay. Sitting around waiting for someone to help you is actually not helpful. It's why I'd rather just do it all myself. It might be more tiring, but at least I can count on me. Waiting for help gives me anxiety. It makes my head hurt. It means I cannot even schedule a haircut because I do not trust that she will be here in time for me to get to the appointment. So now I look like crap and I'm pissed off.

It's just not easy to replace her. The kids love her. She is so patient, and helps with structure and routine with a gentle manner. She is kind.

I know I'm not going to find another me, but of course that's what I look for. I want someone to step in and *be me* when I'm not there, and for there to be two of me when I am home so we can get something done. But I'm not going to chance upon a college-educated, highly motivated, self-starter who successfully began to climb the corporate ladder. I'm not finding a person who now delights in being at home with a kid who sports multiple diagnosis including cerebral palsy, panic disorder, and autism. I'm looking for a kind and gentle-mannered caretaker who thrives on working with a kid who cannot load his own fork, wipe his own face or use the toilet on a regular basis. I'm never going to find that aide because that person doesn't exist.

I am not even that person.

So I keep an eye out all the time. I carry a pen and paper to jot down any leads. I may even place another ad on Craigslist, only this time I'll make sure I'm really clear.

This is it. This is all I really need:

Show up on time.

Make sure my kid doesn't catch fire.

Please, please don't make me cry.

Life Among the Doozies
by Anonymous

It was my first Doozy Conference.

Oops—I guess I'd better back up and provide a little background.

My son David, now forty-two, was born with a neurological condition requiring brain surgery—the first when he was ten days old, and several more times since. Surgical scar tissue led to intermittent grand mal seizures that began when he was eight. He also had learning disabilities that were diagnosed as laziness until 1975, when the public school system discovered disability—by which time David was two years from graduation.

Doozy is the private word we used when my kids were little to refer to David's condition. I invented it when I realized that David's younger sister Sara was having a hard time talking about his condition, especially when other people, upon learning of it, reacted with alarm. Whenever I referred to "David's Doozy," the kids cracked up, releasing some of the tension and fear that surrounded his condition.

I'm resurrecting the term now so I can write about the Doozy Association without (a) publicly trashing an organization that does a lot of good work, and (b) insulting or injuring the individual people who do that good work. After much thought, I decided that the only way for me to be honest about my experience with the Doozy Association is to render it (I hope) unrecognizable. For the same reason, I'm writing anonymously and all names have been changed including those of my children.

So to get back to my first Doozy Conference. David was already a man in his early twenties when I discovered the Association, after moving from the East Coast to the West. Although Doozy had been treated surgically for some fifty years, there were precious few resources for those who had it. Back east, a small group had formed around one of the doctors specializing in Doozy; they sponsored events to raise research money, but that was the extent of their activities. There were no support or educational groups and until I came west, I hadn't known anyone with Doozy, except for two families I hunted down and met briefly when David was a baby. Few people even knew what Doozy was, and so I'd bumbled around, confused and ignorant through the years of David's childhood. If someone had asked me what kind of help or information I needed, I never could have imagined the resources available for people with disabilities today. Isolation, confusion, and fear were par for the Doozy course. This was just the way life with Doozy—or any disability—was back then. I'm talking about 1965 to the 1980s, a time when people didn't speak openly about a lot of topics, and not at all about disability. There was no such thing as early childhood intervention, the Americans with Disabilities Act, the IDEA and IEP. *Accommodations* for *special needs* were not only non-existent, but the words hadn't even been used together yet. People with disabilities were usually referred to as *handicapped, retarded,* or *crippled.* David's Doozy was known as a *birth defect.* Who can be blamed for not wanting to engage in conversations about *defective babies*?

The Disability Rights Movement had its early origins in the 60s, but it wasn't until the 80s that parents of children with disabilities banded together to demand and implement change. By then David was nearly an adult; in his last two years of high school he received special ed—which at that time meant putting him in a classroom for one period a day with kids who covered a wide spectrum from dyslexia to cerebral palsy and everything in between. It wasn't much help, especially since David carried some pretty heavy baggage after twelve years of dysfunctional education. He was born too soon, and the disability rights movement came along too late for him to benefit, at least educationally. Thus, the discovery of a group that advocated for people with Doozy was a major thrill for us. Our whole family—David, his sister Sara and I—had dinner with the founders of the organization. We were all tremendously excited about going to our first conference.

After registering at the hotel and settling in, my kids and I went down to the Doozy Conference welcoming reception. Buffet tables were set up with food and drinks in a large ballroom. Adults and kids milled about nibbling on cheese and crackers. They were expecting about 200 people to attend; today, attendance averages 500. That number looks puny, but it was the highest number of registrants they'd ever had. The Association was over ten years old, but it was still quite small and locally centered, overseen primarily by its two founding families. I'd been impressed with their professionalism, though, as well as the quality of their newsletter and other printed materials, and the connections they'd managed to make with doctors and specialists in the Doozy network.

I entered the ballroom and got a glass of wine. The executive director spotted me and came over. Ellen was a masterful hostess who knew how to make things happen. After a few minutes of chatting she introduced me to someone else, and once the conversation took off she slipped away. I liked how she watched out for me; any time she saw me standing alone and lost, she'd come back and drag me over to another new person, always mentioning something about them or me to get the conversational ball rolling. In this way I managed to meet a fair number of people whose lives had been touched by Doozy in one way or another.

Most of the parents were younger than I was, and most of their kids who had Doozy were infants and toddlers. Because Doozy treatment was relatively new, only a small contingent of people David's age was at the conference—or on this earth. Until around 1955, babies born with Doozy either got over it naturally, or died. It turned out that David, born in 1965, was a Doozy pioneer. I was a pioneer Doozy mother, something I learned at my first Doozy meeting. When I told my story to about a dozen parents, they were in awe, and told me I was remarkable for having survived Doozy almost entirely alone. At first this surprised me: all these years I'd thought of myself more as victim than as remarkable or pioneering. Nor had I seen the big picture—the historical, social and cultural influences that were surrounding my circumstances.

As reality sank in, my sense of myself as a mother began to shift. Where I'd previously been ashamed and embarrassed to talk about Doozy, I slowly developed a matter-of-fact attitude tinged with pride. This transformation didn't happen in a day, but over the course of several years. The way I talk about Doozy now is light years away from my halting attempts as a young mother. Insensitive remarks that once hurt now rouse me to anger and contempt for those who make them.

Midway through the reception, after I'd had two glasses of wine and enough time to calm down, I took a look around at the people with whom I'd be interacting for the next two days. The shock hit me all at once: every single person in the room was white, and they all seemed middle class. Though this was merely a superficial glimpse, the vibe was unmistakable.

Almost everyone was from a background I knew well, one that I'd

229

pejoratively labeled "straight" after walking out of my suburban home back in 1969 wearing a tie-dyed T-shirt and jeans, my two little munchkins in tow. For a while we lived on a commune made up of single mothers and kids. The next year we lived on a mountain dotted with teepees where we worked a communal garden. I went out with men and women of all ethnicities from all walks of life. The kids learned origami, guitar, and Grateful Dead lyrics from the friends and lovers who passed through our home, sometimes staying for dinner, sometimes for three weeks. For awhile, our house was a way station for women in flight from abusive men, or for hippie mothers desperate to leave the city. They stayed until they found their own places, all the kids camping out in the same bedroom. In other words, neither I nor my children had led a typical middle-class life. And though they were choosing more conventional lives as adults, I was still out there seeking adventure, following my instincts to new experiences with offbeat people.

Finding myself alone among "the straights" threw me into panic mode. What if someone asked what I did for a living (phone sex)? How would I answer questions about my marital status (divorced longer than I'd been married) or sexual orientation (bi)? What if my kids innocently let on I was a writer, and they asked me what I'd published (mostly erotica)? Among these well-dressed, well-heeled people who seemed to share a set of moral assumptions, I would have to be very, very careful. The list of data about me that I'd have to hide was long. It included poverty, maternal conflicts, and a scandalous past highlighted by the four years I went AWOL and the kids lived with their father.

Truth be told, I get panicky any time I find myself in a room with all one kind of people. It doesn't matter what kind they are either; if every single person in the group is the same, I immediately focus on the ways I'm different rather than on our commonality. In this case, our only commonality was Doozy—a defining aspect of my life, but hardly enough to define me. I had not allowed it to define me, lest I be diminished—which I would have been in the days when I had no support and knew no other parents of Doozy children. This was before the advent of the Internet, and it would be a few years before I could even look for Doozy people online. Finding this association was empowering. The perspective of those who'd been through a parenting experience similar to mine was invaluable. It was even more empowering for David. Until then, he'd only once met someone else with Doozy; at the conference, there were a dozen or so young adults who looked like him, communicated the way he did, and understood his medical and social history. This group was important to us. After living so long in Doozy isolation, we were grateful to have found them. Which is why, when I realized I was going to feel marginalized—*isolated!*—among these people, my stomach tightened and my heart sank. Finally I was among others who, like me, lived on the fringe of the able-bodied world, and I was still on the fringe. If I couldn't fit in here, there was no hope for me.

Unfortunately, my first cocktail-party impression of the Doozies turned out to be painfully correct. During the five or so years I struggled to find a niche for myself, a place where I could be effective as an advocate for people with Doozy. I never met anyone remotely similar to me except for the year they hired a grant writer, a lesbian who lived an artist's life. I served on the Board, helped organize the next two conferences, and contributed to the newsletter, all the while feeling alienated and marginalized—with good reason. One woman told me she enjoyed having someone "ethnic" (Jewish) like me on the Board. Another cracked a joke about my "marching to the beat of a different drum." They stared blankly at my proposal to do outreach to African-American, Hispanic, and Asian people with Doozy, then promptly shot it down. Even my less ambitious ideas were politely sidelined. And always, at every board or committee meeting, they badgered me for money. Board members were expected to raise money from friends and family, and to donate a percentage of their own income to the organization. I didn't. I couldn't. One board member came up with what she thought was a happy solution: she suggested that I donate my labor by writing whatever needed writing—fundraising letters, fact sheets, grant applications. I didn't. I couldn't. I felt constantly ashamed and humiliated for being poor.

During the planning for my second Doozy conference, I suggested including a support group for mothers only. Previous support groups had thrown mothers and fathers together, and the planning committee didn't see any reason to separate them. Having had experience in both co-ed and single-sex support groups on other issues, I fought long and hard until I just plain wore down the committee.

So many women showed up, the room was overflowing. We crowded around the conference room table, hip to hip, with more women perched on window sills, and went around the room telling our stories. I tend to cry copiously whenever I speak on such occasions, and this was no exception. I was surprised when people were disturbed by my tears. A couple of women tried to give me advice, but I convinced them I didn't need any. Even more surprisingly, nobody else cried. One woman came close, but she managed to hold back her tears. She talked about her Doozy daughter as a burden that weighed heavily on her. The next speaker chastised her; when I interrupted with a reminder of the rule not to judge one another, she was miffed.

About midway through, a woman spoke who uncannily summed up the whole vibe of the Doozy Association. "We were a normal family," she began. I flinched. "A perfectly normal family before this Doozy thing came along and changed everything. We took our boat out on weekends, we went on ski trips ... you know, a typical family life."

I sat there listening, a single mother whose old jalopy used to break down in the snow on the way to post-seizure checkups. I sat there, a pioneer, or so they told me, of Doozy, a mother who'd managed to drag her Doozy kid into his twenties with one hand typing behind her back; who still felt guilty for not hiring a tutor for him; who had to fight tooth and nail just to get us to the beach in the summer; who'd defended my son at school conferences when they belittled him as lazy; who'd threatened a lawsuit to get him into a vocational program. I sat there listening to this smug, middle-class woman lament the way that Doozy had ruined her life, and I thought, "Lady, you should get down on your knees and thank whatever gods there be for bringing Doozy into your life to teach you a thing or two."

I don't mean to romanticize Doozy, or any kind of disability, and I certainly would have preferred not to have had Doozy in my life. But nobody should live an existence of boating and skiing without any glitches in the program. As singer-songwriter-poet Leonard Cohen put it, *There is a crack ... in everything / That's how the light gets in.*

Eventually I resigned from the Doozy board of directors. I stopped going to Doozy conferences several years ago, after attending four of them. I finally found it too painful to listen to parents who were just starting out in the world of Doozy. I felt terrible sympathy for the optimists who, like my younger self, didn't foresee the numerous problems up ahead, but think an operation is the beginning and end of Doozy. On the other hand, I was jealous of these parents' resources, support, and services—yet even knowing all that wasn't available to me, I still felt guilty for not doing more for David.

Ultimately, I might have been able to deal with all the re-stimulation if it wasn't for the lack of space to express and work through these feelings—

the atmosphere at the Doozy conferences remains strangely unemotional. It's that middle-class facade, that brave front of holding it together, chin up and all that sort of thing that I just can't abide.

David still goes, with my help and encouragement, to every conference—he gets a lot out of spending time with other Doozy people. He stands proudly among them for group photographs, and is always sad the day the conference ends. He keeps in touch with one or two people, and his sense of self has benefited tremendously. Ironically, the Association's membership has grown so much that it's now more diverse.

I don't miss the association; I don't seem to have as strong a need for validation and support around the issue of Doozy anymore. Maybe I already got what I needed from them. I would like to be contributing something, but the few times I had an idea or went to a meeting I felt the same old exclusionary vibe.

These days my Doozy work is directly with my son. He lives five minutes from me, and I see him almost daily. I'm working on the karmic plane for now. It's a real doozy.

Glass Houses
by Sarah Talbot

The institution has two large social rooms, two kitchens, and five bed-rooms. The social room upstairs (called the "great room") has two computers, a fireplace, and tables seating up to fourteen indoors and six outdoors. Around the fireplace upstairs, a chair and a couch are arranged into a sitting area. The downstairs collection is less formal: a Ping-Pong table, a library, two study areas, and a sitting area with an old couch a wood stove. Each floor also has a kitchen and bathroom.

Staff members rotate in and out throughout the day and night. The morn-ing shift starts at six and prepares breakfast, then sets up visual schedules. Often there is a midday lull when the residents go to day programs.

One resident, Caleb, has the most intensive needs and requires twenty-four-hour monitoring. Autism makes him impulsive—he's known as a runner and as violent. He has been returned to the institution by the po-lice several times. Once, police retrieved him from underneath the side-walk at a park on the waterfront. The workers thought he had fallen into the water and were looking for him there, but he was just hiding between concrete slabs.

The institution was mostly a therapy space at first. The first therapist to use it worked with Caleb, who is also deaf, to try to help him learn to respond to whatever sound he could perceive. Later, she was joined by a caseworker who used the space weekly, then two deaf volunteers who taught the other residents sign language, then a physical therapist and an occupational therapist who came together and tried to get Caleb to screw lids onto and off of jars. The residents are reported by therapists to have been resistant at that time; they might not show up when therapies were scheduled or might not comply with follow-up instructions. The residents are reported to have seemed resentful. It was a full three years before the institution switched over to part-time staffing.

Now, ten years later, it employs five regular staff plus three itinerate caseworkers, an itinerate nurse, and an HR firm to hire and fire unionized staff positions. A family physician, three neurologists, four psychologists, and a psychiatrist consult on regular rotations. Police, Fire and Emergency Transport are updated about residents' particular behaviors and medical conditions. An onsite management team overseas operations and the state of Washington manages inspections and compliance. Funding comes from state and local agencies, grants, and the families of the residents.

The institution has moved buildings, but the current one is the best. It is yellow and sits high above a residential street. When Caleb first saw it, he loved its pretty wood-look flooring and the quirky chandelier on the second floor. I was most attracted to the size of the space, the light from huge front windows, and the master suite.

I had worried at first that the transition and chaos during the move would traumatize Caleb and the other residents. It wasn't too bad, though. Family photos taken during the transition time show some exhaustion in the residents, but they seem happy and exhibit a sense of humor. Even Caleb seems to be clowning around, stable in his sense of belonging.

Tonight in the institution, the yellow house, Caleb serenely snacks on celery with peanut butter. I let the staff go early—Rebecca was on duty. She's studying to be a teacher, and was happy to have a few more minutes to prepare for her evening class.

Before she left, she filled Caleb's chart with information about his day. Seizure activity? None. Injuries? None. Exercise? A half-mile walk. Physical therapy? Twenty minutes. Violent outbursts? None. She forgot to note food intake. I wonder if he'll wake hungry in the night since he can't tell me what he ate.

Rebecca is the most experienced and skilled of the regular staff, except myself and Yantra, who I don't really count as staff since we're residents. When Rebecca started three years ago, I worried that she could not physically keep up with Caleb. In fact, she once called from a park where she was sitting on Caleb to restrain him from entering the kiddie pool and frightening the little ones. We had to send backups in a car. She stuck with it, though, and Caleb does not feel compelled to push the boundaries with her as much any more.

I know I talk about Caleb far more than the other residents here. It's funny, because it's the opposite of the way I conduct myself in my daily life. When people ask how they are, I focus most on Miranda, Alex, and Michael. They are funny and growing. Alex and Michael are playing summer basketball and Michael is golfing. They are going to sleep-away camp this summer. Miranda is looking for a job and dancing six days a week. She's doing well in school. Caleb? I tell people that he's himself. He's happy. I don't focus on his new neuropathy, the possibility of breakthrough seizures, the speculation about a stroke (disproved after a five-hour ER visit). I don't talk about his boredom or distance, or even the positives, like his artistic endeavors in sidewalk chalk. He's himself. He's the same kind of chaos he's always been.

I also don't talk about the institution much in my daily social interactions. Staff drama, the constant search for new entry-level workers, the funding dilemmas. Because in real life, Yantra and I are more than "house mothers." Yes, we do the greatest number of hours. While no one does more than a six-hour shift while the residents are awake (the work is too taxing—it's too easy to make mistakes and loose tempers after much longer), we do the long overnights. In the early days, that was serious work, but now it's just showering the residents and putting them to bed, then roughly one night a week of wake-up duty.

The reason I don't really count us in considering the staff is because we're really the mothers. The real, unpaid, attached and committed parental mothers. The residents of this institution? That's us and our children. Our family is institutionalized by one child's disability and our desire to keep him home.

I have always known, like most mothers of disabled children, that I wanted to care for Caleb at home. The other kids are typically developing, so whether I wanted their residence in the house, the institution never came into question in my mind. But as Caleb's aggression and physiological impairments grew, we had to bring in more help. State agencies responded favorably, as Caleb is a ringer for another kind of institution—the ones that charge the state upward of $100,000 a year to care for kids like him. We're saving public monies by getting as many services as we can for Caleb here at the institution we call our home.

Our local newspaper's been doing a series on families deciding whether their disabled children should live at home or in an institution. I read an article about a family who institutionalized their disabled thirteen-year-old. They were doing all the care themselves, without help, and were not physically able to do it any more. I thought about what help that boy would have in his institution that Caleb lacks in ours. I couldn't think of a single therapy that he would be offered that Caleb hadn't already had. I couldn't imagine a single advantage that their institution had that mine lacked for Caleb. The disadvantages that came to mind were also quickly dismissed; the newspaper family could visit their son every day. Some days I work such long hours outside our home that I don't even get to see Caleb. Both boys know that they are loved. Both have schedules and the support and care they need. The only difference, in fact, is not in our disabled children and their needs. The family in the newspaper had only one advantage over me—they live outside their son's institution.

We live inside Caleb's. My family is rarely unobserved by professionals for more than twenty-four hours in a row. My typical children know the staff better than they know their extended family. They can't throw a fit or slam a door without an outsider noticing. Similarly, I can't yell or walk around without a bra. Having a glass of wine is a scrutinized activity. Having two? A judged one.

The family in the newspaper who made their difficult choice can walk around the house in their pajamas on Sunday mornings sipping coffee in dirty mugs. They can bicker, fart, cook smelly food without apology, leave a mess in the kitchen, and play annoying music loudly without worrying about some one quitting. They can leave valuables around without worrying that they are tempting underpaid staff. They can yell at their children and curse and scratch themselves without embarrassment.

I was never a terribly private person until I brought mandated reporters into my home.

Their quirks are many, their opinions about how things should be done as real as any employee: Denny won't shower Caleb and thinks it's crazy that we do, even though it's obvious that Caleb cannot shower himself. Eric worries about Caleb abusing the pets. Rebecca thinks we're too permissive, Emmanuel thinks we are too strict. Jeff worries about Caleb needing a father, Summer thought the DAN diet was too restrictive. John worries that Caleb is getting too fat, Brianna thinks he is losing weight. Sharon thinks we are saints, and Mary thinks Caleb is an angel from heaven. Jose thinks we should train the staff better.

Everybody has an opinion about our lives. Every year Audrey (or Janet before her or Kim before her) comes to evaluate our "institution." It's a four-hour meeting that determines our funding for the next year. Every year, we are required to trumpet the new deficits and diagnoses; every year,

Audrey determines what we'll need to keep our family together, to keep Caleb out of that other kind of institution—the one that breaks the state budget. Every year, we fight for a little more help, then watch our lives slip a little more into institutionalization.

I imagine that other family visiting their son in that other institution. I imagine them hearing all the good news—the improvements he's made, the art projects in which he excelled. I imagine the family sharing nothing—not to be difficult, but because it would be inappropriate to share their lives with these professionals. I imagine the family's surprise at their child's new skills, the unfamiliar scent of the institution's laundry detergent when they hug him. I imagine them wondering if any bad things have escaped report. I imagine them in the sitting room of that other institution wondering about the credentials of the workers, the ingredients in the food their son eats, the fiber content of his sheets. Mothers and fathers think about these things. Institutions consider efficiency and effectiveness, comfort and dignity. Mothers and fathers think about their babies.

Caleb sleeps on 200-count cotton sheets with Snoopy on them that were given to him by a family friend. We use the unscented laundry soap. He eats organic peanut butter unless we run out mid-week, and then he might have Adams. On warm days, he has Otter Pops and plays in our plastic pool. He had a fit at the park on Saturday, and tonight was too tired to do much but color. And no one knows more about Caleb's world than Yantra and I do.

The advantage the newspaper family has is privacy, mine is knowledge. My neighbors watch our care providers in the yard and report weird behavior. Our children tell me when people are late, or when they fight on the phone with their boyfriends and burn Caleb's pancakes. I interview all the people who work with him. I can fire them, too. I know them—what they care about, how they work with Caleb, their religions and educations and family backgrounds and police records and dreams for the future. I know the smell of their laundry detergents. And, yes, they know mine.

Audrey came yesterday. I could have told her I can't take the invasion any longer. I could still call her back to tell her that Yantra and I can no longer care for Caleb ourselves, that our typically developing children need more space to be human. I could tell her that having your whole family institutionalized because one child has a difficult disability is just not fair. I could ask her to find a good place that takes kids like him. I could ask her to give me my life back unscrutinized and private and uninstitutional, and

I believe that she could do it. She said this week, when I asked her about supportive care facilities in our area, that she's surprised we've been able to keep him home this long.

For now, though, I think I'll stay in this institution with Caleb. Knowing the smell of his shampoo and the moods of his helpers brings me a peace that weighs more than the worries that my typically developing children will grow secretive and repressed while I am mangled into a strangely private woman. For now, we'll bring the institution to Caleb and live within these glass walls, gathering up a collection of stones.

Small Victories
by Elizabeth Aquino

Sophie is nine and a half years old. She is of average height and build, although the onset of puberty has softened her once skinny frame, lending it subtle curve and roundness. Her head is small and fine, capped with amazing golden brown curls, ringlets that fall elegantly around her shoulders. When she was a baby in New York City, people stopped me on the street to exclaim over her hair. "Is it natural?" they would say, marveling. As if I would use a curling iron or worse, perm my baby's hair. Her face, too, is remarkable in its simple beauty. Full lips, a straight, dignified nose and large, dark brown eyes combine in an easy grace that belies the effort of her being. Sophie has had seizures all day, every day, since she was about three months old.

Aside from trips to the neurologist, acupuncturist, Oriental herbalist, osteopath, homeopath, Kabbalist healer, Guatemalan minister, touch healer, and special needs yoga instructor, we have been diligent in providing Sophie with any therapies that we thought would help her or even to reach her. While Sophie is healthy for the most part, the seizures have taken their toll, generating enough dysfunctional brain activity to thwart speech, easy movement, and facial affect. At the urging of one of Sophie's play therapists (whose job is to encourage social interaction and eye contact), I hired Jackie to be Sophie's music therapist.

I walked into Jackie's music room last month with Sophie and my usual attendant anxiety, kept low and bearable, hovering about and around me like a witch's familiar. Jackie is young, still in her twenties. She had a couple of tattoos and wore distinctive eye make-up. Black outlined them and sparkles twinkle on the lids. I felt decidedly middle-aged, weary in expectation. When we sat cross-legged on the floor, Sophie kept her head up and back, gazing at the ceiling, at nothing. Jackie picked up a guitar and sat down in front of us. She asked me the questions I've answered hundreds of times, dulling me down. *What is her diagnosis? When did it begin? Does she like music? Does she ever make sounds? Does she show pleasure? Is she resistant to anything?* It's simple to answer most of them, just boring because there's nothing, really, good to report.

And then Jackie began to play. I don't know much about music, but her voice was clear and high like an old-time folk singer. The guitar was plucked gently, but each note rose from the burnished instrument like it existed by itself and then floated into nothingness. Jackie inched forward on the floor and rested part of the guitar on Sophie's folded legs. Sophie still looked up, toward the ceiling, using gravity to aid her heavy head.

I felt tense, apologetic, despite the beauty of Jackie's voice and the instrument she had obviously mastered. I wanted to yank Sophie's head down and pivot her eyes myself. I strained against my clothes to move toward her, adjust her, fix her.

Minutes ticked by and Jackie continued to sing. The guitar, resting on Sophie's and Jackie's knees, hummed. I closed my eyes and willed my anxiety down. When I opened them, I looked at Sophie and saw what I can only describe as her appearance. But not the appearance of beautiful skin and curly hair, distant eyes and a mouth not often softened by expression. I saw the essence of her, and it was emerging from deep within her, from the baby that I had once had and that had died in bits and pieces over the years. It was as if her skin had thinned, allowing her soul a surface upon which to light. Jackie's voice, the plucking of the guitar, the vibration of the instrument on her lap had coaxed out an inherent intelligence that I had fixed onto over the years and defiantly and sometimes only half believed in. It seemed less a victory than an acquiescence from the universe.

Dragonflies and Inky Blackness:
Raising a Child with Asperger's Syndrome
by Caryn Mirriam-Goldberg

We're driving home around sunset, late summer. Daniel, age nine, says aloud, "Mom, what do you think is at the end of the universe? Dragonflies? Or just inky blackness?"

I write it down. A good moment when what shines in him shines through, but there are plenty of bad moments, too. Daniel, as exquisitely creative, loving, and intelligent as he is, suffers from what experts label an invisible disability, a chemical imbalance, a little extra electricity in his system.

To kids his own age he's a nuisance. To the school district he's a special needs child. To psychologists he's a quandary. To teachers he's a challenge. To relatives he's a little too hyper. To other parents, he's annoying. To piles of paperwork he's another diagnosis of Asperger's syndrome, epilepsy, hyperactivity. To child-rearing books he's an exception to the rule.

To my husband, Ken, and me, he's just Daniel, but even we can't say what in his behavior is chemical, what's within his control, what he'll outgrow, what will sculpt and contour his growth in ways we cannot see, what's a good sign, what's a bad one. All inky blackness so much of the time, with moments of dragonflies flashing their brilliance across a dulled sky.

◆ ◆ ◆

Nothing about Daniel's life has followed anything I read in child-rearing books or heard about friends who already had kids. Even the birth itself was a surprise. After a long and very painful labor, I finally pushed Daniel out, a baby the color of old-fashioned dark lilacs. The midwife placed him belly-down on my belly, cord still attached, and he opened his eyes for the first time.

His black eyes burned into mine with an intensity that suggested wherever he came from, he brought it along with him.

"I don't care where she is, get the doctor now!" the midwife whisper-yelled to the nurse. I wasn't supposed to hear that something was wrong, that the Apgar score on this baby was only about four out of ten, that my first child was damaged in some way.

"He inhaled amniotic fluid," they told me, "and he's not responding to oxygen enough to breathe on his own." We chose to go to the hospital, hopeful that our wait in the Neonatal Intensive Care Unit would only be a day or so.

A week later, after one minor problem after another, we finally took him home. It was France's bicentennial, and "La Marseillaise" played on the radio. "You're free!" we told him, but was he really? He could only sleep when in our bed, and he needed to be held constantly. We figured such intensity was a reaction to a week in the NICU where he was poked and probed according to a constant explosion of beeps and lights. So we held him. So we slept with him. Being that he was our first baby, his intensity didn't seem unusual.

A year later he almost died when his small intestine telescoped into his large one. Less than a year after that, when he could talk with great skill and a detailed vocabulary, he mainly discussed two topics: death and god.

"Mom, I'm going to die soon," he said.

"No, you can't do that. I'd be broken forever."

He looked at me thoughtfully, and a few days later, said, "Mom, I'm going to die soon, but it'll be okay. I'll have god send you another boy."

"No, it will not be okay. I'd still be broken forever."

I negotiated with this two-year-old over his life for several weeks, until he told me he decided to live, but he also asked, "Do all babies, after they're born, leave their parents to go back to god, and then come back?"

"No, Daniel, all babies don't do that," I told him.

And most toddlers do not approach other kids at the playground swings to ask them where their god monsters are, and what planets they come from.

I wondered if my panic while in labor the first time caused him to inhale amniotic fluid, and that caused him to have problems. I told the midwife this halfway through labor with my second child, a girl who would be very different than Daniel.

"No, that's ridiculous," she reassured me.

But when your child is challenged, you can't help but to blame yourself, as if you have any control. My daughter, born when Daniel was three, is the polar opposite of him. At three months old, she knows how to toss her head-full of dark curls and coyly look almost away when someone shows interest. By the time she's walking, she can work the room of any group, drawing their attention to herself without sacrificing any charm. She's born with an innate sense of knowing about all social situations, the secret language that eluded me as a kid that largely eludes Daniel now, encoded in her DNA.

The third child, another boy, follows her lead, flowing into groups of babies, then toddlers, then preschoolers without a blip. Like his sister, he knows how to work the system, while Daniel, on the other hand, doesn't know without being reminded that there is a system, a way of relating in families, in classes, in clumps of kids who find each other on playground equipment.

Daniel looks past his siblings to me one night in the kitchen, pausing in the middle of a six-hour reading marathon that calms him like nothing else. "I'm feeling rather melancholy tonight," he says, then returns to his book.

◆ ◆ ◆

The first seizure came the last day of May when he was seven. He was standing in the laundry room, chewing on his lip rhythmically, foaming at the mouth. His eyes wouldn't focus. He wouldn't answer.

On the way to the hospital, he started to fall asleep sitting on my lap. I slapped him repeatedly. "Stay awake, Daniel," I called out, afraid he would slip into a coma. I didn't know what just happened was a seizure. I only knew it was something terrible.

The EEG showed an abnormal brain wave. We had to wait to see if he'd never have another seizure before the anti-seizure meds. A week or so passed. No seizure. No worry. Maybe it was nothing. But then I walked in the house one late morning to the answering machine beeping. It was the director of the day-care center he attended that summer. He had just had a grand mal seizure in front of his whole day-care class.

When I got to the center, the staff had closed the office so that the director could sit on the floor next to a sleeping Daniel. His marvelous teachers talked to me repeatedly during the next few days, recounting every detail. They cried when they talked about how well the other kids did, how they watched Daniel as they explained, "Now this is what a seizure can look like. Jack is laying Daniel down so he won't hurt himself, but you can see Daniel's arms and legs moving a lot. It's okay. He's going to be okay."

I cried, too, when I told them that after the grand mal morning, I took him home, by way of the drive-through Chinese restaurant. At our kitchen table, right in front of his hot-and-sour soup, he started having another seizure. It was less dramatic, but longer. I watched him twitching on the floor while I made phone calls. Ken. The doctor. Ken's parents to drive us to the doctor. I carried the twitching Daniel to the car. He twitched until we got there, when he then transitioned to a "fugue state," which made him alternately scream out, then get very quiet and walk quickly into walls.

Finally, on the examining table, the doctor consulted with me about getting him on meds immediately. Once the doctor left the room, my mother-in-law started crying hysterically. "I'm sorry," she said. "I just can't help it."

I don't know why seizures are so frightening to watch, but they are. Most times, I was the one watching. Sometimes his stomach lifted up and down like it was possessed, sometimes his arms jerked in patterns, sometimes he wet his pants; always he fell asleep fast afterwards.

Each time he woke, I would tell him all the details, and he would always have a hard time believing it really happened. A fiction, he thought at first, until I told him the story enough times that he melded it to what he knew of himself.

All summer we tried different meds that made him into the Stepford child, amazingly well-behaved, quiet, focused, but also feverish and covered in a rash. Finally, we found Depakote, an anti-seizure med that both worked and didn't make him disappear.

◆ ◆ ◆

In some cultures, kids who have seizures, see visions, talk about spirit and death and the curve of the universe, are groomed to be visionaries for the community. Shamans who mediate between this world and the one beyond this world.

"In the place I come from," says Cherry, a sixty-year-old African-American woman who grew up in Black community of post-war Detroit, "the old people would watch a child like that very closely. Because they would know he's got something."

When she visits, she and Daniel cuddle up on the couch and read Shel Silverstein poems aloud, together, then alternating who reads each line, their voices creating a harmonics of poetry about washing a butt not your own and losing peanut butter sandwiches.

"What do you see?" my husband asks Daniel one night. Sweet Honey in the Rock music is playing in his room, and Daniel has been staring out into space for some time.

"I see our planet, the water, the land ... I see it getting closer, and then I see a group of women singing and waving their arms. In a circle, dancing, laughing and singing and calling to me."

◆ ◆ ◆

Daniel is in third grade, and I'm on the phone with his after-school day-care provider, who is throwing him out of her day-care center.

"It's not that I'm throwing him out," she explains to me repeatedly, and then goes on about how if Daniel has a sudden breakdown, and she focuses her attention on him and not on the toddlers there, one of the toddlers might get hurt, and then she would lose her business, and then her house. So can't I understand? This is the third after-school program he's been tossed from in two years.

Daniel cannot keep still. He must do his schoolwork and eat his meals while pacing the room, but that doesn't worry me. What does worry me is that the falling down on the floor and crying has dissolved into outbursts of anger, of violence. He kicks a kid who makes fun of him. He rips someone's shirt. "Accidentally," he tells me later.

What does worry me is that he has no friends. That he's been invited to fewer birthday parties than I can count on one hand. That no one ever invites him to their house to play.

What worries me are the looks family members give Ken and me at holiday meals when he yells out at the wrong time—looks that clearly tell us precisely what they say behind our backs.

What does worry me is that I've felt compelled to continually explain the medical terminology for Daniel's conditions to other parents so that they won't think he's a bad child or I'm a bad mother. "He's got Asperger's disorder, that's an autism spectrum disorder that basically means he can't read social cues," I tell them. "And on top of that, he has epilepsy and he's kinda hyperactive. It all goes together—too much electricity in his brain, or he's too inner-directed, or he's too emotional and sensitive. A chemical thing. We can't help it." I buy into the explanations because it gives me some way to convey the impossible, to at least fend off people shunning him because they believe he's bad, although sometimes I wonder if pity is any better than condemnation.

I sit in my room at night, right across from his room, and listen to the incredible stories he tells himself aloud at night when he's falling asleep: long narratives about his life, his birth trauma, places he's visited, how Pluto was formed, or how patterns of electricity work.

No one but those close to him knows he's gifted also. All most people see are the problems—the behavioral problems or the disability, and it takes a long time to see behind that veil, to see that it's not his intention to be obnoxious.

◆ ◆ ◆

I can't see behind that veil myself at times. It's 11:30 pm. He's supposed to have gone to sleep at 8:30 pm. Already, he's woken up the baby, who shares his room, three times by rolling out of his bed and climbing into his brother's bed with him. But he can never sleep still enough to any of us to handle anymore.

He keeps sitting in his doorway, getting what he can of the hall light to read *Calvin and Hobbes*, then screaming and leaping back to bed when I approach. He keeps blasting tape recorder playing Bach.

"Get back to bed now!" I yell. I'm tired, my head hurts, he's been driving me crazy since dinner time.

"NO!" he screams.

I rush his door, "GET INTO BED THIS INSTANT!" He's had a terrible day at school, and tomorrow's another one if he doesn't get rest. I just want to sit in my chair and read the paper.

I just want to watch some stupid sitcom on our miniature black-and-white TV without interruption.

The baby starts crying again. I get up, tuck him in, tell Daniel to get off the floor where he's wound the blanket around himself so tightly that he can't use his arms and legs.

"GET UP NOW!" I try to shovel him into the bed, but he kicks me. I slap the side of his face, fast, instinctively. He howls, spits at me but misses, tries to ram me with his head. I throw him into his bed, against the wall.

He curls up and cries. I go back to my room.

Ten minutes later I'm sitting on his bed. I try to touch him, but he doesn't let me. I ask him to forgive me. "I shouldn't have yelled. I shouldn't have hit you."

I start to leave, but he sits up and yells, "Mom, let's start over again."

"Okay." And so we do.

We start over again and again and again.

◆ ◆ ◆

You wonder how it starts, and you wonder where it came from. I was a kid who probably had Asperger's disorder myself. I had no friends in school: in fact, I was the kid other kids built their reputations upon. So I got beaten up constantly.

I blamed it on growing up in Brooklyn and central Jersey, on being small and a smart-ass, on having parents who slapped me around. But I see now I had the same problem Daniel has: I couldn't read social cues to save my life. I would see a group of kids, want to be part of them, but had no idea what to do, and in fact, what I did do was usually the worst choice.

Negative attention is better than no attention? So I thought.

Where did that come from? Upon hearing what Asperger's disorder is, my stepmother tells me that is absolutely what my father must have. She, his seeing-eye wife into the social world, would know. He has no idea what to say and often says what insults people most. But the more I hear of his childhood, the more I discover someone who grew up friendless and awkward, tormented and ignored. Like his mother behind him. Like her father before her.

I trace the Asperger's line through my family. I stop at Daniel.

Yet I realize how strange it is to call "not reading social cues" a disorder, especially when it's rooted in reading too much from the inside in, instead of the outside in. Yet I collude with the school's category of "other health impaired" so he can get services to help him not turn completely in on himself.

◆ ◆ ◆

"Ritalin, that will cure him."

"No, don't touch that stuff! You need to put him on a no-artificial-anything diet."

"Actually, this herbal mixture will help considerably."

"We're going to have some people, now don't get alarmed by this, from the therapeutic classroom take a look at him. That's for kids with severe psychological challenges."

"I think the best thing would be for him to be privately tutored and not in the class at all."

"He has sensory integration problems and needs a sensory diet. Just brush him every day with this little plastic brush and do joint compressions on him."

"How about the basket in the classroom with squeezie balls and other things to calm him down?"

"Massage will help him."

This is only a partial list. The advice rolls in regularly, the panacea of drug, alternative, and other treatments. We try everything. We visit psychologists, shrinks, neurologists, nurse-practitioners, herbalists, massage therapists, homeopaths, social works, general practitioners, Asperger specialists, occupational therapists. The Ritalin, as well as some other drugs, make him violent and depressed.

"You just have to realize," says a friend of mine whose son suffered from severe learning differences all through his schooling, "that nothing will work. There is no magic pill."

There is no answer. But I can't stop looking. Not when I tuck my kid in at night, and he says, "I'm just a bad person."

"No, you're not. You're a good person."

"That's not true. Something is wrong with me."

But it's not your fault, I want to scream into his bones. You did nothing to deserve this.

◆ ◆ ◆

Both the center of my heart and the edge of my universe contain Daniel. He is the one, more than anyone or anything else in my life, who challenges me to improvise, to forget how it should be, to drop my expectations and ideas about what life is, what a child is, what a parent is.

I make many mistakes with him, moments I wish I could do over. I also do many things right, hold him in the middle of the day on the couch mid-winter for no reason, listen to him carefully.

"Mom, I have to make my own mistakes," he says wisely, like any child would. But it's very hard to watch a kid whose days are spent being shunned by peers, analyzed or dismissed or hoped upon by teachers, medicalized by health professionals, isolated by his own choices and the constant reinforcement of others who chose to isolate him. To watch *your* kid.

Daniel teaches me that all rules are arbitrary, answers are illusionary, future visions are incomplete. He teaches me about the psychic wounds I carry into my parenting, and my only choice is to heal myself. He teaches me to be more patient, more accepting, more tolerant not just of him but of other kids. I see a nine-year-old hyper boy out in public these days, and I don't get irritated with him; instead, I feel empathy and wonder how his parents are doing.

Mostly, Daniel teaches me that love is never arbitrary.

That love leads us into mystery where no one can say what comes next, or how, or why.

◆ ◆ ◆

To my shock, everyone comes to his ninth birthday party, except one boy whose mother doesn't want him to associate with Daniel. We meet in a pizzeria where Daniel opens presents in a haze of joy. Some of the girls argue over who gets to sit next to him. One kisses his cheek every time he opens another gift.

Now it's on to the pool where Daniel, after three years in a row of flunking pre-swimming because he refused to put his face in the water, is jumping in, ducking his head under, rising up, and laughing.

But a few months from now I'll get two phone calls in a day: from his school and Hebrew school, both letting me know he needs "special help" in the classroom.

There will be Daniel wanting to make pickets to go and storm the new chain bookstore that drove our locally owned one out of business. Daniel determined to teach a boy who torments him that "it's not right" and not just. Daniel lecturing the other kids until they lecture us about the evils of McDonald's and the loss of rainforest lands for grazing cattle.

And Daniel at Yom Kippur services with me, hitting his heart as he sings the prayers, determined and utterly earnest in his determination to ask forgiveness, to start again.

◆ ◆ ◆

If we had known, ahead of time or even during the time, how difficult junior high school was for him, we probably would have transferred him, or even home-schooled him. Yet by that time, he had learned enough social cues, thanks for full-time paraprofessionals in grades four through six, to understand he shouldn't tell us everything anymore. Once he was safely in high school, an environment where the other kids were old enough and had known Daniel long enough, he seemed more relaxed despite the sudden bolts of anger and the loneliness over not having much of a social life. At least, by that time, we could blame part of it on him just being a teenager, a time in life when social agony is accepted and even expected.

Now he is at college, a small nest-like college in a small Mennonite Kansas town. Immersed in a community where everyone knows everyone, social activities tend to be all-inclusive, and being a little different and a lot Jewish is seen as exotic, he's thriving. He has friends, he's pursuing his passion for prairie restoration and ecological activism, and he's found a mild form of a Ritalin-like substance, which helps him study more steadily. Somehow he's grown into and through his various diagnoses. A success story, his old special education teachers, autism specialists and paraprofessionals tell me whenever we see each other at the coffee shop.

Still, I worry, surely more than I would have had he not tunneled through rock and steel throughout his childhood. At the same time, I hope what's different about him in the best sense doesn't get sanded off by the life ahead. Yet the life behind us shows me that Daniel has gotten through so far with his Daniel-ness fully intact.

◆ ◆ ◆

Metaphors are ways to contain the uncontainable. Symbols to hold what cannot be held, like fear or hope contained in darkness and dragonflies. Illusions, but what other way can we get close to the center of what's real?

It's like the myriad of names for god in Judaism—all ways to circle around what cannot be touched.

I remember Daniel at age nine: he sits at the kitchen table, and over his pasta, tells us he's convinced the universe does actually end at some point, that space curves into this ending. So there is an end, but he doesn't know what's there. He just knows all things curve into the future, into endings and infinity at once. And he can hold both the endings and the infinity in his head at once.

Like dragonflies in the inky blackness. Like Daniel in this world.

CHAPTER 5

Families:
When the Balancing Act
Induces Vertigo

Family relationships are complex and everchanging. When a family member or multiple family members face challenges that run counter to what society deems as a typical life, their experiences and their struggles influence the day-to-day realities of everyone in the family. We are often called "Down's families," "autistic families," or "wheelchair families." We are highly visible and, as individuals, sometimes completely unseen.

For the parents of special needs children, where is the line between needing to connect with and educate our various "publics" and protecting our children's privacy? How do we adequately parent and protect *all* our children, typical and non-typical, especially when their needs appear to be in conflict with one another? And how do we forgive ourselves when we come face to face with society's limelight and our own limits?

Ultimately, if they are cognitively able, our children find communities of their own. In this process, they discover how their parents' and siblings' various challenges and identities influence their connections to others and how they see themselves. They may have "remember when" stories that are both stinging and hilarious. Like the time when their brother ran down the street in only his underwear and socks and mom ran after him, holding her robe closed, shampoo suds flying off her head as they rounded the corner; or the more frightening moments when he seized on the dinning room floor, and mom relied on them to watch the minute hand so she would know if the emergency anti-seizure medication was needed. They might recall the times they were isolated by difference or the quiet looks and smiles of knowing that helped them walk into the room a bit lighter, knowing that someone had their back.

The writers in this chapter address how the special needs of our children influence family connections and individual identity. They ask how and if parents are to protect their typical and non-typical children from the spotlight of disability. How do parents help their children understand the unique challenges faced by non-typical siblings when they are stumbling over their own grief? These authors explore their intimate realities and insecurities in an effort to figure out how to honor all their children and themselves. Their illusions of control have long been shattered and they are finding hope in closets, grandbabies, growing relationships, love, and forgiveness.

Our Closet

by Diana Robinson

I am always coming out.

I am a woman married to another woman and I am a Jew. Apparently, I look neither queer nor Jewish, for it is always necessary for me to come out. I come out without hesitation whether in a new social situation or in an exchange with a stranger in line at the grocery store. While I never shy away from coming out as a queer woman or a Jew, I don't always choose to come out as the parent of a child with special needs. It is the only component of my identity that I sometimes keep closeted.

Refusing the protection of the closet as a queer woman and as a Jew makes me feel vulnerable yet powerful at the same time. I sacrifice the many privileges passing can afford, but I enjoy the opportunities to educate and to connect with other members of the queer and the Jewish communities by rejecting the closet. But these aspects of my identity and my life—being queer and being a Jew—belong just to me. Anything connected to my children, including but not limited to my daughter's special needs, does not belong only to me.

As an adoptive parent, the line where my story as a parent and my child's story as an individual merge and where our stories diverge, is particularly nebulous. What is mine to share and what belongs only to her? I don't think that line is always clear for biological parents either, but it is even more complex for me as my children's stories do not begin with me, or with my wife. They have in-utero histories, and three of my four children have lived lives after birth without us ranging from seventeen days in a NICU to sixteen years before joining our family. So what is mine and what is theirs? What about my daughters' biological families, their lives before we met and even their journeys to our family is my story to share and what should belong to them?

255

It is with regard to my daughter's special needs that this line is most blurry for me. If I talk about my journey in parenting a child with special needs, I inherently share that she is different from neurotypical children. Will she one day aspire to keep these differences private? Will she be able to choose to pass as neurotypical? Will she want to? If I have already shared her difficult in-utero journey leading to premature delivery, her brain damage at birth, and her terrifying early prognoses with our community, or with readers, then have I stolen her choice?

Even as I write this, I am not sure this is my story to tell. I balance my need to share my journey and honor her privacy by writing about it, but penning it with a pseudonym.

I am an extrovert who is direct with intimates and with strangers alike. I chat with neighbors, grocery store clerks, shoppers in line with me, UPS delivery people. Even the police officer who stops me for speeding will begin to think we're meeting for coffee. The world has always been an anthropological experiment wrapped in a cocktail party just waiting for me to unwrap it. Descartes wrote, "I think, therefore I am." For me it is closer to, "I dialogue, therefore I am."

And being a transracially adoptive lesbian-parented family means strangers ask me the most intimate questions as we stand in grocery store aisles. "Where'd you get her?" is a frequent question in response to seeing one of my kids. Viewing the diverse ethnicities of our family, some ask "Are they all yours?" One of my personal favorite questions is, "Which one of you is the real mom?" My instincts are to enter into dialogue and gently model appropriate language for transracially adoptive families and for lesbian-parented families, but I need to temper these instincts with my mom instincts toward brevity and familial privacy. Of course, I receive the questions because we are visibly "out" as an adoptive family. There is no need to come out about that.

I don't receive questions specifically about Olivia when we are out. At times, Olivia's differences mean we receive stares. Sometimes I receive sympathetic looks from parents who think my preschooler is having a tantrum, or disdainful looks from parents who think the same thing. Sometimes I receive puzzled looks as if the watcher is trying to make all the pieces fit, while at other times there is no indication that Olivia's differences are visible. And, in this way, the closet in which Olivia's differences sometimes hide isn't like the closet I regularly come out of as a queer woman or as a Jew. My closets have solid, heavy doors that I enjoy swinging wide open and hearing the door clang against its frame as I leap out. Olivia's closet has a clear glass door, which sometimes offers no opportunity for privacy and sometimes frosts opaque, thus offering protection. At this point, she does not control whether that closet door is a clear pane of glass or a frosted one from day to day, even hour to hour.

I have four daughters: Catherine, Sophia, Olivia, and Walker. It is Olivia, now three and a half years old, who is our child with special needs. She was born ten weeks prematurely and experienced periventricular leukomalacia. Sadly, her twin sister did not survive their traumatic and early birth. Based on the extent of her brain injury, pediatric neurologists were not certain what we should expect ... will she walk or talk? Time will tell, they said. Now in preschool, Olivia does indeed walk and talk. In fact, she jokes and runs. She is a miracle about whom the neurologist says, "The child in the MRI and the child in my office are two different children!" We are so very grateful. With public and private therapies, daily exercises and a house that looks like a special needs learning center, we are also exhausted. But still grateful.

Sometimes Olivia's challenges are nearly invisible. On good days, her awkward gait, hypotonic muscle tone, and delayed developmental skills might be overlooked. She appears quiet, but is responsive. Since three-year-olds aren't expected to engage in sharp-witted dialogue, her language processing delay might not be noticed. On these days her muscle tone overflow that is occasionally mistaken for a seizure is absent or infrequent enough to go unnoticed. On these days, a strong sensory diet, a series of daily exercises intended to help her maintain self-regulation and a functioning sensory system, renders her biggest challenge (sensory processing dysfunction) seemingly dormant. On these days, I sometimes yearn to pretend I am not the parent of a child with special needs. I yearn to just "pass" as any other parent out at the park with her three young children, to rest in denial for just a moment and enjoy the less intense challenges of plain old parenting. Of course, paradoxically, on these days I am also almost eager to share. I want to shout to the playground audience that this child has only been on the planet for three and a half years but has conquered so much in that short time. I want to hold her up for a round of applause (that would surely trigger a sensory meltdown!) and declare "victory!" and demand that her medal be proudly bestowed upon her.

Sometimes Olivia's challenges are quite visible. Her nineteen-month-old sister has begun to physically outpace her. While Olivia continues to need help both with balance and coordination when roller-skating, Walker confidently roller-skates on her own. When Olivia tries to climb some of the playground equipment alongside other preschoolers, the delay in her motor skills becomes more apparent. When another child takes a toy from her or pushes her out of line, she simply crumples into herself like a paper bag suddenly stepped upon by a heavy boot. She does not protest, or even whine, but simply freezes in time and space. If Olivia has a day when her muscle tone overflow not only presents itself, but also repeats in a loop, her challenges seem not only visible, but illuminated with a spotlight. Her face contorts into a frozen, over-reaching grimace akin to the Joker, and her hands tighten into white-knuckled fists. The force of her muscle contraction causes her face, hands, and sometimes her torso to shake involuntarily like a very young Parkinson's patient. And on days when her sensory system suffers over-stimulation or a misfire of sorts, and she appears to lose language, to lose motor planning, to moan, to yell and sometimes to writhe, flail, and even do a lovely combination of frothing/spitting, well, those differences are not only spotlighted, but under colorful fluorescent and flashing lights as well. On those days, there is no closet in which to hide for her, or for me.

It is on those days that I also sometimes yearn to come out. It is on those days that I have to carry my thirty-five-pound preschooler out of the public library as she flails and screams, yet my toddler walks calmly beside me holding my hand, that I want to not only come out but to come out to each person we see. On those days many people see Olivia's flailing and screaming, but they don't know the reasons why. I want to stop as I carry her twisting body to explain that she is not having a tantrum, that this is not a demo video for *Supernanny*, and that she is so much more than just these painful moments of absent self-regulation. But I don't share any of that. Because it's not mine to share. It's not my closet to decide to come out of.

It's our family closet. I am the parent of a child with special needs, married (albeit not legally) to another parent of a child with special needs. We hold hands in our closet; sometimes we need to hold each other up in our closet. Her sisters are the siblings of a child with special needs. It is their closet too.

While I have the option of choosing to come out of this shared closet, what choices does Olivia have? Will she have the opportunity to come out as a person with different needs? Or will her movements and her speech, will her needs and her differences implicitly and immediately "out" her?

Will my daughter's peers' eyes linger on her glasses, then absorb her movements, and begin to unpeel the nuances of her differences even on the days she could "pass"? Will they bother looking past the differences?

If my daughter continues to make progress in rewiring her brain and looks more and more like a neurotypical individual, will my daughter even want to pass? Or will she announce her differences and claim them as part of her identity? Will she find pride in her differences, in a shared identity and community of others with differences and of her ability to make her own way in this world?

On the days that leave my bones tired, my patience frayed and unraveled, and my energy depleted on the days that I struggle with coming out or respecting her privacy, I try to remember one thing. If it is sometimes hard to be a parent of a child with special needs, it is harder to actually be a child with special needs.

I have lived as a parent of a baby with special needs, a toddler with special needs, and now a preschooler with special needs. How will I feel as a parent of an older child with special needs? Of a teen with special needs? One day as a parent of a woman with special needs? Will I look back and regret the many dialogues I have had—with relatives, friends and even acquaintances—about her challenges and about my fears and hopes for her? Will I be angry with myself for having stolen her privacy? Or will I look back and feel thankful that I sought out and found the support I needed in order to be the best parent I could be? More importantly, how will Olivia feel?

Will Olivia understand my need to come out as her parent? Will she forgive me for my need to vent, to share and to seek support? Will she shrug and choose to come out herself? Or will she be angry that I eliminated her potential of passing with the neighbors or the UPS delivery person?

I finish writing this to find my amazing light-filled child who shuns the spotlight cuddled up with her toy animals to play a complex game of mama and baby animal rescue in the coziness of, yes, our linen closet. We removed the bottom shelf of this closet, and replaced the door to it with a curtain for this purpose. With a curtain hanging where the door should be, you can be both within and outside of it concurrently, with a sense of fluidity to the boundaries of the space. I watch Olivia play in the closet and smile at the irony, hope that her future includes the option of choosing what to share with the world about her differences and her struggles, and remind myself that I need work harder to honor her privacy over my desire to break out of my claustrophobic feeling in our family closet.

"Because He's Retarded, Ass!"
by Amber E. Taylor

When we got the call that we were matched with a baby for adoption, our hearts skipped a beat. When they told us the eleven-month-old who was destined to be ours had Down syndrome, our hearts just about stopped beating all together. What the hell? We didn't sign up for this! We went to our match meeting, and even though we hadn't yet met our son Brave, we knew it was going to be okay. The only thought in our heads was, "That's all right, we'll just buy property with a guest house for him." The saga began.

He has what?

When we told everyone that the much-awaited baby had Down syndrome, we got questions like "what is that, exactly?" We were surprised by people's lack of knowledge. They would say is "Oh, are those the people that all look the same?" We had accepted being "another lesbian couple that adopted a special kid." Yet, I have to admit I didn't expect everyone's ignorance. We bought books for our family to read. We bought advocacy stickers for our cars. We figured if we're going to do this, we're going to do it right!! Yes, our adopted son has Trisomy 21. He is small for his age, he has cute pudgy hands. He was two and a half when he started walking and he still walks funny, but the physical therapist insists that he is fine and doesn't need services.

What does it mean, that Down syndrome stuff? It means he needed heart surgery at four months old. It means he probably will always live at home. It means he will be made fun of. It means he does really goofy stuff and sometimes I laugh and probably shouldn't. It means he doesn't talk yet and may not be coherent when he finally does. It means we have to learn sign language and put up with glares and gawking. It means I have

260

complete breakdowns with tears and rocking and the whole bit because he STILL doesn't know which picture is the "dog" and which is the "cat" even though we have been working on it for months. It means he is making us stronger people and helping us to realize what life is all about.

But why would you do such a thing?

The first time we thought, "Oh dear, this will be challenging," was when our son's Regional Center worker came over to evaluate our new boy. She had been following him since he was born. She asked us a series of questions. "Does he receive SSI?" "No," we replied. "Does he receive WIC?" "No," we replied. "Is he receiving RC monetary support?" "No," we replied. She followed with: "If you're not getting any of these things, can I ask why you would adopt a child like this?"

A child like this. This statement coming from the woman who was looking out for his well-being prior to his arrival in our home. I didn't like this woman, but she was only the first of many. We answered, "because he needs a family and we have the time and patience to make sure he has the best life he can." If I had only known then what we would face. She felt like an ass. I was happy she felt like an ass.

We would get an array of questions and comments along the lines of "When are you going to institutionalize him?" My favorite, "If he were MY son…" and "Why isn't he walking yet!?" To which I would reply, in my most June Cleaver sort of voice "Because he's retarded, you ass!" I blurt it out in that way because when a person is being a jerk and I say "special," or "has needs," "Down syndrome," et cetera, it doesn't seem to sink in. When I blurt out "he's retarded," they get all red-faced and embarrassed, and I enjoy their discomfort.

One of the oddest people to blanket us in negative rhetoric was Mrs. Nun, his preschool teacher. She would say that she thought Brave was very high-functioning and might even be able to spell his name one day. Wow. How exciting. We had higher expectations for our son. He most certainly will spell his name, as well as other words.

Us and THEM, dealing with workers of various sorts...

We had the opportunity to see one of Brave's therapy sessions before we brought him home. We wanted to go to see his routine and what goals he was working on. He was scheduled to have one hour of occupational and physical therapy twice a week at the group home. We got to the home early for the first session so we could play with our baby. One o'clock passed, two o'clock. The therapist never showed up. I asked one of the nurses if that happened often. "Yes," she answered. Apparently there was only one therapist working with all of the group homes in that particular county. We hung out a little bit longer. I rocked him to sleep. The nurses shot me evil glances. If I rocked him to sleep, he might actually enjoy it and then THEY would have to do it, instead of leaving him in his crib and walking away for a few hours. He would have slept all day if they let him.

We came back for his Thursday session. The therapist was late, but she showed up. She only spent thirty minutes with him and got disgusted because he puked all over her therapy toys. The kid has reflux, folks, always has and still does. At this point, she had been "working" with him for about ten months and had managed to never get puked on? DOUBTFUL—he threw up ten times while we were there. She didn't even seem to want to touch him. It killed us to have to leave him in that place for another three days before we could bring him home.

In the infancy of our adoption, we were drowning in a sea of workers. We had our adoption worker (who by the way, remains our favorite worker EVER), our home study worker, Brave's social worker, his RC worker, his Early Start worker (who we later found out is a Catholic nun) and an array of nurses and medical (un)professionals. We were regularly being reminded that he was going to be a challenge and we needed to be ready.

Ready for what?

They did not tell us we needed to be ready for incompetent workers, physical therapists who thought he was fine even though he was twelve months old and couldn't crawl or sit up, or inept school systems. They DID tell us to be careful of judgmental people. This they said as they judged me, the black biracial dyke with head-to-toe visible tattoos and a bald head. This they said as they questioned whether or not my partner and I were old enough to be parents. I was twenty-five, Bee was twenty-two. My mom had me when she was fourteen and I turned out just fine. This being said, I know women who had children in their thirties and all I can think is, poor kids. The legal age to adopt a child in California is eighteen, so surely twenty-two and twenty-five would be just fine.

Our nun is a nice lady. She is a little aloof sometimes, but nice. She has accidentally let things slip like "Oh! You're gonna be Mr. Mom now huh?"

after I told her I was quitting my job and dropping out of school to be with our son full time. I chuckled to myself and said, "No, just mom."

Once, I took Brave to see his cardiologist. The woman who was doing his echocardiogram was acting quite peculiar. Again I was asked, "Why would you adopt this little boy?" I had my token response ready for such things and replied something along the lines of "all children need love and deserve a chance at a normal life, blah blah blah…" After a moment of odd silence she said she asked because she has a twelve-year-old daughter with Down syndrome. She confided in me, saying many days go by where she is upset and this life is hard. Her daughter has very bad arthritis and needed multiple surgeries just to be able to function. She told me how undone she got when she thought her daughter might never be able to ride a bike. It was a reality check for me. Up until that point, I had never considered that these things may happen to my baby. I know they happen, I've read the books. They just couldn't happen to MY baby. She later told me her daughter did eventually learn to ride a bike. She gave me some support group references. I appreciated her honesty and sincerity.

Support(less) groups

I have yet to discover a support group that fits us and I am always looking. Everything seems to be going fine until they find out my son is adopted. I usually get backlash about being there. After all, they are biological parents and didn't have a choice in birthing a special child. The tension is thick. I try to explain choices. I try to explain when we set out to adopt, we didn't expect a special child, just like they didn't expect a special child. I try to explain my grieving for not getting the perfect child I thought we were going to get. Many of the parents are just too bitter to even try to accept my story. I get treated as if I don't have a right to be there. I don't blame them, because I actually DO understand, even if they think I don't.

I tried going to a fost-adopt support group for special kids. That didn't help either. Most of the families there had autistic children, or kids with attachment disorders. They weren't making me feel unwanted. I just didn't fit in because they would talk about typical behaviors their children exhibited and I couldn't relate. No more trips to this group! I do really wish I could find a person with a child Brave's age, with Brave's condition to talk to, but I haven't found anyone yet. So for now, the bulk of my complaining, stressing, confiding, stories of the silly things he does, and developmental firsts, are dumped on to my two closest friends. One of them has two special needs children, so she understands. I listen to her, she listens to me, and we commiserate.

I've got the "my son's retarded and I'm PMSing blues"

Stress, PMS, and loneliness don't mix. It's a difficult job being a stay-at-home parent. It's unbearable having bloating, mood swings, and hot flashes when Aunt Flow comes for a visit. It can be very stressful trying to teach my kid to stop putting everything in his mouth and licking the sidewalk. It is ridiculously frightful when I am ambushed by all of the above, all at once. First, I lash out at my partner. If she didn't work so hard to provide for her ever-growing family, she would be home more. If she were home more, she could help with the kids and teach Brave the color red. Next comes Desolation Road. If only I had more friends. If only I had more friends with young kids. If only I had somebody to talk to that could say more than "da da da ba dubious?" There isn't anybody? So I embark onto my half a dozen blogs. Is anybody out there? Is anybody listening? Finally, Bee gets home from work. All I can do is cry and rock and talk about how big of a mistake I have made because I can't do this and it's too hard and I was wrong and want to go back to work—followed by more tears.

Eventually, she calms me down. She tells me I'm a great mother. She tells me how lucky she is and how lucky the kids are. She lets me know all my hard work is appreciated and Brave is signing so much and it's all because of me. Then, we make passionate love and hold each other...YEAH RIGHT! Who wants to have sex now? I'm freakin' tired! I'm fat! My favorite jeans don't fit and all I can think about is how Brave still doesn't know what color red is and that paper isn't all that easily digested! She does make me feel better, though.

Even Super Mom has a breakdown sometime, right? The pre-child Amber had these aspirations of being June Cleaver or Harriet or Harriet (no Ozzie in this family!). Somehow I ended up more like Roseanne. I guess that's better than Peg Bundy, though, huh? Sometimes I yearn for adult conversations with a person other than my partner. It might be just me, but when I am hormonal, "partner" equals "the enemy." She calls this my "I wanna be single again" phase. I don't want to be single, I hated being single. I love her very much. I just think she doesn't understand what it's like trying to get a child to put the square puzzle piece in the square hole every day for like two months. But it's just the hormones. She understands, she just doesn't have to do it and I guess I get bitter about that. I do often need some solitude around this time. I need to marinate in my solitude. Meditate on my life choices. I need to take comfort in knowing Brave WILL learn the color red, when he is ready. I WILL one day fit my favorite jeans again. Someday, my house will be clean and I will be some artist or writer or fire-spinning, hula-hooping performer. Someday we will have sex regularly again. Someday. Just not today.

The Gap is Closing

When Brave was about eighteen months old, we got an unexpected surprise. A relative of Brave's was born, and needed a new home as well. That wasn't a typo. No matter how much the adoption workers stress that love makes a family, they will take that baby from you if a "real relative" pops up. Anyway, four weeks later, we picked up this beautiful, typically functioning, drug addicted, fit-throwing lil' baby. Between sleep deprivation from Mace (and the recent death of my mother and adoption of my own brother) and the stress of just living, Brave didn't go to school for about six weeks. I really didn't see that big of a difference, with him anyway. Mace is now ten months old; his brother Brave is two and a half. The gap is closing. We knew Brave was behind but until Mace came along, it wasn't as noticeable. Or it was easier to ignore. At ten months, Mace is doing things Brave didn't do until after he was two. We get so excited when he does anything. I feel guilty because I'll see Mace cruising the furniture and crawling and trying to stand by himself and he gets so much admiration because of it.

Soon, Brave will be passed up. I worry for their future together. I know while they are young they will be friends. When they're older, will Mace be protective of his big-little brother? Will he be resentful and embarrassed? Will Brave get his feelings hurt because Mace wants to go out with the girls? Will girls want to go out with Brave? Will Mace get in fights defending our honor? Will Brave be jealous of Mace's accomplishments? Will he be able to accept our lives as they are? How will Brave react to another child, should we choose to expand our family further? Should we go for a typical child or a special child so Brave won't feel lonely? If Mace were not here would these thoughts ever have come into question? I lay in bed at night thinking about the gap in their development closing. What was once a chasm is now a crack in the foundation. What happens when the two sides meet, and continue spreading to create another chasm in the opposite direction?

Guilt, anger, excuses

Having a second, typically functioning kid really accentuates the "short-comings" of my other kid. Even when we go out, people always look at Mace and tell him how cute he is and, "Oh my God, he is such a doll!" All the while Brave is just sitting there, smiling. I feel like shit. What about my other kid, ASS! He's cute too, ya know! And I truly believe this. Just because he has that typical Down's face, doesn't mean Brave isn't just as cute! I find myself constantly reassuring Brave that he is also cute. In reality, he has no idea what is being said to him or his brother, but that's not the point. Eventually, he will understand. What then? Why do I feel obligated to cover up and make excuses for the people in the world that truly are stupid or ignorant or archaic? I expect I will feel this way forever.

Is there really a light at the end of the tunnel?

Raising children is a difficult job. Raising adopted children can be particularly challenging. Raising special needs adopted children when you're a lesbian stay-at-home parent is extremely difficult. So does it ever get better? Nobody wakes up and says, "Man, wouldn't it be totally cool to have a kid that can ride the short bus?" But you know what? That's where we are. We as parents are advocates for our children. It is important for us to remember that we need to be strong. We need to remember that it's okay to cry. We need to remember, nothing in life is guaranteed. We need to hold on to the idea that nothing and no one is ever perfect (not even that Brady Bunch family across the street). So, is there actually a light at the end of the tunnel? Maybe. Or maybe we need to make our own light. When we try to live in people's rigid boxes of social mores, our light dims. Do what works for you and your family and screw everything else. So what if you get stared at when you go into a restaurant with six kids, three special and all under five? Who cares that the drinks have been spilled twice and a plate ended up on the floor? Leave a big tip and laugh it off. That's our light, folks, right there. Like the commercial alludes ... Cost of visiting a mental health professional every month? $200. Cost of candles and red wine to calm down at the end of a hard day? $25. Cost of being Brave's Mama?

Priceless.

I wouldn't have it any other way.

And We Survive

by Nina Packebush

Several years ago my grandma came to terms with the fact that she was not going to get better and that her life was coming to an end. She had doctors and nurses, hospice workers and family, friends and strangers all offering advice on her prognosis, the types of treatment she should accept or not accept, and the best way to die, but in the end it was my grandma that had to make the choices. My grandma was surrounded by a variety of people that had a variety of agendas. The doctors, hospice workers, social workers and nurses had dedicated their lives to their professions and their egos were at stake. Grandma's friends and loved ones had their emotional egos at stake. In many ways it became a competition to see who could get Grandma to follow their advice. In some illogical way that would prove who really understood what Grandma was going through thus making this person more supportive, more heroic, more understanding, more loved by her.

Grandma was surrounded by people with years of experience who were eager to hand out advice and medical expertise and she was surrounded by people that would stroke her hair while she cried, fetch her ice chips, and listen as she relived her life between naps, but at the end of the day it didn't matter how many people had been in that room, Grandma was alone. Alone she had the late night panic attacks, the doubts, the terror, and the tears. She had to weigh all of the advice that was piled upon her and make the choices that best suited her particular situation. She, by herself had to defend her choices to all of the people who claimed to know better. Nobody could possibly feel what she felt or understand what she knew. Nobody—no matter how educated or caring—could understand what she was going through. And so it is with parenting a "special needs" child. We can be surrounded by medical experts, psychologists and psychiatrists, learning specialists and teachers, friends and relatives, therapists and heaps and heaps of information, yet in the end we are still alone with the decisions, the doubts, the fears and the panic, and the consequences. Unlike facing one's own death, knowing how it will end, in parenting a special child, the future is uncertain at best: it is someone else's future that we are responsible for and it all depends on us.

I have three "special" children. My oldest, twenty-two, and my youngest, ten, have pretty significant learning disabilities and ADHD. My oldest is of normal intelligence, yet he didn't learn to read until he was twelve. My youngest is gifted and at ten still can't write her last name dependably. My middle child is eighteen, has absolutely no problems with learning, but is in the process of being diagnosed with schizoaffective disorder. Life is never boring around our house especially since the middle child decided to make me a granny at the ripe old age of thirty-eight!

Throughout my twenty-two years as a parent I have been a "saint," an "angel," "brave," and a "hero." I have had the "patience of Mother Theresa" and the "stamina of an Olympic runner." People have been in awe of me and haven't hesitated to tell me so...at least when my kids were young. You see, the thing about having these special children is that people love the idea of families overcoming their challenges and going on to conquer the world. They love to hear how Mom sat on the floor, rocking back and forth for five straight years, until she finally reached her severely autistic child and brought her back into the world. They love the story of the child with severe learning disabilities that worked hard, whose parents never gave up on him, and he became a millionaire despite being unable to spell or read. They love those Oprah stories in which the underdog succeeds against all odds. What they don't like, however, is when the underdog remains the underdog and the cute little toddler becomes a loud, socially awkward, slightly odd child or teen who will never give friends and family the bragging rights that they feel they deserve. When our special children are young it is easy for people around us to flaunt us as "amazing." As our children age, however, people start to get a little uncomfortable.

When I announced to my family that I was going to homeschool Jason, they were horrified but figured it was just one of my crazy phases and it would soon pass. They decided to make the best of this and see it as a Lifetime for Women movie wherein Mommy decides to sacrifice everything to patiently stay home and nurture her special child into normality. When the crazy homeschool phase didn't pass and my annoying child that couldn't read remained annoying and illiterate my hero status was both elevated and conversely challenged. People would look at me with awe and say, "I don't know how you do it," and in the same breath tell me about how their friend's aunt's son's daughter had trouble with reading, but she just loved school and maybe Jason would too. When I added two more children to the family, and thus our homeschool, my hero status dwindled even further. The psychologist who went to great pains to tell me that I needed to accept the fact that Jason would most likely grow up to be functionally illiterate, had a high probability of dropping out of school, would need to be bussed to special classes for at least part of the day, and might even end up in prison, informed me that homeschooling him would have "catastrophic results." My family and friends just thought I was crazy and suddenly everyone was an expert.

"Have you tried grapeseed extract? I saw this report on the news that says it cures ADHD. You should try it." "So I was telling my hair stylist about Jason and she has a grandson that has the same thing and she said that they are doing biofeedback and her grandson is cured! Have you tried that?" "Last night I couldn't sleep and I saw this commercial for Hooked on Phonics and they guarantee that your child will learn to read. You need to get that for Jason." Yes, biofeedback, grapeseed extract, learning programs, computer programs, public school, private school, special camps, homeopathy, tutors, life coaches, acupuncture, special diets, more exercise, forcing Jason to crawl around on the floor which would supposedly cause the part of the brain that we use for reading to develop in a way that didn't happen when he was an infant, Ritalin, therapy—all of those things were suggested to me by people who had not one ounce of experience with a child like mine. Of course each suggestion chipped away at my confidence as a mother just a little bit more and I had to go and research all of these suggestions no matter how asinine they may have sounded. This was back before the Internet and so to the bookstore I would trudge and hand over another pile of cash that I did not have for an answer that was not there.

I did try a lot of different things. I bought grapeseed extract in bulk, which did nothing but cost me money. I took Jason to a homeopathic doctor who declared bad parenting as the cause of his problems and put him on a "white diet." What is a white diet? It is a diet of only white foods. The boy could have white chicken with no seasoning, cauliflower, milk and a very small selection of veggies with no seasoning whatsoever. That lasted a couple of days. I stopped allowing Jason to eat any artificial food colorings,

MSG or additives and that did help with the hyperactivity, but it did nothing for his learning. I tried Ritalin and Adderall. The Ritalin worked to a degree, but the Adderall made him crazy. The solution of the experts was to try to diagnose Jason with oppositional defiant disorder and prescribe him a bucket of new meds. This med for this and that med for that and those meds to counteract the side effects of these meds and on it went. I made the decision to go med free. This horrified the family, but at the same time made me even more of a martyr.

As time passed and Jason was not emerging as the next Thomas Edison my hero status began to fade even more. Everyone knows that Thomas Edison had learning issues and that his mom homeschooled him and because of that the world was changed. It began to become clear that Jason was most likely not going to be the next Edison and people started to squirm. I realized that nobody had any faith in me. I realized that people thought that I was making up Jason's issues in my head because I had some strange control issue or I was afraid to have him grow up or I was just so fucked up that I was making my kid fucked up. After all, Jason looked normal and talked normal and acted mostly normal. Yes, he was a little wild, but boys will be boys. I had him when I was only a child myself and I did live a rather odd life and I refused to conform and … yes, that's it! The poor boy's mother is whacked and it is all her fault. As I came to this realization I started to believe that maybe they were right. Never mind the fact that I had a bill for $3,000 for private neuro-psych testing that said that he did, in fact, have issues. I was feeling less and less sure of myself.

It is hard to decide which was harder, my days as a hero or my much longer time as a messed-up parent. Heroes do not yell, "Damn it! It isn't that hard! Just write the goddamn words!" Saints do not lie awake at night sobbing and secretly wondering what life would be like if their child hadn't been born. Amazing and brave mommies do not feel such rage when their child falls out of their chair for the fiftieth time that they have to go outside for fear of violence. People with "amazing patience" do not go into their child's room and break things in sobbing frustration when they discover that he has once again drilled a hole in the wall to talk to his sister at night and pushed his mattress out the window because he didn't want it any more. When you are the next goddamn Mother Theresa you aren't allowed to feel and do such things and when you do you sure can't tell anybody, especially when you are homeschooling. On the other hand, when everyone in the world seems to be doubting you and blaming you then every single time you feel rage starting to rise in your chest, just waiting there, and every single time you feel like you want to just grab your dog and your backpack and never come home you are proving them right. Each time you start to think it really was all your fault for whatever reason—whether you didn't take enough prenatal vitamins or you didn't buy the right educational toddler toys or you didn't read to them enough—whatever the reason, you can't tell anyone.

The only thing that saved me was my girls. Hailey appeared to be a normal, average kid that was a little overly attached to me, but basically things came easy to her and she was always calm and well-behaved. Syd, the youngest, was a fireball, but she was so smart. Syd had full sentences at nine months, knew her colors before she could walk, and preferred adults to children. While Jason was bouncing around like a superball and Hailey was hiding behind my leg, Syd, with her blond curls and huge smile, was off making every adult within miles fall in love. People started to relax a little. Surely I couldn't be completely messed up because here was sweet, quiet Hailey and amazingly brilliant Syd; maybe Jason really did have some issues. My girls gave me back a little of my confidence as a parent … at least for a little while.

Syd's vocabulary rivaled most adults' by the time she was six, yet she seemed to be having a really hard time learning her alphabet. I got nervous, but told myself I was creating issues in my head. By eight Sydney still didn't know all of her letters, but she could tell you about all of the animals that inhabited Papua New Guinea. She couldn't spell her last name reliably, but she would be happy to tell you the entire history of El Chupacabra. Syd only slept a few hours a night and was twice as destructive as Jason. I didn't even bother to have her tested. The panic started all over again. Did I do this to her? Was it homeschooling? Was it my parenting? Was it because I came out as a lesbian and left her dad and blew her life up right before her eyes? If you ask my family they would probably whisper yes when they think I am not looking. I fucked up Jason's life by being too young when I had him and now I was fucking up Syd's by becoming a lesbian smack dab in the middle of her childhood. Everyone knew these kinds of things had profound effects on children. I tried to swallow all of those nagging insecurities and just trudged on. At least with Syd I didn't spend years trying things that did not work and I didn't spend hundreds and hundreds of dollars on books about "special" children; after all I had already read them all.

My saving grace was Hailey. She became my poster child. She became the one that validated me. Yes, the family thought that I coddled her and overprotected her on one hand while simultaneously exposing her to far more than was healthy for a child her age, but still she could read and write and, other than math, seemed to learn easily. She was quiet, artistic, and perfectly behaved all of the time. She never got over-stimulated or broke things by being too rough. She never had fits and did I mention that she read really, really well? She was my sidekick. She was the youngest volunteer that the House Rabbit Society had ever had. She went to work with me every day at my farm sanctuary job and participated in the largest animal rescue in the United States when she was only eleven years old. She was given adult responsibilities and earned a letter of recognition from the Red Cross. She stayed up all night reading and writing in journals that she made herself. She painted the living room and the kitchen red and orange and had a clear knack for color and design. She painted amazing murals on her bedroom wall. She learned for fun!

Fast forward just a little bit. Hailey started having visions and fits of mania and depression. It is hard, though, to tell when a teenager is having abnormal mania and depression. Teens are unstable, right? And the visions? Well, all of her friends believed in spirits and saw ghosts; they adored the Ouija board and were sure a zombie apocalypse was inevitable. Teen girls are like that. How was I to know that Hailey *really* saw her dead friend hovering over her bed at night and *really* stayed up all night terrified of the zombies that she sometimes saw looking in her window? The interesting thing is that because Hailey was always the "normal" and easy child, when things started to get a little odd I didn't even notice. She was what I measured normality by, so if she said that the twinkle lights around her Virgin Mary tapestry blinked whenever "Going Once" by Ani came on and that was telling her that we needed to go, well, that was just normal teenage stuff, right? Things were rough around our house at that time because my marriage was breaking up and I was coming out, so the fact that she kept a bag packed next to her bed and stayed up all night because she just knew I was going to abandon her and she wanted to be ready to follow me, that didn't seem overly odd to me. She was my normal kid. This was normal teenage stuff and besides one of our good friends had recently committed suicide so of course she was being a little dramatic. When she got herself pregnant after declaring adamantly that she was a lesbian, I didn't see it as a sign of anything other than normal teenage behavior. There was nothing to worry about. I had my two "special" kids and just because my easy kid was having a rough time did not mean anything. I held fast to the fact that Hail was my normal.

Hailey became angry and had fits of rage, but I attributed that to pregnancy hormones. After baby Felix was born, her detachment, crying fits, and intense paranoia became postpartum depression. As Felix approached his first year, her rollercoaster ride from intense happiness and productivity to crushing depression were withdrawal symptoms of the Zoloft. Then the night came when she very excitedly told me all about how she was going to go to the beach and jump off the pedestrian overpass. It was going to be so much fun. She called her best friend and tried to convince her to come along. She couldn't sit still and she talked so fast I was barely able to understand her. She explained that even if she did die, which she surely wouldn't, but if by some chance she did that would be okay because being dead would be fun. She told me of all the adventures she would have while she was dead. I removed all of the pills and knives from the house and stayed up all night. I was pretty sure this was not normal. Just in time for me to finally become confident and secure in my parenting and just in time for me to finally not even glance at the "special" needs books or hear the relatives when they offered advice or even think about consulting an expert, just when I got to that point, I was thrown headlong into uncertainty and another kid's future to worry about. And again I find myself being handed advice like M&Ms.

We saw doctors, therapists, and psychiatrists, and they all had different ideas. The only thing they could all agree on was that this was most likely bipolar 1. They put her on meds and her mood stabilized, but the visions became stronger and more intense. Her ability to tell fantasy from reality was slipping just a little bit more each month. Now it looks like she may have schizoaffective disorder and everyone has an opinion on how to approach it. I have spent hours on the Internet getting radically conflicting stories about the miracles and the horrors of drugs. The people around me are eager to offer their opinions and advice. Some say she should smoke pot, others say it will trigger psychosis. Some say inpatient treatment, some say outpatient treatment, and some say it is not nearly bad enough to warrant either. I have been told that eating meat is critical and that being vegan is the only way to stabilize her brain. I have been told that she should meditate and let herself go into the visions and I have been told that this is very dangerous. My favorite suggestion so far though is that she just needs a job.

I guess that working for minimum wage is the sure cure for psychosis.

These days she is no longer on an emotional rollercoaster, but she is no longer my easy kid. She is no longer the child I once clung to for reassurance that I was doing things right. This thing with Hailey makes all those years with Jason and Syd seem like nothing. It seems almost silly to me now that I used to worry so much. Often I wake up in the night terrified, worried, and sick to my stomach. The same old fears have come back to me in a whole new way. Did I make Hailey like this by homeschooling her? By overprotecting her? By not protecting her enough? Was it our friend's suicide? Are my genes really that messed up?

Sometimes when I am really torn up I call my son. He has a fiancé, a job, a nice car, a decent place to live, and good credit. My boy calls me almost every day and visits often. He doesn't read well, spells atrociously and struggles with math, but he made it. He gives me advice on his sisters. He tells me when he feels I am coddling Hail too much and when he thinks I should be more forgiving. He reassures me that if I have to take over raising Felix that he will help in any way he can. He warns me when he hears something in Hailey's voice that sounds off to him. And when I whine about how Syd was helping me unload the car and dropped the full box of expensive beer in the driveway he says, "Mom, do you remember what would happen every time I helped you unload the car? I always dropped the apple juice and broke it. Remember? She is just like me, don't let her carry glass!" It took twenty-two years, but I am finally getting some advice I can use. It took twenty-two years but suddenly I no longer feel quite so alone in all of it.

I know my girls will get through their challenges too. It will all turn out okay and I did the best I could. Some of the worst scenes from Jason's childhood have turned into "remember when…" moments. Things that used to eat me up with guilt are funny stories to him. "God, you used to get so mad! Remember the time I made my own skateboard in the garage and spilled paint everywhere and then rode it off the dog house? Oh my god, that was so funny!" I should mention here that Jason takes great pleasure in finally being my "good kid."

A friend of mine and I were talking the other day. She has been in and out of mental hospitals since her early twenties. We were talking about childhood and trauma and the things parents do to their kids. She said, "We all have our stories, Nina. We survive or we don't. Mostly though, we do survive." She is right. Those of us that have special children are just like any other parent. We do the best that we can and make a million mistakes along the way. We might be elevated to saint status or we might be scorned, but in the end we just do the best we can with what we have. My grandma knew she wasn't going to survive and she made the best of the time she had left. I know my kids will survive and I am trying to make the best of the time we have left.

Thanksgiving
by Kim Mahler

When he pulls out his penis and pees
on the carpet everyone has a theory: the right
discipline, cleaner, behavior modification.
Cousins circle my sister, who's scrubbing
the wet-blue patch of her boyfriend's rug.
I'm searching for the right place to hit him.
I've abandoned time outs, but remember
the cheek is reserved for adult betrayal. After three
glasses of wine, I hesitate, consider leaving him
alone, walking out of the house, the holiday.
His forearm is flat, smooth, accessible.
It takes more slaps than seems safe
for his face to register pain. I have no appetite
for punishing the disabled. Isn't there enough dread
without this child's baffled tongue, heavy eyes.
Days later I'm still rattled by my sister's talk
of stains, medication; my hot useless hands.

Dual Parentship Status
by Jennifer Silverman

It was the typical chaos of drop-off at the weekend recreation program: about ten to fifteen kids, mostly boys, with varying degrees of autism, running, jumping, yelling, flapping, and throwing balls around the gym while their parents waited for the day's activities to begin. While my almost ten-year-old son awkwardly peddled a stationary bike, his typically developing two-year-old brother chased a basketball on the floor. Since I had one eye on each kid, I didn't initially notice the woman talking to me above the hullabaloo.* She said something along the lines of "you must be very brave. I've never seen a younger one after a first one with autism."

I knew her comment couldn't possibly be true (I've seen many families with kids of all ages and abilities), but I didn't point that out. Instead I shrugged off the "brave" comment, gestured to Milo and responded that he was developing typically and we were lucky.

She soothingly answered that it was obvious Milo was fine, and then went on. "It must be hard to have your little one pass your big one." By then I had to run off to keep Milo from getting hit in the head by a basketball, so I never got to answer.

She was another mother, one of the parents I never speak to in the program. Although we all saw each other regularly and offered each other weak smiles and nods of understanding, I don't socialize with these other folks. It's too hard to keep the kids safe without trying to make small talk, but I have also never wanted to only be friendly with other autism parents solely on the basis of parenting kids with disabilities. While I no longer have pink-streaked hair and rarely go to drop-off wearing radical political T-shirts, I still stand out among the parents as younger and more urban.

---

* Conversation details as best as my sleep-deprived brain can remember them.

On a surface level (clothing, bumper stickers, and age) it seems like we have very little in common though they seem like nice people. I don't know how much interest they would have in a dyspeptic, anti-establishment mama like me anyways.

I had tried, at the beginning of Luc's diagnosis process, to meet other mamas for some support through a well-meaning parents' service. The first woman I spoke to was too busy for anything other than a phone call, and although she was very nice we didn't connect at all. Their second suggestion was a woman who had seemed okay, but then informed me that she was a born-again Christian who didn't send her kids to school on Halloween because it was the devil's holiday. I never called her back. Since then, I limited my special needs support to online boards, listservs, and the handful of wonderful and funny "special needs" mamas with similar sensibilities who I have met in the years since.

The interaction with the recreation program woman kind of threw me, and stuck in my head for the rest of the day. Brave? Lucky? Possibly foolhardy. I had gone into my second pregnancy, not with the naiveté of a twenty-five-year-old who had assumed a sonogram and negative triple screen test had eliminated the possibility of something going awry, but with the cautious optimism of the thirty-two-year-old I had grown into. Fully aware that there was no prenatal testing for autism, my second husband and I had chosen to have a child and thought through the real possibility of having a second child with a disability. One in a million, the first developmental pediatrician who saw Luc had told me, was that chance of having a child with a disability like his. More like one in one hundred and fifty, as his autism symptoms became clearer and more pronounced, and that became his primary diagnosis.

With the pregnancy that begat Milo, I weighed the odds. Since we were dealing with a new genetic pool, I figured that the odds of autism striking again were fairly low, and there were some factors that I had control over. During pregnancy I stayed away from all fish, didn't have any dental work, and chose to not vaccinate the new baby based on my family history of vaccine reactions. We met with a genetic counselor to make sure there wouldn't be any inherited Jewish diseases to pass on, and then I went through the typical pregnancy screenings. I was thrown for a brief, funny loop when the genetic counselor asked if Ari and I could possibly be cousins (we aren't). Everything looked, as it had with Luc, like it was going to be fine. But Luc wasn't, and there was still that kernel of fear.

I am not a person who would willingly and happily bring a person with a disability into the world. Those people who continue with pregnancies knowing there will be a problem, or the amazingly selfless folks who adopt kids with disabilities have my utmost respect. But I am not naturally patient or noble. Before having Luc I felt that the world was hard enough to grow up in for typical kids, so why make it even more difficult for a child? Part of this stemmed from being raised by a mother with a physical disability—rheumatoid arthritis that got progressively worse, with a host of autoimmune conditions, as I got older. Although we got great parking spaces with the handicapped placard, there was so much that she couldn't do. As a child, I was frustrated by everything that was harder for us than for the average family. Long walks, biking together, roughhousing, painting—those were the kinds of things I didn't get to experience with my mom, though she compensates admirably for her disability. I didn't want my family, the one I created as a mama, to have limitations on us in what we could do together.

I can't say that parenting Luc has made me a saint—far from it, but I've learned to be more patient, found out that I am very adaptable under circumstances I cannot change, and I make a bad-ass mama bear and advocate. Still, I definitely did not want to be a mama of two kids with severe "special needs." Mild ADHD, a learning disability—those were things I could handle, I joked to my husband. I didn't care if our new baby was brilliant. I would be perfectly happy with average.

I'm sure that our families were worried, too. My grandmother went as far as addressing it in a passive aggressive way. "I just don't know why you'd want to make things harder for yourself," she said.

I knew why. As much as I love Luc, I wanted the experience of raising a typically developing child, a combination of me and Ari who would talk, understand the world around him (as much as we did, anyways), and do the things that Luc couldn't. It might sound selfish, but I wanted a child I could make art projects with without forcing it; go to the movies with; who knew when I went to work for the day what I did; who understood what was behind the pomp and circumstance of the marches and rallies we went to; who would grow up to be independent, know the beauty of reading a good book, and would experience the elation of falling in love.

And it looks like we got a pretty neurotypical kid. My progeny both attract attention wherever we go, but for very different reasons. The baby, newly turned three, is all enormous brown eyes, huge smiles, and charm—a natural-born flirt who engages strangers in conversation on the subway. The big boy, ten, is full of recessive genes—tall, blond, blue-eyed and lanky as opposed to his two short, brown-eyed, brown-haired parents. As a baby and toddler, he was gushed over by strangers for his strangely Aryan good looks. For the last six years or so, he's gotten a different kind of attention: stares and rude comments on his jumping, shrieking, and loud tantrums. To be fair, for every twenty or so of those kinds of interactions we do get a kindly person commenting on his sweetness or trying to communicate with him.

The baby turned toddler is ahead on all of his milestones and is really pretty bright. He runs, talks in paragraphs, sings, counts up to twenty, knows his colors, somersaults, and is obsessed with Pete Seeger, going to his music class, the subway system in our city and dressing up in my shoes.

I still don't know what the big kid is capable of, even at age ten. He had known his letters at the age of two but as he's slipped further and further into his own autistic orbit, his use of language has completely disappeared. Much of his second year and into his third was marked by frustration, confusion, anger, and disappointment as we met with unhelpful doctors, watched as the milestones flew by unmet, and eventually had our world turned on its head by the terms *developmentally delayed* and *autism*. We are now starting to look into augmentative communication, which I am (fingers crossed) hoping will help with some of our bigger barriers.

Both my children unquestionably make me happy. As Ari is fond of saying, no one makes me smile like them. But often I feel like I'm caught in two different and almost equally challenging worlds. With the big kid, by the time he was two years old, I had already set up a speech evaluation, concerned about some of his behaviors and deficits that eventually led us to his autism diagnosis. After ignoring my mother's insistence for months that Luc was not developing according to the patterns you would expect, I conferred with our family doctor, and went to a developmental pediatrician. Going in for a speech delay and coming out with an initial diagnosis of global developmental delay definitely wasn't what I expected to happen. Neither was spending the next year in limbo with early intervention specialists until the "A word" was mentioned and special education became our future.

Parenting an insatiably intellectually curious toddler is not something in which I have experience. It's not that autism is easy—by any measure, raising my ten-year-old has been insanely hard. But I'm used to it. I know what to expect, even if it does involve two hours of non-stop screaming or redirecting a self-injurious stimming session. I know how to advocate at an Individualized Education Plan meeting, but not how to interact with other parents at a typical toddler playgroup. There's a comfort level I have yet to reach with parenting my second. Part of this is circumstantial: where I was home with Luc for three veerrrryyyy long years until he started a special needs preschool, I have been at work since Milo was two and a half months old. Ari has done the primary caregiving since then, with help from my extraordinary mother-in-law. His job as a super in a residential building has allowed Ari to take Milo to work, first in a sling, then in a backpack, and now just walking around "assisting" him (no, we do not actually engage in child labor). I have continued to work in nonprofits, swooping through the door in the evening and becoming what we lightheartedly we call "fun dad." Whereas I knew, often to the point of extreme frustration, whether or not Luc had napped that day, what he had eaten, who he had played with, etc., I now have to ask. So there's a kind of disconnect there. Fortunately Milo does not seem to feel that divide—he is almost as attached to me as his brother is, but for nine hours a day, for all intents and purposes I am a memory to him or a voice on the end of the phone.

In most ways, Milo has already developmentally passed his brother. In some ways they're very similar; both were textbook "high needs" babies who were only happy when they were held or nursed for the first six months. They both continue to be fiercely stubborn and equally loving. They share a mutual love of the Beatles, *My Neighbor Totoro*, Veggie Booty, sleeping in the big bed with mama, and a distrust of shirts with buttons. Both are being toilet trained right now, although simultaneously toilet training a preschooler and a preteen is not something that thrills me.

At this time, Milo doesn't yet realize that there's anything unusual about Luc. He just accepts that he doesn't talk, and I've only just started explaining how Luc is different to him. Yesterday Milo called Luc "my brother" for the first time and I beamed for hours afterwards. This is the easy part, I think.

As they get older and it becomes more obvious to Milo, I wonder how he and his peers will react. Will he see his disabled brother as an annoyance? Someone to defend and champion? How will I keep my own frustration in raising Luc enough in check that it won't rub off on how Milo treats him? Because even though I have made peace with who he is, Luc's still a challenge, and like most kids, he saves his worst behavior for his parents. How do we make sure that each child has enough space and individual attention to flourish? Do I send Milo to therapy, or a support group, or scrape up money for sleep-away camps for him to have him his own space? Unlike when Luc was this age and we were pretty poor, or later when we were flat broke and eating via food stamps as a single-parent family, I can now keep on top of our bills. We still live on a lot less than most folks in New York City. In a city apartment of about 850 square feet, which we will be paying off for the next twenty something years, how will I make sure Milo has enough physical room to have friends over, study, or just be when his then teenage brother still acts like a loud toddler? Am I being fair to Milo or do I expect too much of him? These questions are constantly omnipresent and I don't know how to answer them. I don't want him to grow up to resent being the brother of a person with autism, and I also don't want it to hinder him.

For his part, Luc is a really terrific brother. He tolerates Milo's intrusions into his bedroom, helps push the stroller, and patiently lets his baby brother jump on him. He is compassionate, too, something that surprised and pleased me. When Milo was a baby and cried in his car seat, I would glance backwards and see Luc holding his hand, as if to comfort him. Aside from his irritation of being perpetually pestered by Milo, I've seen Luc grow from having the experience of a sibling. He's also become better at communicating his need for interaction with me, and I've seen more of the range of his emotional life. In this way, it has been a growth experience. The same questions apply to him, too, in terms of dividing my time and making sure he gets enough from me. The times when it is just the two of us, he seems more relaxed and sometimes a bit needy—grabbing my hand to come sit with him, sitting himself on my lap—quite a sight, I'm sure, as he's almost the same height as me and has surpassed my shoe size already. Luc's cues are subtler than Milo's, who bangs on the door and yells "Mama, please open the door right now!" anytime I escape for a moment alone, and I hope I don't overlook them.

There was a second set of reasons I wanted Luc to have a sibling, which until now I have only articulated to a small group of people. I wanted to make sure that he had someone to love him and look out for him when we no longer could. There have been, prior to Milo's arrival, many nights where I have stayed up, panic stricken, wondering what will happen to Luc when I die. Who will be there to love him as much as I do? To make sure he's in a good place, well-taken care of, and not lonely? Luc's bio-dad, stepmother, and his other half sibling now live on the other side of the country, and they won't know his day-in, day-out needs like the family he lives with simply by geography.

It seems like there are a hundred questions for every situation I manage to navigate. When Luc was a toddler and I was going through the diagnosis process (while trying to keep my sanity and not cry every ten minutes out of aggravation and crushing sadness mingled with guilt), I was essentially alone. Until I met my friend Karen, another "special needs" parent with a wicked sense of humor almost a year into it, there was no existing friend I could really talk to. Being at home full-time with a toddler who didn't sleep through the night consistently (until he was six), rarely napped, wouldn't sit still unless watching a video, ran away every time we went out, even got kicked out of a special needs music class, and wouldn't engage me back in playing games, was as hard as I thought, and my emotions were justified—I know that now. At the time, I was just *that parent*, at least before the autism label: the one whose kid is always the one not listening, scratching and hitting at other kids, having to be redirected every two seconds, and getting invited to play dates less and less by the few parents I actually knew. I distinctly remember being at an event with a woman I respected whose very verbal three-year-old told her, in front of us, "I don't like that boy." Granted, it was after I disengaged Luc's hands from his head, but it still stung. As it did when neighborhood kids called him retarded, as it still does when people turn around and stare like they've never seem something so freakish before. I can shake it off and say "fuck it," but it's still there.

We were isolated back then, geographically from my support network, and figuratively because of not knowing other parents of kids that we could relate to. By the time Milo arrived, I was back closer to home, surrounded by friends, family, and community and in a relationship with the best step/bio papa I could ever have imagined existed. My mama friends have helped me with the dilemmas of navigating this "typical" babyhood and toddlerhood, and it has made an enormous difference. This group, including honorary aunties and a gay uncle, wonderful step-grandparents, a biological auntie, and bio-grandparents, has also embraced Luc more than I could ever have imagined or hoped for. They make sure he never feels left out, bring him presents and gluten-free treats, and hang out with him at playgrounds and museums, always accepting him for who he is.

But back to the original situation. Are there families who have a second kid after a first with autism? *Of course.* Is it sometimes heart-wrenchingly hard to see Milo grow by leaps and bounds and Luc develop at his own slower pace? Again, of course. I don't know how to properly respond without it turning into a classic catch-22: If I acknowledge that Luc is disabled and Milo isn't, does it look like I am valuing my typical kid over the other? And if I don't, am I doing a disservice to those parents in similar situations by glossing over the struggle? It's like the way you have to choose your answer so carefully when someone says, "I don't know how you do it." My response varies on the situation—to acquaintances: "It's been hard, but I've learned to adapt—and he's really sweet." To strangers—well, most are so put off by our cacophony of noises and movement that they just stay away.

I don't know if I handled the original situation well that Saturday morning, and it was triggering for me on a number of levels. I'm grateful that programs like that recreation one exist to give me time alone with Milo and Luc time to be fussed over by the women on the staff who adore him while having playtime, even if I don't seem super-friendly at drop-off. I'm sure the woman who asked about my kids doesn't remember, and would probably be chagrined to know that her casual observations went beyond that. I wasn't going to tell her about the depression that periodically still comes. Or about the fears, confusion, and feelings of ineptitude that creep in. Other than to recognize it happens, I don't know how to reckon with that. I try to focus on the day-to-day and learn from both of my kids on how to be a better parent and to apologize when I screw it up. And to savor the love from both my boys instead of always waiting for something to go wrong next or think about "what if..." In the meantime, we have been teaching Milo to be kind to Luc by example, in praising Luc for his accomplishments. I hear it reflected it back at me, when Milo says "Good job, Luc-ee!" And for that I am grateful and I don't second guess.

Taking the First Step
by Yantra Bertelli

A broken heart makes everything else seem peripheral. I've been stuck for almost two years now in a place where I do not know how to be. My voice echoes as I talk myself out of bed, down the hall, and out the front door, choking on memories and regret. What if I had done something different or parented in a different way? What if I changed the way I articulated a word or phrase? Dug my heals in even when laws were not on my side? The parenting struggles I have faced thus far find tension around two key quandaries, choice and forgiveness. Now it may be academic or controlling to encapsulate living by the use of two tidy words, but it helps me explain, organize, and contain what my brand of chaos looks like. It is a frame, a container for loss, powerlessness, expectation, and faith.

The pieces of my family are ill fitting. We are definitions that need further explanation, misunderstandings, retarded development, and a collection of individuals who cannot exactly pinpoint the reasons behind the public gawking and hushed commentary we experience. It could be the gay thing? It could be the size of our family? It could be tallness? Or autism? Or misbehavior? Or the occasional break from voice into American Sign Language? As I explain how the pieces fit together, I am defining and sometimes defending what it is like to live inside my skin.

When my youngest son was in kindergarten and first grade he rode the short bus with his stepbrother. It was supposed to be a short-term transportation solution; his stepbrother would be moving on to middle school after my son's first-grade year and our door-to-door service would move with him. We already had a relationship with the school and support staff and I figured this was one more way to take the edge off new-to-school jitters for my growing boy, familiar faces and a few more warm smiles welcoming him to school in the morning. And for the most part he connected. He laughed with the bus driver and attendant, he was helpful when students forgot their jackets in the seat or left their backpacks behind. He was a typically developing sibling riding in the seat behind his neuro-developmentally non-typical stepbrother.

I was naïve in my desire to streamline our lives by sending the children to school together and thus avoiding the car ride over the same six miles to the east side of town. This decision, along with a handful of others, was judged as failure to protect my son from his stepbrother, from the ramifications of his developmental struggles, and from the stigma of the short bus. My decision to be the step parent of a disabled child was framed in family court as selfishness and as disregard for the welfare of my own children. My own children, what did that mean anyway? My own children whose legal bond to me could so easily disintegrate because I am gay. How could I be so thoughtless, so careless with my son's well-being? I must not be his "real mom" or I would have made different parenting decisions? Who did I think I was? Had I forgot my place in society, taking these chances with my children's abilities to grow and learn and feel safe in their own home? I had been allowed to parent on the margin and how dare I jeopardize this opportunity by inviting chaos into my life, making it impossible to slip under the radar and *pass*.

Sitting in the courtroom, as I listened to a lawyer construct all the reasons why my son should live with his other mother, even after I had been the primary parent for his first almost eight years of life, I festered over the ways our society thinks about choice and motherhood. Third wave feminists, women of my own generation who experienced their childhoods during the late sixties, seventies, and eighties, have critiqued the ways the mainstream feminist movement and, perhaps more specifically, middle-class white women defined equality in their civil rights struggles. The critique centers on an equality that is to be achieved through access to existing societal structures and institutions, the goal becoming "equal opportunity." Equality in this instance is equated with equal access to medical and educational institutions, employment, and markets. Choice is understood or experienced through a consumer model or mindset. The concern third wave feminists push forward and question is a fight to demand equal access to existing hierarchies instead of struggling to reshape social structures and institutions to make space for marginalized voices, to include those silenced on the fringes and shift historical power imbalances.

What does this have to do with choice and motherhood or the wringing of my hands in family court?

The connection is found between equality and choice, or to be more specific the idea that choice—reproductive choice, consumer choice, housing choice, educational choice, and career choice lead to a more equal society. A more just society. Choice overshadows connection and human need at various stages of living. One of the problems with this idea is that society gets off the hook when individuals alone are held responsible for these "choices." Here, poverty and abuse occur as a result of a series of wrong choices. Motherhood, parenthood, is no longer a key societal experience and function, but an individualistic act. The importance of attachment, guidance, and care-giving is subverted in the ways we talk about and experience parenting; children become products of their parents instead of part of something greater than themselves or an extension of their families and societies. From this perspective, parents who give birth to non-typically developing and/or physically disabled children are seen as victims of their child's challenges, they often carry a burden of isolation and care, and they are sometimes held responsible for the child's physical and emotional challenges, especially when they question for themselves and for their children society's predetermined molds. Non-typical development is something that happens to a lone child and family, an accident, a punishment, or a challenge to struggle to overcome, instead of another individual for whom society has to stretch in order to accommodate and make room.

During our custody trial, my partner, my stepson's biological mother, garnered sympathy from the judge because the judge saw her motherhood in terms of victimization. Autism was the masked predator and my partner was the hapless victim. She did not actually see the child behind the diagnosis, because she never laid eyes on the boy, as courtrooms are befuddling places for any child. On the other hand, as a step parent, and at this point I had been actively parenting my stepson for over six years, I was held responsible for choosing our lives together. Instead of considering the bond my son and I shared from birth until the present day and the parent I was becoming to my stepson over the years, she concerned herself with the ways the boys' needs might be competing with each other. She saw the limits I had placed on my ability to parent by choosing to be in a relationship with my partner. Attachment was pushed aside, the history of the children's relationship with myself and their other parent was pushed aside, and the fact that my son had another sibling with whom he had bonded and with whom he lived his entire life was marginalized. I was scolded. I had made certain decisions in my past and "what was to be considered now is which home could provide the best support for his everyday needs." Sadly, even my son's guardian ad litem, who was more supportive of our family than the judge, articulated a sort of disillusion that I had "chosen" such a hard situation.

We provided the court with the long list of resources we were able to tap into to assuage fears. We had five to seven days a week in home support. My stepson went to various therapies; we had a mental health social worker, a Department of Developmental Disabilities caseworker, and a nurse who visited our home twice a year. I personally had enough help after school to attend to the other children's homework, their sports activities, and to maintain a regular bedtime routine. However, though we worked to attend to the needs of all of our children and had spent hours advocating for support, agonizing over their needs, and asking our family and friends to pitch in when needed, what the judge heard was the busy pace of our lives. The number of people coming in and out of our home, the four kids, the dog, the two cats. The mom who was in graduate school, the 1,600-square-foot house, the one bathroom, the dog barking, the bickering children, and the concern and honesty in our voices.

Parents of non-typically developing children frequently bump into false conceptions of choice and control. For instance comments like "I could not do what you are doing" or "How do you do it?" or "You are a saint and should be commended" suggest willful decisions and determination that are often fictitious. These words and ideas suggest more individual power than truly exists in the situation that is parenthood. With typical or non-typical children, most parents face situations in which they never thought they would be. So what does it mean to choose parenthood? What is it that we're choosing? Do we know all the possibilities, all the things that could happen? And when we frame parenthood in terms of choice, who is silenced?

Not only am I a stepparent, but I am also gay, queer, a lesbian. The two youngest children that followed me into our blended family started their tiny lives with two moms. Motherhood was a deliberate jumping through hoops and not supported by society as a whole or protected by laws. Right before my son turned a year old, when his sister was two and a half, his moms' relationship dissolved. The three of us remained together, mom, daughter, and son, until the children's other mother invoked biology's privilege two years ago. We did not come to the negotiating table sharing the same power or a similar interpretation of past agreements.

Queer parents frequently bump into false conceptions of choice and control. For instance, comments like, "What will your children call you?" or "Do you have a different bond with your daughter (biological) than with your son (nonbiological)?" or "What if your children are mad at you for putting them in this situation?" or "What if you do not look alike?" These words and ideas suggest more individual power than truly exists in the situation that is parenthood. People can open their hearts to parenthood, to a child, and not know the contours of their child's growing pains and challenges; people can actively parent, caring for a child day in and day out, and slowly recognize that they are only just becoming parents.

My children are not immune to society's critical ways of thinking about our family. In heated moments of anger, I have heard "You are not my real mother," along with "I hate you" and "Please read to me, stay with me, hold me, cuddle me." They try out these rejections and contradictions to watch me flinch, to see if I will cower under the weight of their words because they want to assure themselves that I am not going anywhere. The same almost ten-year-old boy who, in self preservation, hides the years we've held each other just below the surface as he rages against me, has to be reminded now and again that he did not arrive screaming into this world out of my "tummy." When I repeat our family story he says, "oh, that's right," like it almost escaped his memory in the years he spent clutching my hip. And my daughter, now twelve, negotiating the world's biases, questions the capacity of my ability to love them both without condition. She worries that my love for him is a rejection of her and she has not experienced enough of life to reflect on how many siblings share similar fears. Instead, she feels left behind and worries that loving her brother with the same intensity that I love her is a betrayal and I am forcing her to miss the completeness of something that belongs to her as my biological daughter.

I cannot fight for justice in the world and not in my own intimate relationships. My equality is not one of bootstraps and hoops, and choice is a weighty privilege. What I want for all of my children and myself is the opportunity to give our hearts over to the people we love and to be able to share our struggles, our collective contradictions, and the complicated and joyful reality of living. What I want to learn is how to see myself as part of other people and their process of becoming.

In the end my son did not come home.

He began his ninth year of life spending every other weekend and the summer with our family and every weekend with his sister (who goes to her other mother's house every other weekend). Ultimately, it was years and years of inadequate laws to protect children whose parents happen to be gay that triumphed. It was the law's bias toward biological parents over children's and parent's attachments and day-in-day-out parenting that led to the judge's decision. She fundamentally misunderstood the relationship I share with my son and his bond with me, his sister, and stepsiblings and stepmother. She dismissed the lack of legal options we had during the nineties to secure our parental bonds to our children when the relationship first dissolved. She was shortsighted, dismissive of the third parties assigned to the case, and we were out-lawyered. Though I do not believe our abilities to care for my stepson or our other children swayed the judge one way or the other, I do think the judge felt like my son's needs would be better cared for in a home where there was not a child with *special* needs.

Which brings me to a struggle to forgive myself. I continue to experience overwhelming bouts of grief and anger. For all the rage I have for the various participants of our custody trial, I blame myself for not having the power to keep my baby close to me. For the parenting mistakes everyone makes, but which seem so much more high-stakes in my situation. For being blindsided. For being overly optimistic in other people's abilities to show and experience compassion. For not being enough.

Frequently I stare down nights where I cannot get to sleep and I replay all the things I could have done differently. Things I might have altered to change the equation enough to allow me to hear my son breathing in the next room, rustling his covers as he turns. This is when I grieve, when all the questions, all the insecurities, the possibilities overwhelm me. Did I choose one son over the other? Did I choose my happiness over my children's happiness? Was my attachment strong enough with my son? Will he remember our lives, our past? Had I asked too much of the kids? What if I hired a different lawyer, followed different advice? Held on? Held on, knuckles white and drowning out the world with my screams.

As I write, another summer is ending. We are getting ready for the school year, which equates to clothes shopping, scrambling for after school care for my stepson, consulting the calendar weekly, and letting go once again. My son has spent his last summer night under our roof and will live most days of the school year sixty miles away. We will grudgingly find our school-year rhythm. He will come home every other weekend and we may see him at youth sporting events in-between. I will call, I will write him once a week, and we will have holidays. This pattern of letting go, holding my breath, waiting, and bringing him close wears us down. We become desperate. I will cry alone after the drop-off. He will rage. I will convince myself to get out of bed in the morning and push my body down the hall to make coffee, to make lunches, to be cheerful even when I cannot shake the pain. I will feel guilty when I cannot manage to fake joy and when my family witnesses the heaviness of my depression.

My stepson and I are alone this morning, a situation in which I find myself more and more as the kids grow up. My stepdaughter spent the night at her friend's, my son and daughter are with their other mother, and my partner is working. He woke, I made him pancakes, he colored, I gave him a shower, turned the water off five or six times before convincing him to get out, and I helped him dress. Right now he is squinting in my direction trying to avoid seeing me sign "name" over and over again because I want him to write his name at the top of his worksheet before I will give him another. He pushes air through his teeth and across his lips making sounds that he cannot hear. Save for these few oral stimulation tricks, our morning has been a series of silent tasks. Maybe four or five times during the day he will look me directly in my eyes and we will share those brief seconds. He momentarily acknowledges my presence, touching an ache that lingers underneath my skin. Caring for my stepson takes deliberate work and the schedules, routines, worksheets, and forced engagement becomes our opportunity for connection, a back-and-forth exchange.

Daily I bump into my own deeply rooted conceptions of choice and control. I cannot wrap my head around the injustice that surrounds me. I blame myself and try and retrace my steps searching for errors and ways to change the past. I blame myself as a way to recapture some of the power and authority I have lost. How did I get here? The experience of parenthood leaves little room for individual will alone. From the first touch, the relationship flows both ways, attachment hopefully occurs between child and parent and parent and child. The bond is fundamentally about building trust and letting go. Sometimes we release our expectations into the ether or our children are pulled away from us too soon, and sometimes our children leave us for their own versions of adulthood. I never could have imagined a busy morning brimming with silence or how many times a day I would have to rely on intuition because speaking and signing are not options.

I have worked to choose love; however, during these last few years, anger is threatening to swallow me whole. Forgiving myself for things outside of my control and for my own inadequacies seems the only way to save myself. What other option do we have if not love? Even as I mark the path with these words, I do not know when I will find the strength to take the first step.

This is What Love Looks Like
by Andrea S. Givens

This morning Maya cooked scrambled eggs with cheese, ham, and toast. She put cherries in a little black bowl and took the tray upstairs to Zion's room, where he was laying in bed with a headache. She takes care of him, mothers him really, even though she has just turned ten and he is knocking on nine.

It has been like this since Zion was born. After my labor and delivery was over, and Zion was cleaned and dressed and his footprints were recorded, after drops were put in his eyes and a tiny ID bracelet encircled his wrist, Maya walked up to Zion and gave him a kiss, right on his sweet little mouth.

At home she brought me bottles and diapers and rocked Zion gently in his bassinet. When he was two and she was three, they took naps, snuggled together in Maya's blue toddler bed. They held hands. They sat closely and watched TV or listened to stories while Maya stroked Zion's arm or face and sucked her thumb.

When Maya was four and Zion three, we enrolled them at an all-black private school where they could receive academic instruction. At this school, students studied for and took the Iowa Test of Basic Skills; they had spelling words and math tests and homework to turn in every morning. I thought it excessive. My husband thought it good preparation, the sort of education not typically available to black children. Maya excelled in this environment but Zion struggled.

In preschool and pre-kindergarten, Zion's teacher suggested he was not performing like his peers. She showed me the work in comparison: another student's written alphabet, Zion's scrawls on a page. Yet another student's written first name, more scrawls from Zion. I felt he was young, and young for his age, and dismissed their concerns. Boys that age want to be outside running and playing, and it was natural for them to resist sitting quietly.

In kindergarten, Zion's classmates were reading but Zion seemed to have no interest in any academic activities. He couldn't recognize all the letters of the alphabet or their corresponding sounds. He was unable to work well within the confines of the classroom. Skills like raising his hand, having a "quiet body," and waiting his turn eluded him. Our Student Intervention Team meetings considered the dynamics of black boys, how they are often kinesthetic learners, how they sometimes learn best through movement or other opportunities to use their bodies. Kinesthetic learning is a sensory activity developed through music and dance and physical activity. The rhythms and motions somehow work with the brain to assist the learning process. I talked about these dynamics with administrators and told them Zion just needed more time, more intentional instruction. The school had great teachers but I was convinced they hadn't found the way Zion best learned. When they discussed Zion's learning problems, I encouraged them to try a new strategy and stuck my head back in the sand.

Charles, my husband, told me about the history of learning disabilities in his family that plagued at least three generations of men. I allowed Zion might have dyslexia or dysgraphia, but refused to consider anything more complex. We discussed assessment options. He was sure there was something to find, I was equally sure they would only discover Zion brilliant beyond measure, funny and charming and, yes, developing right on schedule.

And that's what happened. We went through our local school district, even though Zion attended private school tens of miles away. A comprehensive assessment was performed and Zion was pronounced typically developing. Right on schedule! Somewhat distractible, but that's normal, too. *Bite me,* I thought about those nice Christian folks at the school. *You don't know anything.*

Zion and Maya received a lot of attention at school. Maya, for being sweet and helpful and an excellent student; Zion, for being funny and handsome and unable to read or write. When they took money to school for field trips or class projects, Maya carried it so Zion wouldn't lose it. Maya would ensure Zion didn't forget his backpack, his coat, a permission slip, a note from the teacher. During the long ride home every afternoon, Maya read to Zion and tried to help him with his homework. She tied his shoes and told him when his clothes were on inside out.

The following year we placed Maya and Zion in our neighborhood public school. Things started off well but went downhill fast. In October, Zion was suspended for a day for kicking his teacher. He was overwhelmed, over-stimulated, and had trouble expressing himself. When this escalated, he would lash out, hitting or kicking his classmates or having meltdowns. We received calls from the school weekly and Zion was put on a behavior plan. Discussions with teachers and administration centered on his behavior and ways Zion could learn to control himself. Academically he performed at a pre-kindergarten level, but in this new environment with larger class-rooms and fewer staff, his behavior was the primary concern.

Maya did well. She made friends and enjoyed second grade. Her class-room, though, was near Zion's and several times she was brought in to help him when he was unable to calm down. Zion didn't trust his teacher: he said he didn't know her, her records, or if she was clean, and he refused to talk to her. Maya was relied on to find out what was going on with Zion so the teacher could determine how to help him. Maya became a caregiver for Zion and monitored his behavior and mood.

In the spring, Zion's teacher thoughtfully mentioned that if Zion were her son, she'd take him to a pediatrician. After what I considered to be the year from hell, I finally acknowledged that there was something going on with Zion that needed attention. We began to seek the advice of experts.

We started with Zion's pediatrician. I showed him a file of Zion's school-work, his IEP, and behavior plan. We discussed at length Zion's struggles, and he listened. We received referrals and began to get Zion tested for speech/language issues, and metabolic, biochemical, and cognitive gaps or deficiencies. He saw a cardiologist, a play therapist, an educational psy-chologist, a urologist, and counselors. After each appointment I gathered the test results and data and put them in a file I could share with the next specialist. I became an expert at managing Zion's medical care.

Maya became an expert, too, at tagging along and sitting in waiting rooms, or being left at school while Zion and I took off for yet another appointment. She smiled and said she understood when Zion came home with a treat because he had his blood drawn, an MRI or EEG performed, or worked with another therapist. She was gracious when I brought her a treat as well—sour Skittles, nail polish, a *High School Musical* poster.

We finally took Zion to a pediatric neurologist. I wanted her to tell me that Zion's brain was fine and that his development was fine, too, not to worry. She looked him over and recommended an EEG. The following week I watched Zion get electrodes hooked up to his head and go to sleep while the EEG was performed. I watched Zion sleep and thought about his strengths. His language and vocabulary were excellent and he had an incredible imagination. I wanted to know why he wasn't like his peers, but I was certain there was nothing wrong some intentional instruction couldn't fix.

Two weeks later I sat in front of the neurologist's computer and she showed me the results of the EEG. Maya and Zion were in the outer office, laughing over a book Maya read out loud. The EEG lines were violent, indicating seizure activity that occurred every two minutes or more. Zion needed an MRI to determine if there was a tumor in his brain causing the seizures, and he would have to take medication to stop them. The neurologist gave me a children's book to read to Zion, *All About Seizures*. I threw it in the trunk and slammed it shut.

Later that evening, I played Uno with Zion and Maya and watched closely for the seizures we saw on the EEG results. I didn't see anything. I tried, I watched carefully, I paid attention to his words and actions and body movements and I saw nothing. Maya caught him hiding cards under his bottom and he laughed and put them back in his pile. He seemed the same to me but I knew the seizures were there. I cried myself to sleep that night and the next night, too.

While Zion's body adjusted to the medication he took to stop the seizures, we did our best to go back to being a regular family. We traded multiple doctor appointments for sports clinics at the YMCA. We made changes we thought were positive. We took Maya and Zion off refined sugar, tightened the schedule so every day was predictable, ensured they drank enough water, got plenty of sleep, and exercised daily. Over time, Zion was less excitable overall and calmed more easily when he was upset. He slept well and woke rested. It was a solid improvement in his countenance but improved his academic performance little.

We took Zion to yet another specialist and found out Zion's seizure activity affected the frontal lobe of his brain, the part responsible for executive functions. Zion's new pediatric neurologist explained it to me like this: executive functions are like the boss of the body. Impulse control, memory, processing, and recall are all affected when there are jolts of electricity—seizures—in the brain. Since Zion had been having seizures for an undetermined length of time, his executive functions were dramatically impacted. This new information brought it all into focus: Zion's inability to manage his own behavior when escalated; why he had so much trouble learning to read and write; why he still suffered from fine and gross motor delays and why he had so much trouble with two- or three-step directions and required constant prompts.

Zion began to resent Maya's endless reminders to put his shoes by the door, his clothes in the laundry room, to use his napkin. He yelled at her and told her she wasn't his mother. They had slept in Zion's room all their lives, but Zion now refused to let Maya in. She slept in her own bed and told me she was lonely.

Meanwhile, I was grieving. I was relentless about making sure Zion's IEP accurately reflected his academic, behavioral, social/emotional, and motor delays. I reviewed every document in his file and highlighted where goals were not measurable or data should be gathered. I met with special education directors at the district and regional levels, researched the type of seizures Zion had and the effects it had on his brain and body. I exercised like a fiend and ignored everyone I knew, focused only on how to help Zion.

At school, Maya and Zion played together at recess. A concerned school administrator told us it was inappropriate because of their different genders and ages and asked us to prevent it. We didn't agree with his perspective. Zion was socially/emotionally delayed and felt more comfortable with Maya, and he had been unable to make and maintain friendships with boys in his class. Maya confirmed that they played together at recess and when I asked her if she minded, she said, "Mommy, Zion doesn't have any friends. If he doesn't play with me, he won't have anyone."

Selfless and tender toward Zion, Maya would get up from her book or TV show to log Zion on to the computer and navigate to his favorite website, or read the text on his Nintendo DS screen so he would know what to do. He needed Maya, yet he resented her when she went to birthday parties or sleepovers, even though she would give him the candy from the treat bags when she came home.

Maya is not perfect. She is emotional and dramatic and more than a little sensitive. She expects Zion to be kind to her and finds it unacceptable when he is rude or dismissive. Maya comforts Zion when he is sad or upset and shuts herself in her room when she is mad at him. A handwritten sign on her door says, "Do not enter unless you knock first ZION!—Maya the Fashion Cat."

Several months ago, my parents helped me realize I had spent almost two years grieving over Zion's diagnosis and disability. I had become narrow in my vision, my actions, my thoughts. I needed to accept our new reality and move forward. No amount of self-pity was going to change it and the furious way I attacked Zion's disability was not going to alter it. I had to let go.

I had to let go and I did, right in that moment. I was sick of myself, sick of rolling around, day after day, in despair and hopelessness. When I came back to myself there was Maya, on the fringes of the family, smart and kind and patient and neglected. I made a standing date with her, every Wednesday evening, just her and me. We watch *America's Next Top Model* or *Wipeout* or we read together. We never miss our date.

Next year, Zion and Maya will go to different schools. Zion needs a creative academic program offered at another elementary school. He will have to establish his own friendships and manage his behavior without Maya intervening. She won't be there to share her lunch if he forgets his, or locate his backpack or coat in the lost and found. He will ride the bus to school; she will walk with friends. They will attend the same after school program.

Meanwhile, I have become deliberate in my relationship with Maya. I call her from work every morning to wish her a good day. She often helps me cook dinner, which gives us time to chat. I let her wear my favorite apron and she calls it an honor. She gets more opportunities to have fun with friends because she has shown so much responsibility and care. I try to demonstrate my appreciation, although I realize that is not enough. I am determined to put as much effort into her education as I have in Zion's. I know I do the best for him; it's long past time to do it for her as well.

Maya still takes care of Zion, and has the tendency to bring him the food she cooks for him. I praise her for her kindness and encourage her to invite Zion to the table. I don't want him to get used to being served by a female. I admire her quiet thoughtfulness, her unquestioning acceptance of Zion and all that he is, her patience, and her ability to take care of him no matter what.

This is what love looks like.

CHAPTER 6

Righteous Resources

What Do You Know: A Little Practical Advice After All

Most of what the *Short Bus* writers know is the truth of our own experiences. Feelings, memories, impulses build the bulk of the previous chapters. This last and shortest chapter reluctantly steps into that region where each of us has often been burned: the land of advice.

We all hear too much about what we should do, could do, might have done. Many of us feel bound to try almost everything for a while. Some of us walked out of those fires scarred by experiences that belittled, frustrated, and disempowered us. Who among us has not vowed to never put another parent through the same experience?

And yet, it's pretty isolating to feel like parents who have lived through something like you're living through won't share the few things we know.

What follows is our endeavor to carefully pick out the few things we feel we can convey without guilt tripping or disrespect for parents' wisdom about their own kids.

First, by way of caution, Mitzi Waltz shares her approach to the volumes of advice available to parents of disabled kids. Then we interview a social worker and disability-rights activist about Special Needs Trusts. Finally, we've compiled a list of resources we found useful.

Our intention is to be generous with those things that have helped. We imagine readers going to this chapter when they have need and desire. We hope that it will never be seen as a "to do" list. Most of all, we intend that it will never cause anyone to feel guilty.

A User's Guide to Self-Help Literature
(Or, Who's the Real Expert Here, Anyway?)
by Dr. Mitzi Waltz

Maybe you know my name. I've written several books on neuro-psychiatric conditions, and even before I could stick PhD on my nametag, that was apparently enough for book reviewers—and far too many parents—to hang a sign saying "expert" around my neck. I'm writing here to let you in on a dirty little secret: YOU, parents of people with disabilities, and people with disabilities themselves, are the real experts. Much of the self-help literature out there is rubbish churned out to make a buck, and some of it doubles the insult by being incredibly patronizing on top of it.

I wrote books because writing is what I did for money, so I can't completely distance myself from that description (in other words, it wasn't rubbish—although I made some mistakes—but I *was* trying to make a buck). Since I was spending half my "working" time trying to solve the mysteries of my two interesting children, I figured I should talk an editor into paying me for it. I also thought that being able to say, "I wrote a book on that," might increase my credibility when dealing with schools and doctors; unfortunately, I was sadly mistaken. But I did learn a lot, and I know that at least some of it has been helpful to other families, too.

One of the things I learned is that deciding what information should be taken seriously is not easy. Particularly in the autism world, where I have spent so much of my life over the past seventeen years, there are scam artists, fast-buck hustlers and well-meaning idiots galore. If they happen to be American, they probably also have a big fat book to sell you, along with some expensive therapy du jour to do to your kid, or to shove down his or her throat. Not all of them give away the game by wearing a cheap suit or saying the C-word ("cure"). Some are articulate, nice, well-connected and, frighteningly enough, employed in places of power where they may actually be making decisions that affect your kid's future.

So without further ado, here are my insider's tips to getting as much as you can out of self-help literature—such as it is.

First off, find out who this "expert" actually is, and whether anyone else has checked over the information in their book or on their web site. Just being "Dr. So-and-So" don't mean a thing. I'd like to name names (but can't because of a cease-and-desist letter), but I know of at least one "Dr." whose doctorate came straight from a diploma mill. Considering that said "expert" got her BA, MA and PhD all within one year, she might as well have gotten it out of a Cracker Jack box. A parent tipped me off and I researched it. Other than the response from her attorney, the only thing that happened when she was outed was that she stopped putting pictures of herself on her website wearing a white coat and a stethoscope. Yes, not only did she have a fake doctorate, she was trying to pass herself off visually as a medical doctor as well. I can't afford the lawyers it would take to put her out of business, so she's still out there—as are many, many more.

It's okay if your "expert" is a parent who has gotten clued up and now wants to share what he or she has learned with you. That describes me fourteen years ago. However, make sure that if a parent is giving you medical, legal, or educational advice, that advice has been checked out by more than one reputable professional. I like my medical advice peer reviewed, and you should, too. That goes double for lawyers. Check those "peer reviewers" out as well: not all MDs, lawyers, and teachers are in good standing, and they can be as uninformed as the rest of us. I get regular emails from doctors who have a pet theory about autism, and most of them are barking up the wrong tree entirely (some of them, on the other hand, are just plain barking mad). The Internet is your friend for expert-vetting, as the most serious offenses, such as lawsuits for malpractice or licenses being taken away, will be part of public documents. I don't take kindly to doctors and lawyers who try to palm off parenting advice either, unless there's evidence that they actually know something about it, perhaps by being a parent of a kid with a disability themselves (although even that's no guarantee).

If your expert recommends a particular intervention, look before you leap. I feel reasonably comfortable about treatments about which you can honestly say, "it won't hurt my child or my family, and it might help." I am a whole lot less comfortable about "it might hurt, but it ought to help." Physical therapy is one of those things that might hurt temporarily, but there's plenty of evidence to show that it is likely to help for many kinds of physical problems and some developmental ones, too. You can find out fairly easily what the potential benefits and risks are. But too many parents feel such pressure to effect a "miracle cure," thanks to our culture's perfection obsession, that we readily accept interventions that actually *do* hurt, and with way less evidence than your friendly physical therapist has to back up such procedures.

Sometimes the pain caused by interventions is very real—ask anyone with cerebral palsy who has been manhandled through Conductive Education* summer camp, or ask the adults with autism who are dealing with post-traumatic stress from lousy applied behavior analysis therapists. Unless you've got absolute proof that it's necessary, "no pain, no gain" is a slogan for gym bunnies, not vulnerable children.

Sometimes the pain is just in your pocketbook, but wouldn't you really rather have cash to pay the rent than another box full of overpriced wonder vitamins (that probably aren't)? Families are bankrupting themselves every day for treatments whose track record is dubious at best. Even those of us who don't have a bank account to raid for this stuff end up with painful "what if" guilt trips.

Another clue to who's on the up and up is what your expert is actually promising. If your child has a condition that actually may be curable—cancer, for example—it's probably worth giving a credible cure story your ear. Most children with disabilities don't fall into that category, but the cure merchants still manage to pick their parents' pockets. I look for information about helping my son have a good life just the way he is, and for anything that might help him build on his abilities. There is stuff he still needs to learn, but learning is different from becoming an entirely different person. The cure merchants tend to promise you a completely different child . . . and all I want is mine: healthy, happy, and as independent as possible since I won't get to live forever.

You would be surprised at how many self-help books are actually pitches for products or consultants in disguise, so keep an eye out for sales pitches as you read. The most popular one is pulling your guilt strings. What a bad parent you are if you don't choose their version of the "gold standard"—your

---

* Conductive Education is a system of physical education for people with disabilities that tries to force them to do things "normally": i.e., walking instead of using a wheelchair.

child will never reach his or her full potential, *and it's all your fault.* They'll trot out tales of kids who have experienced miraculous transformations but, and here's another secret, *some of these kids don't exist.* Press a little, and you may find out that their "examples" are composites of other children (about whom you're given no details). A few practitioners have even been caught out telling outright lies... and a few more would be if anyone could get a real look at the rest of the story. Even seemingly objective sources are not immune to this, including drug studies underwritten by major companies that don't tell you the whole truth about who seemed to benefit (well-nourished middle-class kids whose parents may have been doing other things) and who didn't (poor kids in Costa Rica whose parents were sold false hope by the drug testers). Studies can be constructed to say whatever they want them to, and negative findings are definitely suppressed.

Don't be fooled by the "all-natural" sales pitch either, which sells books but (more importantly to many authors) sells products. I've written a lot about pharmaceuticals over the years, and used them, too, but I'm as dubious about what Big Pharma says as anyone else with a brain. If possible, I'm even *more* dubious about what the branch of Big Pharma/McFood that calls itself the health food business has to say. You would be amazed at just how many of the supplements and special foods with brand names along the lines of "Nature's Natural Organic Good Stuff" are actually made by subsidiaries of either major pharmaceutical companies or the same pseudo-food manufacturers that are trying to sell your kids strangely-dyed pasta shapes with mystery meatballs. These companies especially love the fact that the unregulated nature of the food industry (and supplements are still classed as "food" in most cases) means they can make all sorts of unproven claims, as long as they couch them in weasel words. What they can't say on the package they'll teach their shills to say at sales conferences, so they can hit you with it in mailing-list posts that are supposedly from happy customers or at their next home vitamin-sales party. They'll also use credulous journalists to put their most unsupported claims in the public domain at arm's length.

You probably already know this, but "natural" does not always mean "safer"—and I would be especially careful of Chinese herbal remedies at the moment, as it's not just fake pharmaceuticals that are being produced in China's prison-industrial complex. Several cases have popped up recently of serious problems with these, including lead or arsenic in the "secret formulas."

Oh yes...secrets. To me, secrets are a red rag to a bull. If I'm told that someone has a secret miracle cure, the first thing I want to know is *why*. People do come up with new stuff, of course, but anyone decent would share it with the world. If you've heard the story of the "Lorenzo's Oil" compound developed by parents to treat adrenoleukodystrophy, you can see a different way of dealing with a possible breakthrough. It didn't turn out to be a miracle cure, but as Lorenzo Odone's parents shared it with others, many lives may have been prolonged. Had it been developed by someone a bit more venal, it probably would have been patented and sold at hundreds of bucks per vial. The only logical explanations for someone not sharing their secrets are a) the claim won't stand up to scrutiny or b) the person or company cares more about making a profit than about your kid. Either way, I would avoid like the plague anyone with secrets for sale.

Another popular sales pitch involves saying your product or method comes from somewhere else. "It comes from America" appears to suffice in Europe, and "It comes from Europe" will often convince an American buyer. It's even better if it comes from somewhere so remote and exotic that claims are not easily checked via web searching!

These same cautions should be applied to the claims to scientific proof purveyed by Big Pharma, and for those with educational and therapeutic methods to sell. Whatever promises your author makes should be open to investigation through research, but here again there can be pitfalls. When a certain approach falls afoul of the mainstream (and let's be honest, this doesn't always mean there's some vast corporate conspiracy against it, although saying so can be yet another effective sales pitch), its proponents can simply go create and publish their own proof. I could name at least two interventions touted for autism for which the only positive journal articles I can cite come from journals that exist solely to push that particular approach. All you need to do is find a true-believer academic and a publisher who sees dollar signs. So watch out for that sort of thing—look at what actual processes supposedly underlie the method's effectiveness, and then examine these in the light of what you know about your child's specific condition. Is there a match? It might be worth investigating. Does it appear to work counter-intuitively? Hmm...that's cause for a pause. If you find this kind of research daunting, try to hook up with a science-minded friend.

I'll save my final words for the family fascism of that self-help genre that purports to tell you how to raise perfect children, usually by eliminating or ignoring their differences. If your own are unusual in any way, you've probably had this stuff shoved at you by supposedly well-meaning friends and relations for years. I'm talking about Dr. Dobson's *The Strong-Willed Child* (solution: beat him into submission) and even Emily Perl Kingsley's *Welcome to Holland* (solution: stop worrying about what might have been and enjoy the ride to your exotic new holiday destination). Whether it's from the rabid right wing or the New Age fringe, what this literature tends to have in common is a particular view of family life and children that's rooted in the experiences of upper middle class, straight, white folks: those very families who are perhaps most concerned with the unavoidable deviation from their perfect plans that Johnny or Jennifer's disability represents. It doesn't matter whether they had planned to create perfect little Christians or the perfect products of continuum parenting. For those of us who aren't in their flawless club, their advice is worse than useless. As one of the moms who formed my early support system online used to say, our experience of raising toddlers with autism with no visible means of financial support was more like "Welcome to Beirut" than "Welcome to Holland." So please feel free to use that family fascism literature for winter kindling.

What we outsiders need is a good pair of army boots to kick down doors and kick recalcitrant service providers' asses, not patronizing platitudes or signposts to interventions affordable only by the top 10 percent. We also need to grow enough backbone to insist that our own alternative communities get clued up and skilled up about disability, because in the end the greatest hope for people with disabilities—our kids—is inclusion in truly accepting, nurturing communities that practice mutual aid on an everyday basis. We're not going to get that from the increasingly corporate education or medical systems, as necessary as some of what they offer may be at the moment. The best self-help doesn't come out of a book; it comes from real-world connections, skill-sharing, and organizing to meet our own needs whenever possible. Don't you ever forget it: you and the kid for whom you care are the real experts.

Special Needs Trusts: The Lowdown

Future planning for kids with special needs can be overwhelming, especially if you're coming into it with limited resources. Part of this process is creating a "special needs trust" that contains money to be used by your child once he or she reaches adulthood, as overseen by a guardian. To demystify what a special needs trust is and the process of creating one, SBB (Short Bus book) sat down with New York City–based radical social worker and activist Elliot Madison, who has set up many such trusts.

SBB: *What is a special needs trust?*

EM: The special needs trust that we understand now really comes from 1993 legislation. It's money or wealth or could be property that's set aside for a variety of individuals. The people that qualify to have a special needs trust have a physical or mental disability as defined by the state. What most people don't know is that it also includes people that have a chronic or debilitating disease that at the present many not qualify them to be disabled—for example, progressively poorer eyesight. So you can actually start a special needs trust prior to being disabled. That's important for families because a lot of diseases about are progressive.

SBB: *Why is it important to set one up?*

EM: It's important to set one up, and it's important to set one up early for a couple of reasons. You want to be able to provide for your child in the future, in case something was to happen to you. G-d forbid something happens to you, depending on how you passed away, there could be insurance money that goes to your child. But because there are wealth thresholds or requirements for a whole variety of government programs—SSI, Medicaid, food stamps—you name it, specialized housing, he could actually lose benefits by getting an influx of wealth.

SBB: *What can the special needs trust be spent for?*

EM: The reason to establish a special needs trust is so that the person can keep their benefits, whatever those may be. The idea is the government benefits meet your basic needs. They allow you to live, they allow you to get medicine, pay rent, and get food. So the special needs trust is not supposed to go for basic needs. That's the legalese on that—"basic needs." Trips are obviously fine. Entertainment is obviously fine. Transportation, if somebody wants to buy a car or have a driver, that's fine. You can't use it (special needs trust) for rent, and you can't use it to buy property to live in. For food, you can only use it if you're going out to eat. You can't use it for groceries. How you can think of that is very simple: if you can use food stamps in this place, you can't use your special needs trust.

Clothing is the same way. Clothing has to be above and beyond the basic needs.

SBB: *How do you define what "basic needs" clothing is?*

EM: The government decides every person needs to have this, that and the other. So let's say a person wanted to buy a costume of some sort. Or he wants a top hat just to walk around in. You can do that. What you have to show is that the special needs trust is not going for basic clothing, that you're spending Social Security on basic clothing. If you didn't use Social Security money and bought all of his clothes with special needs trust money that would be a problem. Auditors would basically tell you to stop doing it. It's not like the government comes in and sweeps up all that money.

In a nutshell, other than rent, which is really clear cut, you can spend a special needs trust on a lot of things. And that's where some of the trickiness gets into it. Like if the guardian thinks something is a waste of money and the recipient doesn't.

SBB: *If I were to write a will outside of a special needs trust what would be the maximum amount that I could leave without disqualifying a child from anything?*

EM: This is a great thing—the 1993 law made it very clear that there is no maximum amount in a special needs trust. Prior to 1993, it was a very baroque and complicated system of how much you can leave. In fact I recently worked on a special needs trust that was fifty million dollars.

SBB: *But if I were to leave money just in my will, with no special needs trust established, that would be bad?*

EM: That would possibly be quite a disaster. You might lose medical benefits. If he's of age, he would certainly lose all of his disability benefits.

SBB: *So let's say a relative left money to a disabled person in their will. What would be the maximum amount outside of a special needs trust and their parents' will that could be left to them?*

EM: It depends. For Medicaid it's $13,500, but for other programs it's less than that. What drives parents crazy is that there's not one number. With the special needs trust, you don't have to worry about all of that. It puts money aside and then you don't have to worry about all these caps on everything.

SBB: *So, really, the best thing to do is to try and not leave anything outside of the special needs trust.*

EM: Absolutely. If you have a well-functioning special needs trust there's not reason to leave money outside of it. The other issue is taxing. I'm not an expert on the tax code, but special needs trusts are taxed differently and at the lower amount than what's called the estate tax. So you're actually giving your child more money and the state will get less of it. That's another advantage.

SBB: *So that's fairly consistent from state to state?*

EM: Yes. There are some states that require a lawyer (to set one up). That's the big difference. But as far as the actual law, remember it's a federal law.

SBB: *If someone wants to find out if their state requires a lawyer, how would they know?*

EM: They would probably know because these are states that require lawyers for everything, including wills and guardianship and all that. They can certainly call their state office of disability services.

SBB: *How difficult is it for parents to do this without the help of a lawyer?*

EM: It is moderately difficult. You have to be moderately organized. I think every state has free services to do this. In addition there are books and websites. In fact, there's a website in Massachusetts that's sort of like a turbo tax—they just ask you questions and you put it in and they actually email it to you as the legal form. But if you're just paper and penciling it, your best bet is to get one of those books that already has the legal form in it. You're going to have to buy the legal forms anyway and they're going to cost you anywhere from $10 to $30.

SBB: *How much do you think it would cost with a lawyer?*

EM: Lawyers usually take a percent of the special needs trust. If you really want a lawyer and you have some complications—which usually revolve around things like real estate, you should definitely talk to lawyers. Most of the states require that lawyers get paid in a percentage and there's usually what's called a "hurdle stick." All that means is if you're under a certain amount of money in a special needs trust, they can't charge you. They can still charge you for processing these papers, which you would have to pay on your own.

SBB: *Is it a conflict of interest if multiple family members set up special needs trusts?*

EM: I think it's much easier for an individual to have a consolidated special needs trust. I know a person that i think literally has five special needs trusts. Each time you'd want money from each of these trusts, you'd have to go through the guardian. The paperwork on the special needs trusts multiplied by the number of special needs trusts.

SBB: *Speaking of guardianships, a lawyer friend who does general guardianships has had to take over from a family member when there's been a conflict or some mismanagement. Where is the oversight to ensure a special needs trust cannot be mismanaged by the guardian?*

EM: It's unlikely that a special needs trust will be mismanaged in the way that we tend to think of it—embezzling. What usually happens is that there's a conflict between the trustee and the guardian or they can't get a hold of the guardian. That's not uncommon either, like "I need this money and I can't get a hold of my guardian to get this money," which could be problematic.

There is oversight, like an audit that occurs. How often it occurs is different state by state, though the IRS has an audit too. They want to make sure that it's being used well. And they can audit like they audit taxes—you don't know when you're going to be audited.

SBB: *What about organizations like group homes acting as guardians?*

EM: Some group homes require guardianship to move into it.

SBB: *Does that seem reasonable?*

EM: It depends on the group home. There's another neat thing that's called pooling and what it is, is actually a group of people that create a pooled special needs trust so the organization or person that they chose as the guardian, all that money is put in for the kids.

SBB: *So it's a collective?*

EM: It's a collective, exactly. It serves a variety of other purposes, too. What often happens is that parent groups that have gotten together to start their own group home, but there's no requirement that with pooling you have to provide your own services. In New York, it does require you to be incorporated but that's nothing. That's just a $75 fee—chess clubs are incorporated. It allows maybe eight, ten, twelve people to share one trust. It makes paperwork so much cleaner and much easier. And you're only paying one fee to set it up.

SBB: *Have you seen situations where that has worked?*

EM: None of my people have had that situation, but I've read a lot about different pooling situations. And people who have done it and written about it are very excited about it. I think it's a little bit like a credit union idea in that there are a number of ways that people can do it. I think that people feel more confident, like there's a greater insurance that your child will be provided for as it's drawing on a larger pool of money.

SBB: *So how critical would you say it is for parents to establish a special needs trust?*

EM: They should definitely do it. There's no drawback to doing it. The fact is, life is unpredictable and even when we're all poor and don't expect to come into money, we don't know for sure how things will wind up.

Glossary of Terms

This glossary is designed to give readers a more clinical (and unphilosophical) understanding of some of the conditions and disorders that the writers in this book are facing. Others not listed here are more commonly known or are defined within the essays in which they occur. More detailed information for further reading is listed in the resources section at the end of Chapter Six.

ASPERGER'S SYNDROME (AS) is an autism spectrum disorder that is distinguished by deficiencies in social skills in individuals with normal IQs. The characteristics can range from mild to severe and can include difficulty dealing with transitions, obsessive routines, difficulties in deciphering social appropriate body space, and sensory processing issues. Though language development can appear typical, individuals with Asperger's syndrome often have poor pragmatics (the appropriate use of language in speaking) and prosody (rhythm) in speech.

ATTENTION DEFICIT HYPERACTIVITY DISORDER (ADHD), characterized by impulsiveness, inattention/short attention span, and hyperactivity/restlessness, is diagnosed three times as often in boys than in girls and affects 4 percent to 12 percent of school-aged children. Not all children diagnosed with ADHD have all categories of symptoms. There is no conclusive cause for ADHD.

AUTISM is commonly defined as a pervasive neurodevelopment disorder marked by impairment in social interactions and communication skills, as well as restricted interests and repetitive behaviors. Within the autism spectrum are Asperger's syndrome, hyperlexia and PDD-NOS (pervasive developmental disorder not otherwise specified). There is a saying that if you know one child with autism, you know one child with autism.

Because it is a spectrum disorder, individuals with autism are impacted differently from "high-functioning" to those more profoundly affected. At this point, there is no proven cause for autism, but theories range from genetic mutations to environmental triggers. It is four times more common in boys than girls. The Centers for Disease Control estimates that there are 1 in 150 children in the United States on the autism spectrum. For a complete listing of the diagnostic criteria, visit: http://www.cdc.gov/ncbddd/autism/index.htm.

Individuals with BIPOLAR DISORDER have unusual shifts in mood/temperament and energy levels that allow or interfere with their ability to carry out day-to-day tasks. These shifts are different from the typical ups and downs that most people go through from time to time, resulting in manic or major depressive episodes. Bipolar disorder often develops in a person's late teens or early adult years. At least half of all cases start before age twenty-five.

CEREBRAL PALSY (CP) refers to several disorders of motor function (movement) and muscle tone. Three main types are recognized: spastic (rigid muscles); athetoid (slow and involuntary movement); ataxic (affecting balance and coordination). Mixed CP is a combination of some or all three. CP is non-progressive and is caused by damage to the motor control centers of developing brains, mostly before birth but also can occur as a result of birth injuries, complication of premature birth, or resulting from infection.

CRI DU CHAT SYNDROME (OR 5P) occurs when a piece of chromosome 5 has been deleted. It is not an inherited disorder, and occurs in about 1 in 20,000 to 50,000 babies. Its name comes from a cry that sounds similar to a cat. Other features, which range in severity, include developmental delays, microcephaly (small head size), and hypotonia (low muscle tone).

People with DOWN SYNDROME have forty-seven chromosomes instead of forty-six, with an extra copy of Chromosome 21. Both symptoms of Down syndrome and intellectual impairment can range from mild to severe, and can include health issues like congenital heart defects, reflux, and increased susceptibility of upper respiratory infections. Physically, people with Down syndrome may share common features including upward slanting eyes, a flat nasal bridge, white spots on their irises, and loose muscle tone. Down syndrome occurs in approximately 1 in 800 births in the United States. In the less common and milder mosaic Down syndrome, only some cells in the body have forty-seven chromosomes, while others have forty-six.

The International Dyslexia Association calls DYSLEXIA a specific learning disability that is neurological in origin. It is characterized by difficulties with accurate and/or fluent word recognition and by poor spelling and decoding abilities.

HYPERLEXIA is thought to be on the autism/pervasive developmental disorder spectrum. The American Hyperlexia Association recognizes these defining characteristics: a precocious ability to read words, or an intense fascination with letters or numbers; significant difficulty in understanding verbal language; and abnormal social skills, difficulty in socializing and interacting appropriately with people.

NYSTAGMUS is an unintentional jittery movement of the eyes.

OBSESSIVE-COMPULSIVE DISORDER (OCD) is an anxiety disorder. It is characterized by recurrent, unwanted thoughts (obsessions) and/or repetitive behaviors (compulsions).

OPPOSITIONAL DEFIANT DISORDER (ODD) is a persistent pattern of anger and acting out towards authority figures that interferes with day-to-day functions. Symptoms are seen in multiple settings and might include tantrums, excessive arguing, defiance, deliberate attempts to upset people, blaming others for individual mistakes, being easily annoyed, having frequent expression of anger, hateful and/or mean verbal assaults, and seeking revenge.

PERVASIVE DEVELOPMENTAL DISORDER (PDD) (common US diagnostic category) refers to a group of disorders characterized by delays in the development of socialization and communication skills. Types of PDD include autism, Asperger's Syndrome, childhood disintegrative disorder, and Rett syndrome. Sometimes it is referred to PDD-NOS, the NOS meaning "not otherwise specified."

PERIVENTRICULAR LEUKOMALACIA (PVL) is characterized by the death of the white matter of the brain due to softening of the brain tissue. It is caused by a lack of oxygen or blood flow to the periventricular area of the brain. The periventricular area (the area around the spaces in the brain called ventricles) contains nerve fibers that carry messages from the brain to the body's muscles. Babies with PVL generally have no outward signs or symptoms of the disorder. They are at risk for motor disorders, delayed mental development, coordination problems, and vision and hearing impairments.

People with SENSORY INTEGRATION DYSFUNCTION (DSI) or SENSORY PROCESSING DISORDER have a neurological disability in which the brain cannot accurately process the information coming in from the senses. Individuals may be oversensitive or undersensitive to some sensations. Sensory integration problems can affect touch, hearing, taste, sight, smell, and vestibular sense (which tells us where our body is in space), and the proprioceptive sense (which tells us what position our body is in).

People with SCHIZOPHRENIA typically show one or more of the following: delusions (false beliefs); hallucinations (auditory, sight, smell, taste or tactile); inappropriate behavior; disorganized speech; and Negative symptoms (lack of motivation or interest, diminished cognitive functioning, and decreased emotions). The National Institute of Mental Health calls it a chronic, severe, and disabling brain disorder. Symptoms usually develop in men in their late teens or early twenties and women in the twenties and thirties, but in rare cases, can appear in childhood. SCHIZOAFFECTIVE DISORDER, in which symptoms exist but don't totally warrant a schizophrenia diagnosis, may also have distinct genetic links. It is unknown exactly what causes the disorder. Some experts believe it involves imbalance of serotonin and dopamine in the brain. Serotonin and dopamine are neurotransmitters—chemicals that help relay electronic signals in the brain—and help regulate mood.

SPINA BIFIDA, as defined by the National Institute of Neurological Disorders and Stroke is characterized by the incomplete development of the brain, spinal cord, and/or meninges (the protective covering around the brain and spinal cord). It is the most common neural tube defect in the United States—affecting 1,500 to 2,000 of the more than 4 million babies born in the country each year. Complications of spina bifida can range from minor physical problems to severe physical and mental disabilities like paralysis. The exact cause of spina bifida remains a mystery, but may be genetic, nutritional, and environmental factors. A comprehensive definition available at: http://www.ninds.nih.gov/disorders/spina_bifida/detail_spina_bifida.htm#106443258.

TETRALOGY OF FALLOT (as defined by the American Heart Association) has four key features. A hole exists between the ventricles and there are many levels of obstruction from the right ventricle to the lungs are the most important. Also, the aorta (major artery from the heart to the body) lies directly over the ventricular septal defect, and the right ventricle develops thickened muscle. Because the aorta overrides the ventricular defect and there's pulmonary stenosis, blood from both ventricles (oxygen-rich and oxygen-poor) is pumped into the body. Infants and young children with unrepaired tetralogy of Fallot are often blue as some oxygen-poor blood is pumped to the body.

Resources

These resources are recommended by our editors, contributors, and friends. We hope you find them to be useful!

In addition to what's listed below, there are blogs written by parents and caregivers that are too numerous to mention here, but many are linked through our contributors' blogs (listed in their biographies).

ACADEMIC PROGRAMS

For folks interested in pursuing a degree in disability studies.

School of Disability Studies at Ryerson University
http://www.ryerson.ca/ds

Disability Studies at Syracuse University
http://disabilitystudies.syr.edu/who

University of Illinois at Chicago
http://www.ahs.uic.edu/dhd/about.php

Center on Disability Studies (CDS) at the University of Hawaii
http://www.cds.hawaii.edu

School of Professional Studies, City University of New York
http://sps.cuny.edu/programs/spscourses/
subjectdescription.aspx?sid=DSCP

ADOPTION

A great site for adoptive and foster parents with lots of information and parent-to-parent support.
http://www.fosteringandadoptingolderchildren.yuku.com

ALTERNATIVE COMMUNITIES

Camphill is a movement dedicated to community living that supports and values the contributions of all community participants without regard to their financial assets, or their intellectual or physical capabilities: http://www.camphill.org

L'Arche enables people with and without disabilities to share their lives in communities of faith and friendship. Community members are transformed through relationships of mutuality, respect, and companionship as they live, work, pray, and play together: http://larcheusa.org

ASSISTED/ADAPTIVE TECHNOLOGY

AAC Institute is a not-for-profit, charitable organization dedicated to the most effective communication for people who rely on augmentative and alternative communication (AAC)
http://www.aacinstitute.org

Speak Share is an online AAC community
http://www.speakshare.com

AUTISM

Controversy aside, the Autism Speaks 100 Days kit can help families through the "critical 100 days following an autism diagnosis:"
http://www.autismspeaks.org/community/family_services/100_day_kit.php

The Autism Games site has ideas and activities about engaging autistic children: http://autismgames.googlepages.com

Wrong Planet is a web community designed for individuals (and parents of those) with autism, Asperger's Syndrome, ADHD, PDD, and other neurological differences: http://www.wrongplanet.net

The Autistic Self-Advocacy Network (ASAN) is a non profit organization run by self-described Autistics (those on the autism spectrum), those with other unique neurological types and neurotypical family members, professionals, educators and friends: http://www. autisticadvocacy.org

Senator, Susan. *Making Peace with Autism*. Boston: Trumpeter Press, 2005.

BOOKS FOR CHILDREN TO LEARN
ABOUT DISABILITY/DIFFERENCE

Thomas, Pat. *Don't Call Me Special: A First Look at Disability*. NY: Barron's Educational Series, 2005.

Willis, Jeanne and Tony Ross. *Susan Laughs*. New York: Henry Holt and Co., 2000.

Jackson, Luke. *Freaks, Geeks and Asperger Syndrome: A User Guide to Adolescence*. London: Jessica Kingsley Publishers, 2002.

CEREBRAL PALSY

Editor's note: many of the CP web sites out there are fronts for legal firms who specialize in suing for medical malpractice. Read the fine print.

United Cerebral Palsy's mission is to advance the independence, productivity and full citizenship of people with disabilities through an affiliate network: http://www.ucp.org

Cerebral Palsy Magazine is currently the only publication in the country fully dedicated to issues related to Cerebral Palsy: http://www.cerebralpalsymagazine.com

Bachrach, Steven J. and Freeman Miller. *Cerebral Palsy: A Complete Guide for Caregiving*. Baltimore: The John Hopkins University Press, 1995.

CREATIVE PLAY AND THERAPY

Yoga for kids with special needs: http://www.specialyoga.com

Adapted art projects: http://www.kinderart.com/special

American Music Therapy Association: http://www.musictherapy.org/faqs.html

Voices: A World Forum for Music Therapy: http://www.voices.no

Caleb's favorite toy catalog: http://www.southpawenterprises.com

Independent ratings and reviews of toys for children with special needs: http://www.ableplay.org

BeyondPlay focuses on young children with special needs:
http://www.beyondplay.com

Hippotherapy (horse riding for children with disabilities) explained and
national resources: http://www.americanequestrian.com/
hippotherapy.htm

DIET & NUTRITION
Information about the gluten free and casein free diet:
http://www.gfcfdiet.com

GFCF list-serve: http://health.groups.yahoo.com/group/GFCFKids

The Feingold Diet (eating without artificial coloring, flavoring,
preservatives and Aspartame): http://www.feingold.org

The Body Ecology Diet (focused on restoring yeast balance):
http://www.bodyecology.com/health

DISABILITY ACTIVISM
ADAPT is an advocacy group focused on keeping disabled people in their
own homes and out of nursing homes: http://www.adapt.org

Feminist Response In Disability Activism (F.R.I.D.A.):
http://fridanow.blogspot.com

The Disability Rights Education and Defense Fund:
http://www.dredf.org

Disabled & Proud (while not recently updated, a great source of information about contemporary disability activism):
http://www.disabledandproud.com

The Empowered Fe Fes is a support and action group of young women
with disabilities ages thirteen to twenty-four in Chicago:
http://www.alyouthinfo.org/The_Empowered_Fe_Fes.html.

Fleischer, Doris Zames and Frieda Zames. *The Disability Rights
Movement from Charity to Confrontation*. Philadelphia: Temple
University Press, 2001.

Americans with Disabilities Act: http://www.ada.gov

DEAFNESS

Hands & Voices is a non-biased inclusive organization for families with deaf/hard of hearing and other auditory disorders. It offers support on a local, state and national level: http://www.handsandvoices.org

Rachel Coleman is a musician and writer with two special needs daughters: http://www.signingtime.com

Laurent Clerc National Deaf Education Center: http://clerccenter.gallaudet.edu

Dunsford, Clare. *Spelling Love With an X: A Mother, a Son, and the Gene That Binds Them.* Boston: Beacon Press, 2007.

DOWN SYNDROME

The National Down Syndrome Congress provides information, resources, support, and education, as well as teaching advocacy and networking opportunities: http://www.ndsccenter.org/index.php

This is a clearinghouse of links on the state level for families of kids with Down syndrome: http://specialbilities.net

Kumin, Libby. *Down Syndrome: The First 18 Months.* A DVD resource.

Beck, Martha. *Expecting Adam: A True Story of Birth, Rebirth and Everyday Magic.* New York: Berkley Books, 2000.

Groneberg, Jennifer Graf. *Road Map to Holland: How I Found My Way Through My Son's First Two Years with Down Syndrome.* New York: New American Library, 2008. This book comes highly recommended, despite any reservations you may have about the title.

Bérubé, Michael. *Life As We Know It: A Father, a Family and an Exceptional Child.* New York: Vintage, 1998.

DWARFISM

Little People of America (LPA) is a nonprofit organization that provides support and information to people of short stature and their families: http://www.lpaonline.org

Living Little magazine online: http://www.livinglittlemag.com

Listserv to connect with other parents: http://groups.yahoo.com/group/parentsoflittlepeople2

EPILEPSY

Faces is a non-profit organization that is part of the NYU Medical Center and its Comprehensive Epilepsy Center: http://www.med.nyu.edu/faces

Devinsky, Orrin. *Epilepsy: Patient and Family Guide*. Philadelphia: F. A. Davis Company, 2001.

Fadiman, Anne. *The Spirit Catches You and You Fall Down*. New York: Farrar, Straus and Giroux, 1997. This book is an anthropological analysis of cultural disconnect between a Hmong family raising a daughter with epilepsy and the medical care system that failed to help them.

David B. *Epileptic*. New York: Pantheon, 2005. This graphic novel explores the experience of an epileptic person.

EQUIPMENT FOR KIDS WITH SPECIAL NEEDS

An online group for sharing special needs equipment: http://groups.yahoo.com/group/SpecialChildExchange

The primary focus of Abilitations is serving the needs of individuals with special needs and learning differences: http://www.abilitations.com

Listing of regional places to find used adaptive technology equipment, durable medical supplies, and other gear: http://www.matcoop.org/resources/exchange.htm

FETAL ALCOHOL SYNDROME

This website has lots of information about FASD and also the link to a parent-to-parent support mailing list: http://www.faslink.org

A national organization working to eliminate FAS and support those who live with it: http://www.nofas.org.

Buxton, Bonnie. *Damaged Angels: An Adoptive Mother's Struggle to Understand the Tragic Toll of Alcohol in Pregnancy.* New York: Carroll and Graf, 2004.

FUTURE PLANNING & SPECIAL NEEDS TRUSTS
A legal do-it-yourself pamphlet that explains the ins and outs of special needs trusts: http://www.nolo.com/product.cfm/objectID/C462E0C7-7086-4325-B8227E48F0B16C6C/309/298

Akron Children's Hospital offers a good resource guide for future planning for parents of disabled kids: http://www.medicalhomeinfo.org/tools/future.html

GENERAL DISABILITY
For faith communities, a resource for faith communities as well as parents, teachers, etc. on special needs: http://www.embracechildspirit.org

An explanation of people-first language: http://www.disabilityisnatural.com

Neurodiversity offers resources describing the experience of autistic people with an eye to their strengths and human rights: http://www.neurodiversity.com

Support and resources for sibling of kids with special needs: http://www.siblingsupport.org

The HANDLE Institute provides an effective, non-drug alternative for identifying and treating most neurodevelopmental disorders across the lifespan: http://www.handle.org

Disapedia's mission is to provide the disabled individuals all the community, information and resources they could want or need: http://www.disapedia.com

For a comprehensive catalogue of books and other resources about children and adults with disabilities: http://www.woodbinehouse.com

MotheringDotCommunity has a well-established, supportive special needs parenting section within their message board of which a few of our contributors are members: http://www.mothering.com

This website brings together current news stories and media about disabilities: http://www.patriciaebauer.com

Kids Together, Inc. supports the belief that children with disabilities, like all children, have the need to be welcomed, cherished and embraced in our communities: http://www.kidstogether.org

Kamata, Suzanne, ed. *Love You to Pieces: Creative Writers on Raising a Child with Special Needs.* Boston: Beacon Press, 2008.

HEMOPHILIA

General information and support for families addressing issues around hemophilia: http://www.livingwithhemophilia.ca/en/support.html

A national organization dedicated to helping people with hemophilia and their families: http://www.hemophilia.org

SENSORY INTEGRATION

Also, see Karen Wang's essay for several other suggestions.

Email list for parents of kids with sensory issues: sensoryintegrationgroup@yahoogroups.com.

Biel, Lindsey and Nancy Peske. *Raising a Sensory Smart Child: The Definitive Handbook for Helping Your Child with Sensory Integration Issues.* New York: Penguin Books, 2005. Foreword by Temple Grandin. http://www.sensorysmarts.com.

SPINA BIFIDA

Spina Bifida Association has links, information, and a broad range of resources: http://www.spinabifidaassociation.org

ASBAH is a British organization that provides information and advice about spina bifida and hydrocephalus: http://www.asbah.org

This is an online book to help children learn about spina bifida: http://www.myspinabifidabook.org

Contributors' Biographies

AILEEN MURPHY is the assistant director of creative writing at Virginia Tech, where she has taught creative writing and composition as an instructor in the Department of English for fourteen years. She lives in Blacksburg with her husband and two children, one with Asperger's syndrome, which has inspired these poems.

AMBER E. TAYLOR is a lesbian and stay-at-home parent of three, pursuing a path into midwifery. Her family lives in Southern California. She and her partner have been together for six years. Amber is an activist, a feminist, and a dreamer.

AMY SAXON BOSWORTH was born and raised in central Texas. She now writes from her home in the mountains outside of Nederland, Colorado where she lives with her family. Amy is the mom to three very *special* children. She is a late deafened adult and the recipient of bilateral cochlear implants. Amy's work has appeared in numerous literary publications and trade journals. She is currently working on her third novel.

ANDREA S. GIVENS is a blogger and mixed-genre writer, with work published on innovative websites including momlogic.com and trusera.com. She has been married for fourteen years to the love of her life, Charles Givens, who never asks her to be anything but who she is. She is a mother to Maya Givens, a typically developing sweetie, and Zion Givens, who is not typically developing but is a sweetie nonetheless. Andrea lives and works in the greater Tacoma area.

ANDREA MCDOWELL is a single mother of one in Toronto, Canada. She writes essays and fiction, is currently working on her first novel, and blogs at andreamcdowell.com/Beanie. Once upon a time she enjoyed photography, embroidery, sewing, and beading; now all she has time for is reading and writing. In her free time, she can be found daydreaming about sleep.

ANDREA WINNINGHOFF works, studies, writes and mothers her fourteen-year-old son, Jonah, in Seattle, Washington.

AYUN HALLIDAY is the sole staff member of the quarterly zine the *East Village Inky* and the author of *Dirty Sugar Cookies: Culinary Observations, Questionable Taste, Job Hopper, No Touch Monkey! And Other Travel Lessons Learned Too Late*, and *The Big Rumpus: A Mother's Tale from the Trenches*. Her first children's book, *Always Lots of Heinies at the Zoo,* was published by Hyperion in 2009. She lives in Brooklyn with her husband, playwright Greg Kotis, and their two exceedingly well-documented children. Dare to be heinie and visit www.AyunHalliday.com.

CARYN MIRRIAM-GOLDBERG PhD is the mother of three children, two of whom have IEP files as thick as dictionaries. She's a poet, writer, and teacher, and the author or editor of seven books, including three volumes of poetry (*Lot's Wife* and *Animals in the House*—Woodley Press; *Reading the Body*, Mammoth Publications), and a book on writing (*Write Where You Are*), and she co-edited with Janet Tallman the recent anthology *The Power of Words: A Transformative Language Arts Reader*. She teaches in the Individualized MA Program at Goddard College, where she founded the concentration in Transformative Language Arts: Social and Personal Transformation Through the Written and Spoken Word. She also facilitates writing workshops for many populations, and co-writes songs and co-facilitates Brave Voice: Writing and Singing for Your Life with rhythm and blues singer Kelley Hunt: www.CarynMirriamGoldberg.blogspot.com.

CHRISTINA WITKOWSKI lives with her hubby George, son Gabriel, and daughter SarahAnne in the 'burbs of Chicago. A former Montessori directress, she now stays at home with the kids.

CHRISTY EVERETT lives in Alaska with her husband, Nick, and son Elias. She's spent twenty-one days on a glacier, spoken at Take Back the Night, woken to two black bears outside her cabin door, and faked an orgasm on stage in front of hundreds of people as part of the 2003 National

Poetry Slam, but nothing has scared her as much as the breeched premature arrival of her son, Elias. She writes about life with a former micro-preemie, now special needs preschooler in her blog: www.parents.com/followingelias.

CHLOE EUDALY is a bookseller, publisher, disability advocate, raconteur, chanteuse, and unlikely PTA president. She lives in Portland, Oregon, with her son.

DIANA ROBINSON is a mom in a lesbian-parented, transracially adoptive, interfaith, attachment parenting family. She is the proud mama of Catherine, age twenty-six (who joined our family at age seventeen); Sophia (aged five and a half who united with our family at seven and a half months); Olivia (aged three and a half, joined our family after seventeen days in NICU); and Walker (aged twenty months, united with our family at birth). Diana is an educator who is currently at home full time.

ELIZABETH AQUINO is a writer living in Los Angeles with her husband and three young children. She is currently working on a memoir about her experiences raising a child with a severe seizure disorder and developmental disabilities. Her work has appeared in *Exceptional Parent magazine,* the *Los Angeles Times, Spirituality and Health Magazine,* and *Slow Trains,* an online literary journal. She has reluctantly joined and is now completely seduced by the blogging community, with her own blog: www.elizabethaquino.blogspot.com.

EMILY ZOLTEN is mother to three daughters: Bella and Sadie, and Lucy, who has cri du chat syndrome. In her free time (ha ha) she knits obsessively. She is currently pursuing a change of careers from homebirth midwifery to nursing, and sits in classrooms with people who are much younger than her.

HEATHER NEWMAN is a transplant from New England, now living and learning in Big Sky country with her husband and their three beautiful, energetic boys. She is a freelance illustrator and writer, novice quilter, advocate for her sons, and recovering public school student. This is her first published piece.

JENNIFER BYDE MYERS moved to the Bay Area when she was eighteen, carrying her high school journals with her. She continues to write for large corporations but shares more interesting thoughts on her personal blog www.jennyalice.com. Along with writer Shannon Des Roches Rosa, she manages *Can I Sit With You?*, an ongoing book and blog project, which benefits the special education PTA Jennifer helped found last year: www.CanISitWithYou.org. She is married to a most understanding man, Shawn, and between the two of them, they have managed to keep their kids Jack and Kate alive and well for several years now.

JENNIFER SILVERMAN is an optimist in a pessimist's clothing. She lives, writes and agitates in New York City. There she is surrounded by two exuberant sons, an extraordinarily patient husband, several soundproofed walls, and a constant stream of fairly traded dark roast coffee and Rescue Remedy. Other essays about the wacky hijinks of her family life have appeared in *Hip Mama* and *off our backs*.

JOE DIMINO is married to his wife, Carrie, and has two boys, Miles (three years old) and Zen (ten years old). Born in Kansas City, Missouri, and raised in Liberty, Missouri, he currently lives in Belton, Missouri. His full-time job is in information technology with the Grandview School District as a technician, trainer, and webmaster. In addition, he is a writer, artist, and video producer.

KAREN WANG is doing absolutely nothing at home with her husband, Oliver, and sons Louie (7) and Denny (1). You may have seen them running up the down escalator at the mall, pressing all the buttons on the elevator at the library, or doing very dangerous things with the shopping cart at the grocery store. Karen has no memory of her life before motherhood, but there are framed diplomas and boxes of archaeological slides in her basement.

KATHY BRICETTI's essays have appeared in *The Essential Hipmama: Writing From the Cutting Edge of Parenting*; *The Maternal is Political*; *So to Speak*; *Brain, Child*; *Offspring*; *The Sun*; *Dos Passos Review*; *Under the Sun*; *upstreet*; *Teaching Tolerance*; *Skirt!* and others. One of her essays was nominated for a Pushcart Prize in 2007. Her memoir, *Blood Strangers: A Memoir of Searching*, will be published by Heyday Books in spring 2010.

She has an MFA in creative writing and a doctorate in clinical psychology. She was awarded a residency at the Vermont Center Studios in 2009. Kathy is a Redroom author (www.redroom.com/author/kathy-briccetti) and her website is www.kathybriccetti.com. She also teaches classes at Book Passage bookstore in the San Francisco Bay Area.

KERRY COHEN is the author of *Loose Girl: A Memoir of Promiscuity* (Hyperion) and *Easy* (Simon & Schuster), a young adult novel. Her work has appeared in the *New York Times,* the *Washington Post, Babble.com,* and *Portland Monthly.* "Evaluating Ezra" is adapted from *Seeing Ezra,* a memoir-in-progress.

KIM MAHLER has had poems and work published in *5AM,* the *Cimarron Review, Thought Magazine,* and *DMQ Review.* She edited *Caesura* (from 2006–2008, six issues), the literary magazine for Poetry Center San Jose, for which she also served as secretary of the Board of Directors. Kim has taught writing to college students for fourteen years in the San Francisco Bay Area and is participating in a documentary to raise global autism awareness in Spain where she and her autistic son Harrison will walk 500 miles along the Camino de Santiago. http://www.pilgrimsmovie.com

LISA CARVER is the author of four books including *Drugs Are Nice.* She has two children, two cats, two African clawed frogs, and one lonesome hermit crab.

MAGDALENA BUENO is a mother and artist. She works with the PADS Center, which assists men, women, and families in Cook County who have become or are at risk of becoming homeless. She was also a volunteer at the Northwest Action Against Rape. Recently, she was awarded Community Spirit award for Elk Grove Village. She lives in Elk Grove where she works as an aerobics instructor and freelance artist. Visit her at http://www.paintingsbymaggie.com.

MARCY SHEINER has published many essays and feature stories on disability and other topics. *Perfectly Normal,* her memoir about giving birth to a child with hydrocephalus, is available on iUniverse.com. You can read her blog at http://www.marcys.wordpress.com. She is currently working on several projects, including a memoir of mother/daughterhood.

"Maria June" lives in New England with her wife Laura, their son Mitchell (3), foster daughter Reina (2), and one sweet old dog. Both children are homeschooled, though Mitchell attends a one-day per week Montessori program. Vocationally, Maria serves full-time in a family ministry at a church where she enjoys the opportunity to fully engage in life's great diversity of human experience.

Megan Raines Wingert is a mom of four. So far, she has generally found that working with the "experts" in the medical and educational fields has been about as helpful as trying to place a square peg in a round hole. She is currently interested in the difference in outcomes when children with special needs are homeschooled versus receiving services in a public school setting.

Mitzi Waltz is a lecturer in autism studies at the University of Birmingham in the UK. She has a seventeen-year-old son with autism, and has authored several books, including *Autistic Spectrum Disorders* (O'Reilly, 2002) and *Alternative and Activist Media* (University of Edinburgh Press, 2005). She is also an activist on disability and other issues, and a co-founder of the Anarchist Studies Network. In a former life, she wrote for *Maximum Rocknroll*, published *Incoherent House* zine, and played bass in X-tal and several other bands.

Nina Packebush is a queer, single mom of three amazing kids and one amazing grandbaby. She had been published in a variety of alternative publications and is the creator of several zines including *The Granny Chronicles* and *The True Adventures of the Feminist Snails*. While writing this essay, her youngest child caught her room on fire, her middle child admitted that she has been seeing werewolves, and her oldest called at least four million times to ask for the same hot sauce recipe that only has four ingredients. She can be reached at: revolucinations@gmail.com.

Robert Rummel-Hudson's first book, *Schuyler's Monster: A Father's Journey with His Wordless Daughter*, tells the story of raising a little girl with a disability and learning to become the father she needs. It was published in February 2008 by St. Martin's Press. Robert has been writing online since 1995. He and his family currently live in Plano, Texas, where Schuyler attends a special class for children who use Augmentative and

Alternative Communication devices. Most of her days are now spent in mainstream classes with neurotypical children her age.

SABRINA CHAPADJIEV (http://www.sabrinachap.com) is Magdalena's daughter. She recently edited *Live Through This—On Creativity and Self-Destruction* (Seven Stories Press, 2008), a collection of written and visual essays by women* who've used art to deal with self-destructive tendencies. She is also the editor of *Cliterature—18 Interviews with Women* Writers*. Her first CD came out in winter, 2008. She believes her mom is the best mom ever.

SARAH TALBOT has been raising an autistic deaf punk-rocker since 1994. She and the other five members of her family reside happily in Seattle, Washington where she makes a living as an assistant principal at a comprehensive high school. She has come to be comfortable embodying contradictions—pleading for more services while recognizing progress, advocating for inclusion and protecting teachers, being a mom, and being a writer. Her writing has been published in various places.

SHANNON DES ROCHES ROSA has been writing about autism and parenting since 2003 via the blog "The Adventures of Leelo and His Potty-Mouthed Mom" at http://www.squidalicious.com. Her initial bewilderment about parenting a special needs child has long since evolved into mama-bear, fuck-you righteousness. She is a founding member of her local special education PTA, runs the book and blog project *Can I Sit With You?* (http://www.canisitwithyou.org) with Jennifer Byde Myers, and fully expects people to fall in love with her beautiful son and mischievous daughters (but stay away from her handsome husband).

SHARIS INGRAM lives in the Bronx with her family. Her daughter was diagnosed with Asperger's syndrome in 2005. The final report for her son's evaluation has just arrived with a PDD-NOS diagnosis. You can find her online at http://saltypepper.livejournal.com.

STEPHANIE SLEEPER teaches humanities at a small college in New England. She is parent to a boy-child with a congenital heart defect and

---

* *Anyone who's had the experience of being a woman.*

high-functioning autism, and a heart-healthy, neurotypical girl-child. She is the proud collector of two sewing machines and enough yarn to blanket a small state. This is her first article about anything that happened after the year 1800.

THIDA CORNES lives in the San Francisco Bay area with her husband, two children, two cats, and her service dog. Her son's tumor continues to shrink. He can bend his elbow with help and he has started to run. Both kids thrive in many ways. Thida's essay "Gimp Geek" appears in the anthology *She's Such a Geek*.

YANTRA BERTELLI, the mother of four children, is also an unlikely pet owner. She lives and works in Seattle with her wife and family and thinks up different ways to manage transitions 250,000 times a day. She tends to nudge her children, though a bit lighter than she pushes herself, and always stays up with them until they have finished their homework or puts them to bed over and over again until it finally sticks. Her published writing can be found if you look hard enough.

ZIVA MANN is the mother of two boys, one with hemophilia. She writes the parenting column for *PEN*, a quarterly publication for the bleeding disorder community, and is frankly astonished that anyone wants to let her babble in print. She has an impressively useless MA in medieval literature from Harvard, and a (more useful) forthcoming children's book. She lives in Massachusetts with her husband and sons.

Acknowledgments

Jennifer, Sarah, and Yantra are indebted to the following people without whom this project would certainly not be in your hands: Ariel Gore, Bee Lavender, Liz Baillie, Jeffrey Lewis/Bluestockings Bookstore, Ramsey Kanaan/PM Press, and the 2004 Mama Gathering crew.

...And...

Jennifer is thankful for the many folks who have contributed to the health and well-being of my family over the years. Ari, you are an incredible papa and collaborator every day. Amy Hamilton, your patience and unwavering support is remarkable. I'm so glad to have you both as my partners-in-crime. Maya Gottfried, we are so, so lucky to have you as Luc's godmama and a friend. I am also grateful to Luc's step-grandparents, Ruth and Arnold Silverman, whose love for him is beautifully obvious, bio-grandparents Susan Greenberg and Paul Horenstein, and the irreplaceable "Aunt Do," a.k.a. Jodi Horenstein. And big ups to my mamas Vikki Law and Sasha Luci and our de facto babysitting posse/friends—Lizxnn Disaster, Chris Saldin, Melissa Lorenzana, Marissa Dey, and Gabby Silverman—whether at large or at home, you make everything easier.

Sarah is eternally grateful to her children (step and otherwise) for ruining her plans. Everything is much better than she could have imagined. She sends big love to her wife and co-editor, whose influence is obvious, magnificent, and beneficent. Without the support of Vic, Cheryl, Morgan, and Seth Talbot, Rick and Marcia Bertelli, Monica Miller, Erica Quimby, Jessica Wesch, and John Wilson, Sarah would simply not exist. She appreciates that the Mamas (especially Cherry, Wendy, China, Laurie, Monica, Amber, and Sia) have educated her better than any school ever could.

Yantra wants to thank her parents, Marcia and Richard, for being her original teachers and for their continued love and support. To all my children: you have gifted me with a unique pragmatism and an excruciating ability to love well. And to my wife, you make me laugh even when things are way beyond funny or even comprehensible—I love you.

I would like to appreciate and thank the many friends and family members who prop us up, help us eek through the tight spots, and cheer our entire family on. Thank you to my grandmothers … yes all of you, my in-laws Vic and Cheryl, Uncle Morgan, Quinn, Uncle Seth, Uncle Nazra, Aunt Jennifer, Alannah, Ricky, Lu Lu, Lewis, and Erica and Kaiya Quimby. And a special thanks to the mamas, Anji, Rosanna, Marla, Melissa, Sarah Tavis, Andrea, Trixie, Cherry, and Sia. Finally, I would like to remember the late Allison Crews and her sweet boy who is making his way in the world. You are missed and loved, mama.

Index

"Passim" (literally "scattered") indicates intermittent discussion of a topic over a cluster of pages.

ABA. *See* applied behavior analysis
ADA. *See* Americans with Disabilities Act
ADD. *See* attention deficit disorder
ADHD. *See* attention deficit hyperactivity disorder
ASL. *See* American Sign Language
accessibility of schools, 59–71 passim
achondroplasia, 21
activism, 117–28; resources, 320
adaptive technology information, 318, 322
Adderall, 270
adoption information, 317
adoptive home studies, 124
adoptive parents, 152–57, 255–66
African American boys, 293–98
after-school day-care, 246
aggression, 213–14
aides, 219–26
allergies, food. *See* food: allergies
alternative communities, 318
alternative schools, 63

alternative therapies, 240, 249, 269, 273
American Sign Language, 130, 131, 194, 285
Americans with Disabilities Act, 60, 163, 228
amniocentesis, 22
amputation, 42
Angelman syndrome, 107
anger, 8–15 passim, 155, 196, 246, 251, 273, 289; mothers' and stepmothers', 33, 153, 270–71, 290, 292
Apgar scores, 8, 178–79, 243
applied behavior analysis, 111, 303
Aquino, Elizabeth, 240–41, 327
Asperger's syndrome, 7–19, 54, 137, 141, 150, 242–52; defined, 312
assistive speech devices, 193, 195, 198
assistive technology information, 318, 322
association conferences, 227–33
asthma, 203
attachment, 157, 291

attention deficit disorder, 54

attention deficit hyperactivity
  disorder, 216, 268, 269, 279;
  defined, 312

attorneys. *See* lawyers

auditory processing disorder,
  144–45

autism and autistic children, 7–19,
  32–34 passim, 109, 126, 137–43,
  167–75, 225, 234–38, 277–84;
  Applied Behavior Analysis and,
  303; custody cases and, 285,
  287; defined, 312–13; hyperlexic
  autism, 74; kindergarten
  classes, 212–18; play therapy,
  73; resources, 318; self-help
  literature and, 301, 306. *See
  also* Asperger's syndrome;
  Winkleman v. Parma

autistic spectrum, 33, 54, 110, 137,
  222, 246, 312–13

Axline, Virginia, 7, 10

babysitters, 140

bean bag chairs, 76

bed-wetting, 119

behavioral therapy, 109, 111

behaviorism, 10

Berlin, Charles, 150

Bertelli, Yantra, 285–92, 332

bilateral perisylvian polymicrogyria, 192

bipolar disorder, 1, 273, 313

birth injuries, 69, 313

bisexual mothers, 230

black boys. *See* African American
  boys

blindness, 185

"blue baby" syndrome, 167

boarding schools. *See* residential
  schools

Bosworth, Amy Saxon, 144–51, 325

bottle feeding, 102, 103

brain chemicals, 315

brain diseases: PVL. *See* periventricular leukomalacia (PVL)

brain injury, 256, 257

brain malformations, 192, 201, 209

brain surgery, 227

breast milk pumping, 44–46 passim

breastfeeding, 38–39, 45–49
  passim, 101, 102, 138;
  envisioned by mother-to-be,
  152; of foster children, 156, 157

Bricetti, Kathy, 7–19, 328–29

brothers and sisters. *See* siblings

Bueno, Magdalena, 201–11, 329

Bulgarian immigrants, 201, 202

burnout, fear of. *See* fear of burnout

bus driving, 206–8

bussing, 60, 64, 113, 285–86

California Children's Services
  (CCS), 48

caregiving aides. *See* aides

CART, 148

Carver, Lisa, ix–xi, 329

catheterization, 44, 46

cerebral palsy, 51, 59–71 passim,
  185, 216, 222, 303; defined, 313;
  resources, 319

Chapadjiev, Sabrina, 201–11, 331

chemotherapy, 46–50 passim

child development milestones. *See* developmental milestones

Child Protective Services (CPS), 155

childbirth, 3–4, 42, 242, 243. *See also* birth injuries; natural childbirth

Chinese herbal remedies, 304

choice, 285–87 passim; false conceptions of, 288–89

chronic disease: special needs trusts and, 307

class, 138, 229, 233

classroom presentations, 137–43

cochlear implants, 144, 149

Cohen, Kerry, 32–40, 329

college, 251

coming out, 255–59, 271

Communication Access Realtime Translation. *See* CART

communes, 230

commuting, 65, 67

companion animals. *See* pets

Conductive Education, 303

congenital heart defects, 167

Cornes, Thida, 42–52, 332

co-sleeping, 156

costs. *See* expenses

Craigslist, 222–26 passim

craniosynostosis disorder, 24

cri du chat syndrome, 3–6, 313

Crouzon's syndrome, 24

curfews, 148

custody cases, 285–92

DSI. *See* sensory integration disorder (DSI)

day-care, 156, 220–21, 244–45

deaf children, 129–34, 145–51, 234

deaf mothers, 144–51

deafness information, 323

death and dying, 267; children and, 194–95

depression, 46, 47, 67, 273, 284. *See also* bipolar disorder

Des Roches Rosa, Shannon, 212–18, 331

developmental milestones, 101–12 passim, 220, 280

developmentally disabled children, 188, 203

diabetic mothers, 20

diagnoses: discussing with children, 142–43, 197. *See also* misdiagnosis

diagnostics. *See* tests and testing

Dibs in Search of Self (Axline), 7, 10

diet therapy, 249, 269–70, 273; resources, 320. *See also* sugar-free diet

Dimino, Joe, 101–16, 328

disability: children's books, 319

disability activism, 117–28; resources, 320, 323–24

Disability is Natural (Snow), 70

disability rights movement, 228

disability studies programs, 317

disabled children's choice of schools. *See* school choice: wheelchair users and

discipline, 188

discussing diagnoses with children. *See* diagnoses: discussing with children

divorced mothers, 230

Dobson, James, 306

doctors' referrals. *See* physicians' referrals

doctors' reports. *See* physicians' reports

Down syndrome, 21, 51, 107, 145, 260–66; defined, 313–14; resources, 321

dreams, 196

drug-addicted babies, 265

drug studies, 304

dwarfism, 21, 26; resources, 322

dyslexia, 314

dystonia, 44

EEGs, 244, 295–96

ER visits. *See* emergency room visits

ear infections, 139

ear tube insertion, 139

early childhood centers, 111–13 passim

early intervention, 29, 35, 82, 220–21. *See also* First Steps

Early Start, 49, 50

echocardiograms, 172

Ecuadoran Americans, 201

eczema, 139

Edison, Thomas, 270

electroencephalography. *See* EEG

emergency room visits, 121–22, 161, 164, 203, 204, 236

English as a second language, 202–5 passim, 213

epileptic children, 86–100 passim, 247

epilepsy information, 322

equality, 286–87

Eudaly, Chloe, 59–71, 327

Everett, Christy, 176–85, 326–27

expenses, 142

experts, 301–6

explorers, 192

eye contact and tracking, 16–17

false positive tests, 21, 145

family court, 286–88

father and daughter, 192–98

fear, 153, 176, 284; of burnout, 140; of zombies, 272

feminists, third-wave. *See* third-wave feminists

fetal alcohol syndrome, 322–23

finances. *See* expenses

financial planning, 307–11, 323

first steps. *See* learning to walk

First Steps, 105–11 passim

504. *See* Rehabilitation Act, Section 504

food, 138–39; allergies, 138–39; hoarding of, 119; supplements industry, 304. *See also* bottle feeding; diet therapy; natural food industry; tube feeding

forgiveness, 285. *See also* self-forgiveness

formula feeding, 47, 52

foster parenting, 117–28, 152–57

Fowler, James, 127

friends, 174–75, 189; lack of, 246, 248, 283; monsters as, 193. *See also* making friends

gastroesophageal reflux. *See* reflux
gawking. *See* staring
genetic screening, 138
Givens, Andrea S., 293–98, 325
global developmental delay, 280
government benefits, 307–9 passim
grand mal seizures, 187–88, 227, 244–45
grandmothers, 267
grapeseed extract, 269
grieving, 297
groundings, 148
group homes, 190, 311
guardianship, 310–311
guilt, 158, 172–74 passim, 190, 274, 283, 303

Halliday, Ayun, 86–100, 326
Handle Institute, 127
headaches, 195. *See also* migraines
health food business, 304
health insurance: telephone queries, 86–100
hearing aids, 149, 151
hearing-impaired children, 146
hearing loss, 145
heart defects, 167, 316
heart surgery, 167, 173–75 passim, 185, 260
hemangioma, 42–52 passim
hemophilia, 159–66, 324

herbal remedies, Chinese. *See* Chinese herbal remedies
high-IQ children, 144
Hipmama.com, v
hippie mothers, 187, 230
hiring aides, 219–26
homeopathic remedies, 138–39
homeschooling, 119, 268–74 passim
hyperactivity, 247, 250, 270
hyperlexia, 74, 213, 314
hypersensitivity, 139–41 passim, 146, 168
hypochondroplasia, 21

IDEA. *See* Individuals with Disabilities Education Act (IDEA)
idolatry, 127
illiteracy, 268, 269, 294
immigrant mothers, 201–11
impulsive disorder, 114
independent living, 142
Individualized Education Programs (IEPs), 5, 10, 18, 66, 68, 80, 83, 112–15 passim, 122, 228, 281, 297
Individuals with Disabilities Education Act (IDEA), 60, 186, 228
Ingram, Sharis, 137–43, 331
insurance, 86–100, 146, 204
intensive care units, neonatal. *See* neonatal intensive care units (NICU)
Internet, 230, 273; discussion groups, 49

interpreters, 131, 148, 149
intervention. *See* early intervention
Iraq war, 173

Jewish mothers, 231; daughters
    and, 255–59, 277–84; sons and,
    242–52
joint custody, 290
Judaism, 251

Kasabach Merritt syndrome, 43
kindergarten classes, 212–18, 294
Kingsley, Emily Perl, 306
Kisor, Henry, 150

labels and labeling, 79, 110, 114,
    128, 205, 228, 283
language pathology, 126, 280. *See
    also* dyslexia; hyperlexia
Lasker, Joe, 176
lawyers, 309–10
learning to read, 268, 269
learning to walk, 105–6, 204–5, 260
Leary, Denis, vi
lesbian parents, 117–34, 255–75,
    285–92
letting go, 298
life skills classes, 64–71 passim
lip reading, 149
lobotomy, 188
loneliness, 251, 264
lying to children, 16

MRI, 295, 296
MRSA. *See* methicillin-resistant
    Staphlycoccus aureus
Madison, Elliot, 307–11
magnetic resonance imaging. *See*
    MRI
Mahler, Kim, 41, 72, 276, 329
mainstreaming, 64
making friends, 142, 215–17
Mann, Ziva, 159–66, 332
marriage breakups, 272
McDowell, Andrea, 20–27, 325–26
Medicaid, 307, 309
medication, 114, 171, 249, 251; for
    depression, 273; for hemophilia,
    160, 161; for seizures, 188, 244,
    245; for sleep, 4; stopping, 12
"mental retardation," 51, 203
methamphetamine addicts, 221–22
methicillin-resistant *Staphlycoccus
    aureus*, 222
microcephaly, 313
migraines, 216
milestones. *See* developmental
    milestones
Mirriam-Goldberg, Caryn,
    242–52, 326
miscarriage, 28
misdiagnosis, 25
monsters, 193–94
Montessori schools, 29
mother-only groups, 231–32
Murphy, Aileen, 53–55, 325
music, 189
music therapy, 240–41; resources,
    319
muteness. *See* speechlessness
Myers, Jennifer Byde, 219–26, 328

myringotomy. *See* ear tube
    insertion

nannies, 221
natural childbirth, 102
natural foods industry, 304
neonatal intensive care units
    (NICU), 23, 43–49 passim, 167,
    172, 243
neural tube defects, 315
neurologists, 295–96
newborns, 23, 43–49 passim,
    124–25; siblings and, 208, 210,
    293. *See also* Apgar scores
Newman, Heather, 79–85, 327
Nick Joins In (Lasker), 176–77
nightmares, 141
normality, 160
nurses, 45
nutritional therapy, 171–72
nystagmus, 185, 314

obsessive-compulsive disorder
    (OCD), 314
occupational therapists, 35–36, 49
occupational therapy, 30, 51, 81,
    111, 113
oppositional defiant disorder
    (ODD), 54, 270, 314
organizations, 227–33
ostracism, 141

PTAs, special education. *See*
    special education PTAs
PTOs. *See* parent-teacher
    organizations (PTOs)
PTSD. *See* post-traumatic stress
    disorder
Packebush, Nina, 267–75, 330
panic disorder, 216, 225
parent-teacher organizations
    (PTOs), 68–68. *See also* special
    education PTAs
parents of twins, 152–58
patience, 211
periventricular leukomalacia
    (PVL), 257, 315
pervasive developmental disorders
    (PDD), 39, 54, 147, 314
pets, 119, 237
Pfeiffer's syndrome, 24
phobias, 74
phone conversations, 86–100
physical therapists, 50, 51, 83, 262
physical therapy, 29, 51, 81,
    111, 113, 188, 302–3. *See also*
    occupational therapy
physicians' referrals, 146
physicians' reports, 53–55
Pitocin, 42
play dates, 283
play therapy, 73–78, 155, 170;
    resources, 319–20
police, 14–15, 119, 121, 155, 234
polymicrogyria, 192, 195
Portland, Oregon, 59–71 passim
potty training. *See* toilet training
pregnancy, 20–23, 28, 278. *See
    also* ultrasound screening in
    pregnancy

premature babies, 23, 185, 256, 257, 313

prenatal drug and alcohol exposure, 157

prenatal testing, 138, 145, 278. *See also* amniocentesis; ultrasound testing in pregnancy

preschool, 29, 61, 83, 184, 293

preschool assessment, 178

pride, 229, 259

privacy, 256, 259

psychologists, 7

psychosis, 273–74

public urination, 141, 147

pumping breast milk. *See* breast milk pumping

pyknodysostosis, 25

quacks and quackery, 202, 302

rages. *See* tantrums

reading: learning. *See* learning to read

recess. *See* school recess

reflux, 23–24, 262

Rehabilitation Act, Section 504, 145

Relationship Development Intervention, 171

religion, 149–50, 174, 195–96, 210–11. *See also* Judaism

residential facilities, 210; in private homes, 234–39

residential schools, 131–34

respite care, 137, 139

"retarded" (label), 283

Rett syndrome, 314

rheumatoid arthritis, 279

Ritalin, 249, 270

Robinson, Diana (pseudonym), 255–59, 327

routines, 140, 141, 204; obsessive, 312

Rummel-Hudson, Robert, 192–98, 330–31

rupture of membranes. *See* water breaking

S.E.E. *See* Signed Exact English

scams and scam artists, 301–4

schedules and scheduling, 140, 204, 296

schizoaffective disorder, 268, 273, 315

schizophrenia, 315

school choice: wheelchair users and, 59–71

school recess, 214

school suspensions, 119, 295

schools, residential. *See* residential schools

seizures, 187–88, 227, 236, 240, 244–45, 296–97

self-blame, 244, 291

self-consciousness, 198

self-forgiveness, 290, 292

self-help literature, 301–6

self-identity, 128, 255

self-pity, 298

sensitivity, extreme. *See* hypersensitivity

sensory integration disorder (DSI), 11, 18, 108, 249, 315; resources, 324

sepsis, 46
sex workers, 230
shame, 229, 231
shaving cream play, 75–76
Sheiner, Marcy, 186–91, 329
shopping at supermarkets. *See*
    supermarket shopping
siblings, 208–11 passim, 265,
    281–84, 293–98
sign language, 130–34 passim, 148,
    149, 193, 194, 197, 234, 260, 264
Signed Exact English, 130
Silverman, Jennifer, 277–83, 328
singing, 196–97
single mothers, 59–71, 129–34
sisters and brothers. *See* siblings
sleep, 216
Sleeper, Stephanie, 167–75, 331–31
small girls, 25–27
Snow, Kathie, 70
social anxiety, 142
social class. *See* class
social cues, 247, 248, 251
Social Security, 307, 308
Spanish language, 205
spanking, 18, 31
spastic diplegic cerebral palsy, 51
special education PTAs, 71, 217
special needs trusts, 307–11, 323
speech, 188–89, 205, 207, 280;
    Asperger's syndrome and, 312
speech devices. *See* assistive speech
    devices
speech therapy and speech
    therapists, 35–38 passim, 50, 80,
    111, 113, 147
speechlessness, 192–98, 205

spina bifida, 28–31, 315–16;
    resources, 324
sports, 161–62
staring, 184, 260, 283, 285
Steiner, Marcy, 186–91
stepparenting, 285[a]2
stigmatization, 61, 142, 286
stimming, 7, 281
The Strong-Willed Child (Dobson),
    306
Sturges Weber syndrome, 188
substitute teachers, 145
sugar-free diet, 296
suicidal behavior, 120, 273
suicide, 272, 273
summer camps, 163–66, 175, 236;
    Conductive Education, 303
supermarket shopping, 140, 154,
    219
Supreme Court cases, 186–87
surgery, 42, 67, 185. *See also* brain
    surgery; cochlear implants; ear
    tube insertion; heart surgery
survival, 274–75
swearing, 210

tactile hypersensitivity, 168
Talbot, Sarah, 234–39, 331
talking. *See* speech
tantrums, 8–9, 12–18 passim, 30,
    31, 110, 120, 140–42 passim,
    153, 156, 160, 280; ODD and,
    314; outsiders and, 256, 258
taxation: special needs trusts and,
    309
Taylor, Amber E., 260–66, 325

teachers, substitute. *See* substitute teachers

technology. *See* assistive speech devices; walkers (orthopedic apparatus)

teenage mothers, 129–34

teenage pregnancy, 272–73

tests and testing, 81–82, 106, 114, 208–9; parental consent and, 149. *See also* false positive tests; prenatal testing

Tetralogy of Fallot, 167, 316

third-wave feminists, 286

3M syndrome, 25, 36

time-outs, 8–9, 153, 276

To Kill a Mockingbird (Lee), 198

toe licking, 147

toilet training, 205, 281

tooth brushing, 140

transracially adoptive families, 256

treasure hunts, 76

Trisomy 21, 260

trusts, special needs. *See* special needs trusts

tube feeding, 190

Turner syndrome, 21

twins, 153, 154

U.S. Supreme Court cases. *See* Supreme Court Cases

ultrasound screening in pregnancy, 20–22, 28

underdog stories: people's love for, 268

unschooling, 79–85

urination: on carpets, 276. *See also* public urination

vaccinations, 278

visions, 272, 273

vocabulary, 271

vomiting, 262

walking. *See* learning to walk

walkers (orthopedic apparatus), 59, 176, 180–83 passim, 204

Waltz, Mitzi, 301–6, 330

Wang, Karen, 73, 328

water breaking, 3, 202–3, 209

Welcome to Holland (Kingsley), 306

wheelchair users

bussing of, 207

school and, 59–71

Why We Suck (Leary), vi

Wilbarger technique, 171

Wingert, Megan Raines, 152–58, 330

Winkleman v. Parma, 186–87, 190–91

Winninghoff, Andrea, 129–34, 326

Witkowski, Christine, 28–31, 326

writing, 213

Zoloft, 273

Zolten, Emily, 3, 327

zombies, 272

Girls Are Not Chicks Coloring Book

Twenty-seven pages of feminist fun! This is a coloring book you will never outgrow. Girls Are Not Chicks *is a subversive and playful way to examine how pervasive gender stereotypes are in every aspect of our lives. This book helps to deconstruct the homogeneity of gender expression in children's media by showing diverse pictures that reinforce positive gender roles for girls.*

Color the Rapunzel for a new society. She now has power tools, a roll of duct tape, a Tina Turner album, and a bus pass!

Paint outside the lines with Miss Muffet as she tells that spider off and considers a career as an arachnologist!

Girls are not chicks. Girls are thinkers, creators, fighters, healers and superheroes.

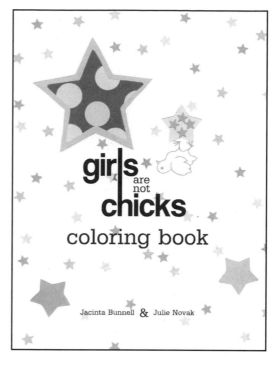

Jacinta Bunnell
and Julie Novak
PM Press/Reach and Teach
978-1-60486-076-4
32 pages
$10.00

PM PRESS PO BOX 23912 OAKLAND CA 94623
510-658-3906 INFO@PMPRESS.ORG WWW.PMPRESS.ORG

The Real Cost of Prisons Comix

One out of every hundred
adults in the U.S. is in prison.
This book provides a crash
course in what drives mass
incarceration, the human and
community costs, and how to
stop the numbers from going
even higher. This volume
collects the three comic books
published by the Real Cost of
Prisons Project—Prison Town:
Paying the Price, Prisoners of
the War on Drugs, Prisoners
of a Hard Life: Women and
Their Children.

The stories and statistical
information in each comic book
is thoroughly researched and
documented.

Over 125,000 copies of the
comic books have been printed
and more than 100,000 have
been sent to families of people
who are incarcerated, people
who are incarcerated, and
to organizers and activists
throughout the country. The
book includes a chapter with
descriptions about how the
comix have been put to use
in the work of organizers
and activists in prison and
in the "free world" by ESL
teachers, high school teachers,
college professors, students,
and health care providers
throughout the country. The
demand for them is constant
and the ways in which they are
being used is inspiring.

Lois Ahrens editor
PM Press
978-1-60486-034-4
104 pages
$12.95

ALSO FROM PM PRESS ●

Vegan Freak: Being Vegan in a Non-Vegan World

Going vegan is easy, and even easier if you have the tools at hand to make it work right. In the second edition of this informative and practical guide, two seasoned vegans help you learn to love your inner vegan freak. Loaded with tips, advice, and stories, this book is the key to helping you thrive as a happy, healthy, and sane vegan in a decidedly non-vegan world that doesn't always get what you're about.

In this sometimes funny, sometimes irreverent, and sometimes serious guide that's not afraid to tell it like it is, you'll find out how to go vegan in three weeks or less with our "cold tofu method"; discover and understand the arguments for ethical, abolitionist veganism; learn how to convince family, friends, and others that you haven't joined a vegetable cult by going vegan; get some advice on dealing with people in your life without creating havoc or hurt feelings; learn to survive restaurants, grocery stores, and meals with omnivores find advice on how to respond when people ask you if you "like, live on apples and twigs."

In a revised and rewritten second edition, Vegan Freak: Being Vegan in a Non-Vegan World *is your guide to embracing vegan freakdom. Come on, get your freak on!*

Bob and Jenna Torres
PM Press/Tofu Hound Press
978-1-60486-015-3
196 pages
$14.95

PM PRESS PO BOX 23912 OAKLAND CA 94623
510-658-3906 INFO@PMPRESS.ORG WWW.PMPRESS.ORG

Resistance Behind Bars:
The Struggles of Incarcerated Women

In 1974, women imprisoned at New York's maximum-security prison at Bedford Hills staged what is known as the August Rebellion. Protesting the brutal beating of a fellow prisoner, the women fought off guards, holding seven of them hostage, and took over sections of the prison.

While many have heard of the 1971 Attica prison uprising, the August Rebellion remains relatively unknown even in activist circles. Resistance Behind Bars *is determined to challenge and change such oversights. Examining daily struggles against appalling prison conditions and injustices,* Resistance *documents both collective organizing and individual resistance among women incarcerated in the U.S. Emphasizing women's agency in resisting the conditions of their confinement through forming peer education groups, clandestinely arranging ways for children to visit mothers in distant prisons and raising public awareness about their lives,* Resistance *seeks to spark further discussion and research into the lives of incarcerated women and galvanize much-needed outside support for their struggles.*

Victoria Law

PM Press

978-1-60486-018-4

288 pages

$20.00

ALSO FROM PM PRESS ●

Friends of PM

These are indisputably momentous times—the financial system is melting down globally and the Empire is stumbling. Now more than ever there is a vital need for radical ideas.

In the year since its founding—and on a mere shoestring—PM Press has risen to the formidable challenge of publishing and distributing knowledge and entertainment for the struggles ahead. We have published an impressive and stimulating array of literature, art, music, politics, and culture. Using every available medium, we've succeeded in connecting those hungry for ideas and information to those putting them into practice.

Friends of PM allows you to directly help impact, amplify, and revitalize the discourse and actions of radical writers, filmmakers, and artists. It provides us with a stable foundation from which we can build upon our early successes and provides a much-needed subsidy for the materials that can't necessarily pay their own way.

It's a bargain for you too. For a minimum of $25 a month (we encourage more, needless to say), you'll get all the audio and video (over a dozen CDs and DVDs in our first year) or all of the print (also over a dozen in our first year). Or for $40 you get everything published in hard copy PLUS the ability to purchase any/all items you've missed at a 50% discount. And what could be better than the thrill of receiving a monthly package of cutting edge political theory, art, literature, ideas and practice delivered to your door?

Your card will be billed once a month, until you tell us to stop. Or until our efforts succeed in bringing the revolution around. Or the financial meltdown of Capital makes plastic redundant. Whichever comes first.

For more information on the Friends of PM, and about sponsoring particular projects, please go to www.pmpress.org, or contact us at info@pmpress.org.

About PM

PM Press was founded at the end of 2007 by a small collection of
folks with decades of publishing, media, and organizing experience.
PM co-founder Ramsey Kanaan started AK Press as a young
teenager in Scotland almost 30 years ago and, together with his
fellow PM Press co-conspirators, has published and distributed
hundreds of books, pamphlets, CDs, and DVDs. Members of PM
have founded enduring book fairs, spearheaded victorious tenant
organizing campaigns, and worked closely with bookstores, academic
conferences, and even rock bands to deliver political and challenging
ideas to all walks of life. We're old enough to know what we're doing
and young enough to know what's at stake.

We seek to create radical and stimulating fiction and non-fiction
books, pamphlets, t-shirts, visual and audio materials to entertain,
educate and inspire you. We aim to distribute these through every
available channel with every available technology - whether that
means you are seeing anarchist classics at our bookfair stalls; reading
our latest vegan cookbook at the café; downloading geeky fiction
e-books; or digging new music and timely videos from our website.

PM Press is always on the lookout for talented and skilled volunteers,
artists, activists and writers to work with. If you have a great idea for
a project or can contribute in some way, please get in touch.

PM Press
PO Box 23912
Oakland CA 94623
510-658-3906
www.pmpress.org